LIBERIA'S
CIVIL WAR

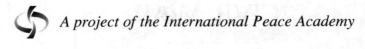 *A project of the International Peace Academy*

LIBERIA'S CIVIL WAR

Nigeria, ECOMOG, and Regional Security in West Africa

Adekeye Adebajo

LYNNE
RIENNER
PUBLISHERS

BOULDER
LONDON

Published in the United States of America in 2002 by
Lynne Rienner Publishers, Inc.
1800 30th Street, Boulder, Colorado 80301
www.rienner.com

and in the United Kingdom by
Lynne Rienner Publishers, Inc.
3 Henrietta Street, Covent Garden, London WC2E 8LU

Library of Congress Cataloging-in-Publication Data
Adebajo, Adekeye, 1966–
Liberia's civil war : Nigeria, ECOMOG, and regional security in West Africa /
Adekeye Adebajo.
      p. cm.
   Includes bibliographical references and index.
   ISBN 1-58826-052-6 (alk. paper)
     1. Liberia—History—Civil War 1989–   2. Liberia—History—Civil War,
1989—Participation, Nigerian. 3. ECOMOG. 4. Peacekeeping forces—Liberia.
I. Title.
DT636.5 .A34   2002
966.6203—dc21   2002017814

British Cataloguing in Publication Data
A Cataloguing in Publication record for this book
is available from the British Library.

Printed and bound in the United States of America

         The paper used in this publication meets the requirements
  ∞   of the American National Standard for Permanence of
         Paper for Printed Library Materials Z39.48-1984.

   5 4 3 2 1

This book is dedicated to
the 200,000 victims of Liberia's horrific civil war
and to the more than
500 ECOMOG soldiers who died
so that Liberia may live

CONTENTS

FOREWORD

David M. Malone

It is with great pleasure that I commend to readers this outstanding volume by the director of the International Peace Academy's (IPA) Africa Program.

Dr. Adekeye Adebajo has been studying conflict in West Africa for the better part of a decade, interspersed with periods of duty for the United Nations (UN) in South Africa, Western Sahara, and Iraq. His in-depth knowledge of the conflicts in Liberia, Sierra Leone, and Guinea-Bissau—raging successively and simultaneously in some cases throughout the 1990s—is rare indeed. The UN has had occasion to draw on his analysis and views, as have several governments. Dr. Adebajo is one of the outstanding representatives of a new, exciting global crop of scholars of international relations and a singularly promising African academic.

In this volume, Dr. Adebajo delves into the complex diplomacy of the Liberian civil war between 1989 and 1996 and examines the postwar years under Charles Taylor's presidency. As a student and advocate of regional approaches to conflict resolution in Africa, Dr. Adebajo pays particular attention to the role of the Economic Community of West African States (ECOWAS), as well as to the leadership of Nigeria, the aspiring subregional hegemon. He is also attentive to the role of several other international actors, not least the United States, the United Nations, and the Organization of African Unity (OAU). In keeping with the IPA's focus on policy-relevant research, this inquiry is rich in lessons for the United Nations, the OAU, ECOWAS, African and other governments, and civil society activists (both Liberian and international). This story is both comprehensive and succinct, representing a tour de force of a conflict much studied but little understood.

We are particularly happy that Professor Amos Sawyer, the only (but very) distinguished recent president of Liberia, has contributed to this volume a more substantive foreword than these brief lines. Liberia's future, highly uncertain today, will need to draw on the civic engagement and selfless commitment of citizens such as Professor Sawyer, if this most ancient independent African country is to regain its place among respectable nations moving toward prosperity and an ethos of service to its population.

—David M. Malone
President, International Peace Academy

FOREWORD

Amos Sawyer

Long before a final settlement was reached in 1996, bringing an end to fighting among the warring parties in Liberia, a stream of publications had begun coming off the presses. The Liberian conflict was one of the first of the post–Cold War era in which subregional, regional, and international efforts were ultimately blended in a single initiative with a subregional organization as the lead entity. With the Economic Community of West African States (ECOWAS) as the lead entity, the ECOWAS Cease-fire Monitoring Group (ECOMOG) became the cornerstone of the peace process and Nigeria its driving force and major pillar. Under the international climate of the time, peace could not have been achieved in Liberia without the involvement of ECOWAS, and ECOMOG would not have been a significant force without the participation of Nigeria. To many observers, the prospect of Nigeria's military government providing leadership for a group of other largely military and authoritarian governments in a mission to help Liberians retain their humanity, end the slaughter, and rescue their society seemed much too ambitious, novel, and riddled with contradictions. Driven by justifiable dislike for military rule, many Africanists and other analysts were quick to dismiss the initiative, impugn its motives, and pronounce its premature failure. Deceived by trappings reminiscent of African liberation struggles of an earlier era and repulsed by the excesses of the Doe regime and the embarrassing image it projected on the international scene, numerous African intellectuals were all too quick to embrace the rebel forces and to extol their perceived revolutionary tendencies.

Dr. Adebajo's book relieves the disquiet caused by many accounts of the Liberian crisis written before the dust had settled or the facts became known. His research is painstaking, his analysis incisive, and his writing lucid. He has meticulously traced the numerous trends of a complex diplomatic odyssey. Although Nigeria's role is one of the book's central concerns, this is the first significant publication that analyzes the interests of the full spectrum of subregional actors.

Dr. Adebajo successfully pursues his main thesis that Nigeria's lead role in Liberia was motivated more by an aspiration to leadership in West Africa than by any other consideration. In convincingly making this point, he also makes a statement of fundamental importance for Nigeria: attaining regional leadership requires the capacity to bring others along and the ability to put one's own house in order. For West African regionalism, he points out some of the hurdles yet to be overcome, especially the hurdle posed by the residuals of colonialism. For Liberians, his account should serve as a reminder of the fragility of the peace attained and the magnitude of the challenge of peacebuilding and reconstruction that lies ahead. Unfortunately, as of the completion of this book, that challenge is yet to be taken up.

As one who was involved in the search for peace in Liberia, I am gratified that in Dr. Adebajo's book we now have an excellent account of a critical dimension of the Liberian tragedy.

—*Amos Sawyer*
President, Liberia's Interim Government
of National Unity, 1990–1994

ACKNOWLEDGMENTS

First, I must acknowledge the enormous support of Gavin Williams at Oxford University. This book has been strengthened in structure, substance, and style as a result of his guidance, and my debt of gratitude to him is immense. I would also like to thank another mentor at Oxford, A.H.M. Kirk-Greene, who encouraged me to study regional security and peacekeeping. In my youthful exuberance, I at first refused to listen to the voice of age and wisdom, but thankfully I heeded this advice and remain forever grateful for it.

I wish to thank the following colleagues, friends, and teachers who read or commented on various chapters of the book: Ladipo Adamolekun, Kweku Ampiah, Daniel Bach, Mats Berdal, Geoffrey Best, Francis Deng, Louise Fawcett, Page Fortna, John Hirsch, David Keen, Chris Landsberg, David M. Malone, James Mayall, Raufu Mustapha, Michael O'Hanlon, Shehu Othman, Donald Rothchild, Amos Sawyer, Stephen Stedman, John Stremlau, W. Scott Thompson, Augustine Toure, Margaret Vogt, Kaye Whiteman, Douglas Yates, and Marie-Joelle Zaher. These individuals gave me invaluable advice that greatly strengthened the work. Any errors that remain are, of course, solely my own.

Amos Sawyer deserves special gratitude for reading the entire manuscript, correcting some factual inaccuracies, and generously contributing a foreword to the book. I wish also to extend a special gratitude to my family, "Auntie," Tilewa, Kemi, and Femi, who were a source of constant encouragement and affection. David Keen was a pillar of support throughout my time at Oxford.

I wish to thank the staff at the Economic Community of West African States and the United Nations secretariats who provided me with primary documents and interviews without which this work would have been less authoritative. I also extend my profound gratitude to the many officials who patiently shared their valuable experiences with me in Liberia, Burkina Faso, Côte d'Ivoire, Ghana, Guinea, Nigeria, Senegal, Sierra Leone, Togo, Iraq, Western Sahara, and the United States, particularly at the U.S. State Department. Most of these diplomats and soldiers spoke on the record, but I must also acknowledge the contribution of sources who for now must remain unnamed. I thank Lynne Rienner and her dedicated staff for their friendly efficiency.

Finally, I wish to acknowledge my good fortune in securing generous financial and other assistance from several institutions for the completion of this study. St. Antony's College, Oxford, offered me an academic home to begin the journey with generous funding provided by the Rhodes Trust, including funding for two research trips to West Africa. Research fellowships at the Brookings Institution in Washington, D.C., and at Stanford University's Center for International Security and Cooperation provided additional funding and stimulating academic homes to complete the journey. The International Peace Academy (IPA), where I now work, and particularly its president, David M. Malone, who did the most to ensure that this book was published, was extremely understanding in allowing me the time to complete the final revisions to the manuscript. The government of the Netherlands also funded an additional research trip to West Africa through a grant to the IPA. The governments of the Netherlands and the UK's Department for International Development provided funding to the IPA's Africa Program, which facilitated the publication and dissemination of this book. I wish to express my deepest appreciation to these institutions for supporting so generously the work of a young scholar.

—*Adekeye Adebajo*

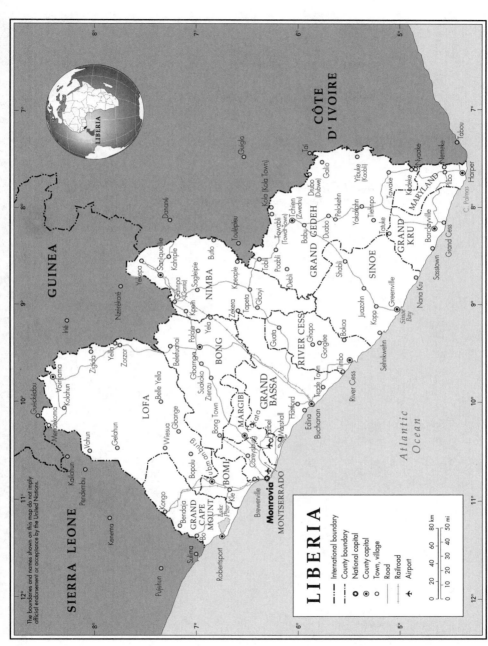

GUINEA

SIERRA LEONE

CÔTE D'IVOIRE

LIBERIA

- ··· International boundary
- ·-·- County boundary
- ⊛ National capital
- ◉ County capital
- ○ Town, village
- Road
- ·+·+· Railroad
- ✈ Airport

| 0 | 20 | 40 | 60 | 80 km |
| 0 | 10 | 20 | 30 | 40 | 50 mi |

Atlantic Ocean

Monrovia
MONTSERRADO

LOFA

BONG

NIMBA

GRAND GEDEH

GRAND CAPE MOUNT

BOMI

MARGIBI

GRAND BASSA

RIVER CESS

SINOE

GRAND KRU

MARYLAND

Robertsport
Brewerville
Careysburg
Kle
Bopolu
Bendaja
Bo
Sulima
Pujehun
Kenema
Pendembu
Kalohun
Mendekoma
Guéckédou
Kongo
Vahun
Gelahun
Kolahun
Voinjama
Zigida
Yella
Zorzor
Belle Yella
Gbange
Wiesua
Suakoko
Bong Town
Zienzu
Lake Piso
Tubmanburg
Kakata
Marshall
Careysburg
Edina
Buchanan
Hartford
Kade Town
River Cess
Timbo
Selnkwehn
Juazohn
Kopo
Nana Kru
Sasstown
Grand Cess
Barclayville
Pleebo
Harper
Nemeke
Nyaake
Tabou
C. Palmas

Gelahun
Irié
Nzérékoré
Danané
Guiglo
Toulepleu
Kola (Kola Town)
Tai
Gbornga
Palala
Belefuanai
Gbange
Gohnpa (Ganta)
Kpein
Yela
Saniquellie
Yekepa
Kahnple
Saglepie
Bullo
Kpeople
Gboyi
Zekera
Tapeta
Yela
Guata
Ghapo
Gonglee
Bokoa
Shabli
Taluke
Yakakahn
Pelokehn
Duabo
Babu
Drubo (Dubwe)
Gollo
Yibuke (Kaabli)
Tuwabli (Tuwah Town)
Tchien (Zwedru)
Debli
Tobli
Poabli
Towoke
Tiethpo
Sinoe Bay
Greenville

Sinkor

Department of Public Information
Cartographic Section

Map No. 3775 Rev. 2   UNITED NATIONS
August 1995

Some fear that ECOMOG is a kind of imperial excuse by Nigeria to interfere in the internal politics of smaller states.
—General Maxwell Khobe,
former ECOMOG Task Force commander

chapter 1

INTRODUCTION

In the twenty-first century . . . France's West African sphere of influence will be filled by Nigeria—a more natural hegemonic power in West Africa. It will be under those circumstances that Nigeria's own boundaries are likely to expand to incorporate the Republic of Niger, the Republic of Benin, and conceivably Cameroon.

—Ali Mazrui

Regional Security in Post–Cold War Africa

"Pax Africana," declared Ali Mazrui in 1967, "asserts that the peace of Africa is to be assured by the exertions of Africans themselves."[1] During the era of the Cold War, many Africans persistently called for African solutions to African problems. They blamed their inability to achieve their aim on the pernicious proxy wars of the Cold War era that engulfed parts of the African continent. Between 1960 and 1990, eighteen civil wars in Africa resulted in about 7 million deaths and spawned 5 million refugees.[2] Though the superpower rivalry of the Cold War fueled many African conflicts, their roots were internal: inept political leadership that manipulated ethnicity to favor or suppress particular groups, unresolved differences from colonially inherited artificial borders, weak and unproductive economies, inefficient bureaucracies, and fragile political authority.[3]

There is a new urgency among African policymakers and scholars in the search for effective mechanisms for resolving African conflicts. As Francis Deng put it: "Africans . . . are recognizing that the world does not care much about them and that they must take their destinies into their own hands."[4] A coincidence of interests now seems to have emerged: Africans,

1

freed of the constraints of the Cold War, are searching for ways to put into practice the concept of Pax Africana; Western powers are urging Africans to keep their own peace in order to avoid being embarrassed by humanitarian considerations intervening in areas where they perceive their interests to be low.[5]

United Nations (UN) peacekeeping assumed an overwhelming importance in post–Cold War Africa in a bid to fill the security vacuum created by the departure of the superpowers.[6] Somalia, Rwanda, Namibia, Western Sahara, Angola, and Mozambique all experienced some form of UN peace-keeping presence, and about half of the UN peacekeeping missions undertaken since 1989 occurred in Africa. The ubiquitous UN presence exposed the institutional weaknesses of the Organization of African Unity (OAU) and subregional organizations in Africa. After the debacle in Somalia where eighteen U.S. soldiers and about 1,000 Somalis were killed in October 1993, UN peacekeepers were forced to withdraw.[7] Since then, the United States and other major powers in the UN Security Council have shown great reluctance to sanction military interventions by the United Nations in Africa. Led by the United States, the Security Council shamefully failed to act decisively in the clear case of genocide against 800,000 people in Rwanda between April and June 1994 despite having a UN military presence on the ground.[8]

Regional organizations in Africa have been forced to fill this void. By far the most significant has been the Economic Community of West African States (ECOWAS) Cease-Fire Monitoring Group (ECOMOG) mission in Liberia, which represents the first full-scale attempt by a subregional organization in Africa to stem conflict largely through the efforts of regional troops, logistics, and funding. The Liberia mission is also the first time that the United Nations has sent peacekeepers to an already established regional peacekeeping effort. ECOMOG was an active manifestation of regional security in the post–Cold War era. Liberia was a country with historical ties to the United States that had served as a Cold War ally. A Nigerian-led intervention would have been difficult to imagine without the end of the Cold War. Liberia perfectly crystallized the growing *indifference* of external actors to Africa and the growing *interest* of African actors in resolving their own conflicts.

ECOMOG also launched a Nigerian-led intervention into Sierra Leone between 1997 and 1999 that involved Ghana, Guinea, and Mali,[9] as well as a brief intervention into Guinea-Bissau between February and May 1999 involving Benin, Gambia, Niger, and Togo.[10] In subregions outside West Africa, efforts have also been made by African actors to promote security: Ethiopia, Tanzania, and Uganda agreed to send troops to Burundi before a coup stalled the idea in July 1996; Burkina Faso, Chad, Gabon, Mali, Senegal, and Togo contributed troops to implement a peace agreement in the Central African Republic in January 1997; the Intergovernmental Authority on Development has attempted to mediate conflicts in the Horn of Africa and Sudan;[11] the Southern African Development Community created the Organ on Politics, Defense, and Security in 1996,[12] whose members have attempted to mediate conflicts in Angola and Mozambique; and South Africa and Botswana intervened militarily in Lesotho in September 1998.[13]

The OAU established the Mechanism for Conflict Prevention, Management, and Resolution at its July 1993 summit in Cairo and sent military observers to Rwanda in 1991, to Burundi in 1994, and the Comoros in 1997.[14] But the organization still suffers from the political, financial, and logistical constraints that hampered its effectiveness during the Cold War, and all three of its observer missions had to be prematurely withdrawn or subsumed under a UN umbrella.[15] In post–Cold War Africa, the subregion seems likely to remain the major arena for conflict management.

Countries most directly affected by refugee flows and other forms of instability resulting from conflicts tend to be more inclined to act swiftly in such situations. Such actors often have the advantage of understanding the complex dynamics of their subregions better and can focus more attention on them than can the OAU and the United Nations, which have many agendas. But as the ECOMOG case in Liberia reveals, there are also clear disadvantages to interventions by subregional actors, including the pursuit of parochial and self-interested goals that sometimes lead to partisanship and a lack of neutrality that could exacerbate rather than alleviate such conflicts.

Since the end of the Cold War, the UN Security Council has been more flexible in defining threats to international peace and security to include refugee flows, humanitarian disasters, and even human rights abuses in places like Liberia, Somalia, northern Iraq, and Yugoslavia. The once sacrosanct legal principles of sovereignty and noninterference in the domestic affairs of states have at least been weakened if not yet abandoned. [16] In his 1992 report *An Agenda For Peace,* former UN Secretary-General Boutros Boutros-Ghali argued that regional security arrangements be used to lighten the heavy peacekeeping burden shouldered by the United Nations.[17] This was consistent with Article 52.2 of the UN Charter, which encourages regional bodies to "make every effort to achieve pacific settlement of local disputes . . . . before referring them to the Security Council." The Security Council is also urged under Article 53.1 to "utilize such regional arrangements or agencies for enforcement action under its authority" with the limiting clause that such enforcement must have the prior authorization of the Council.[18] These arrangements were eventually employed in cases like Liberia, Sierra Leone, and Bosnia.

Main Questions and Arguments

Having thus set out the context within which the ECOMOG intervention in Liberia occurred, we must now focus on the main questions and arguments that will be pursued in this book. There are four main questions that we will attempt to answer: First, why did Nigeria intervene in Liberia, and what factors explain its seven-year commitment to ECOMOG? Second, to what extent was the ECOMOG intervention a Pax Nigeriana shaped by the hegemonic interests and aspirations of Nigeria? Third, what domestic (i.e., Liberian), subregional, and external (i.e., extrasubregional) factors prevented ECOMOG from achieving its stated objectives for seven years? Finally, what domestic, subregional, and external factors eventually led to the achievement of ECOMOG's goals in Liberia?

In this book we address the role of Nigeria, an aspiring hegemon, in security management in West Africa. In response to the four central questions posed above, we pursue four key arguments. First, Pax Nigeriana represents Nigeria's historic attempts to fulfill its political, economic, and military leadership ambitions as an aspiring hegemon in West Africa. Therefore, the key to understanding the ECOMOG intervention in Liberia necessarily involves an understanding of Nigerian foreign policy as well as the hegemonic image that Nigerian military leaders held of their country. The Liberian intervention provided a stage for Nigeria to play out leadership ambitions it had expressed and sometimes sought to fulfill since its independence in 1960. ECOMOG was thus consistent with such foreign policy actions as the creation of ECOWAS in 1975 and the two Nigerian-led interventions in Chad between 1979 and 1982.

Second, we argue that ECOMOG was a Pax Nigeriana in the sense that the intervention was consistent with Nigeria's image of itself as an aspiring hegemon. Yet Nigeria lacked the military resources and political support to act as an effective hegemon, and its legitimacy was questioned by several subregional states. Liberia's neighbors also had far more direct interests than Nigeria in resolving the conflict. We will argue that Nigeria, even though it was the main influence in resolving the conflict, lacked the dominant *capability* and *legitimacy* of a hegemon. ECOMOG represented hegemonic *ambition* rather than hegemonic *achievement*. Nigeria was constrained not only by its own military and domestic difficulties but also opposition to ECOMOG from key francophone states and the National Patriotic Front of Liberia (NPFL), the strongest Liberian faction. We argue further that states like Guinea, Sierra Leone, Gambia, and eventually Côte d'Ivoire had far more direct security interests in resolving the conflict, contradicting widespread claims of a Nigerian effort to impose its parochial interests on Liberia by bullying its neighbors into an intervention.

The third key argument we pursue is that difficulties at the domestic, subregional, and external levels made the conflict intractable for six years.

At the domestic level, enmity between Nigeria and the NPFL, political differences between Liberia's parties, and the determination of all of Liberia's warlords to enrich themselves and buy more arms by exporting the resources of territories under their control rendered disarmament impossible. At the subregional level, ECOWAS members failed to agree on a common policy toward Liberia as Burkina Faso and Côte d'Ivoire backed the NPFL, ECOMOG members supported the United Liberation Movement of Liberia for Democracy (ULIMO), the Liberia Peace Council (LPC), and the Armed Forces of Liberia (AFL), and Nigeria and Ghana disagreed over whether to attack or accommodate Charles Taylor. At the external level, support for ECOWAS's efforts was lackluster. The United States, United Nations, and OAU were involved in humanitarian and diplomatic efforts to resolve the conflict but did nothing significant to improve ECOMOG's logistical deficiencies for six years.

Finally, we will argue that only by obtaining cooperation at these three interdependent levels was the Liberian civil war eventually resolved. At the domestic level, the consent or coercion of Liberian factions was required to ensure successful disarmament, as they controlled about 85 percent of the territory for most of the war. At the subregional level, the diversification of ECOMOG to include more francophone contingents and its increased neutrality after Nigeria's rapprochement with the NPFL were important factors in resolving the conflict. At the external level, the logistical support provided by the United States and other logistical and financial support provided by the United Nations and the European Union (EU) were crucial in achieving success in disarmament and organizing successful elections. Pax Nigeriana was unable to succeed in Liberia without cooperation at these three interdependent levels.

Contingencies and Concepts

The historical approach we adopt highlights the crucial role that contingencies play in analyzing unique cases like the Liberian civil war. We argue that the most crucial factor in explaining the various outcomes of the Liberian civil war can be found in contingencies rather than concepts. Though concepts are helpful as themes to guide our investigation, this study does not attempt to apply the two concepts of hegemony and regional security complexes to the West African case in any formal sense. These concepts have some relevance to aspects of this particular case but do not provide an overarching explanatory framework.

Both concepts—hegemony and regional security complexes—were originally developed for parts of the world outside Africa. If they are to be applied in an African context, they need to be adapted in light of the specific complex dynamics of regional relations. This explains the empirical focus of this book and its strong emphasis on contingencies to explain outcomes. In discussing hegemony, the academic literature has tended to concentrate on the global level of analysis and usually examines states that are capable of creating economic institutions for promoting leadership and maintaining security.[19] We argued above that Nigeria, whatever its aspirations, cannot yet be treated as a regional hegemon because it lacks the *power* and *legitimacy* to act as such.

Barry Buzan's concept of a regional security complex also has limited utility for our case for similar reasons. Buzan argues, for example, that power relations and escalation chains in regional security complexes (described in greater detail below) bind all states together so that they are caught up in the same pattern of alliance and war even if not in direct security interaction with each other.[20] Our Liberia example suggests that such a seemingly mechanistic approach does not apply. Regional states and Liberian factions changed sides in response to altered circumstances without any consistent pattern of alliances being established. Responses to ECOMOG were the result of personal relationships (between the leaders of Burkina Faso and Côte d'Ivoire, Nigeria and Ghana, Nigeria and the NPFL), as well as the impacts of events in Liberia on its neighbors, rather than established linguistic and ideological alignments and rivalries and singular definitions of state interests.

For example, ideologically incompatible Côte d'Ivoire and Libya teamed up to support the NPFL largely due to family reasons on the part of the Ivorian leader, whereas francophone Guinea, Mali, and Senegal broke linguistic ranks to send troops to Anglophone-dominated ECOMOG in the early years of the conflict. As Buzan himself concedes, ECOMOG may foreshadow a potential regional pattern, but a significant pattern of regional security relations has not yet occurred in West Africa.[21] This suggests that it may be useful to focus here on the three levels of analysis—domestic, regional, and extraregional—as suggested by Buzan; still, we must be cautious in adapting this concept to our own limited needs.

No structure or subregional security architecture can explain the chains of consequences resulting from the ECOMOG intervention; the resolution of the Liberian civil war was a highly improvised process. There is no overriding security pattern, and contingencies determined the structure that emerged. Only a detailed chronological historical narrative that focuses on these complex interactions at the domestic, subregional, and external levels can, in our view, capture the changing dynamics between the various actors and adequately explain the sequences of events that occurred during the civil war. Therefore, we address some issues raised by these two concepts without attempting to apply them formally to our case study on Liberia.

According to Graham Evans and Jeffrey Newnham, "Hegemony is a concept meaning primacy or leadership. In an international system this leadership would be exercised by a 'hegemon,' a state possessing sufficient capability to fulfill this role."[22] David Myers defines regional hegemons as "states which possess power sufficient to dominate subordinate state systems."[23] As these definitions illustrate, hegemony requires both *capability* and *power* to exercise primacy or leadership. We argue that Nigeria can best be described as an aspiring or potential hegemon based on its lack of military and economic capability. This was most graphically symbolized by its experience in Liberia, as well as an earlier effort in Chad between 1979 and 1982.[24] France—not Nigeria—has historically played a hegemonic role in West Africa.[25]

Nigeria accounts for roughly 75 percent of West Africa's total gross national product (GNP) and over 50 percent of its population; it maintains a 94,500-strong army. Both its population and army surpass the size of its fifteen ECOWAS neighbors' combined total.[26] Nigeria clearly possesses military and economic resources that would allow it potentially to dominate its subregion. Based on the Liberian experience up until 1994, Clement Adibe, like many authors, opined that "the transformation of ECOWAS is the result of Nigerian hegemony."[27] So why do we argue that Nigeria's role in Liberia was not hegemonic?

Although Nigeria is militarily and politically powerful relative to other ECOWAS states, it lacked the capability to act in an effective manner, and its legitimacy was questioned by several of its neighbors. Nigeria may have been the most influential state in the (temporary) resolution of the Liberian conflict in 1997, but it was far from dominant in handling the challenges from Liberian factions and subregional actors. It eventually needed external logistical and financial support to bring peace to Liberia. Like Clement Adibe, several analysts have argued that Nigeria is a hegemon because the intervention would have been impossible without it. But the fact that the UN intervention in East Timor in 1999 would have been impossible without Australian leadership does not make Australia a hegemon. The key difference in identifying a country like the United States, but not Nigeria, as a hegemon is that it has the *capability* to provide leadership in its sphere of influence in the areas of security, finance, and trade (even if it does not always get its way), and its leadership role is accepted as *legitimate* by its European and Asian allies. It would be more appropriate to describe Nigeria as a "pivotal state" that possesses disproportionate military and economic power and diplomatic influence in its subregion.[28]

We argue that there were both domestic and subregional constraints to Nigeria's hegemonic ambitions in Liberia. Nigeria had to deal with "bargainers" in the form of states like Côte d'Ivoire, Ghana, and Senegal that had the capability significantly to increase the costs of its attempt to impose its will on the subregion. We also examine the domestic constraints faced by Nigerian leaders in their efforts to bring peace to Liberia. Several authors have identified Nigeria's internal divisions, economic dependence, and lack of political cohesion as key reasons in explaining its failure to dominate its subregion.[29] We will examine some of these constraints.

Below, we briefly address the second concept: the regional security complex. Though our main focus is the regional politics of the Liberian civil war, one cannot understand the regional intricacies of the conflict without focusing on the domestic and external levels of analysis that are inextricably linked to the regional aspects. Our Liberian case demonstrates the importance of focusing attention on the significant role of domestic and extrasubregional actors and not treating regions as autonomous subsystems of the global order.

As noted above, the relationship between international, domestic, and regional security has been the subject of close study by, among others,[30] Barry Buzan. Buzan described three levels of analysis in security studies: state (local), subsystem (regional), and system (international). This analytical framework requires one to understand the distinctive security dynamics at all three levels before assessing how they interact. Buzan defines his concept of regional security complexes as "a group of states whose primary security concerns link together sufficiently closely that their national securities cannot realistically be considered apart from one another."[31] The ECOMOG case reveals that West African states did have interdependent security concerns, as evidenced by the intervention of five West African states in Liberia, the instability resulting from the spillover of the civil war into neighboring states, and the five-year civil war triggered in Sierra Leone by a Liberian-backed faction. We, however, will adapt only some relevant aspects of Buzan's approach to the specific case of Liberia.

Contribution to the Existing Literature

No comprehensive study has yet been published on the ECOMOG intervention in Liberia, employing classified ECOWAS reports on Liberia as well as extensive interviews with many of the principal participants. The studies by Colonel Festus Aboaye and Major Innocent Nass present insiders' accounts of the ECOMOG experiences based on their participation in the subregional force.[32] Abiodun Alao describes his own study as an "interim report" rather than a "comprehensive account."[33] Klaas Van Walraven's short monograph does not set out to be exhaustive.[34] Stephen Ellis's account is more interested in using the ECOMOG experience to explain the religious and spiritual aspects of the war.[35] Most of the other published books do not cover more than the first three years of the Liberian civil war. These include a journalistic account by Mark Huband; an edited volume by Earl Conteh-Morgan and Karl Magyar involving African as well as Western scholars; and another collection of essays, edited by Margaret Vogt, mostly by Nigerian scholars, policymakers, and journalists.[36]

This study aims to provide the first comprehensive account of the ECOMOG intervention in Liberia that is uniquely based on still-classified ECOWAS primary documents as well as interviews with many of the principal actors during research trips to nine West African countries. As well as making a meaningful contribution to the literature on regional security, international peacekeeping, and U.S. policy toward Africa, we aim to contribute as well to the study of Nigerian foreign policy. The rich harvest of earlier years of Nigerian foreign policy studies seem to have become something of a drought, watered only by small pockets like the Nigerian Institute of International Affairs. We also attempt to consult widely African as well as Western sources—a glaring deficiency in much of the literature on Liberia, which tends to employ one-sided sources.

Much of the recent literature on regional security has tended to focus on Europe, Asia, and the Middle East. As a result, we aim to contribute to the study of regional security in Africa. The concept of regional security complexes has not yet been discussed in the African context, and in this study we attempt to focus attention on the three interdependent levels of this concept without testing the concept in any formal sense. The link between hegemony and regionalism is also much undertheorized.[37] By focusing on the role of a potential hegemon—Nigeria—in West Africa, we hope to make an empirical contribution to the consideration of such theories.

Through this empirical study of regional security, scholars will be able to develop a comparative perspective on regional security. Some of the issues of regional security are particular to West Africa, but others could have more general application. For example, some individual leaders are strong enough to exert disproportionate influence on their country's foreign policy in West Africa, where institutions are often weak and susceptible to the whims and caprices of regional strongmen. This may not be the case in other regions.

Subregional security relations and dynamics are still not well understood, and only through sufficient empirical knowledge based on cases like this one can this process even begin. Just as the study of African political systems by scholars in the pioneering late 1950s and early 1960s required detailed case studies of countries before generalizations could be drawn, so also does the study of regional interventions in Africa's civil wars in the 1990s and beyond.[38] These studies currently do not exist, and it is this gap that we seek to fill.

There are several weaknesses in the available literature on the Liberian civil war that this study attempts to rectify. The literature rarely employs primary documents from ECOWAS and UN sources, which are crucial to providing important information on the complex closed-door negotiations and other key events that took place during Liberia's civil war. In addition, most scholars have rarely adopted a holistic approach, and much of the literature fails to provide adequate background on Liberian politics and foreign policy while trying to explain the causes of the war. Neither does it provide the historical background on Nigerian foreign policy and the subregional dynamics of the complex diplomacy of West Africa, essential to understanding why Nigeria intervened in Liberia and why other subregional actors opposed or supported the intervention. We address these issues as well as the domestic, subregional, and external factors that first constrained but eventually underpinned Pax Nigeriana. The various works that we challenge in this study are cited in Chapter 3.

There are five other substantive areas in which this study challenges the conventional wisdom or offers a more comprehensive analysis. First, many analysts tend to depict the foreign policies of Nigeria and Côte d'Ivoire as static and unchanging during the civil war, thus failing to note the shift in Nigeria's Liberia policy under General Sani Abacha and the shift in Côte d'Ivoire's Liberia policy under Henri Konan Bédié; this study focuses attention on both changes. Second, analysts tend to overlook the domestic Nigerian environment within which Generals Ibrahim Babangida and Sani Abacha operated; we focus attention on the Nigerian domestic situation during the conflict. Third, this study stresses the importance of bilateral relations between Nigeria and the United States and their effect on Washington's support for ECOMOG. Fourth, we also stress the underanalyzed but crucial alliance between Nigeria and Ghana, which highlights the differences in diplomatic and military approaches of both countries. Finally, we argue that most analysts have an anachronistic view of Franco-Nigerian relations that fails to take into account the more cooperative bilateral relationship that has recently emerged between the two countries; we argue against the belief that France actively tried to frustrate Nigeria's efforts in Liberia, instead noting that Liberia was an area of little military strategic interest for France (though French business interests, like other European and Asian commercial interests, did benefit from the conflict in Liberia).

Many analysts do not place the ECOMOG intervention in a historical context and have thus made several erroneous interpretations. There are two important errors. First, some scholars have downplayed or ignored the external constraints on Nigeria's hegemonic aspirations in West Africa. In so doing they seem to assume that Nigeria has always played the role of military hegemon in West Africa. This role, in fact, belonged to France, and before 1990 Nigeria intervened only twice in a regional civil war and then only as the head of an OAU force. The interventions occurred in Chad between 1979 and 1982, and the peacekeepers were unsuccessful in resolving the conflict.

Second, analysts have talked of a monolithic francophone bloc of pro-French and anti-Nigerian African states. Benin, Niger, and Togo have, in fact, traditionally been close to Nigeria, Senegal has traditionally been a strong supporter of the OAU and ECOWAS, and Sékou Touré's Guinea and

Modibo Keita's Mali were never fully integrated into the Francophonie. It was noteworthy that these last three states were the first francophone states to contribute troops to ECOMOG. This study aims to address these deficiencies while providing a comprehensive analysis of the regional politics surrounding the Liberian civil war.

Approach and Sources

Our overall approach, then, is historical. Yet this is an empirical-analytical study that focuses on a contemporary case study set within the background of Nigerian foreign policy and domestic Liberian politics and foreign policy. Through this historical approach, we attempt to explain why Nigeria intervened in Liberia, showing the extent to which the intervention was consistent with its foreign policy goals since independence in 1960. In the background chapter on Liberia (Chapter 2), we explain the causes of the civil war, situating the explanation in both domestic politics and the loss of external support for Liberian leader, Samuel Doe, who tied his foreign policy closely to that of the United States.

In the other chapters we examine the course of the Liberian civil war through an assessment of the often changing goals, motivations, and interests of the main domestic, subregional, and external actors. Through this approach, we attempt to explain why the Liberian civil war lasted for seven years and to identify the most important factors that finally helped resolve the conflict (at least temporarily). By providing a historical background of the dynamics of Liberian politics and Nigerian foreign policy, and by explaining the interests complicating the resolution of the war, we seek to debunk the myths of "ancient hatreds" and "primordial tribalism" propounded by many Western analysts to explain cases like the Liberian civil war.[39] Many of these authors tend to wallow in the exoticism of African civil wars, often employing crude and simplistic stereotypes of tribal savagery and brutal cannibalism. In similar cases like Bosnia and Kosovo where brutalities occurred, many Western journalists have at least tried to provide a political and socioeconomic context, even if they are not always accurate. In this study, we argue that there were logical political and economic interests involved in the pursuit of the war, as in the Balkans, even though brutal means were often employed to achieve those goals.

Many authors have also sought to demonize ECOMOG, dismissing its peacekeepers as no more than murderers or mercenaries.[40] While pointing out the undoubtedly negative aspects of ECOMOG, we aim to balance some of these prejudiced views with the positive achievements and enormous sacrifices of the peacekeepers. In order to substantiate the main arguments of the book, we will rely on primary documents obtained from the

ECOWAS Secretariat archives relating to more than thirty ECOWAS conferences and diplomatic meetings on Liberia between 1990 and 1997. I visited the Nigerian Foreign Ministry in Abuja, where important speeches and documents on Nigeria's Liberia policy were obtained and interviews conducted with senior Nigerian diplomats. Research trips were undertaken to Liberia, Burkina Faso, Côte d'Ivoire, Ghana, Guinea, Nigeria, Senegal, Sierra Leone, and Togo between 1996 and 1999, during which diplomatic and military officials involved in the ECOMOG mission were interviewed. Senior U.S. State Department and Pentagon officials, as well as West African diplomats, were also interviewed in Washington.

The study also employs primary sources consisting of twenty-six UN Secretary-General reports to the Security Council and other documents published by the United Nations. In New York, interviews were conducted with senior UN officials and West African diplomats. The secondary literature on the Liberian conflict in academic journals and magazines was widely consulted, as was the secondary literature on Nigerian and Liberian politics. Biographies and collected speeches of former Nigerian leaders have also been used.

Organization of the Study

We have already described the basic content of Chapter 2, which provides useful background information on Liberia. Chapters 3–10 are grouped into three parts and cover the seven years of the Liberian civil war. In Part 1 (Chapters 3–5) we cover the period from December 1989 to December 1992, when ECOMOG embarked on a journey without maps, unsure of its mission and logistically ill equipped. The peacekeepers collaborated with the Independent National Patriotic Front of Liberia (INPFL), ULIMO, and the AFL to enforce peace against the NPFL. Seven major peace conferences, mostly in francophone capitals, symbolized efforts to forge subregional consensus by involving ECOWAS's francophone members more in efforts to resolve the conflict.

In Part 2 (Chapters 6–7) we cover the period from January 1993 to August 1994, when ECOMOG embarked on further enforcement action against the NPFL to force it to the negotiating table at Geneva and Cotonou even as ULIMO, the LPC, and the Lofa Defense Force (LDF) seized territory from the NPFL. During this period, UN and OAU peacekeepers were sent to Liberia to assist ECOMOG in disarmament as a divided ECOWAS continued its search for consensus. In Part 3 (Chapters 8–10) we cover the period from September 1994 to July 1997, when Ghana encouraged the new Nigerian military leadership to make peace with Charles Taylor and to appease Liberia's warlords by including them directly in the interim government.

Elections were eventually held in July 1997 after five peace conferences led to successful disarmament.

In Chapter 11 we describe events in Liberia under Charles Taylor's presidency since the (temporary) end of the civil war in 1997 and assess the impact of Taylor's destabilization policies on regional security in West Africa as well as the imposition of economic sanctions on Liberia. In the Conclusion (Chapter 12), we summarize our main arguments and address some broader implications of the ECOMOG experience for subregional security in West Africa.

We now turn our attention to Liberian politics under the leadership of Samuel Doe between 1980 and 1989. We focus on the domestic, regional, and external factors that help explain the causes of the Liberian civil war and help readers contextualize events in Liberia during the subsequent seven years of the post-Doe era.

Notes

1. Ali Mazrui, *Towards a Pax Africana* (Chicago: University of Chicago Press, 1967), p. 203.

2. *Africa Report* 37, no. 3 (May/June 1992): 40.

3. See Robert Jackson, "The Security Dilemma in Africa," in Brian Job (ed.), *The Insecurity Dilemma: National Security of Third World states* (Boulder and London: Lynne Rienner, 1992); and Stephen John Stedman, "Conflict and Conciliation in Sub-Saharan Africa," in Michael Brown (ed.), *The International Dimensions of Internal Conflict* (Cambridge, Mass.: Center for Science and International Affairs, 1996).

4. Francis Deng, "Africa and the New World Dis-Order: Rethinking Colonial Borders," *Brookings Review* 11, no. 2 (Spring 1993).

5. See Richard Joseph, "The International Community and Armed Conflict in Africa: Post-Cold War Dilemmas," in Gunnar Sørbø and Peter Vale (eds.), *Out of Conflict: From War to Peace in Africa* (Uppsala, Sweden: Nordiska Afrikainstitutet, 1997), pp. 9–21; and I. William Zartman, "African Regional Security and Changing Patterns of Relations," in Edmond Keller and Donald Rothchild (eds.), *Africa in the New International Order: Rethinking State Sovereignty and Regional Security* (Boulder and London: Lynne Rienner, 1996), pp. 52–68.

6. See Adekeye Adebajo and Chris Landsberg, "Back to the Future: UN Peacekeeping in Africa," *International Peacekeeping* 7, no. 4 (Winter 2000): pp. 161–188; Christopher Clapham, "The United Nations and Peacekeeping in Africa," in Mark Malan (ed.), *Whither Peacekeeping in Africa?* (Pretoria: Institute for Security Studies, 1999), pp. 25–44; Oliver Furley and Roy May (eds.), *Peacekeeping in Africa* (Aldershot, UK, and Vermont: Ashgate), 1998; Marrack Goulding, "The United Nations and Conflict in Africa since the Cold War," *African Affairs* 98, no. 391 (April 1999): 155–166; and Agostinho Zacarias, *The United Nations and International Peacekeeping* (London: I. B. Tauris, 1996).

7. See Hussein Adam, "Somalia: A Terrible Beauty Being Born?" in I. William Zartman (ed.), *Collapsed States: The Disintegration and Restoration of Legitimate Authority* (Boulder and London: Lynne Rienner, 1995), pp. 69–78; Walter Clarke and Jeffrey Herbst (eds.), *Learning from Somalia: The Lessons of Armed Humanitarian*

Intervention (Boulder and Oxford: Westview, 1997); John L. Hirsch and Robert B. Oakley, *Somalia and Operation Restore Hope: Reflections on Peacemaking and Peacekeeping* (Washington, D.C.: United States Institute of Peace, 1995); and Mohamed Sahnoun, *Somalia: The Missed Opportunities* (Washington, D.C.: United States Institute of Peace, 1994).

8. See Howard Adelman and Astri Suhrke (eds.), *The Path of a Genocide: The Rwanda Crisis from Uganda to Zaire* (New Brunswick and London: Transaction, 1999); Henry Kwami Anyidoho, *Guns over Kigali* (Accra, Ghana: Woeli Publishing Services, 1999); Ami Mpunge, "Crisis and Response in Rwanda," in Malan (ed.), *Whither Peacekeeping in Africa?* pp. 14–24; Organization of African Unity, *The International Panel of Eminent Persons to Investigate the 1994 Genocide in Rwanda and the Surrounding Events* (July 2000); Gérard Prunier, *The Rwanda Crisis: History of a Genocide* (New York: Columbia University Press, 1995); *Report of the Independent Inquiry into the Actions of the United Nations During the 1994 Genocide in Rwanda,* S/1999/1257 (16 December 1999); and Astri Suhrke, "UN Peacekeeping in Rwanda," in Sørbø and Vale (eds.), *Out of Conflict,* pp. 97–113.

9. See Adekeye Adebajo, *Building Peace in West Africa: Liberia, Sierra Leone, and Guinea-Bissau* (Boulder and London: Lynne Rienner, 2002); Colonel Festus Aboagye, *ECOMOG: A Subregional Experience in Conflict Resolution, Management, and Peacekeeping in Liberia* (Accra, Ghana: Sedco Enterprise, 1999), pp. 229–267; Comfort Ero, "The Future of ECOMOG in West Africa," in Jakkie Cilliers and Greg Mills (eds.), *From Peacekeeping to Complex Emergencies: Peace Support Missions in Africa* (Johannesburg and Pretoria: South African Institute of International Affairs and the Institute for Security Studies, 1999), pp. 55–74; and Robert Mortimer, "From ECOMOG to ECOMOG II: Intervention in Sierra Leone," in John W. Harbeson and Donald Rothchild (eds.), *Africa in World Politics: The African State System in Flux,* 3rd ed. (Colorado and Oxford: Westview, 2000), pp. 188–207.

10. See *Economist Intelligence Unit,* Country Report, "Guinea-Bissau"; Eric G. Berman and Katie E. Sams, *Peacekeeping in Africa: Capabilities and Culpabilities* (Geneva and Pretoria: UN Institute for Disarmament Research and Institute for Security Studies, 2000), pp. 128–138; United Nations Development Program, *Report of the Joint Review Mission on the United Nations Post-conflict Peacebuilding Offices,* Department of Political Affairs/UNDP (20 July 2001); and *Reports of the UN Secretary-General pursuant to Security Council Resolution 1216 (1998) Relative to the Situation in Guinea-Bissau.*

11. See Ali Ahmed Saleem, "An Introduction to IGADD," in Martin Doornbos et al. (eds.), *Beyond Conflict in the Horn* (The Hague: Institute of Social Studies, 1992); and Francis Deng, "Africa's Dilemmas in Sudan," *World Today* 54, no. 3 (March 1998).

12. See Jakkie Cilliers, *Building Security in Southern Africa: An Update on the Evolving Architecture,* ISS Monograph Series no. 43 (November 1999); Denis Venter, "Regional Security in Southern Africa in the Post–Cold War Era," in Keller and Rothchild (eds.), *Africa in the New International Order,* pp. 134–148; and Agostinho Zacarias, *Regional Security in Southern Africa* (London: I. B. Tauris, 1999).

13. See Kato Lambrechts (ed.), *Crisis in Lesotho: The Challenge of Managing Conflict in Southern Africa,* Foundation for Global Dialogue African Dialogue Series no. 2 (Braamfontein: Foundation for Global Dialogue, March 1999); Chris Landsberg, "Promoting Democracy: The Mandela-Mbeki Doctrine," *Journal of Democracy* 11, no. 3 (July 2000): 107–121; and Musifiky Mwanasali, "Peacebuilding in the Democratic Republic of the Congo," International Peace Academy Policy Briefing Series (April 1998).

14. See International Peace Academy, "The OAU Mechanism for Conflict Prevention, Management, and Resolution." Report of a conference co-sponsored by the IPA and OAU, Cairo, 7–11 May 1994.

15. See Adekeye Adebajo, "Towards a New *Pax Africana:* Three Decades of the OAU," *Praxis* 10, no. 1 (Spring 1993): 59–71; Chris Bakwesegha, "Conflict Resolution in Africa—A New Role for the Organization of African Unity?" in Sørbø and Vale (eds.), *Out of Conflict*, pp. 79–96; Yassin El-Ayouty and I. William Zartman (eds.), *The OAU after Twenty Years* (New York: Praeger, 1984); Solomon Gomes, "The OAU, State Sovereignty and Regional Security," in Keller and Rothchild (eds.), *Africa in the New International Order*, pp. 37–51; International Peace Academy, *Report of the Joint OAU/IPA Task Force on Peacemaking and Peacekeeping in Africa* (New York: IPA, March 1998); International Peace Academy, *OAU-IPA Seminar on Peacemaking and Peacekeeping,* Addis Ababa, November-December 1998; Monde Muyangwa and Margaret Vogt, *An Assessment of the OAU Mechanism for Conflict Prevention, Management, and Resolution, 1993–2000* (New York: International Peace Academy, November 2000); Organization of African Unity, *The OAU's Programme for Strengthening the Conflict Management Center* (Addis Ababa: OAU, October 1999); and Amadou Sesay (ed.), *The OAU after Twenty-Five Years* (Cambridge, UK: St. Martin's, 1990).

16. See Adekeye Adebajo and Chris Landsberg, "The Heirs of Nkrumah: Africa's New Interventionists," Pugwash Occasional Paper 2, no. 1 (January 2001): 65–90; Kofi Annan, "Two Concepts of Sovereignty," *The Economist,* 18–24 September 1999; Lori Fisler Damrosch, "Introduction," in Lori Fisler Damrosch (ed.), *Enforcing Restraint: Collective Intervention in Internal Conflicts* (New York: Council on Foreign Relations, 1993), pp. 1–26; Francis Mading Deng, "State Collapse: The Humanitarian Challenge to the United Nations," in Zartman (ed.), *Collapsed States,* pp. 207–219; and Eboe Hutchful, "Understanding the African Security Crisis," in Abdel-Fatau Musah and J. Kayode Fayemi (eds.), *Mercenaries: An African Security Dilemma* (London: Pluto, 2000), pp. 210–232.

17. See Boutros Boutros-Ghali, *An Agenda for Peace,* 2nd ed. (New York: UN Department of Public Information, 1995).

18. See Alan Henrikson, "The Growth of Regional Organizations and the Role of the United Nations," in Louise Fawcett and Andrew Hurrell (eds.), *Regionalism in World Politics* (Oxford: Oxford University Press, 1995).

19. See, for example, Robert Gilpin, *War and Change in World Politics* (Cambridge, UK: Cambridge University Press, 1981); Paul Kennedy, *The Rise and Fall of the Great Powers: Economic Change and Military Conflict from 1500 to 2000* (New York: Random House, 1987); and Robert Keohane, *After Hegemony: Cooperation and Discord in World Political Economy* (Princeton, N.J.: Princeton University Press, 1984).

20. Barry Buzan, *People, States, and Fear: An Agenda for International Security Studies in the Post–Cold War Era,* 2nd ed. (Boulder: Lynne Rienner, 1991), p. 188.

21. Barry Buzan, "Third World Regional Security in Structural and Historical Perspective," in Job (ed.), *The Insecurity Dilemma*, p. 184.

22. Graham Evans and Jeffrey Newnham, *The Dictionary of World Politics* (New York and London: Harvester Wheatsheaf, 1990), p. 153.

23. David Myers, "Threat Perception and Strategic Response of the Regional Hegemons: A Conceptual Overview," in David Myers (ed.), *Regional Hegemons: Threat, Perception, and Strategic Response* (Boulder and Oxford: Westview, 1991), p. 5.

24. See Margaret Vogt and Lateef Aminu (eds.), *Peacekeeping as a Security Strategy in Africa: Chad and Liberia as Case Studies,* 2 vols. (Enugu, Nigeria: Fourth Dimension, 1996).

25. See Adekeye Adebajo, "Nigeria: Africa's New Gendarme?" *Security Dialogue* 31, no. 2 (June 2000): 185–199; Bola Akinterinwa, *Nigeria and France, 1960–1995: The Dilemma of Thirty-Five Years of Relationship* (Ibadan, Nigeria: Vantage, 1999); Bassey Ate, "The Presence of France in West-Central Africa as a Fundamental Problem for Nigeria," in Bassey Ate and Bola Akinterinwa (eds.), *Nigeria and Its Immediate Neighbours* (Lagos: Nigerian Institute of International Affairs, 1992), pp. 11–30; Daniel Bach, "Dynamique et contradictions dans la politique africaine de la France: le cas des rapports avec le Nigéria," in Daniel Bach and M.-C. Smouts (eds.), *Politique Africaine* 2, no. 7 (1982): 47–74; Jean-François Bayart, "Endgame South of the Sahara? France's African Policy," in Chris Alden and Jean-Pascal Daloz (eds.), *Paris, Pretoria, and the African Continent* (New York: St. Martin's, 1996); John Chipman, *French Power in Africa* (Oxford: Basil Blackwell, 1989); and Oscar Ede, "Nigeria and Francophone Africa," in Gabriel Olusanya and R. A. Akindele (eds.), *Nigeria's External Relations: The First Twenty-Five Years* (Ibadan, Nigeria: University Press, 1986), pp. 176–195.

26. Mauritania formally withdrew from ECOWAS in December 2000, leaving the organization with fifteen members.

27. Clement Adibe, "Hegemony, Security, and West African Integration: Nigeria, Ghana, and the Transformation of ECOWAS," Ph.D. diss., Queens University, Canada, December 1994.

28. On the concept of pivotal states, see Francis Deng et al., *Sovereignty as Responsibility: Conflict Management in Africa* (Washington, D.C.: Brookings Institution 1996), pp. 131–167; and Adekeye Adebajo and Chris Landsberg, "South Africa and Nigeria as Regional Hegemons," in Mwesiga Baregu and Chris Landsberg, eds., *From Cape to Cairo: Southern Africa's Security Challenges* (Boulder: Lynne Rienner Publishers, forthcoming 2002).

29. See Christopher Clapham, *Africa and the International System: The Politics of State Survival* (Cambridge, UK, and New York: Cambridge University Press, 1996), pp. 21–22; Julius Ihonvbere, "Nigeria as Africa's Great Power: Constraints and Prospects for the 1990s," *International Journal* 46, no. 3 (summer 1991): 510–535; Yusuf Bala Usman, *For the Liberation of Nigeria* (London: New Beacon, 1979); and Anthony V. Williams, "Nigeria in West Africa," in Myers (ed.), *Regional Hegemons*, p. 209.

30. See, for example, James Barber and John Barratt, *South Africa's Foreign Policy, 1948–1988: The Search for Status and Security* (Johannesburg: Southern Book Publishers; Cambridge, UK: Cambridge University Press, 1988); Francis Deng, et al., *Sovereignty as Responsibility: Conflict Management in Africa* (Washington, D.C.: Brookings Institution, 1996); and Thomas Olson and Stephen Stedman, *The New Is Not Yet Born: Conflict Resolution in Southern Africa* (Washington, D.C.: Brookings Institution, 1996).

31. Buzan, *People, States, and Fear,* p. 190.

32. See Aboagye, "ECOMOG," and Major I. A. Nass, *A Study in Internal Conflicts: The Liberian Crisis and the West African Peace Initiative* (Enugu, Nigeria: Fourth Dimension, 2000).

33. Abiodun Alao, *The Burden of Collective Goodwill: The International Involvement in the Liberian Civil War* (Aldershot and Brookfield, UK: Ashgate, 1998), pp. x–xi.

34. Klaas Van Walraven, *The Pretence of Peace-keeping: ECOMOG, West Africa, and Liberia, 1990–1998* (The Hague: Netherlands Institute of International Relations, 1999).

35. Stephen Ellis, *The Mask of Anarchy: The Destruction of Liberia and the Religious Dimensions of an African Civil War* (London: Hurst, 1999).

36. Mark Huband, *The Liberian Civil War* (London and Portland: Frank Cass, 1998); Karl Magyar and Earl Conteh-Morgan (eds.), *Peacekeeping in Africa: ECOMOG in Liberia* (London and New York: Macmillan and St. Martin's, 1998); and M. A. Vogt (ed.), *The Liberian Crisis and ECOMOG: A Bold Attempt at Regional Peacekeeping* (Lagos: Gabumo, 1992).

37. Andrew Hurrell, "Regionalism in Theoretical Perspective," in Fawcett and Hurrell (eds.), *Regionalism in World Politics*, p. 50.

38. See, for example, David Apter, *Ghana in Transition* (New York: Atheneum, 1963); James Coleman, *Nigeria: Background to Nationalism* (Berkeley: University of California Press, 1958); Martin Kilson, *Political Change in a West African State: Study of the Modernization Process in Sierra Leone* (Cambridge: Harvard University Press, 1966); Gus Liebenow, *Liberia: The Evolution of Privilege* (Ithaca: Cornell University Press, 1969); Richard Sklar, *Nigerian Political Parties: Power in an Emergent African Nation* (Princeton, N.J.: Princeton University Press, 1963); Crawford Young, *Politics in the Congo: Decolonization and Independence* (Princeton, N.J.: Princeton University Press, 1965); and Aristide Zolberg, *One Party Government in Ivory Coast* (Princeton, N.J.: Princeton University Press, 1964).

39. See, for example, *The Economist*, "Sharks and Alligators," 13 April 1996; Huband, *The Liberian Civil War;* Robert Kaplan, "The Coming Anarchy," *Atlantic Monthly* (February 1994); Keith Richburg, *Out of America: A Black Man Confronts Africa* (San Diego: Harcourt Brace, 1998); and Phillip van Niekerk, "They Cooked My Brother's Heart and Ate It," *The Observer*, 14 April 1996.

40. The worst example of this sort of writing, in my opinion, is Stephen Ellis's *The Mask of Anarchy*. The sections on ECOMOG in this study appear to be based largely on tendentious claims and unsubstantiated rumors. Interviews with ECOMOG officials explaining their own views are not cited in the book.

chapter 2

A Decade of Troubles: Master-Sergeant Samuel Doe's Liberia, 1980–1989

The real meaning of democracy . . . is to give jobs to somebody who can promote you.
—Master-Sergeant Samuel Doe, Liberian head of state, 1980–1990

In order to understand the roots of the Liberian civil war, as well as the context of the ECOMOG intervention, it is necessary to explain the important political, social, and economic problems in prewar Liberia. Because many of the Liberian actors involved in the civil war—like Charles Taylor, George Boley, Alhaji Kromah, Roosevelt Johnson, Amos Sawyer, Baccus Matthews, Oscar Quiah, Ellen Johnson-Sirleaf, and Ruth Perry—played prominent political roles during this period, we provide this chapter as background for better understanding events that came later.

In this chapter we will assess six key issues that contributed to the causes of the civil war: the exclusionary rule of the Americo-Liberian oligarchy; the brutal and inept rule of Master-Sergeant Samuel Doe; the deleterious effect that Doe's misrule had on the Armed Forces of Liberia; the ethnic rivalries and personal ambitions that resulted from this rule; the subregional tensions and rivalries that resulted from Doe's bloody rise to power; and the destabilizing effect of the sudden withdrawal of U.S. support for Doe, a strategic Cold War ally.

The 133-year rule of the Americo-Liberian oligarchy created deep-seated resentment and divisions within Liberian society and left historical scars on the oppressed indigenous population; the reforms enacted by Presidents William Tubman and William Tolbert (1944–1971; 1971–1980) failed to heal these. Amid growing economic problems, Tolbert was faced with unprecedented political challenges from Liberian opposition groups. The spontaneous jubilation of non–Americo-Liberian indigenous people following the coup of 1980 by low-ranking soldiers graphically symbolized the level of hostility that had welled up against the ruling True Whig Party.

The brutality of Doe's regime was demonstrated by his assassination of Tolbert and thirteen senior officials within a week of taking power. In the next four years, Doe eliminated potential rivals through assassination or enforced exile. Human rights abuses proliferated against students, journalists, and other groups that challenged Doe's rule. The Liberian autocrat's crude tactics, typified by the blatantly rigged 1985 elections, closed off peaceful avenues for dissent and resulted in several military challenges to his regime, culminating in Charles Taylor's 1989 invasion.

Like other Liberian institutions before 1980, the AFL's senior leadership was dominated by Americo-Liberians, creating resentment among the indigenous lower ranks who did not share in the benefits enjoyed by the officer corps. Upon assuming power, Doe perpetuated these divisions by filling the most important military positions with his ethnic Krahn and purging the army of Gios and Manos. He effectively turned a national institution into an instrument of Krahn oppression—a reputation that followed the AFL throughout the civil war.

The brutality of Doe's rule and his parochial, ethnic power base further deepened ethnic divisions within Liberian society. Krahns were also disproportionately represented in the cabinet, and Doe co-opted some Mandingo elements into the political system. This created enemies among important political groups. Many Americo-Liberians felt alienated by the brutal murder of their former leaders, and Gios and Manos felt victimized on several fronts. The incident responsible for igniting the popular uprising that led to civil war was the massacre of an estimated 3,000 Gio and Mano citizens in Nimba County by Doe's Krahn-dominated AFL in 1985. Nimba citizens were also purged from the army, and Gio politician Jackson Doe was robbed of probable electoral victory in 1985. It was an alliance of these two disaffected groups—Americo-Liberians and Nimba citizens—that finally toppled Doe's regime: Americo-Liberian Charles Taylor was able to rally military support among Gios and Manos in Nimba County after his 1989 invasion.

However, ambitious individuals often manipulated group grievances for personal gain. Some Americo-Liberian and Nimba politicians continued to serve the Doe regime. The Liberian state remained the path to power and wealth for ambitious politicians. Politics often became a zero-sum game for control of the state apparatus, and the manipulation of ethnic differences and exclusion of rival ethnic groups from power helped trigger the civil war, which was literally a continuation of politics by other means.

Strong African opposition to Doe's regime, particularly within West Africa, led to his early diplomatic isolation. The killing of Ivorian leader

Félix Houphouët-Boigny's adopted son-in-law by Doe's soldiers in 1980 created a rift between both countries that resulted in Côte d'Ivoire cooperating with the NPFL's attempt to topple Doe in 1989. The strained relationship between Doe and anti-U.S. Libyan leader Muammar Qaddafi also resulted in Libya providing military support to Charles Taylor. Doe had allies in Ibrahim Babangida's Nigeria and Sékou Touré's Guinea. The United States continued its historic relationship with Liberia under Doe, who was regarded as a strategic Cold War ally in Africa. Substantial U.S. military, economic, and diplomatic support helped maintain Doe's autocratic rule. The sudden withdrawal of this support by 1989 had a destabilizing effect on Liberia, leaving a security vacuum that Charles Taylor's invasion attempted to exploit.

The Americo-Liberian Oligarchy

Liberia is Africa's oldest republic. This country of 2.5 million inhabitants was founded on 26 July 1847 by black American settlers who started arriving on the West African coast in 1822. Although representing only 5 percent of the population, this coastal settler elite established a corrupt, nepotistic system that excluded and oppressed the sixteen main "up-country" indigenous ethnic groups: the Bassa, Belle, Dei, Gbandi, Gio, Gola, Grebo, Kissi, Kpelle, Krahn, Kru, Loma, Mandingo, Mano, Mende, and Vai.[1] Most of these groups had ethnic clansmen in neighboring states: Mende, Gola, Kissi, and Vai also resided in Sierra Leone; Loma, Kpelle, Mandingo, Mano, and Gio in Guinea; and Grebo, Kru, and Krahn in Côte d'Ivoire.

The Americo-Liberian oligarchy established the True Whig Party in 1884, which became a vehicle of total control over the state apparatus and oppression of the so-called hinterlanders. The Americo-Liberian rulers were reprimanded by the League of Nations in 1931 for complicity in the forcible recruitment of indigenous Liberians to plantations in the Spanish colony of Fernando Po (now Equatorial Guinea). Under this oligarchic minority, estates of 20,000 acres were acquired for a paltry 50 cents per acre, and politically connected absentee landlords controlled large plantations. The indigenous people were heavily taxed and their crops and livestock requisitioned by corrupt officials, even as settlers themselves refused to pay tax. Like European settlers in the United States who had stripped black Africans of their freedom and dispossessed Native Americans of their land, it can be said that the Americo-Liberian settlers had learned similar lessons with brutal efficiency.

William Tubman was president of Liberia from 1944 to 1971. His unification program attempted to bridge the gap between settlers and indigenous people by broadening political participation of "country people" in the government and encouraging pride in indigenous culture, art, and languages.

He granted suffrage to indigenous people and, in a series of reforms in 1964, extended representation in the legislature to them and increased their access to the civil service. The increasing pool of indigenous people who benefited from expanding high school scholarships meant their continued exclusion from the system became politically inexpedient and economically wasteful. But the one-party system ensured continued Americo-Liberian hegemony. Despite Tubman's efforts at involving the indigenous majority in the political system, "tribal" people continued to be discriminated against in the civil service.

William R. Tolbert became president of Liberia after Tubman's death in 1971. Less charismatic than his predecessor, Tolbert nevertheless continued the reforms. Primary school enrollment increased from 31 percent of the population in 1960 to 60 percent in 1980, and secondary school enrollment increased from 2 percent to 20 percent during the same period. Despite these achievements, Tolbert's Liberia experienced a severe economic crisis when international prices for its two chief exports, iron ore and rubber, dropped in 1975 even as the price of oil imports trebled. Liberia found it increasingly difficult to meet its food needs.

By 1979, the country was importing 25 percent of its total rice needs despite growing the grain domestically. Wages rarely exceeded 50 cents per day for ordinary Liberians, and by 1980 the continuing inequality between Americo-Liberians and indigenous people was symbolized by the fact that 4 percent of the population owned 60 percent of the country's wealth.[2] Liberia's foreign debt increased from $158 million in 1970 to $600 million in 1979. In the midst of this economic crisis, Tolbert decided to host the OAU summit in June 1979, spending an estimated $200 million on a new hotel and conference center.

The Year of Ferment

Tolbert had tried to control dissent by limiting labor and student strikes and restricting public meetings and marches. But he was unable to prevent the emergence of opposition groups calling for an end to his rule. The Progressive Alliance of Liberians (PAL) was founded in 1975 by Liberian students in the United States who called for rapid political reform, a pragmatic African socialism, and a more radical foreign policy toward the rest of Africa. The group strongly criticized the economic inequalities in Liberian society. Its leader was a mercurial, charismatic firebrand, Gabriel Baccus Matthews, an Americo-Liberian graduate of New York's City University. PAL's secretary-general was an indigene of Sinoe County named Oscar Quiah. Its members consisted largely of Liberian students, unemployed Monrovian workers, and small-scale rural farmers.

After Tolbert proposed, in early April 1979, a nearly 50 percent price increase per bag of rice (from $22 to $30), the mainstay of the national diet, a mass demonstration erupted into the violent Rice Riots on 14 April 1979, triggering the so-called Year of Ferment, which would culminate in the fall of the Americo-Liberian oligarchy. In 1979, the average monthly income of urban Liberians was about $80. Following the proposed price increase, a demonstration was organized by PAL involving 2,000 marchers. After police fired into the crowd, rioting and looting ensued, resulting in the death of more than 40 students and the wounding of some 400 demonstrators.

The beleaguered Tolbert appealed to Guinean leader Sékou Touré to send troops to quell the riots, invoking a mutual defense pact signed on 23 January 1979. Touré dispatched 700 Guinean soldiers to Monrovia. Although these troops returned home after three weeks, having helped to restore order, Tolbert was weakened by the incident, appearing as a feeble leader who had to rely on foreigners to keep domestic order. Tolbert soon backed off the rice price increase but ordered the arrest of thirty-three PAL leaders, charging them with treason and attempting to overthrow the government. Habeas corpus was suspended, and the compliant legislature granted Tolbert emergency powers.

On 26 June 1979, Tolbert released the PAL leaders in a general amnesty. Emboldened by its successful demonstration, PAL attempted to register as a political party to challenge the True Whig aristocracy in legislative and presidential elections, scheduled for 1981 and 1983, respectively. After a court prevented its registration, PAL threatened another demonstration. An indecisive Tolbert backed down on 8 January 1980 and agreed to register PAL's Progressive People's Party to contest elections. On 8 March 1980, Baccus Matthews called for a nationwide general strike to force Tolbert to stand down before the 1983 presidential election. Tolbert's reaction this time was swift: he jailed thirty-eight PAL leaders, including Baccus Matthews, claiming he had uncovered a planned armed insurrection to topple his regime. Tolbert set a treason trial for 14 April 1980.

The Movement for Justice in Africa (MOJA) was the other main opposition group to challenge Tolbert's rule. MOJA was founded in 1973 by lecturers and students at the University of Liberia. Togba-Nah Tipoteh, a Kru, was its head. Two of his university colleagues were the other prominent leaders of the group: Amos Sawyer, the Americo-Liberian dean of social sciences and humanities, and Henry Boima Fahnbulleh, a Vai political scientist. MOJA appealed mainly to Liberia's middle class. Its program called for the nationalization of major economic enterprises, the confiscation of the illegal landholdings of the Whig aristocracy, and the punishment of government corruption. It acted as a pressure group, calling for strikes and work slowdowns.

In August 1979, MOJA offered a direct challenge to the True Whig oli-garchy when Amos Sawyer was persuaded to contest the mayoral election in Monrovia. Sawyer's announced participation was met with popular enthusiasm, as it was the first electoral challenge to the Whigs in two decades. Tolbert reacted with characteristic indecisiveness: he first at-tempted to revive moribund property voting criteria, in contradiction of his own reforms, before postponing the election until June 1980. MOJA be-came increasingly vocal in its opposition and, like PAL, applied to register as a political party. MOJA was more cunning than PAL in its opposition to Tolbert but less bold; PAL was more audacious but more opportunistic. Al-though both groups weakened the Tolbert regime, they did not destroy it. The final blow to the Americo-Liberian oligarchy would come from a quite unexpected quarter.

The Men on Horseback

The 6,000-strong Armed Forces of Liberia was a descendant of the notori-ous Frontier Force, which long had a reputation for pillaging local commu-nities and crushing mass uprisings. The army mirrored other institutions in Liberia: its officer corps was almost exclusively Americo-Liberian, and in-digenous Loma, Bassa, Kpelle, Kru, and Krahn were recruited to serve as rank-and-file foot soldiers. Under Tolbert, the officer corps acquired an in-creasing reputation for professionalism, though foiled coup attempts were reported during both the Tubman and Tolbert regimes. Tolbert had unwit-tingly politicized the army by using it to crush various labor and student demonstrations, thus employing military means to solve political problems. Some soldiers had reportedly refused to fire on protestors during the Rice Riots, explaining, in part, the use of Guinean troops.

There were rumblings within the Liberian military in March 1980 after the arrest of some army officers and enlisted men considered sympathetic to the opposition. Rumors of a military coup had spread in Monrovia even before these arrests. Tolbert had earlier alienated junior officers by approv-ing a wage rise for the army in 1976 that disproportionately benefited sen-ior officers. He had also angered some members of the officer corps by bringing in foreign troops to quell a domestic riot.

This provided the backdrop for the coup staged on 12 April 1980 by twenty-eight-year-old Master-Sergeant Samuel Kanyon Doe, along with two staff sergeants, four sergeants, eight corporals, and two privates. In the early hours of the morning of 12 April, these seventeen low-ranking sol-diers stormed the Executive Mansion in Monrovia and assassinated Tolbert along with twenty-six other occupants before announcing their coup over the radio. On 22 April, thirteen True Whig senior officials were executed on a Monrovia beach under the full glare of TV cameras. Doe was so worried about a countercoup that he rarely slept in the same place for two consecutive nights. He maintained a dusk-to-dawn curfew during the first two years of his rule. Like Shakespeare's Macbeth, he seemed haunted by the ghosts of the True Whig oligarchs.

Some of Doe's ill-disciplined troops joined civilians in looting the homes of Whig officials and destroying their grandiloquent Masonic Temple in Monrovia. A jubilant atmosphere engulfed indigenous Liberians after the coup, and the whole country was swept up in a carnival atmosphere: this was their liberation from 133 years of settler domination. The lack of sympathy for the Americo-Liberian leadership could be explained by its brutal rule and the fact that the True Whigs had themselves carried out public beatings and executions. As Doe explained in his first nationwide broadcast of 14 April 1980: "The Tolbert Government had to be removed because, as we all know, it disregarded the civil, human and constitutional rights of the Liberian people. Those who make laws must also live by the laws they make, or they must answer to the people."[3]

Doe became chairman of the People's Redemption Council (PRC) as the most senior-ranking member of the putschists, none of whom had a high school education. This "lumpenmilitariat" released PAL leaders two days before their scheduled treason trial and invited them to join its government.[4] Four cabinet posts went to the PAL and three to MOJA; three of Tolbert's former ministers were retained in an attempt to maintain a broad base of support for the new regime. Baccus Matthews, Togba-Nah Tipoteh, and Henry Fahnbulleh became ministers. Recognizing that it lacked expertise and experience in administration, the PRC co-opted civilians into its government. The early Doe regime was a marriage of convenience that harnessed the brawn of the soldiers to the brain of the politicians: The intelligentsia had experience and expertise but lacked power; the soldiers lacked experience and expertise but had power.

The Limits of a Lumpenmilitariat

In the early days of his rule, Doe tried to present his coup as a victory over an oppressive system rather than an oppressive group, stressing class over ethnicity and criticizing Tolbert's corruption while praising Tubman's achievements. Ironically, the new ruling elite consisted of the indigenous people and lower-income settlers whom the Tubman and Tolbert educational reforms had set out to benefit: the settler class had unwittingly provided the indigenous people with the tools of their own liberation.

Doe moved quickly to consolidate his support within the army by increasing the minimum pay of soldiers and converting low-ranking soldiers to captains, majors, and generals to break the settler domination of the officer corps. The ruling PRC consisted mostly of individuals from Doe's Grand Gedeh County and Sinoe County. Both southeastern counties were among the least developed regions in Liberia. Though the PRC was predominantly Krahn, it also had a sprinkling of Kru, Gio, Grebo, and Loma. Tolbert had diluted the Loma dominance of the army rank-and-file by recruiting more soldiers from Nimba, Grand Gedeh, and Sinoe Counties. But the Loma of Lofa County remained the largest ethnic group in the army in 1980, with 60 percent of the AFL's soldiers.[5] Shortly after his coup, Doe filled strategic positions of the army with his own indigenous Krahns, most notably the Executive Mansion Guards, the 1st Infantry Battalion, and the Special Anti-Terrorist Unit. All four infantry battalions were headed by Krahns. Despite constituting only 5 percent of the Liberian population, Krahns held 31 percent of cabinet posts in 1985.[6]

The Mandingos, a powerful group of Muslim traders with a diaspora stretching from Côte d'Ivoire to Casablanca, had traditionally dominated the transportation and rural retail sectors in Liberia. Doe assiduously courted this group, granting them employment and commercial opportunities. Mandingos dominated the informal crossborder trade with Guinea and Sierra Leone, and Doe offered them protection in return for a cut of their lucrative regional transit trade.[7] The Liberian leader built a mosque in central Monrovia and frequently noted that many of his PRC members were Muslims. Edward Kesselly, a Loma with strong Mandingo family links, was appointed head of the Constitutional Advisory Assembly in 1983. Alhaji Kromah, a Mandingo, was an assistant minister in the Doe regime. Both later fell out with Doe.

Even after the coup, the Americo-Liberian minority was still better-educated and controlled more wealth than the indigenous people. Doe recognized the need to compromise with this group in order to stabilize his regime and prevent a collapse of Liberia's economy and administration. By December 1981, Doe released all political prisoners and returned the confiscated properties of Americo-Liberians, except those of officials executed in the aftermath of the coup. In 1982, Doe brought more Americo-Liberians into his cabinet, encouraged Americo-Liberians who had fled abroad after the coup to return, and courted the Americo-Liberian vote before the 1985 elections by restoring their powerful Masonic Order. The coup had never been a simple overthrow of the Americo-Liberian elite even though its consequence was the loss of their monopoly over state institutions.

Shortly after Doe's putsch, a group of civilian cabinet ministers formed around PRC Vice Chairman Weh Syen. These so-called revisionists urged closer ties to Libya and the Soviet bloc, the continued nonrecognition of Israel, and a radical economic policy. By 1982, the revisionists' defeat was signified by the execution of Weh Syen and four of his PRC colleagues: the Liberian revolution had started to devour its own children. Outspoken civilians like Togba-Nah Tipoteh, Baccus Matthews, and Henry Fahnbulleh also resigned or were forced out of the cabinet. Others were more pragmatic. Oscar Quiah was minister of internal affairs before falling out with Doe in April 1983. Jailed and frustrated in his attempts to enter private business, Quiah would later become secretary-general of Doe's political party. George Boley, a Krahn who served as Doe's education minister, had previously served the Tolbert regime.

Doe and his officials illegally acquired wealth and land as blatantly as the True Whigs once did. Revenue from logging concessions and fuel went straight to Doe's private funds, and even U.S. food assistance was diverted into private pockets.[8] The public sector increased from 18,000 employees in 1979 to 56,000 by 1983 as the state apparatus became a cash cow that Doe milked for political patronage.[9] By the end of his rule, Doe and his cronies had stolen a reported $300 million in public funds.[10]

Human rights abuses became rampant under Doe.[11] Draconian PRC decrees attempted to limit political dissent. In 1984, after students of the University of Liberia demonstrated against the arrest of Amos Sawyer, Doe's riot troops sealed off the campus for five days and embarked on a wanton destruction of life and property. The government admitted that seventy-four students were wounded, and fatalities were reported. Intolerant of media criticism, Doe intimidated the press by fining and imprisoning journalists. He banned issues of the independent Liberian newspapers, the *Daily Observer* and *Footprints Today,* as well as the London-based *West Africa.* Journalist Charles Gbenyon was bayoneted to death in November 1985 while in detention at the executive mansion; Momolu Sirleaf, publisher of *Footprints Today,* was jailed for a total of four months between 1984 and 1985; and the *Daily Observer's* pressroom was burned to the ground in March 1986.

Doe had inherited an economic crisis from the Tolbert administration. During Doe's decade in office, the crisis was exacerbated by a global recession that adversely affected Liberia's three chief exports—iron ore, rubber, and shipping—even as agricultural production continued its downward spiral. Rice imports increased from 42,000 metric tons in 1974 to 126,000 metric tons in 1983.[12] By 1986, Liberia's gross domestic product had declined for six straight years, civil servants were being irregularly paid, and the country's external debt stood at $1.5 billion.

The Metamorphosis of a Master-Sergeant

Within four years Doe, the primus inter pares in 1980, had eliminated all potential rivals and remained unchallenged at the pinnacle of Liberian politics. He had killed more than 50 rivals by 1985.[13] In August 1984, he concocted a plot against three former PRC members, Nicholas Podier, Larry Borteh, and Jerry Friday, and expelled them from the army. Podier, the former PRC deputy chairman and a citizen of Nimba County, was executed on 14 July 1987 after attempting to topple Doe's regime with an invasion from northern Liberia. A three-year ban on political activity was finally lifted after the National Constitutional Commission, chaired by Amos Sawyer, submitted a draft constitution in January 1983 that was approved in a national referendum on 3 July 1984. The constitution enraged Doe by setting a minimum age limit of thirty-five for participation in presidential elections. Doe simply added two years to his date of birth to overcome the inconvenience. He then launched his so-called second coup: a flawed democratic transition that was staged simply to lend a veneer of legitimacy to his autocratic rule and satisfy U.S. demands for an election.

Three months before the 15 October 1985 elections, Doe banned the two most formidable opponents of his NDPL, Baccus Matthews's United People's Party (UPP) and Amos Sawyer's Liberian People's Party (LPP), for espousing what Doe's Special Elections Commission (SECOM) described as "strange and foreign ideologies." Many members of the opposition were intimidated and harassed. Amos Sawyer was jailed for three months at the end of 1984 and remained under virtual house arrest until early 1985. Baccus Matthews, Edward Kesselly, Tuan Wreh, and Harry Greaves were detained for a week in April 1985. Dusty Wolokollie was detained for six weeks in July 1985. Ellen Johnson-Sirleaf was jailed for seven months in November 1985. After the ban on the UPP and LPP, the main opponent of the NDPL became the Liberian Action Party (LAP). Its leader was Jackson Doe (no relation), the Gio former head of the National Port Authority under Samuel Doe.

The October 1985 elections were as unfree as they were unfair. Doe unilaterally removed the entire membership of SECOM and replaced them with more pliant political associates. He appointed Emmet Harmon, a sly Americo-Liberian lawyer with an inexhaustible appetite for nit-picky pedantry, as SECOM chairman. The state-owned ELTV station gave wide coverage to NDPL candidates but paid only scant attention to opposition parties. The chief news editor of the ELWA radio station, Joe Mulbah, was forced out of his job after reporting on electoral fraud. A week before the elections, Doe ordered all civil servants to prove membership in the NDPL in order to retain their jobs. In a famous redefinition of civic responsibility, Liberia's would-be George Washington noted: "The real meaning of democracy . . . is to give jobs to somebody who can promote you."[14] True to his word, Doe removed all non-NDPL members from executive and judicial government jobs.

As exit polls showed Jackson Doe's LAP in the lead in most of Liberia's counties in both presidential and legislative elections, and with the Liberian and foreign press predicting a landslide victory for the LAP, Samuel Doe abruptly stopped the counting on 16 October 1985, citing several reported cases of electoral malpractices. He then ordered all ballot boxes brought to the government's Unity Conference Center on Monrovia's outskirts to be counted in secret by an ad hoc committee of fifty hand-picked Liberians. Twenty members of this committee were from Doe's Grand Gedeh County, and some were relatives and aides of NDPL leaders. None of the three opposition parties were represented on the committee. Doe's vice president until 1990, Harry Moniba, later admitted that the elections were rigged.[15]

As Liberians awaited the results, Doe issued orders to his soldiers to arrest or flog anyone insulting him or predicting an opposition victory, and Justice Minister Jenkins Scott threatened to prosecute anyone who criticized the count as slow. When the results finally appeared out of thin air two weeks later, no one was surprised by the outcome: Samuel Doe had awarded himself a slim 50.9 percent presidential victory and a comfortable 84 percent legislative triumph. Harmon claimed, somewhat implausibly, that the vote had been directed by the hand of God. Public gatherings were disallowed after the elections, for fear, according to the government, that "the jubilation might get out of hand."[16]

Barely a month after the elections, Samuel Doe's nemesis returned to haunt him. General Thomas Quiwonkpa, a Gio from Nimba County and former commander of the AFL, had been credited with restoring discipline to the Liberian army. Concerned about Quiwonkpa's growing popularity, Doe unsuccessfully attempted to transfer him to the post of PRC secretary-general before ordering his arrest in October 1983. After the protests of Nimba chiefs and others, Doe let the popular general go into exile in the United States.

On 12 November 1985, Quiwonkpa returned to Monrovia across the Sierra Leonean border at the head of a band of coup-makers. He attempted to rally support among his former AFL soldiers and announced a coup over the radio. The celebrations that erupted were cut short after Doe announced he was still in charge. Quiwonkpa failed to establish control over the country's communications system and resisted a frontal attack on the Executive Mansion. Both mistakes proved fatal: they gave Doe enough time to mobilize his Krahn-dominated Executive Mansion Guard and 1st Infantry Battalion from Camp Schiefflin to foil the attempted coup. Quiwonkpa was beaten to death, castrated, and dismembered. Other putschists and soldiers were summarily executed. The AFL was purged of Gios.

Quiwonkpa had announced that he was launching the coup to restore the mandate of Jackson Doe, a fellow Gio, who was widely believed to have won the 1985 election. During the coup, Gios and Manos had attacked Krahns and Mandingos in Monrovia.[17] After foiling the attempted coup, Doe's Krahn-dominated soldiers went on a rampage in Nimba County, indiscriminately killing a reported 3,000 Gios and Manos and burning their villages. There were also reported killings of Gios and Manos in Monrovia and Grand Gedeh County. This single incident, more than any other, set the stage for the exploitation of ethnic rivalries that would eventually culminate in the brutal seven-year Liberian civil war.

On 6 January 1986, Doe's metamorphosis was apparently completed upon his inauguration to a six-year term as president. The military fatigues and hand grenades of the early days were dropped in favor of flowing robes and smartly tailored three-piece suits. The government press took to addressing the head of state as "Dr. Doe" after the University of South Korea awarded him an honorary doctorate degree. The shy, skeletal, and apparently dim-witted master-sergeant of 1980 was now transformed into the confident, corpulent, and apparently cerebral civilian president. Christopher Clapham best described the dramatic transformation: "Doe was rapidly metamorphosed from a gaunt and hungry-looking sergeant in ill-fitting battle fatigues, into a plump, immaculately suited figure with a fashionable Afro hair cut."[18]

Doe's Pyrrhic victory had been achieved in the face of immense unpopularity. Gus Liebenow described well the spectacular loss of his early popularity:

> His poor speaking ability was mimicked, his accumulation of personal wealth was compared to the abuses of the True Whig period ("Same Taxi, New Driver" was the popular slogan of the day), and his hypocrisy in calling for a return to constitutional democracy while doing everything possible to undermine that goal, was derided.[19]

The opposition revealed its own lack of unity when thirteen of the eighteen non-NDPL legislators broke ranks with their leader's orders not to legitimize Doe's flawed elections by taking their seats. Among them was a woman who would later play a prominent role in Liberian politics: Ruth Perry, who became head of a transitional government in 1996. Many opposition members also revealed their opportunism during the five years of the Second Republic when they crossed the carpet to join the ruling NDPL in return for access to state patronage.

In August 1988, opposition leader Gabriel Kpolleh was arrested for a second time and sentenced to ten years in prison for allegedly plotting to overthrow the regime. BBC broadcasts were banned, and the Catholic radio station ELCM was shut down in June 1989. Despite holding supposedly democratic elections, Doe continued his autocratic ways. The Second Republic was crippled and deformed at birth. The early signs suggested that the infant monstrosity would not enjoy a healthy life. Amos Sawyer wrote perhaps the most eloquent epitaph to the Doe era:

Murder, torture, and imprisonment became normal instruments of national policy. Similarly, graft and corruption were also perceived as normal business. The combination of ill-trained military people in search of bounties and ambitious former clients of a decaying patronage system seeking to maintain their privileges had produced the right chemistry for ineptitude, plunder, and brutal repression.[20]

From African Pariah to American Puppet

After the 1980 coup, many African states withheld diplomatic recognition from, and tried to isolate, the Doe regime: Liberian Foreign Minister Baccus Matthews was refused permission to land in Lagos by the Nigerian authorities to attend an extraordinary OAU economic summit on 25 April 1980; Liberia was not invited to an ECOWAS defense ministers meeting on 12 May 1980; and the African Development Bank cancelled a 1980 meeting scheduled to take place in Monrovia. The most devastating diplomatic snub occurred when a pair of traditional rivals, Côte d'Ivoire and Nigeria, conspired to exclude Doe's delegation from an ECOWAS summit meeting in Lomé on 27 May 1980. The master-sergeant reacted to this diplomatic affront by recalling his ambassadors from Abidjan, Freetown, and Lagos and suspending Liberia's obligations to ECOWAS and the Mano River Union.

ECOWAS states like Nigeria, Côte d'Ivoire, Sierra Leone, and Upper Volta (now Burkina Faso) were critical of Doe's assassinations following the coup. As Voltaic leader Sangoulé Lamizana put it: "Everybody can change their regime, but the methods used in Liberia are a dishonor to Africa."[21] Sierra Leone's initial hostility to Doe was partly based on the close personal relationship between Siaka Stevens and William Tolbert, who had been a prime mover in the creation of the Mano River Union in 1973. Siaka Steven's successor, Joseph Momoh, allowed his territory to be used by Quiwonkpa to launch his unsuccessful coup against Doe in 1985. Relations rapidly deteriorated between the two countries, and their common border was closed.

Ivorian leader Félix Houphoüet-Boigny had also enjoyed close ties to the murdered President Tolbert. Tolbert was credited with having improved the strained relationship between Houphoüet-Boigny and Guinea's Sékou Touré.[22] More important, Houphoüet-Boigny had a personal stake in the Liberian situation: his adopted daughter, Daisy Delafosse, the daughter of Maurice Delafosse, the deceased cofounder of Houphoüet's ruling party, was married to the late president's son, Adolphus Tolbert.[23] On 14 June 1980, Doe's soldiers dragged the younger Tolbert out of the French embassy in Monrovia, where he had sought refuge, and locked him up in the notorious Belle Yella prison. Houphoüet-Boigny sent a delegation to plead with Doe to spare his life, which Doe promised to do. But while Doe was on a trip abroad, his soldiers killed Adolphus Tolbert.[24] Doe refused to return any of Tolbert's assets to his widow. The Ivorian leader, *le vieux* (the old man), would never forgive the young Doe for this act. After the 1980 coup, many anti-Doe dissidents were granted political asylum in Abidjan: Tolbert's vice president, Benny Warner, for example, advocated the toppling of Doe's regime from his Ivorian sanctuary. Doe accused Houphouët of involvement in the recruiting of mercenaries for Quiwonkpa's botched 1985 coup attempt.

Nigerian President Shehu Shagari expressed his country's displeasure at Doe's coup by closing its embassy in Monrovia. Shagari was almost certainly under pressure from his own powerful military, which had reacted to Jerry Rawlings's execution, after a military coup, of three former military heads of state in 1979 by freezing Nigerian oil sales to Ghana. Nigeria's generals were clearly worried about the increasing precedents of the execution of former rulers by lower-ranking soldiers. But under General Ibrahim Babangida's regime after 1985, relations improved dramatically between Lagos and Monrovia, with Doe establishing close political and economic ties to Nigeria and naming a graduate school of international studies at the University of Liberia after Babangida (see Chapter 3).

The highly personalized nature of African politics explains the cold response to Doe's regime. In the cozy club of African heads of state known as the OAU, Tolbert had been a popular incumbent chairman after hosting a lavish summit in June 1979. But the ostracism of Doe by African leaders smacked of hypocrisy considering the lack of democratic credentials of most of these leaders and their own human rights violations. Doe's early years were in fact similar to Rawlings's early years in Ghana: a purportedly revolutionary council killed members of the ancien régime, established "people's courts," proclaimed a radical path, co-opted socialist academics, and courted the Eastern bloc and Libya. But faced with a declining economic situation, both leaders eventually eased out left-leaning policymakers and adopted Western-oriented economic policies.[25]

Doe eventually found an ally in Guinea's Sékou Touré, who ironically had sent troops to rescue Tolbert's regime during the 1979 Rice Riots. Touré became the first African leader to invite Doe on a state visit. He then organized a subregional reconciliation meeting in Abidjan on 16 June 1980 involving the leaders of Côte d'Ivoire, Guinea, Togo, Sierra Leone, and Liberia and arranged a follow-up meeting in Monrovia on the eve of the OAU summit in Freetown in July 1980, to which Doe finally gained access. The Guinean leader's early embrace of Doe was not entirely selfless. It was based largely on strategic considerations: the Guinean port of Conakry needed access to Monrovia's Freeport and the new port in Buchanan for Guinea's iron ore and other exports.[26] Doe's early isolation and humiliating battle for recognition by African states had left deep scars. He gazed beyond Africa for diplomatic support and eventually came to rely almost entirely for his regime's survival on Liberia's most enduring external ally: the United States.

Uncle Sam's Frankenstein

The Liberian capital, Monrovia, is named after James Monroe, the fifth U.S. president. Monrovia's large Memorial Hospital was named in honor of slain President John F. Kennedy. The Liberian constitution, currency, and flag are modeled after those of the United States. As Gus Liebenow put it, "Liberia is the only country in Africa which has enjoyed a sustained relationship with the United States over a period of more than 160 years."[27] But this is a hopelessly one-sided special relationship. Liberians obviously value the relationship much more than do the Americans, most of whom are either totally oblivious of, or do not place much value on, the relationship.

James Monroe was one of the supporters of the American Colonization Society, which transported the first black American settlers (mostly freed slaves) to Liberia in 1822. The trips were financed by the U.S. Treasury, and the settlers arrived in vessels of the U.S. Navy. The U.S. Congress approved funds for the purchase of land, the building of homes, and the payment of teachers.[28] The U.S. government, however, did not officially sponsor this colonial enterprise, sending the first group of settlers to Liberia under the guise of being artisans and carpenters to construct a receptacle to shelter slaves intercepted on the high seas.[29] But even after the Liberian declaration of independence in 1847, U.S. warships helped quell numerous indigenous uprisings against Americo-Liberian rule. President Abraham Lincoln and other U.S. politicians who supported the repatriation of black Americans to Liberia had naively hoped that the country's politically divisive problems of slavery might be solved through such actions.[30] By 1860, the United States had already become Liberia's main trading partner. In 1912, President William Taft sent black American officers to head the Liberian Frontier Force, thus beginning a military relationship that would last for eight decades. In the same year, Washington extended a loan to Liberia that forced Monrovia to surrender its tax proceeds to a general receiver appointed by President Taft.

The U.S. multinational rubber company, Firestone, established the world's largest rubber plantation at Harbel in 1926. After it signed a ninety-nine-year lease and extended a loan to the Liberian government in 1926, Liberia became informally known as the "Firestone Republic." Republic Steel, another U.S. firm, became an early player in the exploitation of Liberia's iron ore deposits.[31] The U.S. government also extended loans to the Liberian government for the construction of an airport and seaport in Monrovia.

In 1956, the Liberian ambassador to Washington was bluntly told by the U.S. State Department that a planned visit by President Tubman to Moscow would "unfavorably reflect on the prestige of the U.S. government."[32] Tubman cancelled the trip. In 1959, Washington signed a mutual defense pact with Liberia. During the next decade, the United States built two communications facilities in Monrovia: a telecommunications relay station to handle diplomatic and intelligence traffic in Africa, and a Voice of America (VOA) transmitter for radio broadcasts to Africa, the Middle East, and parts of Southwest Asia. In 1976, Washington built the Omega navigational station in Monrovia to direct shipping traffic in the eastern Atlantic and along Africa's West Coast. President Jimmy Carter stopped over in Monrovia in 1978 for a brief official visit and praised Liberia's "individual human freedom." But some Liberians did not fail to notice that it had taken 131 years for a U.S. president to visit Liberia.

The initial U.S. response to Doe's regime was hesitant. At the time of the coup, the United States had 3,000 citizens in Liberia and private investments of $350 million; Firestone, Goodrich, and Uniroyal had rubber plantations; Bethlehem Steel had an iron ore mine; Chase Manhattan, Citibank, and Chemical Bank had local branches; U.S. bank loans to Liberia totaled $100 million; and loans from the U.S. Agency for International Development (USAID) stood at $76 million.[33] After the debacle with revolutionary Iran in 1979, Washington was keen to avoid being caught on the wrong side of a popular revolution that would destroy its influence and harm its interests. U.S. officials therefore adopted a cautious wait-and-see approach to developments in Liberia.

Washington urged Doe to avoid a bloodbath before the 22 April 1980 executions. U.S. officials later expressed displeasure at the assassination of True Whig officials. After the killings, foreign aid of $10.5 million was slowed down, new U.S. investments were stopped, and the International Monetary Fund (IMF) and World Bank imposed stricter borrowing conditions. By contrast, Libya, the Soviet Union, Cuba, and Eastern bloc countries reacted warmly to the Doe regime. Tolbert had expelled some Soviet diplomats from Monrovia months before the 1980 coup, and Moscow especially welcomed Doe's regime. Doe sent officials to these countries in the early days of his regime.

Largely due to strategic Cold War calculations and fears of Liberia falling into the Soviet camp, Washington sent Assistant Secretary of State for African Affairs Richard Moose to Monrovia in June 1980 to meet with Doe. After the visit, Moose recommended increased U.S. economic and military aid to Liberia. Ambassador Vernon Walters was dispatched to Monrovia in 1984 to urge Doe not to visit Tripoli in return for $5 million in U.S. economic assistance.[34] By the time Doe seized power, 52 percent of government revenues was provided by two U.S. firms, Firestone and the

Liberian Iron Mining Company, making it difficult for him to sustain the leftist tilt that some of his civilian and military advisers were encouraging in the early years of his regime.[35] After eliminating the so-called radicals from his cabinet, Doe closed the Libyan embassy in Monrovia in May 1981 and the Soviet embassy in July 1985. He established diplomatic relations with Israel and visited Jerusalem in September 1983 in defiance of an OAU boycott. Doe stoutly defended U.S. policies at the United Nations, summits of the Non-Aligned Movement, and other international fora. He was rewarded with a state visit to Washington in 1982, during which President Ronald Reagan famously referred to him as "Chairman Moe."

Liberia's foreign policy under Doe was now in tune with that of the new Reagan administration in Washington. Reagan met Doe again after a UN General Assembly session in 1983 and described the Liberian autocrat as "a dependable ally—a friend in need."[36] Doe granted the newly created U.S. Rapid Deployment Force staging rights to Liberia's seaports and airports with twenty-four hours' notice. Robertsfield Airport was used to transit arms to the U.S.-backed UNITA rebels in Angola, and Doe became a key ally in U.S. efforts to thwart the regional ambitions of Washington's bête noire, Muammar Qaddafi. In return, Doe was granted special security protection by the Central Intelligence Agency (CIA).[37] By 1984, Washington was assisting Doe in the payment of teachers' salaries, and U.S. private investment in Liberia, at $5 billion, was the third largest such investment in Africa.[38] U.S. provision of rice aid to Liberia also prevented a repetition of the Rice Riots that had proved so fatal to Tolbert.

Despite Uncle Sam's generosity, Doe was notoriously rude to U.S. officials like Ambassadors William Swing (1981–1985) and James Bishop (1987–1990). Both Swing and Bishop left Monrovia barely on speaking terms with the Liberian leader.[39] After Swing tried to pressure Doe to return to the barracks, the master-sergeant asked for his recall and threatened to bundle him on a plane. Washington's plenipotentiaries persevered in pushing Doe to hold elections in 1985. After the elections, U.S. officials fell over themselves in the rush to justify their support for the farcical charade. Assistant Secretary of State for African Affairs Chester Crocker described the elections as "the beginning . . . of a democratic experience that Liberia and its friends can use as a benchmark for future elections" and "a rare achievement in Africa and elsewhere in the Third World."[40] In condoning clearly fraudulent elections, Crocker demonstrated a patronizing and paternalistic attitude typical of many U.S. officials in their dealings with Africa. His insensitive remarks were often deeply offensive to Liberians and other Africans.

In the era of the Cold War, U.S. strategic interests in Liberia appeared to be more important to Washington than did niceties about human rights and democracy. The Reagan administration increased aid to Liberia from

$20 million in 1979 to $90 million by 1986, eventually sinking over $500 million into the Liberian "rat hole," including an annual $14 million in military assistance.[41] After the 1985 Liberian elections, Reagan continued to reward Doe by extending $65 million in economic assistance, $11 million in food assistance, and $4.7 million in military aid.[42] By 1986, Washington provided a third of the Liberian government's total revenue.[43] The Democratic-controlled U.S. Congress, however, attempted to exert some pressure on the executive. The House and Senate passed nonbinding resolutions in December 1986 and January 1987 requesting that further U.S. aid to Liberia be tied to progress on human rights and democracy.

By 1987, the Reagan administration was deeply embroiled in the Iran-contra scandal. The Cold War was also coming to an end, and military assistance to sub-Saharan Africa was drastically reduced, from $147.6 million in 1985 to $25.25 million in 1988.[44] Doe was forced to turn to countries like Israel, Romania, and South Korea for arms. But key U.S. officials maintained their support for Doe, with visiting Secretary of State George Shultz making a curious remark in 1987: "There is freedom of the press here, there is an opposition, there are no political prisoners. So there is genuine progress."[45]

In 1986, the IMF denied Liberia access to its special drawing rights for defaulting on a $900 million debt, forcing Doe to reduce all government jobs and salaries by 25 percent. The World Bank had stopped loans to Liberia the same year. Liberia was placed under virtual international receivership when U.S. financial experts arrived in 1988 to oversee government spending. Doe, however, scuttled the agreement within months. The Congress's Brooke Amendment, preventing loans to countries that fall a year behind in servicing their U.S. debts, was hanging over Liberia like a sword of Damocles in 1988. Despite Doe's efforts to prevent its enactment through a belated national rally to raise funds, the amendment was applied to Liberia in May 1989, and military assistance was cut the same year. Uncle Sam had finally abandoned his monstrous nephew.

With the crumbling of the Berlin Wall and the end of the Cold War, Doe had become a political dinosaur, living out his last days in a Cold War museum. He had outlived his strategic usefulness to Washington. Master-Sergeant Doe was a caricature of the archetypal African autocrat.[46] In his semiliterate buffoonery, he resembled Field Marshal Idi Amin and Emperor Bokassa. The Doe saga itself was like the chronicle of a death foretold. A violent orgy of killings had unleashed a decade of troubles during which Doe repeatedly resorted to bloodletting to keep himself in power. But in retrospect there was something almost inevitable about the fate of the Macbethian master-sergeant. Having spilled so much blood and made so many enemies in his rise to the top, a bloody end seemed like a predictable outcome for this tragicomic figure. Even as Liberia's economy tottered on the brink of total collapse by the end of 1989, a political crisis of catastrophic proportions loomed just over the horizon.

Notes

1. See G. E. Saigbe Boley, *Liberia: The Rise and Fall of the First Republic* (New York: St. Martin's, 1983); Christopher Clapham (ed.), *Private Patronage and Public Power: Political Clientelism in the Modern State* (London: Frances Pinter, 1982); Gus Liebenow, *The Evolution of Privilege* (Ithaca: Cornell University Press, 1969); Eghosa Osaghae, *Ethnicity, Class, and the Struggle for State Power in Liberia* (Dakar: CODESRIA, 1996); and Amos Sawyer, *The Emergence of Autocracy in Liberia: Tragedy and Challenge* (San Francisco: ICS, 1992).

2. Gus Liebenow, *Liberia: The Quest for a Democracy* (Bloomington, Ind.: Indiana University Press, 1987), p. 170.

3. Quoted in Mobolade Omonijo, *Doe: The Liberian Tragedy* (Lagos: Sahel, 1990), p. 64.

4. Christopher Clapham coined this memorable phrase.

5. Emmanuel Dolo, *Democracy Versus Dictatorship: The Quest for Freedom and Justice in Africa's Oldest Republic* (Lanham, Md., and London: University Press of America, 1996), p. 265.

6. D. Elwood Dunn and S. Byron Tarr, *Liberia: A National Polity in Transition* (Metuchen, N.J.: Scarecrow Press, 1988), pp. 199–200.

7. William Reno, *Warlord Politics and African States* (Boulder and London: Lynne Rienner, 1998), p. 92.

8. Paul Gifford, *Christianity and Politics in Doe's Liberia* (Cambridge, UK: Cambridge University Press, 1993), pp. 36–37.

9. Dunn and Tarr, *Liberia*, pp. 126–127.

10. Bill Berkeley, "Between Repression and Slaughter," *Atlantic Monthly* (December 1992): 54.

11. See Robert Kappel and Werner Korte (eds.), *Human Rights Violations in Liberia, 1980–1990: A Documentation* (Bremen, Germany: Liberia Working Group, 1990); Lawyers Committee for Human Rights, *Liberia: A Promise Betrayed* (New York: Lawyers Committee For Human Rights, 1986); and Amos Sawyer, *Effective Immediately: Dictatorship in Liberia, 1980–1986—A Personal Perspective* (Bremen, Germany: Liberia Working Group, 1987).

12. Liebenow, *Liberia*, p. 2.

13. Lawyers Committee for Human Rights, *Promise Betrayed*, p. 7.

14. Quoted in Liebenow, *Liberia*, p. 281.

15. Mark Huband, *The Liberian Civil War* (London and Portland: Frank Cass, 1998), p. 37.

16. Cited in Liebenow, *Liberia*, p. 298.

17. Dolo, *Democracy Versus Dictatorship*, p. 63.

18. Christopher Clapham, "Liberia," in Donal Cruise O'Brien, John Dunn, and Richard Rathbone (eds.), *Contemporary West African States* (Cambridge, UK: Cambridge University Press, 1989), p. 108.

19. Liebenow, *Liberia*, p. 263.

20. Sawyer, *The Emergence of Autocracy in Liberia*, p. 296.

21. Quoted in Liebenow, *Liberia,* p. 209.

22. Hassan B. Sisay, *Big Powers and Small Nations: A Case Study of United States–Liberian Relations* (Lanham, Md., and London: University Press of America, 1985), p. 160.

23. Following Stephen Ellis's article "Liberia 1989–1994: A Study of Ethnic and Spiritual Violence," *African Affairs,* 94, no. 375 (April 1995): 165–197, many scholars have erroneously stated that Daisy Delafosse married Burkinabè leader Blaise Compaoré, making Houphoüet his adopted son-in-law. But Compaoré is married to a different Ivorian woman, Chantal Terrasson de Fougrès, sister of a former Ivorian health minister.

24. Herman Cohen, *Intervening in Africa: Superpower Peacemaking in a Troubled Continent* (Hampshire, UK: Macmillan; and New York: St. Martin's, 2000), pp. 126–127.

25. See Henry Bienen, *Armed Forces, Conflict, and Change in Africa* (Boulder, San Francisco and London: Westview, 1989).

26. Liebenow, *Liberia,* p. 210.

27. Ibid., p. 3.

28. Ibid., p. 13.

29. The author thanks Amos Sawyer for this point.

30. Katherine Harris, *African and American Values: Liberia and West Africa* (Lanham, Md. and London: University Press of America, 1985), p. 70.

31. Reed Kramer, "Liberia: A Casualty of the Cold War's End?" *CSIS Africa Notes,* no. 174 (July 1995): 2–4.

32. Quoted in Dunn and Tarr, *Liberia,* p. 191.

33. Ibid., p. 176.

34. Huband, *The Liberian Civil War,* p. 34.

35. Reno, *Warlord Politics,* p. 84.

36. Quoted in Gifford, *Christianity and Politics in Doe's Liberia,* p. 234.

37. Kramer, "Liberia," p. 6.

38. Harris, *African and American Values,* p. 76.

39. Personal interview with Ambassador James Bishop, Washington, D.C., July 1997.

40. Quoted in Liebenow, *Liberia,* p. 293.

41. This expression was coined by Jesse Helms, the conservative former chairman of the U.S. Senate Foreign Affairs Committee and a vociferous critic of foreign aid.

42. Liebenow, *Liberia,* p. 306.

43. Ibid., p. 304.

44. Gifford, *Christiany and Politics in Doe's Liberia,* p. 234.

45. Quoted in ibid., p. 236.

46. See Wole Soyinka, *A Play of Giants* (London: Methuen, 1984).

part 1

Journey Without Maps,
December 1989–December 1992

chapter 3

Things Fall Apart,
December 1989–August 1990

If you see a next-door neighbour's house on fire, you must act speedily to help put it out, because you do not know when the resulting conflagration may spread to your home.
— *Gnassingbé Eyadéma, Togolese head of state*

In this chapter we discuss the outbreak of the Liberian civil war in December 1989, the early mediation efforts, and the decision to deploy ECOMOG in August 1990. We address two main issues. First the chapter assesses the often conflicting goals and interests of the main players by looking at the main Liberian, subregional, and external actors involved in the conflict. A key contention here is that difficulties at the domestic, subregional, and external levels made the resolution of the conflict difficult; we therefore assess the roots of these difficulties. Charles Taylor's NPFL was able to manipulate ethnic rivalries fueled by Doe, as discussed in Chapter 2, in order to build a civilian army. Key ECOWAS states like Côte d'Ivoire and Burkina Faso supported the NPFL, and Togo, Senegal, and Mali opposed the establishment of ECOMOG, causing a split between the subregion's anglophone and francophone members. The United States abandoned Doe, a former Cold War ally, and decided that its interests were no longer vital enough to warrant a military intervention in Liberia. The UN, OAU, and European Economic Community (EEC, now the EU) offered ECOMOG early diplomatic but not military or financial support.

The second issue addressed here is whether ECOMOG was a Pax Nigeriana, in the sense of Nigeria imposing its narrow, hegemonic interests on Liberia, or whether Nigeria acted in pursuit of broader interests. We provide historical background to explain the roots of Pax Nigeriana in a broader foreign policy context before explaining Nigeria's specific role in Liberia. This chapter seeks to demonstrate that there were subregional actors like Guinea, Gambia, Sierra Leone, and Ghana who pushed for and supported ECOMOG from the start and were, in most cases, more directly affected by the conflict than Nigeria. This contradicts the commonly expressed view in the academic literature that Nigeria was imposing its own parochial interests on the rest of the subregion and somehow coerced other subregional states into supporting its self-interested intervention. We offer an explanation for Nigeria's intervention, focusing on General Ibrahim Babangida, the Nigerian head of state who played a key role in launching ECOMOG, the Nigerian army, and Nigeria's historical quest for a leadership role in Africa. We focus on these three aspects of Pax Nigeriana to challenge more conventional explanations. We also highlight domestic opposition in Nigeria to the ECOMOG intervention in Liberia.

The Christmas Eve Invasion

As Liberians prepared for Christmas on 24 December 1989, a band of 168 armed men, calling themselves the National Patriotic Front of Liberia, crossed into Liberia's Nimba County from Côte d'Ivoire. The express purpose of the group was to topple the regime of Samuel Doe. The rebels quickly reached the Nimba capital of Saniquellie before Doe dispatched his Armed Forces of Liberia to the region with tanks and mortars on 29 December. In its attempt to crush the rebellion, the rampaging AFL burned villages and executed civilians, but Liberia's dense rainforests and the army's lack of vehicles and ammunition made it difficult to contain the guerrilla insurgency.

Having survived several previous attempts to overthrow him (see Chapter 2), Doe badly misjudged the danger posed to his regime by this latest effort. He underestimated the level of resentment against him in a county where his army had massacred an estimated 3,000 Gio and Mano civilians after General Thomas Quiwonkpa's foiled invasion in November 1985. Nimba County was a hotbed of discontent, seething with rage, and hungry for revenge against Doe's Krahn-dominated army. The NPFL had little difficulty finding recruits to whom it provided arms. In order to gain Gio and Mano support in Nimba County, the invasion's leader, Charles Taylor, presented it as a continuation of General Quiwonkpa's failed coup. The murdered Quiwonkpa, a Gio from Nimba County, enjoyed widespread popularity in his home region. This manipulation of ethnic differences predictably led to NPFL attacks on Krahns and Mandingos in its march to the Monrovian capital, and many Krahn civilians were killed in the early stages of the war.

Desperate, Doe scrambled to control the situation by broadening his political base. He released political prisoners, unbanned political parties, deproscribed some newspapers, increased civil service salaries, and promised free and fair elections in 1991. This was as much for domestic consumption as it was to gain crucial support in Washington. But any support was compromised by the increasingly horrendous atrocities committed by Doe's undisciplined army. Doe's Krahn-dominated army killed Gio and Mano soldiers in the AFL.[1] On 30 May 1990, AFL elements stormed the UN compound in Monrovia, abducting thirty Gios and Manos and killing four others. In a more horrific act, 600 mostly Gio and Mano civilians sheltering in Monrovia's St. Peter's Lutheran Church were machine-gunned to death by AFL soldiers in July 1990,[2] including the father of NPFL warlord Charles Taylor.

As U.S. and European civilians were being evacuated from Monrovia, Doe went to Lagos on 7 May 1990 to ask his friend, Nigerian leader General Ibrahim Babangida, for assistance. Returning quickly to Monrovia, Doe was besieged in his Executive Mansion with a battalion of his AFL troops. The beleaguered leader downed gallons of French brandy even as his country burned around him. No less than seven of his ministers deserted him. In a pathetic plea to U.S. President George Bush, published in the *Washington Post* in August 1990, Doe pleaded:

> Our capital is named after your President Monroe. Our flag is a replica of yours. Our laws are patterned after your laws. We in Liberia have always considered ourselves "stepchildren" of the United States. We implore you to come help your stepchildren who are in danger of losing their lives and freedom.[3]

But the world had changed with the fall of the Berlin Wall in 1989. Doe had lost his strategic value to Washington and become an orphan of the Cold War.

The Roots of Pax Nigeriana

Because Nigeria's role in Liberia has often been misunderstood and rarely been adequately explained, it is important to provide some background on Nigeria's foreign policy goals and interests before explaining the country's specific role in Liberia. Pax Nigeriana is the attempt by Nigeria to establish itself as a regional leader in Africa through political, economic, and military actions taken in Africa or on issues related to Africa.[4] Politically, Nigeria has attempted to act as Africa's spokesperson at the United Nations, the OAU, and other international fora; militarily, it has sent peacekeepers to the Congo, Chad, Liberia, Somalia, and Sierra Leone, provided military training to armies from Gambia to Tanzania, and supplied military assistance to liberation movements in southern Africa; economically, it has promoted subregional integration through ECOWAS and provided bilateral aid and technical assistance to African countries. A particularly important aspect of Pax Nigeriana is Nigeria's attempts to act as a regional peacemaker and peacekeeper by sending soldiers abroad and attempting to mediate conflicts involving African states.

Pax Nigeriana is reflected in the utterances of Nigerian soldiers, politicians, diplomats, scholars, students, and journalists. These Nigerians share a common belief in their country's manifest destiny as the Giant of Africa with special responsibilities to act as a regional big brother by providing moral and political leadership and economic and military assistance to other African states. The metaphor of a benevolent older brother with more experience and power to protect and assist younger siblings has been widely used in Nigeria's diplomatic lexicon. During Nigeria's First Republic (1960–1966), the National Council of Nigerian Citizens parliamentarian E. C. Akwiwu opined: "It is necessary, that those whom we stand a chance of leading should be able to look up to Nigeria as a senior brother, an elder brother that is capable of looking after their affairs and is very interested in their well-being." The big-brother syndrome has afflicted Nigerian leaders since independence. It implies a sense of responsibility and a feeling of protectiveness toward weaker inexperienced siblings and smacks of a paternalism that has sometimes irritated other African countries. Nigeria's leaders almost gave the impression that all the country had to do was simply appear on the African stage and all other states would bow in deference at the splendor of the new African colossus that the gods had sent to fulfill their messianic mission in Africa.

Shehu Shagari, Nigeria's president from 1979 to 1983, made an explicit comparison between Nigeria's hegemonic aspirations and the role of the United States in the Americas: "Just as . . . President Monroe proclaimed the American hemisphere free from the military incursions of European empire builders and adventurers, so also do we . . . in Nigeria and in Africa insist that African affairs be left to Africa to settle."[5] Nigeria's former ambassador to Washington, Olu Sanu, expressed a similar sentiment: "We have to be recognized as a regional power in West Africa. This is our region and we have a right to go to war. It is a Monroe Doctrine of a sort."[6] Nigeria's first President, Nnamdi Azikiwe, talked of "the historic and manifest destiny of Nigeria on the African continent,"[7] and a Nigerian ambassadors' conference in June 1966 noted that "Africa is Nigeria's natural sphere of influence. To shirk this manifest destiny is not to heed the logic of history."[8] These themes have been consistently championed by Nigerian leaders since the country's independence in 1960.

Pax Nigeriana, unlike Pax Britannica or Pax Americana, has not entailed militarily expansionist imperialism. There were a few calls from Nigerian politicians in the 1960s for the country to annex the island of Fernando Po in the Spanish colony of Equatorial Guinea and to incorporate the Yoruba-speaking parts of Dahomey (Benin). But these were not taken seriously by Nigerian rulers. They defined their hegemonic ambitions in terms of providing prosperity and security as a public good rather than imposing their will on weaker neighbors. West African states are more wary of the *potential* threat posed by Nigerian hegemony than its *actual* threat. As Matthew Mbu, a former Nigeria foreign minister, put it: "We have no ambition to annex Liberia. We have no ambition whatsoever to explore our territorial expansion. We are quite happy where we are."[9]

We are not suggesting that Pax Nigeriana is purely altruistic. Nigeria has historically sought to extend its influence in West Africa by loosening French economic, military, and political dominance over its former colonies in order to gain more security and create a larger market for Nigeria's goods and industries. However, one has to seek the explanation for Nigeria's intervention in Liberia not in terms of *military* aggrandizement for the political control of Liberia but instead in terms of *political* aggrandizement for long-term economic and military influence in West Africa. Nigeria did not intervene to colonize Liberia but in order to expand its influence in West Africa and bolster its image as the Giant of Africa. In the case of Liberia, Pax Nigeriana was neither expansionist nor altruistic. ECOMOG also served the practical purpose of deflecting international criticism of the Sani Abacha military junta's human rights policies, and Nigeria's generals benefited from occult state revenues that were costed out as ECOMOG expenses.

In order to understand the Nigerian intervention in Liberia, one must appreciate the self-image its military rulers have historically held. They have a profound concern for their place in history, and some have even tried to write this history themselves. Yakubu Gowon, Emeka Ojukwu, Olusegun Obasanjo, and Joe Garba have all written accounts related to their experiences. Others have had mostly laudatory biographies published about them: Ibrahim Babangida, Yakubu Gowon, and Joshua Dogonyaro. Almost all of Nigeria's military leaders have published books of collected speeches. Babangida had a lavish seven-volume collection published on various aspects of his regime.[10] Sani Abacha set up the Foundation for International Peace.

Many of Nigeria's military officers see their institution as exemplifying positive values like self-discipline, comradeship, honesty, and patriotism. These soldiers regard themselves as guardians of national integrity and guarantors of national unity with a responsibility to save the country from the decadence of corrupt politicians. They see their institution as more cohesive and detribalized than any other in the country. As Robin Luckham put it in 1970:

> When the military took part in politics, it did so on a vaguely articulated premise that it was desirable for it to attempt to reconstruct government

and society in its own image, in accordance with the values of which it was believed to be the unique standard-bearer.[11]

During his first coup broadcast in January 1966, Major Kaduna Nzeogwu railed against politicians who "make the country look big for nothing before international circles." It has always mattered to the soldiers how Nigeria is regarded abroad. Nigeria's foreign policy is closely tied to the military's image of the country as a regional giant and its own role in promoting and defending this image. Gallantry, honor, and heroism are aspects of glory associated with the military. Nigeria's generals have used such virtues to justify their intervention in Liberia.

Most of Nigeria's senior military officers had fought the civil war and served on international peacekeeping missions. This group shares similar views about the country's leadership position in Africa. As commander of the Nigerian division in Jos during Chadian military attacks on Nigerian villages in the Lake Chad region, General Muhammadu Buhari, Nigeria's leader between 1983 and 1985, launched military reprisals against Hissene Habré's forces in 1983 that went beyond the orders of civilian President Shehu Shagari. Nigeria's generals were also angered by what they perceived as Shagari's weak response after Cameroonian soldiers killed Nigerian citizens in disputed border areas in 1981. They were stung by domestic criticism of their military performance in Chad between 1979 and 1982.

Pax Nigeriana involved all regimes from Abubakar Tafawa Balewa in the 1960s to General Ibrahim Babangida in the early 1990s, placing Africa at the center of their foreign policy. The influence Nigeria sought in West Africa could be achieved only if it were regarded as a credible regional leader. This leadership was expressed in the subregion through Nigeria's dominance of ECOWAS,[12] and Nigeria also played an active part in the liberation struggles in southern Africa.[13] Nigeria's leadership aspirations in the 1960s were certainly not realized. Though its views were respected in intra-African diplomacy, where it exerted some influence, Nigeria's descent into civil war at the end of the decade weakened its case for African leadership. Its leadership ambitions had to await reunification and a fortuitous oil boom.

By the 1970s, Nigeria had Africa's largest population, black Africa's richest economy, and its biggest army. Washington courted Nigeria as part of its African policy;[14] the Frontline States invited Nigeria to their meetings; Nigeria was instrumental in formulating OAU positions; and ECOWAS grudgingly accepted its leadership. Five francophone states, Côte d'Ivoire, Mali, Mauritania, Niger, and Upper Volta (Burkina Faso), backed by France, attempted to balance Nigeria's strength within ECOWAS by creating the Communauté Economique de l'Afrique de l'Ouest in April 1973. The continued acceptance of French military intervention in Africa by most francophone African states, as well as the stationing of French troops in Africa, exposed the military weakness of African states despite ECOWAS's increasing efforts at institutionalizing military cooperation.[15]

Unlike during the 1960s, however, Nigerian foreign policy by the late 1970s won the political support of articulate domestic groups like students, trade unions, and the media. The country was at last playing the role expected of it after gaining independence, and Nigerians could take pride in its leadership role without having to envy Ghana, its rival in the 1960s under the charismatic leadership of Kwame Nkrumah.[16] Nigeria increasingly employed "oil diplomacy": it sold oil to its neighbors at concessionary rates; cut off oil supplies to Ghana after Jerry Rawlings's violent coup in 1979; and nationalized the assets of British Petroleum in August 1979 in a bid to influence London's Rhodesia policy.

Nigeria's greatest influence was, however, achieved within its own subregion. Lagos extended its influence in West Africa through the creation of ECOWAS in 1975 and became a respected actor on the wider continental scene. ECOWAS remained Nigeria's greatest foreign policy achievement until 1990. Overcoming the opposition of France and the vast majority of francophone states, Lagos created a vehicle through which it could extend its political, economic, and military influence in the subregion. ECOWAS was thus the very embodiment of Pax Nigeriana: it provided a forum through which Nigeria could mobilize support for its goal of forging closer subregional economic and military cooperation in order to lessen French influence in West Africa. But this demonstrated Nigeria's increasing influence rather than its dominance. Nigeria's hegemonic ambitions remained unfulfilled amid the continuing French presence and ECOWAS's political divisions and poor economic performance.

By the 1980s, then, Pax Nigeriana was becoming more difficult to pursue as a domestic economic crisis and increased dependence on Western financial institutions forced Nigeria to scale back its generous economic assistance to African states and its high-profile political role of the 1970s. The increasing nationalism of Nigerian foreign policy was reflected in the mass expulsions of nearly 3 million mainly West African citizens in 1983 and 1985.[17] Despite such economic problems, in 1984 Nigeria's GNP was still more than twice as large as that of Côte d'Ivoire, Ghana, and Senegal combined. It was clear that Lagos would still continue to bear the burden of regional integration and other efforts at military cooperation in West Africa. This explains why Nigeria was still able to embark on a policy of "hegemony on a shoestring" with its intervention in Liberia in 1990.

Pax Nigeriana became difficult with such a small purse, and it was clear that ECOMOG would encounter enormous difficulties. The Chad interventions launched during the oil boom of the 1970s had, after all, failed to achieve their objectives and exposed the logistical shortcomings of the

Nigerian army. By 1990, Nigeria had accumulated an external debt of $33 billion. Whereas Nigeria had relied on cocoa, groundnuts, and palm oil in the 1960s, its overreliance on the shaky foundations of a monocrop economy was evident in the 1990s, when it relied on a richer but no less volatile and erratic source of income.

Nigeria's Role in Liberia

In explaining Nigeria's role in Liberia, one is also seeking to explain why the ECOMOG intervention occurred, because without Nigeria there would have been no ECOMOG. Nigeria eventually provided 75 percent of the troops and 90 percent of the funding for ECOMOG and was the only contingent whose withdrawal would have meant the end of the mission. It was also the only country that had the capacity and resources to undertake the intervention alone, but it chose to secure some political cover by involving other ECOWAS members in the mission, this in a subregion already profoundly suspicious of Nigeria's hegemonic ambitions.

Most analysts have identified four main reasons for Nigeria's decision to intervene in Liberia: Babangida's close relationship with Doe; the holding of Nigerian hostages by the NPFL; Nigeria's fear of Libyan adventurism in Liberia and the possibility of an anti-Nigerian alliance of Libya, Burkina Faso, and Côte d'Ivoire; and Nigeria's suspicion of French political motives and economic interests in orchestrating an anti-ECOMOG alliance.[18] We will explain the origins of these in turn, questioning the validity of each, before offering our own explanation for Nigeria's involvement in Liberia.

One can point to several reasons why Babangida wished to keep his friend, Doe, in power. General Babangida had contributed $1 million to establishing the Ibrahim Babangida Graduate School of International Studies at the University of Liberia.[19] Babangida also sent military supplies (rifles and machine guns) to Doe to quell the rebellion.[20] Nigeria and Liberia had signed the Economic, Scientific, and Technical agreement in 1988. Babangida had often mediated disputes between his friends Samuel Doe and Sierra Leone's Joseph Momoh. Nigeria had also paid for the Liberian section of the Trans-African Highway, which was named after Babangida.[21] Nigeria settled Liberia's debt to the African Development Bank in December 1989.[22] And Nigeria invested $25 million in the joint Liberia-Guinea Mifergui iron ore project, as well as $4.5 million in the Liberian National Oil Corporation.[23]

Although most of these are indisputable facts, the "special relationship" between Babangida and Doe has often been exaggerated. The reality is that General Babangida was often condescending toward Doe, a master-sergeant who had promoted himself to general without rising through the ranks.[24] Doe had, in fact, become an embarrassment to Babangida by 1990.[25] In addition, Nigeria had far more economic and political ties to neighboring Benin, Togo, and Niger than with Liberia. If economic investments and diplomatic camaraderie suffice to subsume broader interests into personal ones, Washington's abandonment of Doe—despite having far more political, economic, and military investments in Liberia than did Nigeria—would be difficult to explain. Although Babangida's supplying of military equipment to Doe early in the conflict raised serious questions about Nigeria's neutrality, Babangida was forced to commit himself to Doe's resignation soon after in order to ensure the support of his ECOMOG allies and Liberian political groups for the intervention. He quickly withdrew military support when he realized that Doe could not crush the NPFL rebellion as easily as he had claimed.

Moreover, Doe rejected the ECOMOG intervention when he realized that the peace plan called for his resignation. Babangida also claimed that he urged Doe to leave office in the interest of his country.[26] Finally, the fact that Doe was murdered barely two weeks after ECOMOG entered Liberia— without a precipitate Nigerian withdrawal—and the fact that Doe's confessed murderer, Prince Yeduo Johnson, was granted asylum in Nigeria in 1992 by the Babangida regime, cast doubt on the claims that Nigeria intervened in Liberia mainly to protect Doe.

The issue of hostages certainly influenced Nigeria's decision to intervene in Liberia. Some 3,000 Nigerian citizens were trapped in Liberia, and many had sought refuge in the Nigerian embassy in Monrovia. Having threatened to kill the Nigerian ambassador and Nigerian professors at the University of Liberia, the NPFL attacked the Nigerian embassy on 12 July and 8 August 1990, killing some of its citizens. Babangida has been rightly criticized for his lackadaisical approach to evacuating Nigerian citizens from Liberia when the Americans and Europeans were evacuating their citizens in May 1990. He claimed, implausibly at the time, that such a move would create divisions among Africans. But it was a grave miscalculation, and Babangida fiddled while Liberia burned. He not only should have evacuated his citizens but also, like the Americans, sent troops to guard his Monrovian embassy. Though Nigeria deployed troops to Liberia partly to correct this flaw and eventually evacuated its citizens from Liberia, the fact that its ECOMOG contingent stayed in Liberia for the entire duration of the seven-year civil war, having rescued its citizens, suggests that other considerations were more important in explaining Nigeria's intervention. ECOMOG troops could, after all, have simply rescued Nigerian nationals and left Monrovia.

Scholars like Ademola Adeleke, Stephen Ellis, Terry Mays, W. Ofuatey-Kodjoe, and Klaas Van Walraven have argued that Nigeria intervened in

Liberia to prevent an anti-Nigeria alliance of Burkina Faso, Côte d'Ivoire, and Libya in Liberia.[27] But although Ouagadougou and Tripoli enjoyed close relations, Abidjan and much of francophone West Africa have traditionally opposed Libya's Africa policies and strongly backed Paris against Tripoli in Chad. Côte d'Ivoire's anti-Doe policy in Liberia, unlike Burkina Faso's, was in no way coordinated with Libya's. It was merely a coincidence of interests between two ideologically incompatible regimes. Nigeria's diplomats conversant with the Liberia dossier have argued convincingly that the Chadian case between 1979 and 1982, and not Liberia, raised fears about Libya's role, explaining Nigeria's peacekeeping efforts in Chad by its proximity to a country with which it shares a common border.[28] According to Nigerian diplomats, then, the fear of Libyan expansionism in Liberia was not a significant consideration for Nigerian policy.

As for the widely held belief that Nigeria intervened in Liberia to stem French influence, though French commercial interests benefited from trade with Taylor in NPFL areas, the French government showed little interest in Liberia, an anglophone country outside the French sphere of influence.[29] Many scholars have failed to distinguish between private French interests (admittedly often backed by the government), which benefited from trade in NPFL areas, and French foreign policy, which not only declined to give military support to the pro-NPFL camp but also provided military support to ECOMOG through the UN Trust Fund established in 1993. The allegations of France's anti-ECOMOG stance are somewhat inconsistent when one considers that no one has accused the Japanese, Malaysian, and other European countries like Germany of being pro-NPFL or anti-ECOMOG because their private interests benefited financially from NPFL-controlled areas. These analysts have also ignored the improved political relations between France and Nigeria, which saw General Babangida undertake an unprecedented state visit to Paris in February 1990. Nigeria's ambassador to Paris at the time, Olu Adeniji, noted that French policymakers were coming to the realization that West Africa needed a strong Nigeria and did not oppose ECOMOG.[30]

We can offer three arguments to explain Nigeria's participation in ECOMOG: the idea of Pax Nigeriana and Nigeria's leadership aspirations (already discussed above); General Babangida's self-image as a great leader and his desire to leave an indelible mark on Nigerian history; and the aspirations of the Nigerian army to enhance its status and prove its worth as a national and subregional asset. Thus, Nigeria, Babangida, and the army wanted to make history through their intervention in Liberia.

Ever since Nigerian Premier Abubakar Tafawa Balewa severed diplomatic relations with Paris in 1961 to protest French nuclear tests in the Sahara, Nigeria has always sought to play a leadership role in Africa. As Babangida explained, "[Nigeria's] participation in ECOMOG fell in line with Nigeria's foreign policy over the past three decades."[31] The changed international environment after the Cold War made the pursuit of a Pax Nigeriana possible. With less external interest in Africa, Nigeria could intervene in Liberia, where previously U.S. interests would have made this impossible. Nigeria was a restless giant in a volatile subregion in search of a role it had long sought but had never been able to play. Liberia offered the first opportunity to flex Nigeria's subregional muscle.

Babangida perceived himself as a charismatic leader. Whereas every Nigerian military ruler had adopted the title of head of state, Babangida insisted on being referred to as the president. And whereas every Nigerian military leader was primus inter pares in the ruling junta (Mohammed/Obasanjo; Obasanjo/Yar'Adua/Danjuma; and Buhari/Idiagbon) or relied on other power centers like the civil service (Ironsi and Gowon), Babangida reigned supreme, shuffling even the most senior officers around like a pack of cards and dissolving the cabinet and Armed Forces Ruling Council (AFRC) at will. As Shehu Othman noted: "No previous Nigerian leader has established a firmer grip over the military hierarchy and indeed the country than Babangida has done. . . . Babangida relishes, indeed glories, in his personal contribution to recent Nigerian history."[32] Nobel laureate Wole Soyinka also noted:

> Babangida's love of power was visualised in actual terms: power over Nigeria, over the nation's impressive size, its potential, over the nation's powerful status within the community of nations. The potency of Nigeria, in short, was an augmentation of his own sense of personal power.[33]

With Babangida having amassed more power than any other Nigerian leader at home, Liberia was to be his foreign policy showpiece. He adopted a hands-on approach to Liberia policy, stamping his personal authority on decisionmaking and exacerbating the already strained relationship with Charles Taylor rather than presenting himself as a statesman in contrast to Taylor's warlordism. The Nigerian Ministry of Foreign Affairs was merely an instrument rather than an originator of policy, used as much or as little as was required, and no one in that key ministry knew how much Nigeria was spending on Liberia.[34] Babangida's quest for international recognition was also evidenced by his chairmanship of the ECOWAS Authority of Heads of State and Government for an unprecedented three consecutive terms between 1985 and 1988 and his chairmanship of the OAU in 1991.

Finally, even though most of the military was excluded from decisionmaking on Liberia policy and many soldiers privately opposed the intervention, some senior members of the 94,500-member Nigerian army eventually became keen to prove their worth to a country that had for long questioned their professionalism.[35] They wished to demonstrate that the

army was more than an avenue for coup-making soldiers to embark on political careers. As General Ishola Williams, commander of the Nigerian
army's training and doctrine center at Minna in 1990, put it in 1997, "Nigeria is the superpower of the subregion. . . . Here you have a situation in
which you do not want to lose face."[36]

Before the Nigerian civil war (1967–1970), the army was a light infantry of 6,000 soldiers, its air force had no frontline jets or airlift capability, and its navy could not provide support for the army.[37] By 1990, the air
force had 95 fighter jets, including Hercules C-130s, Jaguars, and AlphaJets,
and it had developed close air support capability; the army had two mechanized divisions, two light rapid deployment divisions, one armored division,
modern artillery pieces, antiaircraft guns, fighting vessels, and 257 armored
battle tanks; the navy had acquired a flagship, a landing ship, a fast patrol
craft, minesweepers, and Lynx helicopters.[38] The Nigerian military was especially concerned with developing its maritime capacity in order to defend
its vulnerable offshore oil in the possible event of conflict.[39]

In the early 1990s, the Nigerian army sent its troops on international
peacekeeping missions with the United Nations in the Balkans, Lebanon,
Kuwait, Western Sahara, Somalia, and Rwanda. Seeking a permanent seat
on the UN Security Council to enhance Nigeria's image as a regional power
and be recognized as such, Nigeria's military rulers wished to portray
the country as a responsible global citizen. But there were also practical
considerations behind the Nigerian military establishment's support for
ECOMOG. As Adedoyin Jolaade Omede noted after discussions with members of the Nigerian armed forces, "It is felt within the Nigerian Army, that
the ECOMOG mission will be used as a testing ground for both the effectiveness and viability of its arsenals and act also as a deterrent to any hypothetical enemy."[40]

Having embarked on a twenty-year arms buildup fueled by the oil
boom of the 1970s, some senior members of the Nigerian army were keen
to test out both their new weaponry and the battle-preparedness of their
troops: an estimated 75 percent of Nigeria's soldiers had not been involved
in armed combat in 1990.[41] It was also felt that the intervention could help
deter countries like Cameroon and Chad, with which Nigeria has had
clashes over disputed border areas. Senior members of the Nigerian army,
led by Babangida, thus staked their honor and professional reputation on
success in Liberia. This helps to explain Nigeria's single-minded determination to bring peace to Liberia even at great economic cost to itself at a
time when the country had an external debt of $33 billion and against a
growing tide of domestic public opinion.

Babangida's regime forcefully presented its case for the necessity of
the intervention at home and abroad. In the international arena, Nigerian
Foreign Minister Rilwanu Lukman and its permanent representative to the

United Nations, Ibrahim Gambari, were instructed to push the ECOWAS peace plan (discussed below) aggressively at the world's highest diplomatic body. Addressing the UN Security Council on 8 August 1990, Rilwanu Lukman explained ECOMOG's reasons for intervening in Liberia as "first and foremost to stop the senseless killings of innocent civilians—nationals and foreigners—and to help the Liberian people to restore their democratic institutions." He went on to offer the assurance that "ECOWAS intervention is in no way designed to back one party or punish another."[42]

Babangida used his ability to forge personal relationships to good effect with key countries like Ghana, Gambia, and Sierra Leone. The personal chemistry between Babangida and Jerry Rawlings cemented the Abuja-Accra axis, which was the most crucial alliance for the establishment of ECOMOG and remained the most important partnership for the subregional initiative throughout the seven-year civil war. Babangida also had a good relationship with Dawda Jawara. The Gambian leader's support for ECOMOG was essential, for he was chairman of both the ECOWAS Authority and of its Standing Mediation Committee (SMC). Nigeria had previously sent its judges to work in the Gambian judiciary, and the head of the Gambian army in 1990, Colonel Abubakar Dada, was a Nigerian. Finally, Sierra Leonean leader Joseph Momoh had been a classmate of Babangida's at the Nigerian Army Staff College, and they remained good friends ever since.

Babangida, however, discovered that domestic support was much harder to secure than subregional support. There was much hostility in Nigeria toward the establishment of the multinational force. Many habitually skeptical Nigerians feared that Babangida, whom they had nicknamed "Machiavelli" for his manipulative cunning, was attempting to use the Liberia intervention as an excuse to remain in power and derail his own transition program.[43] No fewer than six organizations—the Nigerian Union of Journalists, Civil Liberties Organization, Committee for the Defense of Human Rights, the Gani Fawehinmi Solidarity Association, the National Association of Nigerian Students, and Women in Nigeria—issued a joint statement calling for the withdrawal of Nigerian troops from Liberia. The Nigerian Labor Congress condemned Nigeria's participation in ECOMOG, saying it was an unnecessary strain on the country's weak economy. Much of Nigeria's press also criticized the intervention, citing factors like the $80 million OAU debt that Nigeria had been forced to write off during its involvement in the Chad peacekeeping debacle and referring to Liberia as "Nigeria's Vietnam."[44]

Two respected Nigerian jurists added their voices to the dissent. Akinola Aguda expressed doubt at the possibility of "colonising Liberia and decolonising it in twelve months,"[45] and Akin Oyebode warned that "if ECOWAS sends a peacekeeping force without the agreement of the two parties, that could mean intervention in the internal affairs of the country."[46] A surprising voice of dissent came from a serving Nigerian official in New York, in the form of its permanent representative to the UN, Ibrahim Gambari, who wrote: "The ECOWAS Mediation Committee may have bitten off more [than] it could chew. . . . ECOMOG is a poorly thought-out quick-fix effort—a rush job."[47]

But ECOMOG also had a few domestic supporters. The Nigeria Bar Association noted the importance of an active Nigeria in its immediate sphere of influence, and the *National Concord* of 19 October 1990 warned:

> If ECOMOG finally pulls out in disgrace, other countries within the region will go home with the dangerous impression that ours is a big-for-nothing country, incapable of upholding its foreign policy priorities in ECOWAS and undeserving of respect around the world.[48]

Margaret Vogt, head of strategic studies at the Nigerian Institute of International Affairs at the time, used a similar argument to justify the intervention:

> A premature withdrawal, in disgrace, would be perceived as a failure of Nigeria's military and diplomatic initiative, the impression would be created of a country with a huge and sophisticated armed forces that could not deal with a minor armed resistance by the largely untrained forces of Charles Taylor.[49]

Babangida himself put up a stout and sometimes vituperative defense of ECOMOG:

> To those involved in false historical comparison, intellectual intoxication and phantom analysis, I ask, should Nigeria and other responsible countries in this subregion stand by, and watch the whole of Liberia turned into one massive graveyard?[50]

But it was clear that many Nigerians were opposed to their country's participation in ECOMOG, though the lack of a democratic government prevented them from forcing a change of policy (as occurred, for example, in the United States over Somalia in 1993). This, combined with a lack of detailed information on ECOMOG, as well as economic concerns at home during an era of a tortuous political transition, meant that the Nigerian public could voice its disapproval only from the sidelines.

Côte d'Ivoire, Burkina Faso, and Libya

Soon after news of the rebel invasion reached Monrovia at the end of December 1989, Doe accused Côte d'Ivoire, Burkina Faso, and Libya of conspiring with the NPFL to topple him. The rebels had entered Liberia through the Ivorian border, and Ouagadougou and Tripoli had provided training bases and arms to the NPFL. These actions had their roots in an intricate web of personal networks. As noted in Chapter 2, Ivorian leader Félix Houphoüet-Boigny had never forgiven Doe for executing Adolphus Tolbert, the husband of his adopted daughter, Daisy Delafosse. Houphoüet also wanted to restore the close relations his country had enjoyed with Tolbert's Liberia and gain access to the world's richest iron ore deposits in Nimba County.[51] Burkinabè leader Blaise Compaoré, who enjoyed close relations with Houphoüet-Boigny, had introduced Charles Taylor to Libyan leader Colonel Muammar Qaddafi. Houphoüet-Boigny's relationship with Compaoré was cemented by the Ivorian leader's fear in the early 1980s of being encircled by a revolutionary axis between Burkina Faso's Thomas Sankara, Ghana's Jerry Rawlings, and Libya's Muammar Qaddafi. Houphoüet-Boigny enthusiastically embraced Compaoré after his 1987 coup. Burkina Faso's dependence on Côte d'Ivoire for jobs for its migrant workers and access to the sea provided a further bond between the neighbors.

After the NPFL invasion, Abidjan denied reports that it was assisting the rebels. But criticism from the official Ivorian press of AFL "genocide" in Nimba County; calls from Ivorian opposition leader at the time and current president, Laurent Gbagbo, for the government to stop arming the rebels; and, most significant, the fact that Houphoüet-Boigny had let his territory be used for launching the invasion—all cast doubt on the authenticity of these denials.[52] Ivorian-based commercial interests would soon start benefiting from NPFL mineral and timber concessions, and such economic gains further cemented Abidjan's support for Taylor.[53]

Burkina Faso's relationship with the NPFL was even closer. In the late 1980s, Compaoré had obtained Charles Taylor's release from a Ghanaian jail and introduced Taylor to Qaddafi.[54] Compaoré remained close to Qaddafi after Sankara's death, visiting Tripoli frequently, condemning U.S. air strikes against Libya as "terrorist" in 1989, maintaining close military ties to Tripoli, and establishing the joint Banque Arabe-Libyenne du Burkina.[55] Ouagadougou remained the main source of NPFL arms throughout Liberia's civil war, and as Compaoré himself admitted in September 1991, 700 soldiers of the Burkinabè army assisted Taylor in the early stages of the war.[56] Compaoré benefited from trade ties to the NPFL leader during the war and hoped for future influence over a Taylor-controlled Liberia.

Doe had ruptured his country's relations with Qaddafi by closing down the Libyan embassy in Monrovia in May 1981 and by supporting Washington in its anti-Qaddafi policies in Africa. Libya also had a record of supporting insurgency in West Africa: it reportedly backed a 1981 coup that narrowly failed in Gambia and provided military training to dissident Liberians and Sierra Leoneans in Libya. In the Liberian case, Tripoli and Ouagadougou provided arms and military bases for training NPFL fighters.

The United States

Testifying before the U.S. House of Representatives Foreign Affairs Sub-committee on Africa in June 1990, Herman Cohen, the assistant secretary of state for African affairs, summed up his country's Liberia policy: "Our policy seeks to achieve a cease-fire, to avoid the bloody battle for Monrovia, and to bring the senseless killings to an end. . . . We also seek freely-held, internationally-monitored elections at the earliest practical moment."[57] As the Liberian conflict escalated, Samuel Doe sent a delegation to Washington on 1 May 1990. U.S. officials impressed upon Doe's emissaries the importance of an early democratic election in Liberia, suggesting that elections, originally scheduled for October 1991, be moved forward to January 1991.

The U.S. State Department signified Washington's intentions to remain neutral and not intervene in the fighting to save Doe, a former ally. U.S. officials met the NPFL's Tom Woewiyu in Washington on 14 May 1990; on 3 June 1990 Washington sent 2,500 U.S. Marines to Liberia with strict instructions only to guard strategic U.S. installations and protect the 1,100 Americans left in Monrovia; the United States evacuated the rest of its citizens from Liberia on 5 August 1990. Washington had, however, briefly considered supporting Doe. On 2 January 1990, the United States had sent two military observers to the AFL camp in Nimba County once it discovered that the NPFL rebels had been armed and trained by Muammar Qaddafi. As Herman Cohen later admitted, "We wanted the AFL to be able to contain this insurgency because of the Libyan connection."[58]

But with mounting reports of AFL atrocities, a congressional outcry forced the speedy withdrawal of the two military advisers, and the United States reverted to its policy of maintaining contact with all three Liberian factions. Washington's desire to protect its VOA and CIA relay stations and navigational station in Monrovia, and the NPFL's control of 90 percent of Liberia, however, soon led to U.S. support for a Taylor-led interim government to organize national elections.[59] As the rebels descended on Monrovia, senior Liberian politicians implored Washington to send in its soldiers to restore order, and even some of America's European allies called for U.S. military intervention.[60]

But Washington limited its assistance to diplomatic measures, publicly throwing its weight behind the ECOWAS peace plan, which it endorsed in July 1990. It also supported humanitarian assistance efforts, contributing 60 percent of the $2.8 million of international relief to Liberia in 1990.[61] U.S. Ambassador to Nigeria Lannon Walker was asked by Nigeria's army chief, General Sani Abacha, to explain U.S. policy in Liberia. Walker informed his Nigerian hosts that Washington would not intervene in the conflict and opined that any solution to the crisis would have to come from the subregion, in which Nigeria was the only country capable of projecting power. However, he also stressed that he was not instructed by Washington to ask for a Nigerian-led intervention.[62] Nigeria had effectively received assurance that the United States would not oppose a subregional military intervention into Liberia.

Herman Cohen was prevented by political superiors in Washington from taking a more high-profile role in resolving the conflict. On 20 April 1990, Cohen secured agreement from a reluctant Gnassingbé Eyadéma to grant Doe political asylum in Togo.[63] At a critical policy meeting in Washington on 24 May, Deputy National Security Adviser Robert Gates adamantly rejected the view that the United States had a historical responsibility to intervene in Liberia. Representatives of the CIA, U.S. Information Agency, and Defense Department who had earlier argued for the need to protect "vital" U.S. installations in Monrovia were brow-beaten into silence by Gates's outburst.[64] On 5 June, Deputy Secretary of State Lawrence Eagleburger informed his colleagues that President Bush had decided that Washington should not take the lead in Liberia, and Cohen was ordered not to travel to Monrovia to convince Doe to go into exile.[65] U.S. installations in Monrovia were soon destroyed by Liberia's warring factions, and any active U.S. role became a forlorn hope.

Liberia had outlived its strategic usefulness to the United States in a deideologized post–Cold War era. Tunji Lardner best described the dramatic change in Washington's Liberia policy: "Master-Sergeant Doe is the latest victim of imperial euthanasia. He died because his treatment was withheld by the United States and his life-support system shut off."[66] The Iraqi invasion of Kuwait on 2 August 1990 ended any lingering hopes of a distracted U.S. intervening militarily in Liberia. Washington was to stand aside in 1990 and 1991 and watch regimes collapse in Liberia, Chad, and Somalia—African countries in which it had invested heavily during the Cold War.[67]

The National Patriotic Front of Liberia

The NPFL had been founded by General Thomas Quiwonkpa before his abortive coup in 1985. It was later revived by survivors of the coup attempt and consisted largely of anti-Doe Liberian exiles in West Africa.[68] The nucleus of the NPFL consisted of Gio soldiers and farmers recruited by Charles Taylor from Nimba County,[69] as well as Burkinabès, Gambians, and Sierra Leoneans, all of whom had received training in guerrilla warfare in Libyan and Burkinabè military camps. It was this motley crew of farmers, soldiers, and mercenaries that was to pose the most formidable challenge to Samuel Doe's ten-year rule. Even by the standards of West Africa's coup-ridden history, the NPFL was a rather unusual phenomenon: a band of 168 fighters had launched an invasion from a neighboring state, armed an ethnic coalition of disgruntled civilians as they marched, and descended on the capital to topple the head of state.

Charles McArthur Taylor, the forty-eight-year-old leader of the NPFL, was born in Liberia of an Americo-Liberian father and Gola mother. During the Liberian civil war, he often brandished a Kalashnikov and dressed in combat fatigues with the words "Commander-in-Chief" emblazoned on his chest. A skillful manipulator of the press and a ruthless, egocentric leader, he had obtained an economics degree from Bentley College in the United States, where he had headed the 35,000-member student movement known as the Union of Liberian Associations in the Americas. Taylor returned to Liberia shortly after Doe's 1980 putsch and rose rapidly to serve as chief of the General Services Agency, the Liberian government's procurement office. Appointed deputy minister of commerce after falling out with Doe, Taylor was accused of involvement in the embezzlement of $900,000 while in his former post and fled Liberia for the United States in 1983 to avoid punishment.

Because Washington had an extradition treaty with Monrovia, Taylor was arrested on 24 May 1984, at Doe's request, and detained in the Plymouth County House of Corrections in Massachusetts. Taylor's escape from prison is now part of Liberian political folklore. Having spent fifteen months in detention, he reportedly sawed through the bars of his cell with a hacksaw blade and lowered himself from the third-floor window to freedom with a rope made of bedsheets.[70] A less spectacular version noted that Taylor was simply allowed to walk out of prison by his Massachusetts jailers.[71] However he escaped, Taylor set off on a voyage through Mexico, Spain, and France, arriving in Accra in 1986. He became particularly close to the Burkinabè ambassador in Accra, Memunu Ouattara, a cousin of Blaise Compaoré. Taylor became a connoisseur of West African jails, spending time in Ghanaian, Guinean, and Sierra Leonean prisons before settling in Compaoré's Burkina Faso by 1987.[72]

The NPFL was simply a vehicle for Taylor's political ambitions, and it had no clearly defined ideological identity beyond its leader's description of himself as a "cold-blooded capitalist" and "worshipper of Reaganomics." Taylor established a cult of personality, and his leadership style was autocratic. The NPFL, though, did have some of Liberia's most experienced politicians in men like Laveli Supuwood, Tom Woewiyu, Sam Dokie, and Ernest Eastman, many of whom had held high office under Doe.[73]

By the time it captured Buchanan and Gbarnga at the end of May 1990, the NPFL had built up an estimated 10,000 fighters; Doe's rapidly disintegrating 6,000-strong army could muster only about 2,000 soldiers. But as the NPFL marched into Monrovia in July 1990, one of its commanders, Prince Yeduo Johnson, abandoned Taylor to form his own splinter group, the Independent National Patriotic Front of Liberia with about 6,000 mostly Gio NPFL fighters. Johnson, himself a Gio, was a former commander of Liberia's military police. He had taken part in Quiwonkpa's unsuccessful 1985 invasion and trained NPFL fighters in Libya. Johnson said that he broke away from the NPFL after Taylor ordered the assassination of some senior NPFL commanders. Taylor claimed that Johnson deserted to avoid a court-martial for executing seven NPFL fighters.

On 2 July 1990, the rebels cut off the supply of water and electricity to Monrovia and started to pound the city with heavy artillery and rocket fire, forcing Doe to offer a cease-fire and a half-hearted resignation. On 25 July, the NPFL launched attacks on the Executive Mansion as Doe's final hideout stood tantalizingly within Taylor's grasp. Taylor hesitated, apparently wishing not to destroy the Executive Mansion in order to enter his new home intact[74] and in deference, Taylor later claimed, to U.S. wishes of avoiding a bloodbath in Monrovia.[75] The INPFL engaged the remnants of the AFL in pitched battles on the streets of Monrovia, turning the city into a graveyard of ethnic slaughter. Taylor declared himself president of Liberia on 28 July 1990 and, in a blatant appeal to U.S. support, announced elections in six months, though he had previously talked of a five-year transition.

The Exiled Liberian Opposition

Amos Sawyer and Ellen Johnson-Sirleaf were the most prominent Liberian political exiles at the time of the NPFL invasion. Both were members of the Association for Constitutional Democracy in Liberia (ACDL), an umbrella organization with about 2,200 members from various Liberian political groupings in the United States. Sawyer was executive director of the organization and Johnson-Sirleaf a leading member; both had been jailed for brief periods under Doe. There were also other exile groups in the United States, Europe, and West Africa with which the ACDL maintained contact.

The NPFL invasion had left the ACDL without a clear policy. The exiles had previously decided on a strategy of uniting behind a single candidate for the October 1991 elections, hoping that the new international climate after the Cold War would leave Doe with no other choice but to ensure free and fair elections. Charles Taylor's invasion split the nine-member ACDL executive committee. Ellen Johnson-Sirleaf and Harry Greaves, the ACDL's treasurer, initially supported Taylor. Greaves and some other members felt so strongly about this support that they printed new ACDL letterheads and solicited funds for the NPFL without the approval of the executive committee. Amos Sawyer, Patrick Seyon, and Joseph Woah-Tee were among the ACDL leadership that opposed the NPFL from the start.[76] After reports of NPFL atrocities against civilians, many ACDL members who backed the invasion withdrew support. They instead called for Doe's resignation, a cease-fire, and a nonpartisan interim government. Talks between the ACDL and NPFL broke down in April 1990 due to the insistence of the exiles on Taylor postponing his leadership ambitions until an interim government organized elections. Taylor, however, insisted on heading any new government in Liberia.

The Liberian exile opposition, perhaps rather naively, expected Charles Taylor, an Americo-Liberian unsure of his electoral support but on the verge of military victory, to surrender the fruits of his labor, probably to one of its own candidates. Taylor did not mask his hostility toward the ACDL, describing its members as "a bunch of cowards . . . [who] run and hide under beds as soon as Doe talks."[77] The NPFL leader threw down a challenge to the exiles, saying, "We are bleeding and dying in this forest to remove Doe. They want to talk? Let them come to Liberia and fight."[78] The urbane group of cosmopolitan exiles was certainly a stark contrast to Charles Taylor, a former jailbird and escaped convict. His warlordism contrasted sharply with the ACDL's arcane concerns with the intricacies of constitutional democracy and its abhorrence of violence.

The exiles seemed unsure of how to respond to the situation in Liberia. Johnson-Sirleaf, director of the United Nations Development Programme (UNDP) Regional Bureau for Africa at the time, opposed external intervention and regarded ECOMOG as an invasion force that would keep Doe in power. As the situation worsened, she reportedly asked the State Department for a U.S. intervention force.[79] Amos Sawyer was more pragmatic, expressing support for ECOMOG if a U.S. intervention could not be staged.

ECOWAS

The first point that should be made about ECOWAS is that its West African subregion already contained many divisions before the Liberian conflict erupted. The attempts of some ECOWAS members to intervene directly in Liberia not only deepened these divisions but also threatened the organization with possible extinction. The acrimonious relationship between Doe's Liberia and Côte d'Ivoire and Burkina Faso has already been discussed. The plethora of diplomatic and border disputes involving other ECOWAS members in 1990 included: Senegal and Gambia, Senegal and Mauritania, Senegal and Guinea-Bissau, Ghana and Togo, Ghana and Burkina Faso, and Burkina Faso and Mali. A further source of subregional disunity lay in the fact that only four out of sixteen ECOWAS states had paid their arrears to the subregional body in June 1990, and the organization was $17 million in debt.[80] These hardly seemed the most auspicious circumstances to undertake a precedent-setting peacekeeping mission to Liberia.

Less than half of ECOWAS's heads of state attended the thirteenth summit of the ECOWAS Authority in Banjul during 28–30 May 1990. Two days before the summit, General Babangida visited and conferred with the outgoing ECOWAS chairman, Blaise Compaoré. At the summit, Babangida proposed the establishment of a five-member Standing Mediation Committee with a mandate to mediate the Liberian conflict and report its findings back to the full ECOWAS Authority. Nigeria, Ghana, Gambia, Mali, and Togo were elected as the first members of the SMC. The body was to enjoy a three-year lifespan, after which its members would be replaced. Ghana, Gambia, Guinea, and Sierra Leone pressured Nigeria to take the lead on Liberia, even as Babangida remained uncertain of subregional support.[81] Doe sent apologies to the summiteers, citing pressing state matters as the reason for his inability to attend the summit.

Meanwhile, Liberia's Inter-Faith Mediation Committee, composed of religious leaders, organized peace talks at the U.S. Embassy in Freetown during 12–16 June 1990. The NPFL failed to send representatives, insisting that Doe resign before any talks could be held.[82] At another meeting in Freetown on 12 July 1990 chaired by ECOWAS foreign ministers, the NPFL rejected proposals for an interim government not headed by Doe and a regional peacekeeping force. Its representatives at first agreed to a peacekeeping force without Nigeria before rejecting the proposal after consulting with Taylor.[83] Furthermore, a more predictable stalemate occurred: Doe insisted the NPFL give up its guns before talks, whereas NPFL representatives insisted Doe give up his presidency before talks.

The SMC meeting in Banjul (6–7 August 1990) proved momentous. It was attended by ECOWAS's Gambian chairman Dawda Jawara, General Babangida (Nigeria), Flight Lieutenant Jerry Rawlings (Ghana), and Generals Lansana Conté (Guinea) and Joseph Momoh (Sierra Leone). Guinea, Sierra Leone, and Côte d'Ivoire were invited as observers, being hosts to the majority of Liberian refugees fleeing the conflict. Although Conté and Momoh attended, Houphoüet declined. The rapidly deteriorating situation in Liberia provided the backdrop to the meeting. By August 1990, 225,000 Liberian refugees had flooded into Guinea, 150,000 into Côte d'Ivoire, and 69,000 into Sierra Leone; about 5,000 people had been killed, and about 3,000 Nigerian, Ghanaian, and Sierra Leonean citizens were being held hostage by the NPFL, making the intervention force that Taylor was opposing more likely.

The outcome of the meeting was a plan, based on that of the Inter-Faith Mediation Committee's earlier proposal, to establish the Economic Community of West African States Cease-fire Monitoring Group of military peacekeepers from the five SMC states as well as Guinea and Sierra Leone. This ECOMOG force would supervise a cease-fire, and an interim government was to be established, following Doe's resignation, to organize elections after twelve months. None of the faction leaders would be eligible to head the interim government. A $50 million Special Emergency Fund was also to be established to finance both ECOMOG and the Election Observer Group and to provide for the immediate humanitarian needs of Liberians. ECOWAS, the OAU, and members of the international community would be asked to contribute to the emergency fund.[84]

Jawara sent letters to the other ECOWAS heads of state not present in Banjul to inform them of these decisions. Jawara, the civilian leader of Gambia for twenty-five years, was renowned for his abilities at consensus-building. But even his skills were unable to assuage the anger of his francophone counterparts, who felt that they had been presented with an unacceptable fait accompli. Jawara was at pains to explain that ECOWAS was not sending an invasion force. But some suspected that he had self-interested motives in backing the ECOMOG intervention. Among Taylor's NPFL were individuals who had been involved in the unsuccessful Gambian coup in 1981, including its leader, Samba Kukoi Sanyang. Burkina Faso, a chief supporter of the NPFL, was suspected of sheltering Gambian dissidents.[85] And the 1981 coup had been sponsored by Libya, which had provided arms and training facilities to the NPFL.

Guinea and Sierra ¦Leone also had strong reasons for supporting the ECOMOG intervention. Not only were they among the three states most directly affected by the spillover of refugees into their territories, but Guinea had 30,000 citizens trapped in Liberia, and NPFL guerrillas had launched a brief incursion into the Macenta Province in July 1990.[86] Guinea's General Lansana Conté was threatening to launch a unilateral intervention into Liberia if ECOMOG did not intervene, and Conakry historically had strained ties to Abidjan, a major NPFL supporter. Freetown had similar reasons to be concerned about Liberia, for the NPFL had Sierra Leonean dissidents within its ranks who were vowing to destabilize it. These fears later proved to be well founded, as some NPFL Sierra Leonean elements took the war into Sierra Leone in March 1991. Sierra Leone had a weak economy and an ill-equipped army, and its national security would soon become inextricably tied to its support for ECOMOG.[87] The fact that Sierra Leone's Momoh had an acrimonious relationship with Doe—he had allowed his country to be used for Quiwonkpa's 1985 invasion—provided further evidence that national security interests were more important than joining a Nigerian-led effort to save Doe's regime.

Ghana's Jerry Rawlings arrived in Banjul with his military planners, including the proposed force commander of ECOMOG, General Arnold Quainoo. Quainoo had visited Babangida on 3 August 1990 and was told that if Ghana took the lead on the intervention force Nigeria would follow.[88] Babangida insisted that Ghana provide ECOMOG's force commander to assuage NPFL fears.[89] Ghanaian citizens had been attacked in the Barnesville estate near Monrovia.[90] As Obed Asamoah, the Ghanaian foreign minister in 1990, said, "It does matter to Ghana if 10,000 Ghanaians get killed."[91] Within Ghana itself, a strong public voice was the former force commander of the United Nations Force in Lebanon, General Emmanuel Erskine, who argued strongly for intervention to prevent regional instability and the spillover of refugees into neighboring states. Erskine also argued that ECOMOG conformed with ECOWAS protocols because external actors like Burkina Faso and Côte d'Ivoire were involved in fueling the conflict in Liberia.[92]

The national interests that these ECOWAS states had in the ECOMOG intervention in Liberia certainly contradicts the claims of Neil Macfarlane and Thomas Weiss, who criticized what they described as "Nigeria's manipulation of ECOWAS" and argued that "it was Nigerian insistence that caused ECOWAS to ignore its restrictions on involvement in the internal affairs of member states."[93] Robert Mortimer also argued that "the intervention was essentially a Nigerian *fait accompli.*"[94] The evidence above suggests that the situation in Liberia was somewhat more complex than these views of an overbearing Pax Nigeriana imply.

Present at Banjul when the decision to establish ECOMOG was made were UN Assistant Secretary-General James Jonah and OAU Secretary-General Salim Ahmed Salim. Salim pledged OAU support to ECOMOG and asked the United Nations to do likewise. He brushed aside the legal arguments against ECOMOG, saying, "to argue that there was no legal base for any intervention in Liberia is surprising. Should the countries in West Africa . . . just leave the Liberians to fight each other? Will that be more legitimate?"[95] The OAU chairman, Ugandan President Yoweri Museveni, also lent his weight to the pro-ECOMOG camp, saying: "The ECOWAS experiment could indeed be emulated by other regional organizations when calamities of this kind strike member states. . . . ECOMOG should be congratulated for having prevented a bad situation from getting worse."[96] The EEC (now the EU) provided early diplomatic support and some humanitarian relief.

But ECOMOG enjoyed more support externally than it did from within its own subregion. A nervous Abass Bundu, the energetic and pugnacious Sierra Leonean ECOWAS executive secretary, requested that ECOMOG's deployment be delayed while further negotiations were given a chance to work.[97] Several of ECOWAS's francophone members, especially Burkina Faso, Côte d'Ivoire, and Senegal, were opposed to what they regarded as a usurpation of the ECOWAS Authority's powers by the SMC. Abidjan accused Nigeria of attempting to extend its sphere of influence in West Africa, Ouagadougou considered Nigeria an instrument of U.S. policy in Liberia,[98] and Senegalese Foreign Minister Seydina Oumar Sy argued that any intervention in the name of ECOWAS must be referred to an extraordinary summit of the ECOWAS Authority.[99]

The two francophone members of the SMC, Mali and Togo, declined to contribute troops to ECOMOG, with Lomé arguing that the intervention could result in more bloodshed.[100] Compaoré had developed close ties to Eyadéma, who was an early supporter of his regime, and the Burkinabè leader had mediated between Togo's domestic groups and sent his troops to monitor Togolese elections in 1993.[101] Burkina Faso also had some influence over Mali and Niger as a result of Compaoré's efforts as a mediator in the Tuareg rebellions in both countries.[102] The Malian foreign minister, N'golo Traoré, complained that the intervention had been prepared in a military commission without its participation;[103] Niger opposed the intervention less noisily.[104] ECOWAS's historic anglophone-francophone divide, which had been carefully bandaged, now became an open wound vulnerable to an infection that, if allowed to spread, could have spelled the death of the organization.

The most strident and persistent critic of ECOMOG was the Burkinabè leader, Blaise Compaoré, who argued that "the [SMC] is not competent to interfere in a member states' internal conflict; but only if there is a conflict between one member state and another."[105] Compaoré's minister of external affairs, Prosper Vokouma, was even more blunt, declaring that "the military conflict should be resolved by Liberians and not by outsiders. . . . Burkina does not recognise the forces of [ECOMOG]."[106]

Putting aside Compaoré's self-interested motives in wishing to protect the NPFL, there was some merit in his argument that the establishment of ECOMOG did not conform to the constitutional legal requirements of ECOWAS.[107] The arguments used in establishing ECOMOG, in fact, had a more solid basis in politics than law, and ECOMOG was justified largely on humanitarian grounds, as Abass Bundu himself later admitted.[108] Neither the 1978 ECOWAS Protocol on Non-Aggression nor the 1981 Protocol Relating to Mutual Assistance on Defense provided clear legal justification for ECOMOG's intervention in Liberia. The 1978 protocol commits members to settling disputes peacefully (article 1), refraining from supporting subversion or aggression (article 2), and preventing foreigners and nonresident foreigners from perpetrating such acts against members (articles 3 and 4) while promising to refer disputes to a committee of the ECOWAS Authority (article 5).

The 1981 protocol called for the creation of the Allied Armed Forces of the Community, consisting of specially earmarked units of national armies (article 13) and a Defense Council consisting of a deputy executive secretary (article 12) and ministers of defence and foreign affairs to discuss intervention strategies (articles 7 and 8). None of these bodies had been created by 1990. Furthermore, the 1981 Protocol permitted intervention in internal conflicts only in cases of (1) an externally directed threat (article 16); (2) a conflict between two ECOWAS states (article 17); or (3) an internal conflict that is externally sustained (article 18).

Even if one argued that Liberia's situation had extrasubregional support from Libya that could justify intervention, the fact that two of its members—Burkina Faso and Côte d'Ivoire—were primarily involved in providing this support makes this argument difficult to justify. By the time of ECOMOG's intervention, the 1981 protocol had not yet been ratified by some members, due in part to fears about Nigeria's preponderant weight in the military structure. Mali and Cape Verde had refused to sign the protocol; Benin, Gambia, and Mauritania had not yet ratified it.[109]

Even the body that took the decision to establish ECOMOG was on shaky legal foundations. The SMC was intended, as its name suggests, only to *mediate* rather than attempt to impose solutions on conflicts. Article 4 of the document establishing the SMC talks only of mediation procedures, and nowhere does it refer to military action. Compaoré was himself chairman of the ECOWAS Authority of heads of state at the time of the establishment of the SMC in May 1990, and it was he who signed the document establishing it. He was therefore in a particularly privileged position to know what the mandate of the SMC entailed. But as noted in the Introduction (see Chapter 1), there were other efforts, which remain highly contested, to establish a legal basis for humanitarian interventions in places like Somalia, northern Iraq, and Bosnia. Liberia was part of this post–Cold War trend.

Doe had sent a letter to Jawara requesting military intervention but had withdrawn this request after he realized that the Banjul plan required his own resignation. The NPFL at first seemed unexpectedly to have agreed to the Banjul plan, calling for wider OAU representation in ECOMOG and insisting that Taylor head an interim government; it did not reject the ECOMOG force outright. But an NPFL communiqué issued shortly after Banjul warned that "the concept of a Peace-keeping Force . . . must have prior commitment of all . . . parties to a cease-fire or else it could exacerbate rather than resolve problems."[110]

Even as Amos Sawyer was elected interim president in Banjul on 29 August 1990 by seventeen of Liberia's political parties and interest groups, Charles Taylor sent an ominous warning by refusing to dispatch any representatives to Banjul and insisting that he be made head of any interim government. Taylor denounced ECOMOG as illegal and vowed to resist foreign intervention by force. He established his own rival twenty-member National Patriotic Reconstruction Assembly Government in Gbarnga and declared himself president of Greater Liberia.

Notes

1. Stephen Ellis, "Liberia's Warlord Insurgency," in Christopher Clapham (ed.), *African Guerrillas* (Oxford: James Currey; and Indiana: Indiana University Press: Fountain, 1998), p. 155.

2. See Segun Aderiye, "ECOMOG Landing," in M. A. Vogt (ed.), *The Liberian Crisis and ECOMOG: A Bold Attempt at Regional Peacekeeping* (Lagos: Gabumo, 1992), p. 115.

3. Cited in *Africa Report* 35, no. 5 (November-December 1990): 15.

4. The phrase "Pax Nigeriana" was, we believe, coined by Bolaji Akinyemi in *Foreign Policy and Federalism* (Ibadan, Nigeria: Ibadan University Press, 1974). Akinyemi, who was Nigeria's foreign minister from 1985 to 1987, used it to describe Nigeria's influence in the crafting of the OAU charter.

5. Shehu Shagari, *My Vision of Nigeria* (London and Toronto: Frank Cass, 1981), pp. 75–76.

6. Quoted in Terry Mays, "Nigeria's Foreign Policy and Its Participation in ECOMOG," in Karl Magyar and Earl Conteh-Morgan, eds., *Peacekeeping in Africa: ECOMOG in Liberia* (Hampshire, UK: Macmillan; and New York: St. Martin's, 1998), p. 112.

7. Nnamdi Azikiwe, *Zik* (Cambridge, UK: Cambridge University Press, 1960), p. 71.

8. Quoted in John Stremlau, *The International Politics of the Nigerian Civil War, 1967–1970* (Princeton, N.J.: Princeton University Press, 1977), p. 12.

9. Personal interview with Matthew Mbu, Lagos, 13 January 1997.

10. See Ade Adefuye, et al., *Seven Years of IBB,* 7 vols. (Lagos: Daily Times of Nigeria, 1993); Nkem Agetua, *Operation Liberty: The Story of Major-General Joshua Nimyel Dogonyaro* (Lagos: Hona Communications, 1992); Chidi Amuta, *Prince of the Niger: The Babangida Years* (Lagos: Tanus Communications, 1992); J. Isawa Elaigwu, *Gowon* (Ibadan, Nigeria: West Books, 1986); Joseph Garba, *Diplomatic Soldiering: Nigerian Foreign Policy, 1975–1979* (Ibadan, Nigeria: Spectrum, 1987); Frederick Forsyth, *Emeka* (Ibadan, Nigeria: Spectrum, 1982); Yakubu Gowon, "The Economic Community of West African States: A Study of Political and Economic Integration," Ph.D. diss., Warwick University, UK, February 1984; Olusegun Obasanjo, *My Command* (London, Ibadan, and Nairobi: Heinemann, 1980); and Olusegun Obasanjo, *Not My Will* (Ibadan, Nigeria: University Press, 1990).

11. Robin Luckham, *The Nigerian Military: A Sociological Analysis of Authority and Revolt, 1960–1967* (London and New York: Cambridge University Press, 1971), p. 279. For a more recent study, see Shehu Othman, "Nigeria: Power for Profit—Class, Corporatism, and Factionalism in the Military," in Donal Cruise O'Brien, John Dunn, and Richard Rathbone (eds.), *Contemporary West African States* (Cambridge, UK: Cambridge University Press, 1989), pp. 113–144.

12. See Gowon, "The Economic Community of West African States"; Anthony Kirk-Greene and Douglas Rimmer, *Nigeria since 1970: A Political and Economic Outline* (London: Hodder and Stoughton, 1981); James Mayall, "Oil and Nigerian Foreign Policy," *African Affairs* 75, no. 300 (July 1976); Omotayo Olaniyan, "Nigeria and ECOWAS: A Role and Problem Analysis," in Gabriel Olusanya and R. A. Akindele (eds.), *Nigeria's External Relations: The First Twenty-Five Years* (Ibadan, Nigeria: University Press, 1986); Olatunde Ojo, "Nigeria and the Formation of ECOWAS," *International Organization* 34, no. 4 (Autumn 1980); Olatunde Ojo, "Nigeria," in Timothy Shaw and Olajide Aluko (eds.), *The Political Economy of African Foreign Policy* (Aldershot, UK: Gower, 1984); and Ralph Onwuka, *Development and Integration in Africa: The Case of the Economic Community of West African States* (Ile-Ife, Nigeria: University of Ife Press, 1982).

13. See, for example, James Polhemus, "Nigeria and Southern Africa: Interest, Policy and Means," *Canadian Journal of African Studies* 11, no. 1 (1977); and Abiodun O. Sotunmbi, *Nigeria's Recognition of the MPLA Government of Angola:*

A Case-study in Decision-making and Implementation (Lagos: Nigerian Institute of International Affairs, 1981).

14. See, for example, Jean Herskovits, "Nigeria and the U.S.: An Historical View," in Olajide Aluko (ed.), *Africa and the Great Powers* (Lanham, Md.: University Press of America, 1987); Olujimi Jolaoso, *In the Shadows: Recollections of a Pioneer Diplomat* (Lagos and Oxford: Malthouse, 1991); and George Obiozor, *Uneasy Friendship: Nigeria/U.S. Relations* (Enugu, Nigeria: Fourth Dimension, 1992).

15. See, for example, Bola Akinterinwa, "French Security Arrangements with Francophone Africa: Implications for Nigeria's Relations with Its Immediate Neighbors," in Bassey Ate and Bola Akinterinwa (eds.), *Nigeria and Its Immediate Neighbours* (Lagos: Nigerian Institute of International Affairs, 1992); S.K.B. Asante, "ECOWAS/CEAO: Conflict and Cooperation in West Africa," in R. I. Onwuka and A. Sesay (eds.), *The Future of Regionalism in Africa* (London: Macmillan, 1985); Daniel Bach, "The Politics of West African Economic Cooperation: CEAO and ECOWAS," *Journal of Modern African Studies* 21, no. 4 (1983); Daniel Bach, "Francophone Regional Organizations and ECOWAS," in Julius Okolo and Stephen Wright (eds.), *West African Regional Cooperation and Development* (Boulder, San Francisco and Oxford: Westview, 1990); and Emeka Nwokedi, "Nigeria and France," in G. O. Olusanya and R. A. Akindele (eds.), *Nigeria's External Relations: The First Twenty-five Years* (Ibadan, Nigeria: University Press, 1986).

16. See Olajide Aluko, *Ghana and Nigeria, 1957–1970: A Study of Inter-African Discord* (London: Rex Collings, 1976); A.H.M. Kirk-Greene, "West Africa: Nigeria and Ghana," in Peter Duignan and Robert H. Jackson (eds.), *Politics and Government in African States, 1960–1985* (Stanford: Hoover Institution, 1986); and W. Scott Thompson, *Ghana's Foreign Policy, 1957–1966* (Princeton, N.J.: Princeton University Press, 1969).

17. See Olajide Aluko, "The Expulsion of Illegal Aliens from Nigeria: A Study in Decision-making," *African Affairs* 84, no. 337 (October 1985).

18. See Ademola Adeleke, "The Politics and Diplomacy of Peacekeeping in West Africa: The ECOWAS Operation in Liberia," *Journal of Modern African Studies* 33, no. 4 (1995); Stephen Ellis, *The Mask of Anarchy: The Destruction of Liberia and the Religious Dimension of an African Civil War* (London: Hurst, 1999); Terry Mays, "Nigerian Foreign Policy and Its Participation in ECOMOG," in Karl Magyar and Earl Conteh-Morgan (eds.), *Peacekeeping in Africa: ECOMOG in Liberia* (Hampshire, UK: Macmillan; and New York: St. Martin's, 1998); W. Ofuatey-Kodjoe, "Regional Organizations and the Resolution of Internal Conflicts: The ECOWAS Intervention in Liberia," *International Peacekeeping* 1, no. 3 (Autumn 1994): 273; Max Sesay, "Civil War and Collective Intervention in Liberia," *Review of African Political Economy* 23, no. 67 (March 1996); Byron Tarr, "Extra-African Interests in the Liberian Conflict," in Magyar and Conteh-Morgan (eds.), *Peacekeeping in Africa*; William Reno, "Reinvention of an African Patrimonial State: Charles Taylor's Liberia," *Third World Quarterly* 16, no. 1 (1995): 115; and Klaas Van Walraven, *The Pretence of Peace-keeping: ECOMOG, West Africa, and Liberia, 1990–1998* (The Hague: Netherlands Institute of International Relations, 1999).

19. Personal correspondence with Amos Sawyer.

20. Personal interview with General Hezekiah Bowen, former AFL Chief of Staff, Monrovia, 14 July 1999; D. Elwood Dunn, "Liberia's Internal Responses to ECOMOG's Interventionist Efforts," in Magyar and Earl-Conteh (eds.), *Peacekeeping in Africa,* p. 89; and Emeka Nwokedi, "Regional Integration and Regional Security: ECOMOG, Nigeria, and the Liberian Crisis," *Travaux et Documents,* no. 35 (Bordeaux, France: Centre d'Etude d'Afrique Noire, 1992), p. 11.

21. Ibrahim James, "ECOMOG under Attack," in Vogt (ed.), *The Liberian Crisis and ECOMOG*, p. 127.

22. *West Africa*, no. 3800, 25 June–1 July 1990, p. 1089.

23. Emmanuel Kwezi Aning, "Managing Regional Security in West Africa: ECOWAS, ECOMOG, and Liberia," Working Paper 94.2 (Copenhagen: Center for Development Research, February 1994), p. 15.

24. Personal interview with Admiral Augustus Aikhomu, former Nigerian Chief of General Staff, Lagos, December 1996.

25. Personal interview with Herman Cohen, former U.S. Assistant Secretary of State for African Affairs, Washington, D.C., July 1997.

26. "The Babangida Interview," *West Africa*, no. 3814, 1–7 October 1990, p. 2578.

27. Adeleke, "The Politics and Diplomacy of Peacekeeping in West Africa," pp. 577–579; Mays, "Nigerian Foreign Policy," p. 114; and Ofuatey-Kodjoe, "Regional Organizations," p. 272.

28. These views were gleaned during personal interviews at the Nigerian Ministry of Foreign Affairs in Abuja between November and December 1995.

29. Tarr, "Extra-African Interests," pp. 150–170.

30. Personal interview with Ambassador Olu Adeniji, Lagos, 13 January 1997.

31. Quoted in Mays, "Nigerian Foreign Policy," p. 112.

32. Shehu Othman, "Nigeria: Power for Profit—Class, Corporatism, and Factionalism in the Military," in Donal Cruise O'Brien et al., (eds.), *Contemporary West African States* (Cambridge, UK: Cambridge University Press, 1989), pp. 142–143.

33. Wole Soyinka, *The Open Sore of a Continent: A Personal Narrative of the Nigerian Crisis* (Oxford and New York: Oxford University Press, 1996), p. 14.

34. Personal interviews, Nigerian Ministry of Foreign Affairs, Abuja, November and December 1995.

35. Personal interviews with Nigerian military officers, Lagos, January 1997.

36. Personal interview with General Ishola Williams, Lagos, 6 January 1997.

37. *Africa Confidential*, 32 no. 422 (22 February 1991): 5.

38. Ibid., and Herbert Howe, "Lessons of Liberia: ECOMOG and Regional Peacekeeping," *International Security*, 21, no. 3 (Winter 1996/1997): 167–168.

39. Brigadier R. M. Kupolati, "Strategic Doctrines: Joint Operations," in A. E. Ekoko and M. A. Vogt (eds.), *Nigerian Defence Policy: Issues and Problems* (Lagos and Oxford: Malthouse, 1990), p. 327.

40. Adedoyin Jolaade Omede, "Nigeria's Military-Security Role in Liberia," *African Journal of International Affairs and Development* 1, no. 1 (1995): 51.

41. Personal interview with a former ECOMOG officer, Lagos, 7 January 1997. This view was also confirmed by General Timothy Shelpidi, former ECOMOG force commander, during a personal interview with him in Abuja, 4 August 1999.

42. Quoted in Ibrahim A. Gambari, *Political and Comparative Dimensions of Regional Integration: The Case of ECOWAS* (Atlantic Highlands, N.J., and London: Humanities Press International, 1991), p. 132.

43. See Chidi Amuta, *Prince of the Niger: The Babangida Years* (Lagos: Tanus Communications, 1992).

44. See Austin Iyashere, "Making of a Vietnam," *African Guardian* 5, no. 36 (17 September 1990); Nnamdi Obasi, "Perceptions of the ECOMOG Peace Initiative," in Vogt (ed.), *The Liberian Crisis and ECOMOG;* and Bayo Onanuga, "A Giant Blunders," *African Concord* 5, no. 17 (27 August 1990).

45. Quoted in Jinmi Adisa, "The Politics of Regional Military Co-operation," in Vogt (ed.), *The Liberian Crisis and ECOMOG*, p. 223. For a fuller discussion, see

Akinola Aguda, "The Concept of Sovereignty and Non-intervention in the Internal Affairs of States and the Phenomenon of Peacekeeping Forces in Africa," in M. A. Vogt and L. S. Aminu (eds.), *Peacekeeping as a Security Strategy in Africa: Chad and Liberia as Case Studies*, 2 vols. (Enugu, Nigeria: Fourth Dimension, 1996).

46. Quoted in *West Africa,* no. 3804, 23–29 July 1990, p. 2165.

47. Gambari, *Political and Comparative Dimensions of Regional Integration,* p. 131.

48. Obasi, "Perceptions of the ECOMOG Peace Initiative," in Vogt (ed.), *The Liberian Crisis and ECOMOG,* p. 335.

49. Margaret Vogt, "Nigeria's Participation in the ECOWAS Monitoring Group (ECOMOG)," *Nigerian Journal of International Affairs* 17, no. 1 (1991): 116.

50. Quoted in Obasi, "Perceptions of the ECOMOG Peace Initiative," in Vogt (ed.), *The Liberian Crisis and ECOMOG,* p. 337.

51. Ellis, "Liberia's Warlord Insurgency," p. 166.

52. Cited in *West Africa,* no. 3798, 11–17 June 1990, p. 981.

53. Paul Richards, "Rebellion in Liberia and Sierra Leone: A Crisis of Youth?" in Oliver Furley (ed.), *Conflict in Africa* (New York and London: Tauris Academic Studies, 1995), p. 143.

54. Stephen Ellis, "Liberia, 1989–1994: A Study of Ethnic and Spiritual Violence," *African Affairs* 94, no. 375 (April 1995): 181.

55. Pierre Englebert, *Burkina Faso: Unsteady Statehood in West Africa* (Boulder and Oxford: Westview, 1996), pp. 163–164.

56. Ibid., p. 159.

57. "U.S. Policy and the Crisis in Liberia," Hearings Before the Subcommittee on Africa of the Committee of Foreign Affairs House of Representatives, 19 June 1990 (Washington, D.C.: U.S. Government Printing Office, 1990), p. 8.

58. Personal interview with Herman J. Cohen.

59. Herman J. Cohen, *Intervening in Africa: Superpower Peacemaking in a Troubled Continent* (New York: St. Martin's, 2000), p. 144.

60. E. John Inegbedion, "ECOMOG in Comparative Perspective," in Timothy M. Shaw and Julius Emeka Okolo (eds.), *The Political Economy of Foreign Policy in ECOWAS* (London: Macmillan, 1994), p. 227.

61. Aning, "Managing Regional Security in West Africa," p. 15.

62. Personal interview with Lannon Walker, former U.S. Ambassador to Côte d'Ivoire, U.S. Embassy, Abidjan, August 1996.

63. Personal interview with Herman J. Cohen.

64. Cohen, *Intervening in Africa,* p. 143.

65. Ibid., p. 144.

66. Lardner, "An African Tragedy," *Africa Report* 35, no. 5 (November-December 1990): 15.

67. Jeffrey Herbst, *U.S. Economic Policy Toward Africa* (New York: Council on Foreign Relations, 1992), p. 14. See also Michael Clough, *Free at Last? U.S. Policy Toward Africa and the End of the Cold War* (New York: Council on Foreign Relations, 1992); and Peter Schraeder, "Removing the Shackles? U.S. Foreign Policy Toward Africa after the End of the Cold War," in Edmond Keller and Donald Rothchild (eds.), *Africa in the New International Order: Rethinking State Sovereignty and Regional Security* (Boulder and London: Lynne Rienner, 1996).

68. Ellis, "Liberia's Warlord Insurgency," p. 158.

69. Ellis, "Liberia, 1989–1984," p. 182.

70. *Africa Report* 35, no. 3 (July-August 1990): 48; and *Africa Confidential* 38, no. 14 (4 July 1997): 8.

71. Personal interview with Herman J. Cohen.

72. Ellis, "Liberia, 1989–1994," pp. 180–181.

73. See "Taylor's One Man Band," *Africa Confidential* 31, no. 15 (27 July 1990).

74. Personal interview, Nigerian Ministry of Foreign Affairs, Abuja, 30 November 1995.

75. *West Africa,* no. 3891, 13–19 April 1992, p. 674.

76. Personal interview with Amos Sawyer, Monrovia, 14 July 1999.

77. Quoted in *West Africa,* no. 3796, 28 May–3 June 1990, p. 880.

78. Ibid.

79. *West Africa,* no. 3803, 21–26 July 1990, p. 2126; and no. 3806, 6–12 August 1990, p. 2231.

80. *West Africa,* no. 3798, 11–17 June 1990, p. 981.

81. Personal interview with Omar Sey, the former Gambian Foreign Minister, 1987–1994, Baghdad, 14 December 1997.

82. See Samuel Kofi Woods, "Civic Initiatives in the Peace Process," in Jeremy Armon and Andy Carl (eds.), *The Liberian Peace Process, 1990–1996* (London: Conciliation Resources, 1996), pp. 27–32.

83. Personal interview with Omar Sey.

84. "Final Communiqué," First Session of the ECOWAS Standing Mediation Committee, Banjul, 6–7 August 1990, pp. 4–6.

85. *West Africa,* no. 3894, 4–10 May 1992, p. 756.

86. Mays, "Nigerian Foreign Policy," p. 114.

87. See Earl Conteh-Morgan and Shireen Kadivar, "Sierra Leone's Response to ECOMOG: The Imperative of Geographical Proximity," in Magyar and Conteh-Morgan (eds.), *Peacekeeping in Africa.*

88. Personal interview with General Quainoo, Accra, Ghana, 7 August 1996.

89. Personal interview with Omar Sey.

90. *African Guardian* 15, no. 36 (17 September 1990): 14–15.

91. "A New Role for ECOWAS," *Africa Report* 35, no. 5 (November-December 1990): 19.

92. Personal interview with General Emmanuel Erskine, Accra, Ghana, 13 August 1996.

93. Neil Macfarlane and Thomas Weiss, "Regional Organizations and Regional Security," *Security Studies* 2, no. 1 (Autumn 1992): 20.

94. Robert Mortimer, "ECOMOG, Liberia, and Regional Security in West Africa," in Edmond Keller and Donald Rothchild (eds.), *Africa in the New International Order: Rethinking State Sovereignty* (Boulder and London: Lynne Rienner, 1996), p. 152.

95. Quoted in *West Africa,* no. 3817, 22–28 October 1990, p. 2690.

96. Statement by H. E. Yoweri Kaguta Museveni to the Kampala Forum, 19 May 1991, in Olusegun Obasanjo and Felix Mosha (eds.), *Africa: Rise to Challenge* (New York: Africa Leadership Forum, 1993), p. 269.

97. *West Africa,* no. 3809, 27 August–2 September 1990, p. 2355.

98. Personal interview with Prosper Vokouma, the former Foreign Minister of Burkina Faso, 1989–1991, Ouagadougou, 22 July 1999.

99. *Jeune Afrique,* no. 1552, 26 September–2 October 1990, p. 29.

100. *African Guardian* 5, no. 35 (10 September 1995): 10.

101. Englebert, *Burkina Faso,* p. 156.

102. Personal interview at the Burkinabè Permanent Mission to the United Nations, New York, July 1998.

103. *Jeune Afrique,* no. 1552, 26 September–2 October 1990, p. 29.

104. Englebert, *Burkina Faso,* p. 158.

105. Quoted in Aning, "Managing Regional Security in West Africa," p. 11.

106. Quoted in *West Africa,* no. 3817, 22–28 October 1990, p. 2714.

107. For an excellent discussion of the legal issues, see David Wippman, "Enforcing Peace: ECOWAS and the Liberian Civil War," in Lori Fisler Damrosch (ed.), *Enforcing Restraint: Collective Intervention in Internal Conflicts* (New York: Council on Foreign Relations, 1993), pp. 157–203.

108. See Abass Bundu, "The Case Against Intervention," *West Africa,* no. 4156, 30 June-6 July 1997.

109. Olu Adeniji, "Mechanisms for Conflict Management in West Africa: Politics of Harmonization," *ACCORD* Occasional Paper, January 1997, p. 4.

110. Quoted in *West Africa,* no. 3807, 13–19 August 1990, p. 2289.

chapter 4

Seamen from Renaissance Africa, August 1990–December 1991

> *Military maps were not available except the tourist maps of Monrovia which was what the initial planning was based on.*
> —*Brigadier Cyril Iweze, ECOMOG chief of staff,*
> *August–November 1990*

In this chapter we will assess ECOMOG's performance during the first sixteen months of its existence. We focus on Pax Nigeriana and the domestic, subregional, and external constraints to its attainment. The chapter assesses the military difficulties encountered by ECOMOG, including opposition from the NPFL as well as its own logistical shortcomings.

At the domestic level, Charles Taylor controlled 90 percent of the country and derived resources from the lucrative export trade in areas under his control. The NPFL provided a strong military challenge to ECOMOG's ill-equipped peacekeepers, and ECOMOG's alliance with the INPFL and AFL compromised its stated neutrality. Another faction, ULIMO, emerged in September 1991 to challenge NPFL control of territory and resources and further complicated peacemaking efforts.

At the subregional level, we analyze the diplomatic difficulties encountered by ECOWAS as it tried to bridge its diplomatic divisions through peace conferences at Bamako, Lomé, and Yamoussoukro, where francophone states were given the lead role in peacemaking. Despite Mali and Togo playing a more supportive role, Burkina Faso and Côte d'Ivoire continued to support the NPFL while Guinea, Sierra Leone, and Nigeria furnished military support to ULIMO. Tension erupted between ECOMOG's two main contingents, Ghana and Nigeria, after a Nigerian general replaced the Ghanaian force commander in September 1990. Accra also opposed

Abuja's enforcement actions against the NPFL and was able to influence, if not determine, Nigeria's approach in the knowledge that it did not want the withdrawal of ECOMOG's second-largest contingent. The spread of the Liberian war into Sierra Leone in March 1991 exposed the limits of Pax Nigeriana and forced Nigeria to send troops to Sierra Leone to prevent other vulnerable regimes like Guinea and Gambia from withdrawing troops from ECOMOG.

At the external level, the United States provided the bulk of humanitarian assistance and supported ECOWAS's diplomatic efforts. However, it failed to contribute crucial logistical support to ECOMOG. In short, then, we argue that the limits of Pax Nigeriana were exposed by the NPFL's continued military control of much of Liberia; the failure of ECOMOG to prevent the war spreading to Sierra Leone in early 1991; the realization that the francophone states had to be included in peacemaking to promote subregional unity and NPFL cooperation; and the increasing calls by ECOWAS states for greater external contributions from the United States and United Nations.

We further argue that Nigeria's preponderance was not evident at the start of the intervention when it had a similar number of troops as Ghana, which supplied ECOMOG's force commander and made most of the early military decisions in Liberia. Guinea's deputy force commander was also able to influence military decisionmaking. The replacement of the Ghanaian force commander with a Nigerian in September 1990 and the doubling of Nigerian troops, however, marked the beginning of Nigeria's military dominance of ECOMOG. From that point on, all of ECOMOG's commanders and the majority of troops remained Nigerian for the duration of the seven-year conflict. The internal policymaking debate within Nigeria further revealed the limits of Pax Nigeriana. Amid continuing domestic opposition in Nigeria to the ECOMOG intervention and the increasing costs of the mission, several senior ECOMOG officials advocated accommodation with Taylor as the only way to resolve the conflict.

The ECOMOG Landing

Graham Greene's famous travelogue *Journey Without Maps* recounted his trek across Liberia in 1935. As the British author noted: "It would have been easier if I had been able to obtain maps. But the Republic is almost entirely covered by forest, and has never been properly mapped."[1] Nearly six decades later, ECOMOG was embarking on another unprecedented journey without maps into the same country. Not only had ECOMOG secured its photocopied maps of Liberia from the U.S. Embassy in Freetown, where its troops had assembled before setting sail for Monrovia, but its troops were also sailing into uncharted waters following the controversial decision to intervene militarily in a member state's civil war.[2] ECOMOG's peacekeepers were sailing to Liberia on their own *mission civilisatrice:* as they perceived it, they were bringing reason and enlightenment to truculent tribes engaged in senseless warfare.

A Nigerian team, led by Lieutenant Tunde Tebowie, had visited Monrovia to negotiate ECOMOG's safe entry with the INPFL's mercurial Prince Yeduo Johnson on 6 August 1990. Johnson had given his support after difficult negotiations.[3] The 3,000-strong ECOMOG contingent that assembled in Freetown in the second week of August 1990 consisted of a battalion each from Ghana, Guinea, Nigeria, and Sierra Leone, as well as a rifle convoy from Gambia. It also included a Nigerian naval fleet (NNS *Ambe,* NNS *Ekpe,* NNS *Damisa,* the *Dolphin Mira* tugboat, and the MT *Northern Navigator* oil tanker); a Ghanaian naval fleet (GNS *Achimota,* GNS *Yogaga,* and the MV *River Tano* merchant ship); the Nigerian air force's four AlphaJets, two Super Puma helicopters, and nine Hercules C-130 planes; and four Ghanaian air force jets. This armada set sail from Freetown on 23 August 1990 at 12:30 P.M. and, nearly thirty hours later, made an amphibious landing in Monrovia's Freeport on 24 August. ECOMOG troops were disgorged from the ships amid fierce fighting between the INPFL and NPFL on the outside perimeter of the port. They were enthusiastically welcomed ashore by the embattled Prince Johnson, whose INPFL was at the time in danger of being driven out of the port by the NPFL.

ECOMOG's political leaders had been careful to maintain a political balance in the composition of the force's High Command. Its force commander was General Arnold Quainoo, who had served as commanding general officer of the Ghanaian army and was a member of Ghana's ruling Provisional National Defense Council. Quainoo's deputy force commander came from Guinea, his chief of operations from Sierra Leone, and his chief of personnel and camp commandant from Gambia; Nigerians held the key positions of chief of staff, chief logistics officer, chief intelligence officer, and chief of communications.

Even before leaving Freetown, Quainoo had publicly expressed doubts about the wisdom of sailing to Liberia without having established a ceasefire and securing the full consent of the NPFL for the intervention. He felt from the outset that if Doe could be forced to leave Liberia, the INPFL and AFL could be persuaded to disarm, and popular support for Taylor would be undermined by the removal of his casus belli.[4] This reflected ECOMOG's overconfidence as it entered Liberia, and many of its soldiers were convinced that Charles Taylor's ill-trained ragtag NPFL force would flee at the sight of professional soldiers.[5]

Tension had already been evident in Freetown between the Nigerian and Ghanaian contingents, as the Ghanaian battalion commander refused to take orders from his Nigerian chief of staff.[6] Quainoo also received a letter from the Nigerian army chief, General Sani Abacha, requesting that all Nigerian officers above the rank of colonel return home because the Guinean deputy force commander, Lamine Magasoumba, was only a lieutenant colonel and thus senior Nigerian officers could not serve under him.[7] Magasoumba was promoted to major general in Freetown, and the Nigerian officers remained in place.

The initial military plan was for the Ghanaians and Nigerians to secure Monrovia's Freeport. The Ghanaians would then move east to secure Stockton Creek and Mesurado River, the Nigerians would go west and north to secure St. Paul's River, the Guineans would proceed centrally to capture Gardensville, and the Sierra Leoneans and the Gambians would remain behind to defend the port. Meanwhile, naval patrols would provide gunfire support while the air force would carry out reconnaissance and, if necessary, air strikes on designated military targets.[8]

As ECOMOG moved into position, the NPFL launched coordinated small-arms and artillery attacks. ECOMOG suffered some casualties but managed largely to secure its initial military aims on the first day. ECOMOG's NNS *Damisa,* under Nigerian Commander Gani Adekeye, captured the NPFL's sole Mano River ship on 26 August, with some troops and arms aboard, and thus incapacitated the NPFL naval "fleet" for the rest of the war.[9]

But the first major problem arose when the Guinean contingent failed to secure its position in Gardensville and kept withdrawing to the Freeport, where ECOMOG had established its base. The Guineans and Sierra Leoneans became increasingly notorious among other ECOMOG troops for turning and fleeing at the sight of NPFL fighters.[10] Subregional politics then came into play, as the Guinean deputy force commander, Lamine Magasoumba, complained that his francophone troops were being given more difficult assignments than their anglophone counterparts and saw this as a conspiracy to eliminate the only francophone contingent.[11] He insisted that ECOMOG troops be arranged in multinational rather than national units and suggested that each battalion commander determine military objectives without prior approval from the ECOMOG High Command.[12]

Caving in to political rather than military logic, Quainoo allowed the Guineans to go to Spriggs Payne Airport, the dividing line between the NPFL and AFL, where Ghanaian troops were already stationed. Contingents were, however, retained within national units. But rather than holding their positions, the Guineans proceeded straight to their embassy in Monrovia to rescue their besieged nationals. As they rejoiced with their kinsmen at the embassy, they were saved from annihilation from an NPFL ambush only by a swift Ghanaian intervention. But four ECOMOG soldiers died in the attack.[13] Aside from these political and military difficulties, ECOMOG also suffered from logistical, communications, and financial problems that were to hamper its effectiveness throughout most of the civil war: Many troops arrived without weapons; the Nigerians provided some military equipment and transportation to the Gambian contingent;[14] the force lacked adequate intelligence information and effective communications with its ECOWAS political leaders and secretariat; and the contingents that had radios could not communicate with others because the brands were incompatible.[15]

Furthermore, the peacekeepers did not have enough logistics officers, military equipment was not properly maintained, and ECOMOG lacked much of the necessary requirements for efficient counterinsurgency operations, including helicopters, spotters, and tanks suited to Liberia's dense forests.[16] ECOMOG also lacked adequate trucks, helicopters, uniforms, boots, blankets, water rehabilitation units, medical supplies, and tents. The $5 daily stipend for the peacekeepers often arrived months late, and troops were infrequently rotated.

The peacekeepers, however, made some early progress with the factions. The Nigerian chief intelligence officer, Major Chris Otulana, started secret negotiations with the NPFL.[17] ECOMOG opened a channel of communications with Doe's Executive Mansion through the AFL chief of staff, General David Brapoh.[18] Quainoo secured a cease-fire between the INPFL and AFL. Another early success included the launching of Operation Exodus, beginning with the evacuation of 7,500 Ghanaians on 31 August 1990 and eventually resulting in the evacuation of thousands of ECOWAS and Liberian citizens to various West African destinations. ECOMOG also fed and protected thousands of refugees who sought safe haven at its Freeport headquarters.

Despite these initial successes, the NPFL continued to present the most persistent threat to ECOMOG's peacekeeping ambitions. Shortly before ECOMOG's arrival in Liberia, Charles Taylor had warned: "They will have to kill all of us or we will kill all of them. When they use guns, we shall use knives."[19] Upon ECOMOG's arrival, Taylor welcomed the peacekeepers with a barrage of artillery fire and launched a virulent anti-ECOMOG campaign on his NPFL radio station, urging Liberians to resist "Nigerian colonisation" and dubbing ECOMOG "armed bandits." The irony of ECOMOG attempting to restore democracy to Liberia with only one member, Gambia, that could plausibly claim to have a democratically elected government, was not lost on Taylor, and he constantly referred to ECOMOG as a "Club of Dictators." Taylor particularly criticized Nigeria's General Ibrahim Babangida, whom he described as a "mad dictator" bent on inflicting genocide against Liberians.

ECOMOG was also not helped by the perception that it had compromised its stated neutrality through interactions with the various parties. As earlier mentioned, Prince Johnson had welcomed ECOMOG into Liberia and given up areas he controlled around the Freeport for the peacekeepers to establish their headquarters. Johnson provided boots and other gifts to the ill-equipped ECOMOG peacekeepers,[20] the INPFL continued to maintain checkpoints with ECOMOG,[21] and ECOMOG relied on INPFL intelligence to provide information on NPFL positions.[22] As General Quainoo later explained, "The enemy of your enemy is your friend."[23] This early intimacy permitted the INPFL uninhibited access to ECOMOG's base, and Prince Johnson would often arrive at the Freeport with his band of merry men, strumming a guitar and singing. The erratic and temperamental Johnson briefly held some foreigners and sixty Nigerian soldiers hostage, and he executed some of his own fighters in full view of ECOMOG soldiers.[24]

But General Quainoo appeared frightened of Johnson, whom he privately referred to as a "terrorist,"[25] and took no action to curb his excesses or create a safe distance between ECOMOG and the INPFL. ECOMOG's Nigerian chief of staff, Brigadier Cyril Iweze, described ECOMOG's predicament with particular eloquence:

> AFL was accusing us of supporting Prince Johnson by allowing him free access into the Freeport while we were not according them the same treatment. INPFL on the other hand was accusing ECOMOG of not fighting NPFL and we were therefore useless. NPFL on the other hand established a radio station accusing ECOMOG of being foreign invaders, mercenaries and looters.[26]

The failure to curb the excesses of the INPFL was to cost ECOMOG dearly in the next major episode of the war. Samuel Doe had not ventured out of his Executive Mansion for three months when, on 9 September 1990, he decided to go to the ECOMOG base at the Freeport with his soldiers in his limousine adorned with the Liberian flag. Upon seeing Arnold Quainoo, Doe told the general, "As an African, you know our tradition; when you enter a village or town, the first thing you do is you go and call on the chief."[27] As Doe berated Quainoo, trouble erupted when Prince Johnson arrived at the Freeport with armed fighters. Doe's soldiers had been disarmed by ECOMOG before they entered the base.

After one of Doe's men referred to Johnson as a "rebel," the INPFL fighters started a shooting spree that killed about sixty AFL soldiers. Johnson stormed the building, shot Doe in the leg, bundled him into the back of the presidential limousine, and drove away with his quarry.[28] Quainoo later talked of a ruse involving Nigeria and Guinea to lure Doe into exile in Conakry via a Guinean ship that had arrived in Monrovia on the morning of Doe's visit.[29] Twenty-four hours later, Doe was dead. The home video that Prince Johnson made of the torture of the late autocrat was already enjoying wide distribution: INPFL fighters cut off Doe's ears in a macabre interrogation, even as Doe desperately pleaded for his life to be spared. Doe was locked up in a bathroom, where he bled to death.[30]

Johnson's abduction of Doe at ECOMOG headquarters and ECOMOG's failure to protect him greatly undermined the credibility of the entire peace-keeping mission. Prince Johnson declared himself president of Liberia, riding into ECOMOG headquarters in the presidential limousine ostentatiously waving the Liberian flag. He now demanded to be addressed by dual titles— acting president of Liberia and field marshal of the INPFL—in a grandiloquent fit of *folie des grandeurs* (delusions of grandeur). During Doe's arrest, Quainoo had mysteriously disappeared into a Ghanaian ship, reappearing only after Johnson's departure. He called a meeting of his High Command in Monrovia, informing them that he was going to see the ECOWAS chairman, Dawda Jawara, to advise the latter that he withdraw ECOMOG from Liberia. [31] Quainoo never returned to Liberia to lead the mission.

From Peacekeeping to Peace Enforcement

On 14 September 1990, two Ghanaian sailors and three Nigerian nurses were killed when NPFL artillery shells hit the GNS *Achimota* carrying a Ghanaian fact-finding mission to Monrovia. An enraged Jerry Rawlings ordered the bombing of NPFL positions by Ghanaian air force jets. This attack also provided the pretext for the military pacification of Monrovia. One week later, the ECOMOG mandate was changed by its political leaders from peacekeeping to peace enforcement. Its peacekeepers were ordered to establish a buffer zone in Monrovia against NPFL attacks. Traditional UN peacekeeping doctrine assumed the consent of the parties to the conflict and lightly armed peacekeepers to implement an agreed cease-fire.[32] These prior conditions were unfulfilled in the case of ECOMOG.

Sent to carry out the new mandate was Nigeria's Major General Joshua Dogonyaro, a member of Nigeria's ruling AFRC and an ally of General Ibrahim Babangida. General Quainoo's title of force commander was changed to field commander for General Dogonyaro. It was thought at first that the Ghanaian would continue in Freetown as force commander in overall charge of coordinating the political side of the mission with ECOWAS's leaders while leaving the field commander in charge of the military operations on the ground.[33] But Dogonyaro refused to accept anything less than total command of ECOMOG, and the position of force commander became moribund. Rawlings later informed Quainoo that Nigeria's generals were in "open" revolt against Babangida for appointing a Ghanaian commander and insisted on a Nigerian replacement.[34]

Arriving in Monrovia at the end of September 1990, Dogonyaro seemed determined to correct the impression of weakness associated with his ineffectual predecessor. He told his troops to prepare for a full-scale attack on the NPFL on the first day of his arrival in Monrovia and was credited with improving the sagging morale and discipline of his troops.[35] Known as the "Enforcer," Dogonyaro was a Rambo in military attire—a no-nonsense general who thought his mandate was to use as much force as required to enforce peace. He referred to his methods as a "limited offensive" and implausibly claimed to be pursuing "positive neutrality." On 29 September, two extra battalions arrived from Nigeria and Ghana, doubling ECOMOG's troop strength to 6,300, and on 1 October—Nigeria's Independence Day—ECOMOG launched Operation Liberty—an offensive to flush out the NPFL from Monrovia.

Guided through the swamps of the capital by the INPFL, Dogonyaro's claims to neutrality appeared hollow. But the general did manage to achieve his objectives: after a sustained three-week offensive, the NPFL was repelled from central Monrovia, a buffer zone was secured, Spriggs Payne Airport was captured from the NPFL to stem the flow of its arms imports, and the port of Buchanan was blockaded.[36] A shell-shocked Charles Taylor accepted a cease-fire in November 1990. ECOMOG established a secure headquarters, electricity and water were restored to the capital by early November 1990, and humanitarian assistance was resumed to the city.

Dogonyaro's ruthless approach was revealed again in early December 1990 when INPFL fighters tried to attack the AFL's Barclay training camp in Monrovia: no less than sixty INPFL fighters were killed by a crack Nigerian-Ghanaian squad, and an INPFL home was petrol-bombed.[37] Some 500 of Prince Johnson's men were also disarmed.[38] But Dogonyaro did suffer some setbacks: fifteen of his soldiers died, and forty were injured after the attacks on Monrovia;[39] and ECOMOG troops were accused of looting and raiding in Monrovia by the Washington-based human rights group Africa Watch in November 1990.

Dogonyaro felt he needed two or three more battalions to complete the task of establishing a cease-fire across Liberia, but Lagos denied his request after a powerful faction within the military, led by General Ike Nwachukwu, fearing heavy casualties and wary of Dogonyaro's growing popularity, opposed the move.[40] The Malian leader, Moussa Traoré, had also prevailed upon Babangida to halt the military operation with the assurance that he had obtained Charles Taylor's agreement to negotiate an end to the conflict and the establishment of an interim government at a peace conference in Bamako.[41]

Dogonyaro later said ruefully, "The whole thing could have been finished a long time ago but political considerations are naturally superior to military decisions."[42] But it is unlikely that Dogonyaro could have finished the job with such ease in the light of the events of 1993, after ECOMOG's strength was increased to the numbers he had requested. Dogonyaro was replaced as field commander after five months, leaving Liberia with Charles Taylor's opprobrium ringing in his ears. But for many ECOMOG soldiers and Monrovians, his time is fondly remembered as a brief golden age that ushered in a two-year reign of peace in the capital.

All *seven* ECOMOG commanders after Dogonyaro came from Nigeria. Dogonyaro's replacement arrived in February 1991. He was Major General Rufus Kupolati, a member of Nigeria's AFRC and the former Nigerian contingent commander of the OAU mission to Chad. Jinmi Adisa described his tenure in Liberia thus: "An officer and a gentleman, he was irritated by the level of mendacity, chicanery, duplicity and fraud that pervaded the Liberian political arena."[43] Kupolati, a U.S.-trained mechanical engineer, was considered something of an intellectual soldier. In contrast to Dogonyaro, he was quiet, unassuming, and diplomatic. Kupolati saw his main task as establishing a classic peacekeeping operation, avoiding peace enforcement, and opening a dialogue with all parties. He innovated "confidence visits" by all parties, including the NPFL, to ECOMOG's headquarters, lifted the blockade of the Buchanan port, and opened highways leading to and from NPFL areas to human and aid traffic.[44] As Kupolati himself put it: "My job is to build, not to destroy."[45]

Kupolati's relationship with Liberia's interim president, Amos Sawyer, worsened as the new commander appeared to attach more importance to building the NPFL's confidence in ECOMOG than in supporting Sawyer's interim government. Sawyer was alarmed after Kupolati reminded him that Nigeria had withdrawn its troops from Chad in 1982 after the capital was attacked by an armed faction. As Sawyer later noted, "This neither inspired confidence nor bred friendship. I could not understand this strategy. We all knew that Taylor was building up an arsenal."[46] For his part, General Kupolati felt that Sawyer favored the status quo over a peace deal. He accused Sawyer of involvement in a press report that Kupolati was sending arms to the NPFL. The level of distrust between both men was so high that Kupolati always took an aide with him to meetings with Sawyer and rejected a Liberian national honor that the Liberian interim president had tried to bestow on him.[47] Charles Taylor struck up a good relationship with Kupolati, whom he described admiringly as a "pan-African." The ECOMOG commander met Taylor three times. Kupolati's critics, however, noted that his conciliatory approach merely allowed Taylor time to continue to derive economic benefits from NPFL areas, launch an incursion into Sierra Leone, and rearm for another assault on Monrovia without any NPFL concessions in return. Kupolati underestimated Taylor's ambitions, which ECOMOG still obstructed. Due to these irreconcilable differences he was unable to secure long-term peace.

On 4 October 1991, Major General Ishaya Bakut arrived in Liberia to replace Kupolati. Bakut was a veteran of the UN force in Lebanon and was chief of army operations in the Nigerian army before his appointment. Bakut took over

a force threatening to break into pockets of nationalist sentiment, with
Ghanaians adhering to one set of rules, Guineans to another, and Sierra
Leoneans and Gambians marginalised by their numerical inferiority. Nigerians were becoming overlords of a badly disenchanted and demoralised
force.[48]

The Nigerian general set about trying to restore troop morale and discipline. He arrived just as NPFL elements launched attacks into Sierra Leone
on 23 March 1991. Nigeria sent 1,200 troops to Sierra Leone to bolster its
security. Guinea also sent troops and, along with Sierra Leone, cooperated
with a new faction—ULIMO—to launch military attacks against the NPFL.
Nigerian and Sierra Leonean instructors were involved in training ULIMO
fighters.[49]

The Abuja-Accra Axis

This period saw tensions rise between Nigeria and Ghana on ECOMOG
policy. Ghana complained that it had not been properly consulted on the removal of its force commander, General Arnold Quainoo. Brigadier Francis
Agyemfra, Ghana's army chief of staff from 1992 to 1996, later complained
that Ghana had heard this news through BBC radio.[50] With the Ghanaian
press calling for its contingent to be brought back home, Accra started attaching conditions to the use of its troops, insisting that it be consulted before any changes were made to ECOMOG's mandate.[51] Quainoo returned
to Ghana a bitter man in October 1990, recommending that Ghana withdraw its 2,000 men, warships, and planes from ECOMOG unless better
Nigerian cooperation could be assured.[52]

Addressing his military officers in November 1990, Jerry Rawlings
made clear that Ghana would remain neutral in the conflict and did not object to anyone becoming president.[53] In a similar vein, the Ghanaian foreign
minister, Obed Asamoah, said: "ECOMOG is completely neutral as to what
the outcome should be, as to who should be leader of Liberia. . . . We are
not against any particular individual."[54] Asamoah sent a letter to the
ECOWAS executive secretary, Abass Bundu, in April 1991, informing him
that Ghana was rethinking its ECOMOG policy and expressing a wish for
its troops to "maintain only a defensive posture" rather than engage in offensive fighting. Asamoah continued by noting that the "realities on the
ground" should determine the political arrangement that emerged in
Liberia.[55] General Kupolati received a letter from Ghana's defense headquarters warning that Ghanaiian troops not be used to undertake any military "adventures" in Liberia.[56] Also, Baffour Assasie-Gyimah, Ghana's former ambassador to Burkina Faso and a deputy security adviser at the time,
later noted: "We are practical. Nigeria saw things differently. We had not

come to impose someone there as a ruler. We had come as peacekeepers. We did not go there with any preferences."[57]

Accra, unlike Abuja, was prepared to tolerate a Taylor presidency and wanted its troops to engage strictly in peacekeeping functions, not in a peace-enforcement role. Ghana objected to what it saw as Nigeria's obsession with eliminating Taylor, and this policy division remained a feature of ECOMOG's presence in Liberia under the Babangida regime. Accra reportedly was also under pressure from its old Libyan ally not to frustrate Taylor's presidential ambitions.[58]

Nigeria was worried about the possible withdrawal of ECOMOG's second-largest contingent. As Ambassador A. O. Esan, former director of the West Africa division of the Nigerian foreign ministry, put it: "If Ghana withdrew, it would be a totally Nigerian affair, which we didn't want."[59] Though some senior Nigerian military officials saw Ghanaian preparedness to accommodate Charles Taylor as anti-Nigerian, Abuja's approach was to make all necessary efforts to keep Ghanaian troops in Liberia. General Babangida stopped over in Accra during a visit to Uganda in September 1990 to heal the widening rift. Nigeria provided fuel to the Ghanaian troops, and there were reports that Nigeria threatened to cut off commercial oil sales if Ghana withdrew its troops from ECOMOG.[60]

Nigeria

At this time, there appeared to be three distinct views within Nigerian policymaking. The hawks, epitomized by the chief of general staff, Admiral Augustus Aikhomu, General Joshua Dogonyaro, and Ambassador Joshua Iroha (the special representative of the ECOWAS executive secretary to Liberia), saw the elimination or military defeat of Taylor as the only way to resolve the conflict. The doves, epitomized by Nigerian Foreign Minister General Ike Nwachukwu, ECOMOG Commander General Kupolati, and the Nigerian ambassador to Liberia, Ayo Ajakaiye, considered ECOMOG an unnecessary burden on Nigeria's finances. They called for greater burden-sharing with other ECOWAS states and the United Nations, sought a rapprochement with Taylor for pragmatic cost-saving reasons, and sought to avoid further alienating an already hostile Nigerian public. These distinctions were not always clear cut: the dovish General Nwachukwu was close to the hawkish Ambassador Iroha, whom he had nominated as ambassador to Brussels while serving as military governor of Imo State. [61] There was friction between Kupolati and Ambassador Iroha, who complained that Kupolati did not listen to his advice and took his instructions directly from General Sani Abacha, Nigeria's chief of army staff.[62] Kupolati, for his part, accused Iroha of colluding with Amos Sawyer and ECOWAS executive secretary, Abass Bundu, to wreck peace talks in March 1991. Kupolati also accused Iroha of urging General Nwachukwu to ignore the force commander's advice.[63] With the replacement of Dogonyaro and Kupolati, it seemed that a third group of pragmatists, led by General Babangida, favored a middle course between cooperation and confrontation, the policy General Bakut was attempting to implement.

Nigeria reopened its embassy in Monrovia in 1991 during a time when only Washington still maintained a diplomatic presence in Liberia. The experienced diplomat Ayo Ajakaiye was appointed Nigeria's ambassador to Liberia in May 1991. Ajakaiye was widely respected for his eloquence and impressive analytical skills but was known to push his positions to obdurate extremes once he decided on the right course to follow. The new Nigerian ambassador felt that the period of peace secured by the cease-fire in November 1990 was being squandered and that Charles Taylor held the key to the resolution of the Liberian conflict. He therefore advocated a policy of dialogue with Taylor, which was extremely unpopular in some influential military circles in Nigeria. Some even insinuated that Ajakaiye had personal commercial interests in seeking a rapprochement with Taylor.

Upon arriving in Monrovia in May 1991, Ajakaiye delayed presenting his credentials to Sawyer's Interim Government of National Unity (IGNU) for fear of being declared persona non grata by the NPFL. This was done apparently on the advice of General Kupolati.[64] Within four days of his arrival, Ajakaiye went to Gbarnga to meet Charles Taylor, explaining that presenting credentials to the IGNU—a government recognized by Nigeria—did not mean Abuja would not be evenhanded in its approach to the Liberian conflict. Several powerful ambassadors in Nigeria's foreign ministry, who refused to acknowledge Ambassador Iroha's role in Liberia, also opposed recognition of the IGNU.[65] Ajakaiye met several times with Taylor in Gbarnga and Ouagadougou at a time when Nigeria's diplomatic and military policies in Liberia converged; the conciliatory General Kupolati was also urging dialogue with Taylor. This approach doubtless contributed to Taylor's decision to release 781 Nigerian hostages in September 1991.

Ajakaiye, the intrepid Nigerian envoy, undertook these missions to NPFL areas at great personal risk: he once overheard someone calling for his lynching at the Gbarnga market. But Ajakaiye was seeking a rapprochement with the NPFL while the Nigerian press was maintaining a rabid anti-Taylor stance and, as earlier noted, while powerful voices within military policymaking circles were calling for Taylor's elimination. Ajakaiye's conciliatory gestures were out of step with the mood of some of his political masters. He was removed under controversial circumstances in November 1992, a month after Taylor's attack on Monrovia (see Chapter 5) had revealed the failure of the policy of dialogue.[66]

By October 1990, Nigeria had already spent a reported $50 million on ECOMOG.[67] Its foreign minister, General Ike Nwachukwu, admitted in

May 1991, "Our economies are so weak, and this particular operation is biting deep into our finances."[68] Nwachukwu met secretly with a senior NPFL official, Cyril Allen, in Ouagadougou at the end of 1991 in a bid to end the conflict. Allen, who had attended school in Nigeria and whose grandparent came from eastern Nigeria, spoke Igbo to Nwachukwu and tried to offer Nigeria a stake in Bong Mines in return for recognizing Taylor's presidential claim.[69] Nwachukwu was unimpressed.

The continuing ECOMOG mission was also complicated by the fact that General Babingida was preparing plans to establish a national guard, which many felt was intended as a private army to perpetuate his rule. Keeping Nigerian soldiers abroad would, it was felt, facilitate this agenda. Meanwhile, press reports that $250–500 million in oil windfalls from the Gulf War were reported as ECOMOG expenses, despite the continuing logistical and financial shortcomings of the troops, increased domestic opposition to the mission. Suspicions grew that Liberia was being used to enrich Nigerian military leaders.[70] Nigerian Chief of Army Staff General Sani Abacha had taken over the feeding of ECOMOG troops and was said to be profiting from these contracts.[71] But General Babangida and many of his senior officers could not contemplate a humiliating withdrawal from Liberia and were prepared to see the mission through to a successful conclusion regardless of the cost to the country's treasury. As General Nwachukwu later noted, "The country had made a commitment and there was no way we could pull back. . . . We had our national pride at stake at the time. We had lost so many lives that an inconclusive withdrawal from Liberia would have meant all the resources and human lives were expended for nothing."[72]

The Nigerian media continued to play an important role in shaping popular perceptions about Liberia. A report in the *African Concord* in January 1991 citing 750 Nigerian casualties in Liberia met with official denial and insistence that the government figure of fifty was more accurate. But the NPFL's execution of two Nigerian journalists, the *Daily Champion*'s Tayo Awotusin and the *Guardian*'s Krees Imodibie, at the end of 1990 united the Nigerian press in its anti-Taylor crusade. The government-owned *Daily Times* noted that "Taylor is intent on sacrificing the peace and security of Liberia on the altar of his personal ambition,"[73] and the independent *Daily Champion* asked ECOMOG to "annihilate the rebel armies, especially that of the NPFL."[74] General Dogonyaro later noted that anti-NPFL reports in the Nigerian media during the captivity of the two journalists had probably contributed to their deaths.[75]

There was a tendency to demonize Charles Taylor and depict him simply as an obstructionist, power-hungry warlord. Many Nigerian journalists and policymakers failed to understand that Taylor had genuine grievances of his own: he felt that illegitimate interlopers were denying him the fruits of his meticulous military planning, which had secured the NPFL control of 90 percent of Liberia in six months.

From Bamako to Yamoussoukro

There were still signs of a lack of francophone support for ECOMOG. On 6 September 1990, the Burkinabè leader Blaise Compaoré asked the visiting ECOWAS chairman, Dawda Jawara, to convene an extraordinary ECOWAS summit on Liberia.[76] In the same month, Compaoré visited his close friend, Gnassingbé Eyadéma, in Lomé, admitting publicly for the first time what many had long known: Ouagadougou was supporting the NPFL militarily.[77] Both leaders issued a joint statement describing ECOMOG as a violation of the 1981 ECOWAS protocol and calling for an extraordinary ECOWAS summit. Senegal continued to express grave doubts about ECOMOG's ability to resolve the conflict. Houphouët-Boigny took up Compaoré's call for an extraordinary ECOWAS summit in early October. ECOMOG members vowed to boycott the proposed summit, arguing that only Jawara was authorized to call such a meeting.

Some bridges started to span the anglophone-francophone divide when Eyadéma, in a dramatic diplomatic reversal, went to Lagos at the end of October 1990 and pledged full support for ECOMOG, urging other states to stop assisting the NPFL.[78] In the same month, the Malian foreign minister, N'golo Traoré, agreed to send troops to ECOMOG during an SMC foreign minister's meeting (22–24 October 1990; six Malian officers would arrive in Liberia in April 1991). At this meeting, the NPFL refused to sign a cease-fire unless ECOMOG's composition was expanded, but an agreement was reached to hold an extraordinary ECOWAS summit.[79]

The first-ever extraordinary ECOWAS summit took place in Bamako on 27 November 1990 and saw the heads of state of Benin, Burkina Faso, Côte d'Ivoire, Gambia, Ghana, Mali, Niger, Nigeria, Senegal, and Togo attending. One week before Bamako, a delegation of ECOWAS foreign ministers had gone to Tripoli to urge Muammar Qaddafi to halt military support to the NPFL. Charles Taylor, whose faction had by this time been repelled from Monrovia by Dogonyaro, also attended the summit with forty Burkinabè bodyguards. After acrimonious disputes with the ECOWAS foreign ministers, Taylor was pressured into signing the Bamako agreement by Compaoré, who in turn was being encouraged by Eyadéma to play a more constructive role.[80]

The Bamako summit encouraged more ECOWAS states to contribute troops to ECOMOG, urged Liberia's warring parties to work out modalities for implementing a cease-fire and establishing an interim government, and called on all members to abide by their obligations to the ECOWAS Protocol on Non-Aggression.[81] During the summit, the ECOWAS Authority finally endorsed the Banjul peace plan that the five-member SMC had devised. ECOWAS received a further boost when the UN Security Council endorsed the peace plan on 22 January 1991.

A fourth SMC meeting in Banjul on 20–21 December appointed a technical subcommittee, chaired by Dogonyaro, to examine the modalities for implementing the Bamako cease-fire within thirty days and organizing a national conference to establish an interim government within sixty days. The subcommittee met in Monrovia from 18 to 22 January 1991. At the meeting, disagreements remained on the confinement and disarming of troops, and the NPFL insisted that it would commit to a cease-fire only after a successful national conference.[82]

The tortuous, winding ECOWAS diplomatic road soon veered toward Lomé, where Presidents Diouf, Babangida, and Eyadéma met on 28–29 January 1991 and called on ECOWAS members to support ECOMOG. At the SMC meeting of 12–13 February 1991, Liberia's three warring factions—the NPFL, INPFL, and AFL—signed the Lomé agreement, which called for the confinement and disarming of their troops under ECOWAS's auspices after the establishment of an interim government. A cease-fire was signed on 13 February, and a national conference was set for 15 March 1991.[83] The meeting witnessed an irate Eyadéma screaming at Charles Taylor in frustration at the warlord's unpredictable and intransigent character.[84] A diplomatic stalemate, however, remained: the NPFL insisted on a new interim government before disarmament, whereas the IGNU insisted on disarmament before another interim government could be installed. This stalemate would remain a key diplomatic impasse at every negotiation conference during Liberia's seven-year civil war.

The ECOWAS-sponsored All-Liberia Conference, which took place in Monrovia from 15 March to 20 April 1991, highlighted the failure of Bamako. Taylor refused to attend, citing fears of assassination, and visits by the foreign ministers of Nigeria, Ike Nwachukwu, and Togo, Yaovi Adodo, to Kakata and Gbarnga, respectively, failed to change his mind. The NPFL had been offered one of two vice presidential positions in the interim government and 40 percent of the seats in the fifty-one-member interim legislature. But Taylor continued to insist on personally heading the interim government; his representatives walked out of the conference on 27 March. As a result, Amos Sawyer was reelected interim president, and new elections were optimistically scheduled for October 1991.[85]

After Bamako and Lomé came Yamoussoukro. The newly acquired prominence of francophone capitals for ECOWAS's peacemaking attempts, the selection of the new Committee of Five (comprised of francophone Côte d'Ivoire, Senegal, and Togo, as well as Gambia and Guinea-Bissau) to monitor the cease-fire and electoral process, and the election of Senegal's Abdou Diouf, a strong advocate of regional integration, as ECOWAS chairman in July 1991—all confirmed the ascendancy of the francophone states in subregional mediation. Babangida and Jawara had played an instrumental part in Diouf's election.[86] A division of labor was emerging within

ECOWAS: the francophones took the lead in peacemaking and left the peacekeeping largely to the anglophones.

Lurking behind the mediation efforts was, however, continuing sub-regional instability caused by the Liberian war: in July 1991 there were 342,000 Liberian refugees in Guinea, 227,000 in Côte d'Ivoire, 10,000 in Sierra Leone, 6,000 in Ghana,[87] and 4,000 in Nigeria. Four meetings took place in Houphoüet-Boigny's new showpiece capital of Yamoussoukro between 29 June and 30 October 1991. The first meeting was attended by the heads of state of Burkina Faso, Côte d'Ivoire, Gambia, Togo, and Nigeria. The spirit of Yamoussoukro was vividly captured by the symbolic embrace of Taylor and Sawyer, and a delighted Houphoüet exclaimed, "We'll declare that there's only one winner, Liberia, which must find peace."[88] Babangida left centerstage to his Ivorian host, who staked his enormous personal prestige on the success of Yamoussoukro. Known respectfully as *le vieux* or *le sage* (the old man or the wise man), Houphoüet-Boigny had established a legendary reputation as the wise man and doyen of francophone African diplomacy, the bridge between Africa and the former metropolis.

Although Côte d'Ivoire publicly appeared to have reversed its policy of requesting UN troops to replace ECOMOG, Houphoüet refrained from closing his border with Liberia, and arms were still reaching the NPFL from Burkina Faso in December 1991.[89] During the Yamoussoukro negotiations, the ECOMOG field commander, General Bakut, provided well-documented evidence of the movement of personnel and cargo across the Ivorian border to Liberia.[90] Leaked documents of correspondence dated 23 October 1992 between the U.S. Embassy in Abidjan and the State Department in Washington[91] also revealed that Houphoüet was attempting to use Yamoussoukro to install Taylor as president,[92] casting further doubts on his role as an impartial mediator. But several Nigerian diplomats regarded Houphoüet as genuinely concerned about the destabilizing effects of the NPFL on subregional stability, and they felt that senior Ivorian military officials conducted the NPFL arms trade without the aged Houphoüet's support or knowledge.[93]

Despite the display of unanimity at Yamoussoukro, the four rounds of talks suffered difficulties. Guinea and Sierra Leone refused to attend until the last round in October 1991 because they were invited only as observers. Conakry also accused NPFL troops of launching incursions into Guinea, and Houphoüet had to warn Taylor against such incursions under threat of closing his border with Liberia.[94] During the fourth round of talks (16–17 September 1991), Houphoüet publicly expressed irritation at the nonattendance of Babangida, Rawlings, and Eyadéma.[95] Finally, there was continuing tension between Nigeria and the NPFL as Nigeria's Admiral Augustus Aikhomu took Taylor aside during negotiations and threatened him with something unpleasant if he did not agree to peace proposals in five minutes.[96]

The main points of the Yamoussoukro agreement included: the deployment of ECOMOG to all parts of Liberia; the encampment and disarming of factions under ECOMOG's supervision, with members of former U.S. President Jimmy Carter's International Negotiations Network visiting the camps; the creation of a buffer zone on the Liberia–Sierra Leone border; monitoring of all Liberian air and seaports by ECOMOG; an expansion of ECOMOG, with the addition of 1,500 Senegalese troops; resettlement of refugees; and the creation of an interim government, elections commission, and ad hoc supreme court to organize elections in six months. Disarmament was to occur between 15 November 1991 and 14 January 1992.[97] Taylor was allowed to continue administering areas under his control during the transition.

But Yamoussoukro was flawed in its very conception: it was ambiguous in talking of "encampment" of the NPFL rather than full demobilization and in granting ECOMOG only a "supervisory" rather than monitoring role in disarmament, allowing Taylor to claim that the NPFL, and not ECOMOG, would disarm his fighters.[98] In addition, timetables were too short (e.g., only one week was granted for storing weapons); details on demobilization, reintegration of fighters into civilian life, and equipment sites were vague; there was not enough emphasis on full disarmament before elections, allowing Taylor to hold the "Savimbi card"[99] in reserve; and ULIMO was not brought into the process, even though it controlled territory seized from the NPFL.

The agreement was in fact creating problems that would hamper future peacemaking efforts. The NPFL and IGNU had successfully resisted Ivorian attempts at including ULIMO in the peace process.[100] The United States, which played a key role in facilitating the Yamoussoukro process (see discussion below), also argued that ULIMO's participation in the peace talks would only complicate matters. Washington was convinced that ULIMO, whose leaders it had remained in contact with since its creation in the Freetown, would support any agreement reached in Yamoussoukro.[101]

The Domestic Liberian Actors

Having signed and broken several previous accords, Charles Taylor could certainly not be trusted to implement the Yamoussoukro agreement. He continued to call for UN troops and a reduction of ECOMOG troops from 6,000 to 1,500. Taylor was devising a series of different strategies in response to the growing consensus within ECOWAS. After Dogonyaro's offensive of October 1990, he sent his "justice minister," Laveli Supuwood, to the eleven non–troop contributing ECOWAS states, as well as to London and Washington, to seek diplomatic pressure against ECOMOG to end its military attacks.

Regarding militarily weak Sierra Leone as ECOMOG's Achilles' heel and in fulfillment of an earlier deal with rebel leader, Foday Sankoh, Taylor encouraged NPFL elements, mainly led by a group of Sierra Leoneans calling themselves the Revolutionary United Front (RUF), to enter Sierra Leone on 23 March 1991 in an attempt to replicate his own efforts at toppling the established government.[102] This caused 107,000 refugees to flee into Guinea from Sierra Leone in four months.[103] Sierra Leone's public and press reacted by asking the head of state, Joseph Momoh, to withdraw his troops from ECOMOG. Nigerian and Guinean troops were rushed in to support the Sierra Leonean army.[104] In a conciliatory gesture, Taylor sent his "foreign minister," Ernest Eastman, to Lagos in January 1991 to open a channel of communication with ECOMOG's most powerful member. In September 1991, Taylor also released the 995 Ghanaian, 781 Nigerian, and twenty-eight Sierra Leonean hostages he had held since 1990.[105]

The rationale behind Taylor's strategy was to increase the costs of ECOMOG'S intervention while preventing his own diplomatic isolation.[106] He attempted this by inflicting large casualties on ECOMOG; destabilizing Sierra Leone and Guinea to splinter the ECOMOG coalition and force a withdrawal of either or both countries from the conflict; and demonstrating ECOMOG's raison d'être to be a sham because it could neither keep the peace nor prevent the war from spreading to the subregion.

Though Taylor partly succeeded in some of his goals, he was suffering militarily from the newly emerged ULIMO faction, even as his diplomatic isolation grew. He failed to convert early military successes into diplomatic capital. Taylor's anxiety about ULIMO's military success against the NPFL was demonstrated by his refusal to disarm until ULIMO had halted its advances. Part of the NPFL leader's support for Yamoussoukro was based on his expectation that ECOMOG's creation of a buffer zone between Liberia and Sierra Leone would ease ULIMO's military pressure on the NPFL.

Five NPFL commandos were executed on 5 September 1991 after reportedly trying to unseat Taylor.[107] The NPFL leader surrounded himself with Burkinabè bodyguards, having reportedly ordered his NPFL commandos to kill prominent Gio politicians Moses Duopo, who had challenged his autocratic leadership of the NPFL, and Jackson Doe.[108] This reflected Taylor's personal insecurity as an Americo-Liberian who was unsure of his supporters and feared political challengers who might gain the support of his largely Nimba fighters.

Taylor's relationship with the RUF and Compaoré remained strong, with Burkinabè soldiers reportedly assisting the NPFL during incursions into Sierra Leone.[109] The NPFL leader sustained the war and enriched himself through commercial ties to foreign corporations, exploiting gold, diamonds, timber, iron ore, and rubber in areas under his control. A consortium of European, U.S., and Japanese steel producers paid Taylor an estimated $10 million per month for iron ore exports, and logging levies for exports through Greenville fetched Taylor an estimated $500,000 in the first half of 1991.[110] This reduced his incentive to disarm his fighters and surrender areas under his control to ECOMOG.

The United Liberation Movement of Liberia for Democracy was founded on 29 May 1991. It described itself as "a non-tribal and non-sectarian organisation born out of the desire of displaced Liberians to return home and continue their search for democratic freedom"; its members aimed to free Liberia "from the plunder of Charles Taylor."[111] ULIMO was a coalition of former AFL soldiers and mostly Krahn and Mandingo anti-NPFL refugees in Sierra Leone; it had an army of some 3,000 men, and most of its key commanders were former AFL soldiers. ULIMO helped defend Sierra Leone against RUF attacks and launched military attacks against NPFL positions beginning on 5 September 1991, two months before the end of the Yamoussoukro peace talks. Having been excluded from Yamoussoukro, ULIMO objected especially to Côte d'Ivoire's role in the peace process and considered Houphoüet-Boigny to be less than an honest broker due to his earlier support of the NPFL.

ULIMO's leadership included Alhaji Kromah, an ambitious former assistant minister for information under Doe who controlled the Conakry-based Movement for the Redemption of Liberian Muslims consisting largely of Mandingos. Having earlier fallen out with Doe, Kromah had appeared in Nimba County at the start of the Liberian civil war to urge Mandingos to support Doe.[112] He accused the NPFL of killing 10,000 of his kinsmen at the start of the conflict. The Mandingos have a large ethnic presence in Guinea, whose government provided support and a base for Kromah. ULIMO also had two Freetown-based Krahn leaders who had served in Doe's cabinet: General Albert Karpeh, who led the Liberia United Democratic Force, and George Boley, who later formed the Liberia Peace Council.

The president of the IGNU, Amos Sawyer, was a pragmatic intellectual who felt that he had to do *something* to help his country. As the only interested party in Liberia who had no army, he was totally dependent on ECOMOG to provide security in Monrovia, creating the perception that the IGNU was an instrument of ECOMOG's political control. But Sawyer felt that this dependence was preferable to leaving the future of the country to be determined by power-seeking warlords like Charles Taylor and Prince Johnson. Sawyer tried to exert influence on ECOMOG through its field commanders. Under pressure from Ghana, he urged General Dogonyaro to halt his attacks on NPFL positions and adopt a defensive posture, and he warned General Kupolati of the dangers of intimacy with Charles Taylor.[113]

Sawyer moved the interim government from Banjul to Monrovia on 22 November 1990 and, as he took the oath of office, told Liberians: "We must now find a way to bring ourselves up before we despair and do greater damage to our country. It is the only country we have. Whether we like it or not, it belongs to all of us."[114] But the cerebral professor was in a situation where madness and mayhem reigned over order and oratory; one sometimes had the impression that he was in over his head. Sawyer travelled the subregion in search of diplomatic recognition, shuttling most often between Abuja, Accra, Banjul, Conakry, and Freetown. His efforts were rewarded by his recognition as Liberia's president at OAU meetings, and he addressed the UN General Assembly in 1991.

Sawyer's domestic priorities included ending the war; repatriating Liberia's 589,000 refugees from neighboring countries; resettling its 600,000 internally displaced persons; and providing administration for the needs of the 500,000 people living in Monrovia by the end of 1990. By March 1991, the death toll from the war had risen to 20,000.[115] Having inherited a $3 billion debt from the Doe regime, and with most income-generating revenue based in NPFL-controlled areas, the IGNU had great difficulty fulfilling these needs. The IGNU's unity was shaken on 15 August 1991 by the resignation of Peter Naigow, the INPFL vice president and Doe's former minister of labor, after Sawyer criticized Prince Johnson for executing seven of his men at his Caldwell base in Monrovia.

Like Charles Taylor, Sawyer called for Jimmy Carter's mediation in the conflict, hoping to reduce his dependence on ECOMOG by attracting greater U.S. involvement. But Sawyer tired of what he saw as Carter's naivety in depicting Taylor as a good Christian family man. As Sawyer later noted: "Jimmy Carter was a very naive man. He brought elements of simplistic notions of redemption to a problem steeped in a culture he did not understand."[116] Sawyer tacitly backed ULIMO's entry onto the scene as a way of reducing the NPFL's strength and forcing Taylor to compromise.[117] His acrimonious relations with Taylor dated back to the NPFL leader's imprisonment in Ghana in the late 1980s, which Taylor blamed on the machinations of Liberian exiles, including Sawyer.[118] But Sawyer swore that he never met Taylor or discussed him during two visits to Accra between 1987 and 1990.[119] Accra's close ties to Sawyer, however, increased Taylor's distrust of ECOMOG.[120] Sawyer's approach with Taylor was one of carrots and sticks: he offered his own resignation if Taylor agreed to disarm and take part in the IGNU. Irked by Taylor's intransigence and the economic benefits the NPFL derived from the continued control of 90 percent of Liberia, Sawyer finally imposed economic sanctions on NPFL areas on 20 December 1991, preventing nonessential goods from going into and out of Monrovia.

The United States

During this period U.S. involvement in Liberia remained sporadic, as it had been during the outbreak of the civil war. Though U.S. officials publicly praised ECOMOG for driving the NPFL out of Monrovia and facilitating the delivery of humanitarian relief to the city, it was clear that Washington did not wholeheartedly back the ECOMOG effort. U.S. policy was based on three key goals: maintaining contact with ECOMOG without identifying too closely with it; withholding full recognition from the interim government until the NPFL was included in it; and maintaining contact with Taylor to prod him to negotiate with ECOMOG while denying him the right to take power without elections.[121]

U.S. diplomats complained that ECOMOG was supporting ULIMO; regarded the IGNU as a partisan instrument of ECOMOG;[122] and felt that the interim government was riddled with corruption.[123] These problems partly explain the lackluster U.S. financial support for ECOMOG's special operating budget, support that stood at $2.8 million by the end of 1991. Washington preferred instead to channel most of its resources into humanitarian assistance, which by contrast had reached $130 million in the same period.[124] Though wary of Taylor, U.S. officials privately admitted that they could have learned to live with him, and many, along with numerous U.S. analysts, felt in retrospect that an NPFL victory would have been more conclusive than the ECOMOG intervention.[125] Thus, it is worth noting what Herman Cohen, the former U.S. assistant secretary of state, said in this regard: "Taylor's troops had no experience with frontal assaults, and Prince Johnson's NPFL forces were harassing them. They failed to capture Monrovia because they did not have the capability."[126] As historian Eric Hobsbawn also noted: "Arguments about counterfactual alternatives cannot be settled by evidence, since evidence is about what happened and hypothetical situations do not happen. They belong to politics or ideology and not to history."[127]

Some U.S. officials felt guilty over their abandonment of a former African ally with long-standing historical ties to the United States, and there was some recognition that U.S. support for Doe during the 1980s had contributed to Liberia's civil war (see Chapter 2). U.S. Ambassador to Liberia Peter de Vos admitted to his Nigerian counterpart, Ayo Ajakaiye, that ECOMOG was fulfilling Washington's responsibilities in Liberia.[128] This guilt partly explains the continuing U.S. diplomatic efforts despite the reservations regarding ECOMOG. Herman Cohen obtained a cease-fire from the NPFL on 22 September 1990 after meeting Taylor, but the NPFL resumed violence a week later. Cohen visited Lagos on 19 September 1990, and Babangida asked Washington to persuade Compaoré to stop supplying arms to Taylor.[129] The United States threatened to suspend aid to Burkina Faso in December 1990, but Ouagadougou continued to supply arms to Taylor. U.S. Ambassador de Vos went to Gbarnga after the NPFL entered Sierra Leone in March 1991 to ask Taylor to withdraw his troops, but Taylor refused. U.S. emissaries in Liberia thus talked loudly but wielded a small stick. Washington's diplomatic standing was not helped by the admission that it had shared military intelligence with the NPFL in 1991.[130]

Jimmy Carter, the former U.S. president, was an important one-man diplomatic team, and for the most part he operated independently of the U.S. State Department while keeping its officials informed.[131] Throughout the civil war, he attended peace meetings and travelled to various West African capitals on peace-brokering missions. Carter went to Lagos in October 1991 to discuss the Liberian situation with General Babangida. He also established the Carter Center as a permanent mediation presence in Monrovia for most of the civil war. He attended the second Yamoussoukro meeting on 29 and 30 July 1991 and regarded disarmament before elections as a sine qua non of any successful agreement. Much to the annoyance of Abuja, Carter supported Taylor's calls for a reduction of ECOMOG's troops, the removal of some of its heavy weapons from Liberia, and the establishment of a more representative interim government.[132]

Washington played a key role in arranging the Yamoussoukro round of talks. Confidential State Department documents, leaked in November 1992, showed that U.S. Vice President Dan Quayle's visit to Abidjan in June 1991 involved pressuring Houphoüet-Boigny to take a leading role in subregional mediation.[133] In September 1991, Quayle visited Nigeria to encourage the idea of an expanded ECOMOG with greater francophone participation. Such pressure, sweetened by a promise of logistics and funding as well as the cancellation of Senegal's $42 million U.S. debt, secured Senegal's promise to send troops to ECOMOG.[134] This decision was announced by Abdou Diouf during a state visit to Washington in September 1991, with President George Bush using his close friendship with Diouf, established during visits to Dakar as vice president, to good effect.[135] Washington also sent nonlethal military support to Sierra Leone to help Momoh in his efforts to control the rebellion in his country. In December 1991, Washington suspended its military training program with Burkina Faso in a bid to pressure Compaoré to stop sending arms to the NPFL from Libya. Herman Cohen acknowledged based on his sources that Burkina Faso was supplying arms to the NPFL through Libya.[136] But unwilling to take the lead in Liberia and distrusting the military solution sometimes pursued by ECOMOG, Washington confined itself to supporting subregional diplomatic efforts and to providing humanitarian relief. With no prospect of Pax Americana in sight, Liberia was stuck with the continuing frustrations and deficiencies of Pax Nigeriana.

Notes

1. Graham Greene, *Journey Without Maps* (London and New York: Penguin, 1978), p. 45.

2. Personal interview with a Ghanaian officer on the initial ECOMOG contingent, Laayoune, Western Sahara, 22 June 1995.

3. Segun Aderiye, "ECOMOG Landing," in M. A. Vogt (ed.), *The Liberian Crisis and ECOMOG: A Bold Attempt at Regional Peacekeeping* (Lagos: Gabumo, 1992), p. 104; and Mark Huband, *The Liberian Civil War* (London and Portland: Fank Cass, 1998), p. 183.

4. Personal interview with General Arnold Quainoo, Accra, Ghana, 7 August 1996.

5. C. Y. Iweze, "Nigeria in Liberia: The Military Operations of ECOMOG," in M. A. Vogt and A. E. Ekoko (eds.), *Nigeria in International Peacekeeping, 1960–1992* (Lagos and Oxford: Malthouse, 1993), p. 220.

6. Ibid., p. 223.

7. Personal interview with General Quainoo.

8. Iweze, "Nigeria in Liberia," p. 223.

9. See Gani Adekeye, "The Role of Naval Power in Peacekeeping Operations in Liberia," in M. A. Vogt and L. S. Aminu (eds.), *Peacekeeping as a Security Strategy in Africa: Chad and Liberia as Case Studies* (Enugu, Nigeria: Fourth Dimension, 1996), pp. 422–437.

10. Personal interview with Ghanaian ECOMOG officer, June 1995.

11. Iweze, "Nigeria in Liberia," p. 226.

12. Ibid.

13. Ibid., pp. 226–227.

14. Personal interview with Omar Sey, former Gambian Foreign Minister, 1987–1994, Baghdad, 14 December 1997.

15. Iweze, "Nigeria in Liberia," pp. 220–241.

16. Herbert Howe, "Lessons of Liberia: ECOMOG and Regional Peacekeeping," *International Security* 21, no. 3 (Winter 1996/1997): 167–169.

17. *Africa Confidential* 31, no. 19 (2–8 September 1990): 1.

18. Iweze, "Nigeria in Liberia," p. 228.

19. Quoted in Jinmi Adisa, "ECOMOG Force Commanders" in Vogt (ed.), *The Liberian Crisis and ECOMOG,* p. 242.

20. Ibid., p. 231.

21. Personal interview with a Ghanaian ECOMOG officer, June 1995.

22. Adedoyin Jolaade Omede, "Nigeria's Military-Security Role in Liberia," *African Journal of International Affairs and Development* 1, no. 1 (1995): 52.

23. Personal interview with General Quainoo.

24. Aderiye, "ECOMOG Landing," p. 110.

25. Iweze, "Nigeria in Liberia," p. 224.

26. Ibid., p. 228.

27. Quoted in *West Africa*, no. 3816, 15–21 October 1990, p. 2650.

28. Personal interview with Cyril Iweze, Lagos, December 1996.

29. Personal interview with General Quainoo.

30. Huband, *The Liberian Civil War,* p. 194.

31. Personal interview with Cyril Iweze.

32. See Alan James, *Peacekeeping in International Politics* (London: Chatto and Windus, 1990).

33. Personal interview with General Quainoo.

34. Ibid.

35. Adisa, "ECOMOG Force Commanders," p. 251.

36. See Nkem Agetua, *Operation Liberty: The Story of Major-General Joshua Nimyel Dogonyaro* (Lagos: Hona Communications, 1992), pp. 81–87; and Karl Magyar, "ECOMOG's Operations: Lessons for Peacekeeping," in Karl Magyar and Earl Conteh-Morgan (eds.), *Peacekeeping in Africa: ECOMOG in Liberia* (London: Macmillan; and New York: St. Martin's, 1998), pp. 59–65.

37. Personal interview with a Ghanaian ECOMOG officer, June 1995.

38. Agetua, *Operation Liberty*, p. 105.

39. *West Africa*, no. 3813, 24–30 September 1990, p. 2532.

40. *Africa Confidential* 33, no. 2, (24 January 1992): 1.

41. Personal interview with Omar Sey.

42. Quoted in Adisa, "ECOMOG Force Commanders," p. 252.

43. Ibid., p. 258.

44. Ibid., p. 256.

45. Quoted in *West Africa,* no. 3851, 1–7 July 1991, p. 1077.

46. Personal interview with Amos Sawyer, Monrovia, 14 July 1999.

47. Personal interview with General Rufus Kupolati, Lagos, 13 July 2001.

48. *Africa Confidential* 33, no. 2 (24 January 1992): 2.

49. Ibrahim Abdullah and Patrick Muana, "The Revolutionary United Front of Sierra Leone: A Revolt of the Lumpenproletariat," in Christopher Clapham (ed.), *African Guerrillas* (Oxford: James Currey; Kampala: Fountain; and Bloomington: Indiana University Press, 1998), p. 178.

50. Personal interview with Brigadier Francis Agyemfra, Monrovia, 18 July 1999.

51. M. A. Vogt, "The Problems and Challenges of Peace-Making: From Peace-Keeping to Peace Enforcement" in Vogt (ed.), *The Liberian Crisis and ECOMOG,* p. 168.

52. *Africa Confidential* 31, no. 21 (26 October 1990): 8.

53. *West Africa,* no. 3819, 5–11 November 1990, p. 2793.

54. "A New Role for ECOWAS," *Africa Report* 35, no. 5 (November-December 1990): 18.

55. *Africa Report* 36, no. 4 (July-August 1991): 41.

56. Personal interview with General Rufus Kupolati, Lagos, 13 July 2001.

57. Personal interview with Baffour Assasie-Gyimah, Ghana's former Ambassador to Burkina Faso, Ouagadougou, 20 July 1999.

58. Personal interview with Omar Sey.

59. Personal interview with Ambassador A. O. Esan. Nigerian Ministry of Foreign Affairs, Abuja, 6 December 1995.

60. Emmanuel Kwezi Aning, "Managing Regional Security in West Africa: ECOWAS, ECOMOG, and Liberia," Working Paper 94.2 (Copenhagen: Center for Development Research, February 1994), pp. 16–17.

61. Personal interview with General Ike Nwachukwu, former Nigerian Foreign Minister, New York, 3 August 2001.

62. Personal interview with Ambassador Joshua Iroha, former Special Representative of ECOWAS to Liberia, Lagos, 28 July 1999.

63. Personal interview with General Rufus Kupolati, Lagos, 13 July 2001.

64. Personal interview with Ambassador Joshua Iroha.

65. Ibid.

66. The information on Ajakaiye's tenure in Liberia was obtained during a personal interview with him at the Nigerian Ministry of Foreign Affairs in Abuja in December 1995.

67. *West Africa,* no. 3818 (29 October–4 November 1990): 2742.

68. "Towards a More Relevant Africa: Interview with Major-General Ike Nwachukwu," *West Africa,* no. 3846 (27 May–2 June 1991): 842.

69. Personal interview with Cyril Allen, Monrovia, 12 July 1999.

70. See, for example, Austin Iyashore, "The Price of Peacekeeping," *African Guardian* 5, no. 42 (29 October 1990).

71. Personal interview with General Rufus Kupolati, Lagos, 13 July 2001; See also General Chris Alli, *The Federal Republic of Nigerian Army: The Siege of a Nation* (Lagos, Nigeria: Malthouse Press, 2001), pp. 346–347.

72. Personal interview with General Ike Nwachukwu, New York, 3 August 2001.

73. Nnamdi Obasi, "Perceptions of the ECOMOG Peace Initiative," in Vogt (ed.), *The Liberian Crisis and ECOMOG*, p. 341.

74. Ibid., p. 342.

75. *West Africa*, no. 3831 (4–10 February 1991): 140.

76. "Final Report," Third Ministerial Meeting of the ECOWAS Standing Mediation Committee, Banjul, 22–24 October 1990, ECW/SMC/FM/III/4Rev.1, p. 11.

77. *West Africa*, no. 3814 (1–7 October 1990): 2590.

78. *West Africa*, no. 3818 (29 October–4 November 1990): 2755.

79. Third Ministerial Meeting of the ECOWAS Standing Mediation Committee, 22–24 October 1990, pp. 12–14.

80. Personal interview with Prosper Vokouma, former Foreign Minister of Burkina Faso, 1989–1991, Ouagadougou, 22 July 1999.

81. "Final Communiqué," First Extraordinary Session of the ECOWAS Authority of Heads of State and Government, Bamako, 27–28 November 1990, pp. 6–8.

82. "Final Report," Fifth Ministerial Meeting of the ECOWAS Standing Mediation Committee, Lomé, 11 February 1991, ECW/SMC/EM/V/3, pp. 5–7.

83. "Final Communiqué," Third Summit Meeting of the ECOWAS Standing Mediation Committee, Lomé, 12–13 February 1991, pp. 5–6.

84. Personal interview with Omar Sey.

85. See "Final Report," Proceedings of the All-Liberia National Conference, Virginia, Liberia, 15 March–20 April 1991.

86. Personal interview with Omar Sey.

87. "Crisis in Liberia: The Regional Impact," Hearing Before the Subcommittee on Africa of the Committee of Foreign Affairs House of Representatives, 16 July 1991 (Washington, D.C.: U.S. Government Printing Office, 1992), p. 11.

88. Quoted in *West Africa*, no. 3852 (8–14 July 1991): 1123.

89. *West Africa*, no. 3874 (9–15 December 1991): 2069.

90. Personal interview with J. Coker, former Nigerian Ambassador to Côte d'Ivoire, Abidjan, August 1996.

91. These documents were later authenticated, and a Washington-based Cameroonian journalist was arrested and charged with stealing them, along with a State Department official from whom the documents had been obtained.

92. *Africa Confidential* 33, no. 23 (20 November 1992): 7.

93. Personal interview, Nigerian Ministry of Foreign Affairs, Abuja, December 1995.

94. Mariam Diallo, "La CEDEAO au chevet du Liberia," *Jeune Afrique*, no. 1604 (25 September–1 October 1991): 24–25.

95. Ibid., p. 24.

96. *Africa Confidential* 32, no. 23 (22 November 1991): 6.

97. "Final Communiqué," Third Meeting of the ECOWAS Committee of Five on the Liberian Crisis, Yamoussoukro, 29–30 October 1991, pp. 4–5 and annex.

98. Peter da Costa, "Good Neighbors," *Africa Report* 36, no. 6 November–December 1991): 22.

99. Jonas Savimbi was the UNITA rebel leader in Angola whose troops were only partly disarmed by UN peacekeepers, allowing him to return swiftly to war after he had lost elections in 1992. Savimbi was killed by government troops in February 2002.

100. Personal interview with Ambassador Ahmadou Traoré, Director of Africa, Asia, and the Middle East, Ivorian Foreign Ministry, Abidjan, July 1996.

101. Personal interview with Amos Sawyer, Monrovia, 14 July 1999.

102. See Paul Richards, *Fighting for the Rainforest: War, Youth, and Resources in Sierra Leone* (Oxford: James Currey, 1996); Ibrahim Abdullah and Patrick Muana, "The Revolutionary United Front of Sierra Leone"; and David Keen, "'Sell-game': The Economics of Conflict in Sierra Leone," paper presented at University College of London, 21 October 1995.

103. "Crisis in Liberia," Hearing Before the Subcommittee on Africa of the Committee of Foreign Affairs, House of Representatives, p. 12.

104. See Janet Mba, "Nigeria to the Rescue," *Newswatch* 13, no. 18 (29 April 1991): 26.

105. *Africa Confidential* 32, no. 7 (5 April 1991): 8.

106. Personal interview with Daniel Chea, Liberian Defense Minister, Monrovia, 13 July 1999.

107. *West Africa,* no. 3862 (16–22 September 1991): 1537.

108. Stephen Ellis, "Liberia's Warlord Insurgency," in Clapham (ed.), *African Guerrillas,* p. 159.

109. Pierre Englebert, *Burkina Faso: Unsteady Statehood in West Africa* (Boulder and Oxford: Westview, 1996), p. 159.

110. William Reno, *Warlord Politics and African States* (Boulder and London: Lynne Rienner, 1998), pp. 96–100; see also Valéry Laramée, "Charles Taylor fait des affaires," *Jeune Afrique,* no. 1633 (23–29 April 1992): 12.

111. See *West Africa,* no. 3850 (24–30 June 1991): 1035.

112. Stephen Ellis, "Liberia, 1989–1994: A Study of Ethnic and Spiritual Violence," *African Affairs* 94, no. 375 (April 1995): 182.

113. Personal interview with Gabriel Baccus Matthews, former IGNU Foreign Minister, 1990–1994, Monrovia, 17 July 1999.

114. Quoted in *West Africa,* no. 3824 (10–16 December 1990): 2988.

115. *Africa Report* 36, no. 2 March-April 1991): 11.

116. Personal interview with Amos Sawyer, Monrovia, 14 July 1999.

117. Personal interview at the Nigerian Ministry of Foreign Affairs, Abuja, December 1995.

118. Paul Richards, "Rebellion in Liberia and Sierra Leone," in Oliver Furley (ed.), *Conflict in Africa* (New York and London: Tauris Academic Studies, 1995), p. 138.

119. Personal interview with Amos Sawyer.

120. D. Elwood Dunn, "Liberia's Internal Responses to ECOMOG's Interventionist Efforts," in Magyar and Earl-Conteh (eds.), *Peacekeeping in Africa,* p. 87.

121. Herman Cohen, *Intervening in Africa: Superpower Peacemaking in a Troubled Continent* (Hampshire, UK: Macmillan; and New York: St. Martin's, 2000), p. 153.

122. Personal interview at the Nigerian Ministry of Foreign Affairs, Abuja, December 1995.

123. Personal interview with James Bishop, former U.S. Ambassador to Liberia, 1987–1990, Washington, D.C., July 1997.

124. "Crisis in Liberia," Hearing Before the Subcommittee on Africa of the Committee of Foreign Affairs, House of Representatives, p. 12.

125. Personal interview with Charles Stonecipher, U.S. State Department Liberia Desk Officer, Laayoune, Western Sahara, 7 September 1995.

126. Cohen, *Intervening in Africa,* pp. 243–244.

127. Eric Hobsbawn, *On History* (London: Abacus, 1997), p. 307.

128. Personal interview with Ambassador Ayo Ajakaiye, Nigerian Ministry of Foreign Affairs, Abuja, December 1995.

129. Cohen, *Intervening in Africa,* p. 154.

130. W. Ofuatey-Kodjoe, "Regional Organizations and the Resolution of Internal Conflicts," *International Peacekeeping* 1, no. 3 (Autumn 1994): 269.

131. Personal interview with Herman J. Cohen, Washington, D.C., July 1997.

132. *West Africa,* no. 3870 (11–17 November 1991): 1900.

133. *Africa Confidential* 32, no. 23 (20 November 1992): 7.

134. Robert Mortimer, "Senegal's Role in ECOMOG: The Francophone Dimension," *Journal of Modern African Studies* 34, no. 2 (1996): 297.

135. Cohen, *Intervening in Africa,* p. 158.

136. Ibid., p. 154.

chapter 5

Annus Horribilis:
The Death of Yamoussoukro,
January–December 1992

> *Instead of ECOMOG encamping and disarming the NPFL, the NPFL*
> *wants to encamp and disarm ECOMOG.*
> —Amos Sawyer, Liberia's interim president, 1990–1994

In this chapter we examine ECOMOG's difficulties in implementing the Yamoussoukro accord of October 1991, which eventually led to the failure to implement the accord at the end of 1992. We argue against the common perception that ECOMOG was the parochial concern of hegemonic Nigeria. The deleterious effects of the Liberian conflict on neighboring Côte d'Ivoire, Sierra Leone, and Guinea demonstrated that those states had a more direct interest than Nigeria in resolving the conflict. Sierra Leone was still enduring a two-year civil war triggered from Liberia, Guinea remained part of ECOMOG, and Côte d'Ivoire closed its border with Liberia to stem the flow of arms across its territory. We also argue that continuing differences at the domestic, subregional, and external levels once again frustrated the achievement of a Pax Nigeriana.

At the domestic level, Charles Taylor's intransigence increased as he continued to lose territory and access to resources to ULIMO, which he accused ECOMOG of supporting. The personalized nature of Taylor's rivalry with Nigeria was again evident after verbal clashes with Nigeria's chief of general staff, Admiral Augustus Aikhomu, during peace negotiations, and with Babangida's consistently tough stance against the NPFL. The continuing distrust between ECOMOG's dominant contingent and Liberia's strongest faction remained a major obstacle to the resolution of the Liberian conflict. Taylor's conviction that Nigeria was determined to deny him political power led him again to pursue the military option. This was a desperate bid to achieve outright military victory or, more likely, to force ECOMOG's withdrawal by inflicting heavy military costs and drawing ECOMOG into a politically costly enforcement action that would result in casualties and further questioning of its peacekeeping role. With the failure of the NPFL's military assault on Monrovia, the military and political stalemate continued: Taylor could not defeat ECOMOG militarily in Monrovia, and ECOMOG lacked the troops, logistics, and political support to defeat Taylor militarily in the countryside.

At the subregional level, Pax Nigeriana was frustrated by the continuing lack of subregional consensus for the Nigerian-led effort. Despite the inclusion of the first major francophone state, Senegal, in ECOMOG, and the lead role of Côte d'Ivoire and Benin in mediation efforts, Burkina Faso continued to provide military support to Taylor, Benin was reluctant to adopt ECOWAS sanctions against the NPFL, and Côte d'Ivoire and Benin showed little confidence in the ability of ECOMOG to resolve the conflict, calling instead for UN intervention. Nigeria was constrained from taking tough action against the NPFL for fear that the subregional consensus painstakingly stitched together would fly apart. Abuja ceded leadership in mediation to francophone Côte d'Ivoire and Benin and acceded to Senegal's request to play a role in determining ECOMOG's military strategy. Like Ghana, Senegal successfully challenged Nigeria's ability to impose its will on ECOMOG unilaterally.

At the external level, the United States adopted an increasingly tough stance against the NPFL and Burkina Faso after the killing of Senegalese peacekeepers revealed Taylor's lack of commitment to disarmament. But the bulk of U.S. resources continued to be channeled to humanitarian relief, not to ECOMOG peacekeepers. Washington's continuing distrust of ECOMOG neutrality, and the low priority accorded to Africa in the U.S. Congress, deprived other ECOMOG contingents the vital logistical support the United States provided to the favored Senegalese contingent. The support of several ECOWAS members for a UN role in Liberia further revealed the limits of Pax Nigeriana. These subregional states hoped that the United Nations would provide some of the logistical and financial support that ECOMOG clearly lacked and dilute Nigeria's preponderant strength.

From Geneva to Abuja

By March 1992, the sole requirement of the Yamoussoukro accord that had been fulfilled was the nomination of members of the elections commission and ad hoc supreme court. The encampment and disarmament of the factions, the establishment of buffer zones on the Liberia–Sierra Leone border, the monitoring of Liberia's airports and seaports by ECOMOG, and the installation of a new interim government were all behind schedule. With continued NPFL intransigence amid military losses to ULIMO, Taylor's erstwhile Ivorian backers, whose honor was at stake as hosts of the Yamoussoukro accord, seemed to be tiring of his failure to implement peace agreements. As Côte d'Ivoire's exasperated foreign minister, Amara Essy, warned: "Taylor cannot be taking everyone for a ride . . . we are prepared to act against him."[1]

The first of only two ECOWAS peace conferences on Liberia held outside Africa took place in ailing Ivorian leader Félix Houphoüet-Boigny's winter home in Geneva between 6 and 7 April 1992. The meeting merely confirmed what had been agreed in Yamoussoukro; revised the timetables for the deployment of ECOMOG to 30 April 1992 and for the completion of disarmament to 8 June 1992; and acceded to Taylor's requests to send unarmed observers to the Liberia–Sierra Leone buffer zone and to maintain a personal security detail of company strength.[2] The Geneva meeting was characterized by another clash between Taylor and Nigeria's Admiral Augutus Aikhomu. After Taylor made insulting remarks about Nigeria, its chief of general staff described him as a "rebel" who had no locus standi and should long ago have been tried and eliminated.[3] Aikhomu went on to tell the self-proclaimed president of Greater Liberia that "Liberia lost [its] sovereignty during the civil war."[4]

After the conference, Taylor complained that he had been pressured to sign the Geneva agreement. As had become customary with other previous accords, within a week Taylor dismissed Geneva as a "rat-trap" that was as unbalanced as it was unsatisfactory; he described the agreement as "the colonisation of Liberia with the Field Commander of ECOMOG as the Governor-General."[5] At a week-long national conference in Gbarnga that began on 21 April, Taylor repeated his call for a reduction of ECOMOG forces to 1,500 and insisted that his fighters retain control over disarmament sites. Houphoüet's failure to deliver Taylor at Geneva was the final proof—if any was needed—that the NPFL puppeteer's residence was in Gbarnga and not Abidjan, Yamoussoukro, or Geneva. This lack of influence was confirmed in confidential correspondence between the U.S. Embassy in Abidjan and the State Department in Washington, D.C.[6]

From 27 to 29 July, ECOWAS held its annual summit in Dakar. Before the summit, Nigerian leader General Ibrahim Babangida had consistently called for economic sanctions against the NPFL.[7] A new leader appeared at the summit in the form of twenty-seven-year old Captain Valentine Strasser, a former ECOMOG soldier who had seized power from Joseph Momoh through a military putsch in Sierra Leone. With Taylor obstructing disarmament, Strasser set the tone at the summit by telling his fellow leaders, "All we require now is to match force with force if that would bring peace to the country."[8] By August 1992, Sierra Leone's civil war had displaced 417,500 persons internally and spilled 169,500 refugees into Guinea and 12,000 into Liberia.[9] Guinea's granting of political exile to Joseph Momoh, and the former leader's public boasts from Conakry that he would reinstate himself to power forcibly, caused friction between the two ECOMOG members.[10]

Coming two months after the killing of six Senegalese peacekeepers by the NPFL (see discussion below), the ECOWAS summit explicitly blamed the NPFL for failing to cooperate with ECOMOG and stated that Taylor's actions "continued to constitute a serious threat to the peace, stability and security of the West African region."[11] The summit issued a thirty-day ultimatum for the NPFL to cooperate with disarmament or face comprehensive economic sanctions. It agreed to dispatch a team of ECOWAS foreign ministers to the UN Security Council to make sanctions binding on all members.[12] This delegation went to New York in November 1992.

The ECOWAS summit in July elected Benin's president, Nicéphore Soglo, as ECOWAS chairman. This was a continuation of the policy of giving the francophones more prominence in peacemaking to make up for its lack of representation in peacekeeping. But despite the public display of unanimity, it was clear that ECOWAS was still unable to devise a common approach to the Liberian conflict. Abdou Diouf and Blaise Compaoré had a heated exchange in Dakar over Liberia policy.[13] Compaoré, who had earlier promised troops to ECOMOG, broke that promise, citing the distrust that Sierra Leone held toward his country. As noted in Chapter 4, Burkinabè soldiers had reportedly assisted the NPFL in its incursions into Sierra Leone in March 1991. Moreover, four months before the ECOWAS summit Gambia was accusing Compaoré of colluding with Libya to train Gambian rebels to invade its country.[14] And finally, Soglo exacerbated ECOWAS divisions by unilaterally shelving the imposition of economic sanctions on the NPFL after the expiration of the thirty-day deadline on the grounds that fighting between the NPFL and ULIMO had created a new situation.

Leaked U.S. State Department documents would later reveal that Soglo and Houphoüet, who were in regular contact, preferred U.S. or UN troops to replace those of ECOMOG. A confidential memorandum from the U.S. ambassador in Cotonou to the State Department, dated 27 October 1992, also talked of Soglo's abdication of responsibility for mediation to others due to Benin's financial constraints. More damaging, the U.S. ambassador observed that Soglo felt Nigeria had taken over ECOMOG and that the body was too divided to fight. Soglo was quoted as saying that the best solution was to leave the factions to fight until they were exhausted.[15] The same documents further revealed that even Côte d'Ivoire, the most prominent ECOWAS peacemaker between 1991 and 1992, considered the ECOMOG approach unrealistic. As a 23 October 1992 correspondence between the U.S. ambassador in Abidjan and the State Department noted, "The Ivorians see Nigeria's deployment of war planes, warships and 6,000 soldiers as effectively substituting for the Yamoussoukro accords."[16]

A less serious split was the dismissal by Abass Bundu, ECOWAS executive secretary, of his Nigerian special representative, Ambassador Joshua Iroha, in October after nearly two years as political adviser. This followed an apparent row between the two. During his tenure, Iroha had exerted great influence on General Ishaya Bakut, the ECOMOG field commander, and was credited with the adoption of a firm approach toward Taylor, which had earned the Nigerian envoy a death threat from the NPFL leader. With Iroha's departure, ECOMOG lost an important political presence on the ground, leaving difficult negotiations in the hands of field commanders with little or no experience in diplomacy.

Soglo's unilateral decision to shelve automatic sanctions against the NPFL after expiration of the thirty-day ultimatum, coupled with his public call for UN peacekeepers to replace ECOMOG, led to the absence of the leaders of Nigeria, Ghana, Guinea, and Senegal at the first joint meeting of the Committee of Five and SMC in Cotonou on 20 October.[17] The meeting called on the NPFL and ULIMO to declare an immediate cease-fire, and a Committee of Nine (Benin, Burkina Faso, Côte d'Ivoire, Gambia, Ghana, Guinea, Nigeria, Senegal, and Togo) was established to monitor the implementation of Yamoussoukro and to impose sanctions on the warring factions for noncompliance. Sanctions would include a blockade of all entry points into Liberia to deny factions access to the sinews of war and the export of commodities from Liberia.

Following former U.S. President Jimmy Carter's letter to ECOWAS members proposing that a UN observer group be sent to Liberia to monitor ECOMOG's neutrality, the October ECOWAS summit requested UN assistance for ECOWAS disarmament and electoral tasks.[18] A month later, the UN Security Council adopted Resolution 788, imposing an arms embargo on all factions in Liberia. France, however, resisted economic sanctions due to continuing commercial ties of French firms to the NPFL, mostly timber and iron ore.[19] Trevor Gordon-Somers, a Jamaican economist with the UNDP, was also appointed as the UN Secretary-General's special representative for Liberia on 20 November 1992.

On 7 November, the ECOWAS Committee of Nine held an acrimonious meeting in Abuja. Babangida revealed Nigeria's continuing animosity toward the NPFL, telling his fellow leaders that "Taylor . . . represents the madness that we all really abhor and condemn."[20] Compaoré was widely criticized for his continued support of the NPFL, and Guinea's Lansana Conté openly attacked Houphouët, asking, "Why should we respect him just because he is old?"[21] Host Babangida and the youthful Strasser reprimanded Conté for breaching the African tradition of respect for age.[22] Despite such criticism, Abidjan had started to show concern over the destabilizing effects of the Liberian civil war on its territory, asking Washington for $2.2 million to patrol its border with Liberia and then announcing the closure of the border at the end of November 1992.[23] Houphoüet also sent 500 troops to guard the border. Abidjan had started to distance itself from Ouagadougou's continued support for the NPFL.

During 1992, IGNU President Amos Sawyer continued efforts to weaken support for the NPFL by traveling to Tripoli, Abidjan, and Ouagadougou in an attempt to sway Taylor's backers. Though he lifted the economic embargo on goods entering NPFL areas, Sawyer introduced new five-dollar bills in January 1992 to weaken Taylor's economic base. He also started training 450 black berets in Guinea in a bid to lessen his military dependence on ECOMOG. These soldiers were expected to form the nucleus of a new, ethnically diverse national army. They did not, however, play a significant military role during the civil war, though they did help defend Monrovia from an NPFL invasion in October 1992 (see discussion below).

The United States

The United States had still not recognized the IGNU by 1992. Leaked State Department documents revealed a fear that it would be accused of being a party to the conflict. As the U.S. ambassador in Abidjan warned, "Like everyone else involved up to now in Liberia's conflict, we, too, could assume the appearance of belligerent."[24] But the United States did pressure Blaise Compaoré to desist support for the NPFL by recalling the U.S. ambassador from Ouagadougou on 4 November and by rejecting the new Burkinabè ambassador to Washington, Prosper Vokouma. Although Burkina Faso was a poor country heavily dependent on foreign aid, French assistance was more crucial than U.S. aid, and Compaoré retained close political ties to Paris. In 1990, for example, French development assistance to Burkina Faso was $93.8 million, compared to the U.S. figure of $11 million.[25] By mid-1993, Washington sent a new ambassador to Ouagadougou despite Compaoré's continuing arms supplies to Taylor.

Washington eventually lost all faith in Charles Taylor and adopted an increasingly tough stance against the NPFL. A gruesome incident involving American citizens particularly angered policymakers: the murder of five nuns by NPFL fighters between 20 and 23 October 1992. This followed the killing of six Senegalese peacekeepers that Washington had been so instrumental in dispatching to Liberia. Leonard Robinson, the deputy U.S. assistant secretary of state for African affairs, reflected the hardening U.S. position during a hearing before the House of Representatives. He described the NPFL as "essentially an internal army of occupation, sustaining an environment of brutality and coercion and prolonging the misery of the Liberian people."[26]

Uncharacteristically for a U.S. official, Robinson lavished ECOMOG with praise, noting that "ECOMOG ended the killing, separated the warring factions, allowed relief assistance to flow to avert starvation, and established a cease-fire and framework for peaceful negotiations."[27] But praise did not translate into increased support for the peacekeepers. By November 1992, Washington had provided only $8.6 million to ECOMOG compared to $200 million for humanitarian assistance.[28] Although the United States condemned the NPFL, it was not prepared to embrace ECOMOG, which was still cooperating militarily with ULIMO, the AFL, and INPFL.

The Road to Vahun

Two hundred Senegalese peacekeepers arrived in Liberia in October 1991, fulfilling the Yamoussoukro accord's call for ECOMOG expansion. By March 1992, 1,200 Senegalese troops had joined. The United States, still grateful that Senegal had sent 500 troops to the Gulf War Coalition in 1991, contributed $15 million to the Senegalese contingent, provided logistical and transportation needs, and supplied weaponry, vehicles, radios, uniforms, helmets, shoes, and stipends that other contingents lacked. France had advised Diouf to stay out of Liberia.[29] Paris was to have provided one-third of Senegal's logistical support while the United States provided two-thirds, but the French eventually decided not to contribute.[30] Though some have argued this was due to a rivalry with Nigeria, it is more likely that France was wary of the increasing influence that Washington was exerting in its backyard, U.S. calls for democracy and economic reform in francophone Africa being a continuing irritant to Paris.

Ibrahim Babangida and Abdou Diouf had a good personal relationship, and Babangida had backed Diouf for the ECOWAS chairmanship in 1991.[31] This, coupled with Abuja's promise to meet the fuel needs of the Senegalese contingent, also influenced its decision to participate in ECOMOG.[32] The cordial relations between Abuja and Dakar did not, however, immediately translate into the smooth integration of the Senegalese contingent into ECOMOG. Senior Senegalese officers were at first reluctant to take orders from ECOMOG's High Command.[33] The commander of Senegal's army, General Mamadou Seck, insisted that Senegal take part in conceptualizing the military operation rather than leave it solely to the dominant Nigerian military leadership.[34] The Senegalese contingent commander, Colonel Diallo Mountiaga, privately disagreed with Bakut's decision to cave in to NPFL pressure to disallow logistical support for deploying Senegalese troops. Publicly, Mountiaga remained loyal and went along with the order.[35] Leaked U.S. State Department documents noted that General Seck suggested to Diouf that Senegal withdraw from ECOMOG because "the Nigerians and the Ghanaians won't fight."[36]

It was Charles Taylor who first suggested that Senegalese troops join an expanded ECOMOG in order to dilute its anglophone dominance. With the arrival of the Senegalese, however, Taylor expressed fear at what he described as "the massive troop build-up" and complained that "the [United States] is using the Senegalese for their surrogate activities in Liberia."[37] Despite this outburst, the disarmament process got off to a good start, with the NPFL opening the Monrovia highways with Kakata and Bomi on 10 January. On 30 April, ECOMOG started deploying its troops to the Liberian countryside, with the Ghanaians going to Kakata, Harbel, and Buchanan, the Nigerians going to Bong, Nimba, Maryland, and Grand Gedeh Counties, and the Senegalese to Grand Cape Mount and Lofa Counties. The Nigerians and Senegalese were instructed to establish the buffer zone along the Liberia–Sierra Leone border.

ECOMOG still lacked vital logistical support like vehicles, helicopters, radios, tents, and armored protection, and there were many difficulties in deployment: Continuing ULIMO incursions into NPFL areas caused delays and forced ECOMOG to withdraw from the Liberia–Sierra Leone border zone; ECOMOG troops were kept under surveillance by the NPFL; their freedom of movement was restricted; they were denied accommodation; and their heavy weapons were disallowed. Worse events would follow.

On 28 May, a crowd of NPFL supporters surrounded Senegalese peacekeepers in the Lofa County village of Vahun and demanded their Jeep and weapons. In the ensuing scuffle, six Senegalese peacekeepers were killed.[38] An enraged General Mamadou Seck told U.S. Assistant Secretary of Defense James Lilley that "the best solution to the Liberian problem would be to eliminate Taylor."[39] The commander of the Senegalese army was expressing the same frustrations that several Nigerian generals had expressed earlier. The Vahun incident ended any hopes for a sustained Senegalese presence in Liberia.

In August, two Nigerian soldiers were killed in fighting near the Po River. The total number of ECOMOG troops killed in Liberia by August 1992 had reached almost 100, including fifty-eight Nigerians, twenty-four Guineans, nine Ghanaians, four Sierra Leoneans, and two Gambians.[40] With the military situation growing increasingly perilous, ECOMOG field commander General Bakut ordered all his peacekeepers back to Monrovia. His worst fears were confirmed when Charles Taylor held 500 of them hostage and stripped them of their weapons, uniforms, and personal effects. They were released unharmed after one week, following Jimmy Carter's personal intervention. As Bakut lamented, "I now realise that I was wrong about Taylor's intention. It is quite clear that Taylor is not sincere about disarmament nor is he willing to let anything stand between him and the Executive Mansion."[41] Bakut was not the first or the last ECOMOG commander to underestimate Taylor's ambition and duplicity.

The military situation in Liberia was complicated by tensions within ULIMO. Roosevelt Johnson tried unsuccessfully to replace Arma Youlou as field commander with Lieutenant Colonel David Johnson in October. Youlou and Alhaji Kromah were accused of the murder of ULIMO chieftain General Albert Karpeh, even as Raleigh Seekie's leadership was being challenged. Despite this internal disunity, however, ULIMO managed to gain military control of Grand Cape Mount County, as well as parts of Lofa and Bomi Counties, and reduced NPFL control of Liberian territory to 75 percent by August.[42] ULIMO was barely forty kilometers from Taylor's Gbarnga headquarters by the end of 1992.

Operation Octopus

The period of relative tranquility since November 1990 that Liberians had come to describe as "no peace, no war" was about to change dramatically. Earlier in the year, it looked as if the NPFL would await a change of regime in the two main ECOMOG countries, Nigeria and Ghana (both scheduled to hold presidential elections in 1992), hoping that new civilian regimes would not tolerate the economic and political costs of maintaining ECOMOG in Liberia. After ECOMOG stopped a ship believed to be transporting arms to the NPFL on 8 October, Charles Taylor decided on a different strategy: he declared war on ECOMOG yet again.

On the morning of 15 October 1992, the NPFL launched Operation Octopus, which involved a persistent twelve-hour shelling of Monrovia, with ECOMOG headquarters, Monrovia Freeport, the Ducor Hotel (seat of the IGNU), and the Nigerian embassy as the main targets. The NPFL then launched a three-pronged attack on the capital, sending hundreds of young troops in waves as cannon fodder in a sustained attack. The headquarters of the Nigerian and Sierra Leonean troops in Topoe village, on Monrovia's outskirts, were overrun, and the NPFL attacked ECOMOG at Spriggs Payne Airport with mortars.[43] Nigerian infantry units suffered heavy casualties in the fighting.

The offensive took ECOMOG completely by surprise, revealing once again its lack of military intelligence. A Nigerian battalion had also been stationed in Monrovia since August 1992 without sufficient arms and ammunition, and frequent requests for military supplies had been ignored by Abuja.[44] It was not until 22 October that the peacekeepers started a coordinated counterattack, sending warplanes to bomb Harbel, Buchanan, Kakata, and Robertsfield Airport, ordering its navy to shell Harper and blockade NPFL-controlled ports, and beating back the attack with more accurate firepower than the NPFL. The fighting was brought under control by the end of October 1992, as more Nigerian and Ghanaian reinforcements arrived, bringing ECOMOG's troop strength to about 10,000, with 7,000 Nigerians.[45] On

6 November, Nigerian Alpha Jets bombed the NPFL headquarters in Gbarnga, and during a bombing raid on Buchanan that month ECOMOG mistakenly hit a building belonging to the Catholic Relief Services.[46] In late November, ECOMOG blew up a cargo ship in Buchanan suspected of carrying arms to the NPFL, and the peacekeepers battled Taylor for control of Spriggs Payne airport.

Units of the AFL and ULIMO fought alongside ECOMOG to defend Monrovia, as they had done in October 1990, again raising serious questions about ECOMOG's impartiality. There were unconfirmed reports of diamond-trading between ULIMO's Alhaji Kromah and senior Guinean officials, and Conakry and Freetown continued to cooperate militarily with ULIMO against the NPFL.[47] ECOMOG's image was also tarnished by reports of Nigerian troops in Monrovia shipping home looted refrigerators, air-conditioners, and other goods.[48]

By the end of Operation Octopus in December 1992, 3,000 people had died in Monrovia.[49] Just two weeks before the operation, General Adetunji Olurin, a Babangida loyalist and commander of the 3d Armored Division of the Nigerian army, had been appointed field commander to replace Bakut. Olurin had briefed Nigeria's Armed Forces Ruling Council in Abuja about the gravity of the situation in Liberia on 14 October 1992 following a visit there four days earlier. The general had warned Nigeria's most powerful decisionmaking body that this was not just another idle threat by Charles Taylor, that an attack on Monrovia was imminent, and that ECOMOG could be overwhelmed. A day later the AFRC met again and made the decision to defend the capital.[50] The changeover of command from Bakut to Olurin was effected on 19 October amid the siege of Monrovia, and Olurin immediately ordered troop and armored reinforcements to defend the city.

Amid this chaos ECOMOG bundled Yeduo Johnson, whose Caldwell base had been overrun by the NPFL, on a ship and banished him to comfortable exile in Lagos, thereby eliminating the INPFL as a factor in the Liberian civil war. Some INPFL fighters rejoined the NPFL, but others bid farewell to arms. Earlier Bakut had accused the INPFL leader of military collaboration with the NPFL. Johnson has since made the transition from warlord to born-again Christian, living an apparently changed life in Lagos's plush Victoria Island.

Thus, 1992 was truly an *annus horriblis* for ECOMOG: 500 peacekeepers were held hostage; its ill-equipped troops were ignominiously withdrawn from their disarmament tasks; the killing of six Senegalese troops precipitated a decision to withdraw the main contingent that provided ECOMOG vital francophone presence it hitherto lacked; the profound political divisions within ECOWAS were embarrassingly laid bare at ECOWAS summits and in leaked State Department documents; and in the final blow, Taylor launched an end-of-year assault that almost ended in the fall of

Monrovia. The accord painstakingly crafted at Yamoussoukro was rendered a dead letter.

* * *

The first phase of the ECOMOG intervention in Liberia, from August 1990 to December 1992, saw inexperienced and ill-equipped peacekeepers embark on a journey without maps. They were unsure of their mandate, and the efforts at Pax Nigeriana were constrained by internal challenges by the NPFL, subregional divisions within ECOWAS, and a lack of external logistical and financial support from the United States and United Nations.

The most formidable challenge to Pax Nigeriana at the domestic level was the NPFL, which ECOMOG had to confront militarily in 1990 and 1992. With the appearance of ULIMO in May 1991, the militarization of ethnicity worsened a complicated situation. By making an outright NPFL military victory more difficult, ULIMO ensured the war became a protracted struggle. Amos Sawyer's Interim Government of National Unity was widely considered an instrument of ECOMOG policy, as it depended entirely on the peacekeepers for security. This weakened its legitimacy, and its claims of sovereignty were contradicted by the fact it lacked any authority beyond Monrovia.

From the outset, ECOMOG entered a volatile situation. It was trying to keep peace where none was to be kept, and its nebulous mandate was inherently flawed. It was logistically unprepared for the mission and overconfident in assuming it could achieve a quick cease-fire; it also overestimated its military capabilities against the largely untrained Liberian factions. ECOMOG compromised its neutrality by cooperating militarily with the INPFL, AFL, and ULIMO. It damaged its credibility by failing to protect Samuel Doe at its headquarters; there were reports of looting by its peacekeepers.

By changing its mandate from peacekeeping to peace enforcement in September 1990, ECOMOG recognized the confusion of its original mandate. One could plausibly argue that the change was necessitated by the peacekeepers being attacked, but it reflects a more fundamental misconception: the failure to secure NPFL agreement before the intervention surely meant that ECOMOG could not simply enter Liberia as a cease-fire monitoring group. The fact that Generals Dogonyaro and Olurin had to increase ECOMOG's troop strength to enforce peace, in 1990 and 1992, respectively, was an admission that ECOMOG was improvising its strategy as it went along. ECOMOG's experience in Liberia, like much during the course of the war, was a series of contingencies. The peacekeepers were reacting to situations rather than anticipating them.

Other problems exposed the limitations of Pax Nigeriana in Liberia. The danger of deploying troops to disarm factions without adequate logistical support proved fatal: peacekeepers were killed and held hostage. ECOMOG lacked common rules of engagement, leading to problems between Nigeria and both Ghana and Senegal, as well as complaints by the Guinean contingent. ECOMOG's armies were accustomed to different military cultures in training techniques and command structures.

Continuing subregional divisions also hampered ECOMOG's efforts. Guinea was the only francophone member in the initial ECOMOG intervention force. The fact that the two francophone members of the ECOWAS Standing Mediation Committee, Togo and Mali, refused to contribute troops to ECOMOG revealed the political split in the subregion. Francophone Burkina Faso, Côte d'Ivoire, Senegal, Togo, and Niger all initially opposed the ECOMOG intervention. Even after several francophone-led peace conferences, ECOWAS remained divided over the best approach to achieve peace in Liberia. Côte d'Ivoire and Burkina Faso backed the NPFL; Benin and Côte d'Ivoire called for UN troops to replace ECOMOG; Sierra Leone, Guinea, and Nigeria cooperated militarily with ULIMO; Nigeria favored an aggressive stance against Charles Taylor; and Ghana favored political accommodation with him.

Arguments by leaders of ECOMOG states that the Liberian civil war had ceased to be a purely internal affair and thus affected subregional stability were not unreasonable: 600,000 Liberian refugees spilled into Côte d'Ivoire, Guinea, and Sierra Leone at the start of the war; the war triggered a decade-long civil war in Sierra Leone in 1991, and 181,500 refugees spilled into Guinea and Liberia from Sierra Leone after it started; Burkinabè soldiers fought with the NPFL in both Liberia and Sierra Leone; Burkina Faso and Libya provided military training and arms to the NPFL and the RUF; Côte d'Ivoire provided a staging post and arms-supply route for the NPFL; and Sierra Leonean, Guinean, and Gambian dissidents were fighting with the NPFL.

In order to win subregional consensus for ECOMOG and end military and diplomatic support for the NPFL, ECOWAS members attempted to bridge the diplomatic divide between francophone and anglophone members: Mali and Senegal contributed troops to ECOMOG; peace conferences were held in francophone capitals Bamako, Lomé, and Yamoussoukro; Ivorian leader Félix Houphoüet-Boigny was made chairman of five mediation efforts; Senegal's Abdou Diouf and Benin's Nicéphore Soglo were elected ECOWAS chairmen; and a Committee of Nine was established in October 1992 with six francophone members. Though Côte d'Ivoire started distancing itself from Taylor, and the killing of Senegalese peacekeepers convinced most ECOWAS states to support sanctions, Burkina Faso remained a staunch military supporter of the NPFL.

The ECOWAS peace conferences reflected fundamental problems that could not be overcome solely by diplomatic bridge-building. Many agreements lacked a viable implementation mechanism, and they often seemed to be hastily drafted documents with loopholes that the warlords exploited. There was no incentive for the NPFL—which still controlled most of Liberia's territory—to disarm without any guarantee that it could reap the fruits of its military labor at the ballot box. More significant, Charles Taylor and ULIMO leaders derived revenues from lucrative commercial exports of iron ore, rubber, timber, gold, and diamonds in areas under their control, further reducing any incentive to disarm.

Increasing calls by ECOWAS states for U.S. and UN assistance reflected the urgent need for financial and logistical resources that the subregion simply lacked. Washington adopted a low-risk, low-cost approach by supporting the ECOWAS peace plan and contributing humanitarian assistance to Liberia. Its distrust of ECOMOG's neutrality, the exclusion of the NPFL from the IGNU, and the low priority given to Africa by the U.S. political leadership prevented substantial financial and logistical support. Unwilling to intervene directly, Washington continued to support ECOMOG for lack of a better alternative. Contrary to the frequent claims in much of the academic literature regarding French influence over its former West African colonies, in fact Washington was the most dominant external influence on the Liberia policies of these countries: it pushed Houphoüet to host the Yamoussoukro meetings in 1991 and convinced Diouf to send Senegalese peacekeepers to Liberia in 1992 by providing for their logistical and financial needs. Its diplomatic pressure against Burkina Faso was less successful.

The diplomatic support of the OAU and United Nations was important in legitimizing the ECOMOG intervention. OAU support was to some extent a recognition of its own weakness; it was grateful that ECOMOG was fulfilling a task that the OAU has often been accused of abdicating. The United Nations also supported ECOMOG for similar reasons: with peacekeeping commitments already in Angola, Mozambique, and Western Sahara and mounting calls for intervention in Somalia and Rwanda, the United Nations was grateful that a subregional body had assumed the UN's own responsibilities. The United Nations became more active in Liberia in 1992, imposing an arms embargo on all Liberian factions and appointing Trevor Gordon-Somers as the UN Secretary-General's special representative for Liberia.

Having assessed the first two years of the Liberian civil war, we now turn to the years 1993–1994, during which ECOMOG adopted a tougher stance against Charles Taylor's NPFL.

Notes

1. Quoted in *Newswatch* 15, no. 18 (4 May 1992): 24.
2. Informal Consultative Group Meeting of the ECOWAS Committee of Five on Liberia, Geneva, 6–7 April 1992, pp. 1–3.

3. Personal interview with Admiral Augustus Aikhomu, Lagos, 9 January 1997.

4. *West Africa,* no. 3893 (27 April–3 May 1992): 728.

5. *Jeune Afrique,* no. 1633 (23–29 April 1992): 12.

6. *Africa Confidential* 33, no. 23 (20 November 1992): 7.

7. *African Concord* 7, no. 24 (2 November 1992): 17.

8. Quoted in Osisioma Nwolise, "Implementation of Yamoussoukro and Geneva Agreements," in M. A. Vogt (ed.), *The Liberian Crisis and ECOMOG: A Bold Attempt at Regional Peacekeeping* (Lagos: Gabumo, 1992), p. 301.

9. Earl Conteh-Morgan and Shireen Kadivar, "Sierra Leone's Response to ECOMOG: The Imperative of Geographical Proximity," in Karl Magyar and Earl Conteh-Morgan (eds.), *Peacekeeping in Africa: ECOMOG in Liberia* (London: Macmillan; and New York: St. Martin's, 1998), p. 142.

10. Ibid., p. 146.

11. "Final Communiqué," Fifteenth Session of the ECOWAS Authority of Heads of State and Government, Dakar, 27–29 July 1992, p. 8.

12. Ibid., pp. 8–9.

13. Personal interview with James Jonah, former UN Special Envoy for Liberia, New York, May 1997.

14. Pierre Englebert, *Burkina Faso: Unsteady Statehood in West Africa* (Boulder and Oxford: Westview, 1996), p. 159.

15. *Africa Confidential* 33, no. 23 (20 November 1992): 6–7.

16. Ibid., p. 7.

17. Matthias Igbarumah, "Playing the Judas," *Newswatch* 16, no. 17 (26 October 1992): 30.

18. "Final Communiqué," First Joint Meeting of the ECOWAS Standing Mediation Committee and the Committee of Five, Cotonou, 20 October 1992, pp. 4–7.

19. David Wippmann, "Enforcing Peace: ECOWAS and the Liberian Civil War," in Lori Fisler Damrosch (ed.), *Enforcing Restraint: Collective Intervention in Internal Conflicts* (New York: Council on Foreign Relations, 1993), p. 174.

20. Quoted in *West Africa,* no. 3922 (16–22 November 1992): 1908.

21. Quoted in *Africa Confidential* 33, no. 23 (20 November 1992): 7.

22. Ibid.

23. *African Concord* 7, no. 28 (30 November 1992): 14.

24. Quoted in *Africa Confidential* 33, no. 23 (20 November 1992): 6.

25. Englebert, *Burkina Faso,* pp. 160–162.

26. "The Ongoing Civil War and Crisis in Liberia," Hearing Before the Subcommittee on Foreign Affairs, House of Representatives, 19 November 1992 (Washington, D.C.: U.S. Government Printing Office, 1993), p. 3.

27. Ibid., p. 4.

28. Ibid.

29. Robert Mortimer, "Senegal's Role in ECOMOG: The Francophone Dimension," *Journal of Modern African Studies* 34, no. 2 (1996): 297.

30. Personal interview with General (Ambassador) Mamadou Seck, Embassy of Senegal, Washington, D.C., 21 July 1997.

31. Personal interview with Ibrahima Fall, former Senegalese Foreign Minister, 1984–1990, United Nations Secretariat, New York, July 1998.

32. Personal interview, Nigerian Ministry of Foreign Affairs, Abuja, December 1995.

33. *Africa Confidential* 32, no. 23 (22 November 1991): 7.

34. Personal interview with General Mamadou Seck.

35. Lindsay Barrett, "Why Senegal Withdrew," *West Africa*, no. 3931 (25–31 January 1993): 103.

36. *West Africa*, no. 3922 (16–22 November 1992): 1967.

37. "Taylor Explains," *West Africa*, no. 3892 (20–26 April 1992): 674.

38. Personal interview with General Mamadou Seck.

39. Quoted in *Africa Report* 38, no. 1 (January/February 1993): 21.

40. *West Africa*, no. 3911 (31 August–6 September 1992): 1471.

41. Quoted in Herbert Howe, "Lessons of Liberia: ECOMOG and Regional Peacekeeping," *International Security* 21, no. 3 (Winter 1996/1997): 158.

42. Géraldine Faes, "Taylor perd du terrain," *Jeune Afrique*, no. 1652 (3–9 September 1992): 22.

43. Lindsay Barrett, "The Siege of Monrovia," *West Africa*, no. 3923 (23–29 November 1992): 2008–2011; and Karl Magyar, "ECOMOG's Operations: Lessons for Peacekeeping," in Magyar and Earl-Conteh (eds.), *Peacekeeping in Africa*, pp. 69–70.

44. Personal interview with General Victor Malu, former ECOMOG force commander, Lagos, 2 October 2001.

45. *Economist Intelligence Unit*, Country Report, "Liberia," no. 1 (1993): 29.

46. Ibid., pp. 29–30.

47. Stephen Ellis, "Liberia's Warlord Insurgency," in Christopher Clapham (ed.), *African Guerrillas* (Oxford: James Currey; Bloomington: Indiana University Press; and Kampala: Fountain, 1998), p. 164.

48. *Africa Report* 39, no. 3 (May-June 1994): 64.

49. Magyar, "ECOMOG's Operations," p. 69.

50. Personal interview with General Adetunji Olurin, former ECOMOG commander Lagos, 9 August 1999.

part 2

Waging War to Keep Peace,
January 1993–August 1994

chapter 6

The Bloody Road to Cotonou, January–July 1993

If a faction decides to take us on and challenge the peacekeepers, then the enforcement role comes in. We must make all factions comply with the collective wisdom of others. . . . Then, we will return to our peacekeeping posture.

—*General Adetunji Olurin,
ECOMOG field commander, 1992–1993*

In this chapter we assess ECOMOG peace-enforcement measures against Charles Taylor and the NPFL, which culminated in a peace agreement in Cotonou in July 1993. As in the previous chapters, we argue that the problems at the domestic, subregional, and external levels continued to impede efforts to resolve the civil war.

At the domestic level, ECOMOG's military offensive against the NPFL gave ULIMO a chance to capitalize on Taylor's problems. But this did not resolve the question of how factions would be convinced to give up territory that provided resources for export. Nigeria's difficult relations with the NPFL also continued to impede progress: ECOMOG was able to bomb Taylor to the negotiating table but still lacked the military capability and subregional unity to force him to abide by peace agreements. ULIMO accused Côte d'Ivoire and Burkina Faso of supporting the NPFL. This lack of trust further complicated ECOWAS mediation efforts.

At the subregional level, ECOMOG's aggressive bombing of NPFL territories led to disagreements between Nigeria and two important ECOWAS states: Ghana and Côte d'Ivoire. Ghana continued to oppose Nigeria's anti-NPFL stance and sought support from Sierra Leone to balance Nigeria's dominant role in ECOMOG. Côte d'Ivoire was increasingly concerned about the deleterious effects of the Liberian conflict. Having seen the

119

Liberian civil war trigger a conflict in neighboring Sierra Leone, Abidjan was keen to avoid a similar fate. Explicit calls within the Cotonou agreement to establish a buffer zone on Liberia's borders with Côte d'Ivoire, Guinea, and Sierra Leone, and to repatriate non-Liberian mercenaries from Liberia, challenged the conventional wisdom that Nigeria was merely using ECOMOG to pursue parochial interests and impose its will on weaker states. Liberia's neighbors were far more directly affected by the war than was Nigeria: Sierra Leone was in the second year of a civil war; Côte d'Ivoire was suffering increasing incursions that necessitated a deployment of troops to its border with Liberia; and these two states and Guinea continued to host hundreds of thousands of Liberian refugees.

At the external level, the United Nations took a more active role in Liberia, with UN Special Representative Trevor Gordon-Somers taking the lead in peacemaking efforts at Cotonou. For its part, the OAU appointed Reverend Canaan Banana as its eminent person for Liberia. Both envoys presented themselves to Liberia's parties as more neutral than the mediators from ECOWAS states. This was a recognition of the need for impartial extrasubregional mediation in a conflict in which several ECOWAS states were compromised by their support for different Liberian factions. At Cotonou, both the United Nations and OAU agreed to send peacekeepers to Liberia, a further sign of the military weakness and political difficulties of Pax Nigeriana. The lackluster U.S. support for ECOMOG continued to deny the peacekeepers the logistical support they needed to disarm the factions.

Enforcing Peace

While ECOMOG reeled from the NPFL's military attack on Monrovia at the end of 1992, its Senegalese contingent was preparing to return home; by mid-January 1993 all 1,500 Senegalese soldiers had left Liberia. This represented a double blow for ECOMOG: politically, Senegal had provided ECOMOG with a solid francophone presence that ensured wider subregional support for the mission; militarily, the Senegalese peacekeepers had earned a glowing reputation for being a professional, disciplined, and effective force during their fifteen-month mission in Liberia. Dakar gave two reasons for withdrawing. First, it said its men were needed to fulfill their constitutional role of guarding polling stations during upcoming presidential elections (21 February 1993); second, President Abdou Diouf explained that his soldiers were required to keep peace in Senegal's separatist Casamance region.[1] Senegal was also involved in border disputes with Mauritania and Guinea-Bissau. Furthermore, Senegal's top brass voiced doubts about ECOMOG's ability to succeed in Liberia.

Senegal's departure coincided with another dramatic change in ECOMOG's strategy. ECOMOG was, ironically, about to adopt the tough stance toward

Charles Taylor that the commander of the Senegalese army, General Mamadou Seck, had advocated earlier. General Adetunji Olurin, the newly arrived Nigerian ECOMOG field commander, obtained more troops to push the NPFL out of Monrovia and all the way back to Charles Taylor's base in Gbarnga. General Dogonyaro's limited offensive of October 1990 was now to be replaced by General Olurin's defensive offensive. The new ECOMOG Commander vowed, "I won't stop until I get to Saniquellie [capital of Nimba County]."

After Operation Octopus began in October 1992, Olurin had used his position as trusted adviser to General Babangida to convince the Nigerian head of state, during several trips to Abuja, to commit more troops to Liberia to take the war to Charles Taylor. By January 1993, ECOMOG's troop strength stood at 16,000, of which 12,000 were Nigerian, with Ghana, Guinea, and Sierra Leone also sending troops. This now gave ECOMOG the offensive strength to take on the NPFL's 10,000 combatants. The arrival of the new troops, coupled with General Olurin's aggressive leadership, considerably improved the sagging morale and performance of the Nigerian contingent. The new field commander approached his enforcement tasks with the unnerving equanimity of a general who was shielded from political pressures, saying, "We are professional soldiers and fully aware that when we go into any action, we know that there [will] be casualties."[2]

During this period, with U.S. Marines launching air strikes against targets in Mogadishu in a frantic search for Somali warlord Mohammed Farah Aideed, the international climate seemed propitious for enforcement action. Olurin launched a ten-day offensive at the end of January 1993, capturing several strategic NPFL assets: the Firestone rubber plantation near Harbel, Robertsfield International Airport, and the Bassa highway leading from Monrovia to Buchanan. The Nigerian field commander warned, "I want to make it clear to the remaining NPFL leadership still in Liberia that this is the time to call off their senseless adventure and embrace the ECOWAS peace accord before it is too late."[3] In the next three months, ECOMOG jets conducted aerial bombardments on Harper, its ships blockaded Buchanan port, and its infantry captured Kakata. By May 1993, ECOMOG had gained control of the Buchanan port and expelled the NPFL from all positions between Buchanan and Monrovia, creating a larger buffer zone and making any NPFL attack on Monrovia more difficult. ECOMOG had taken the war to Taylor, engaging in a long, bloody march toward Gbarnga.

Under pressure from Amos Sawyer, Liberia's interim president, Olurin personally led a convoy of ECOMOG vehicles, tanks, and helicopters to disarm 200 AFL and 160 ULIMO combatants in Monrovia. These men had fought alongside ECOMOG during Operation Octopus. Olurin imposed a dusk-to-dawn curfew in Monrovia, with a chilling order for his men to shoot any violators on sight. Monrovians nicknamed him "the hurricane" and started comparing his ruthless style favorably with that of General Dogonyaro, the military enforcer who had established two years of peace in the capital. Even Janet Fleischman, Human Rights Watch/Africa research associate and a strong critic of ECOMOG, was forced to admit after a March 1993 visit to Monrovia, "One would be hard-pressed to visit Monrovia without hearing, time and again, 'Thank God for [ECOMOG].'"[4]

The fall of strategic NPFL assets to ECOMOG was a serious blow to Charles Taylor: Robertsfield Airport was the entry point for NPFL arms and ammunition, the Firestone plantation was the source of much income and taxation, the Buchanan port was the loading point for NPFL iron ore, rubber, and timber exports, and Kakata was a key supply route between Gbarnga and Monrovia. With growing military losses, Taylor also lost the support of his French and Lebanese logging interests in Côte d'Ivoire.[5] An incensed Taylor exclaimed, "We win every day that we kill an ECOMOG soldier. . . . ECOMOG is a warring party. They have brought genocide to our people. We will talk when Nigeria is out of here."[6]

With the failure of Operation Octopus, Taylor's previous military preponderance had shrunk even more. By the end of February 1993, ULIMO was making gains in Lofa County from a distracted NPFL that was reeling from ECOMOG attacks. ULIMO added to earlier gains in Bomi and Grand Cape Mount Counties, thereby winning control of virtually all of northwestern Liberia. By early March, ULIMO, having cut off the NPFL from its RUF allies in Sierra Leone, was fighting with the Sierra Leonean army to capture Bo Bridge on the Mano River. ULIMO also captured Bong Mines from the NPFL.

The NPFL's military response to the ECOMOG assault was threefold. First, it attempted to infiltrate Monrovia with combatants disguised as refugees, using its superior intelligence over ECOMOG to launch a terrorist campaign of bombings and assassinations. This forced ECOMOG to tighten its curfew and embark on daily house-to-house searches.[7] Second, the NPFL resorted to guerrilla tactics, launching surprise attacks against isolated ECOMOG battalions. Finally, the NPFL used civilians as human shields in a desperate attempt to prevent ECOMOG's aerial bombardment.[8]

In April 1993, Taylor's fighters destroyed bridges on the Bassa highway to slow ECOMOG's advance and tried unsuccessfully to recapture Kakata. In the last week of May, they launched successful guerrilla attacks on ECOMOG positions on the outskirts of Monrovia, using dirt tracks unfamiliar to the peacekeepers and attacking by night. The NPFL failed, however, in its attempt to capture the Paynesville suburb of Monrovia, but Taylor took comfort in the knowledge that the dense forests in the Liberian countryside prevented an ECOMOG infantry attack, which would almost certainly have resulted in high casualties for the peacekeepers.[9]

Whatever military successes that ECOMOG achieved were gradually eroded by the political damage to its professed image as an impartial peacekeeper. General Olurin had worked closely with AFL Chief of Staff General

Hezekiah Bowen in the military operation that repelled the NPFL from Monrovia.[10] Large sections of the international media and Western human rights groups were especially critical of ECOMOG's decision to wage war against one party, even though it had been attacked by the NPFL, and condemned the increasing civilian casualties resulting from ECOMOG bombing raids. These critics did not always seem as evenhanded in their criticisms of U.S. actions in Somalia during the same period, which resulted in far more civilian casualties. The NPFL accused ECOMOG of bombing civilians, hospitals, and relief convoys in Buchanan, Harbel, Greenville, and Kakata. Nigerian jets bombed Phebe hospital on 10 March, injuring five people; bombed Greenville on 18 March, killing fifteen people; and attacked a Médecins sans Frontières aid convoy near Saniquellie on 18 April, which Olurin accused of transporting arms to the NPFL.[11] Some ECOMOG troops were also accused of looting and occasional harassment of civilians.[12]

General Olurin vigorously defended his tactics, denying that he was targeting civilians and explaining that his targets were military supply routes and arms caches. But there was no denying that civilian casualties had resulted. Even as Nigerian jets bombed NPFL areas, Nigeria continued its diplomatic contacts with the NPFL. Emmanuel Otaokun, Nigeria's ambassador to Liberia, met frequently with Taylor spokesman John Richardson in Monrovia. Otaokun complained about the anti-Nigerian propaganda emanating from Gbarnga, and Richardson assured him that he would inform Taylor of his concern. But the broadcasts continued unabated.[13]

Les Frères Ennemis: Nigeria and Côte D'Ivoire

Côte d'Ivoire's evolving Liberia policy was reflected in a January 1993 meeting between Félix Houphoüet-Boigny and the new UN special representative for Liberia, Trevor Gordon-Somers. During the meeting, the Ivorian leader complained that the 580-kilometer border with Liberia was difficult to police and expressed concern about the pernicious effects of the Liberian conflict. Houphoüet also expressed full support for the arms and economic embargos imposed on Liberia's factions in 1992.[14] ECOWAS's economic sanctions of July 1992 and its military actions of early 1993 were already showing some results, having reduced commercial exports from Liberia.[15] But despite the converging interest in the Liberia policies of Côte d'Ivoire and Nigeria, this period saw increased tension in relations between the traditional subregional rivals.

ECOMOG's aggressive military tactics brought political repercussions on 27 February 1993 when its jets strayed into Ivorian airspace and bombed the Loguato Bridge on the Ivorian-Liberian border. ECOMOG had always argued that Taylor's arms came through the Ivorian coastal town of San

Pedro, and there were reports that the NPFL had a base in the Ivorian border town of Danané. But Nigeria's diplomats doubted that Houphoüet-Boigny was himself personally involved in such activities, blaming NPFL sympathizers in his administration and corrupt officials for breaching the official policy of closing the border to such arms.[16] Matthew Mbu, Nigeria's external affairs minister, noted that Houphoüet was appalled by Taylor's treachery[17] and explained that "given the tortuous terrain of our brothers, it is not easy to effectively control every nook and corner of such a large terrain."[18]

Abidjan showed less understanding for what it considered a breach of its sovereignty by ECOMOG. A day after the bombing incident of February 1993, Amara Essy, the Ivorian foreign minister, sent a strongly worded letter to the ECOWAS chairman, Nicéphore Soglo, complaining of a violation of Ivorian sovereignty in an area in which, Essy said, there were no NPFL combatants. Before the NPFL could try to exploit a potential rift between ECOWAS's most influential anglophone and francophone states, General Ibrahim Babangida dispatched Matthew Mbu, Chief of General Staff Admiral Augustus Aikhomu, and General Olurin to Abidjan on 5 March to reassure Houphoüet-Boigny. At this meeting, the Nigerian delegation explained that the incident had been an operational error. After a briefing from General Olurin about the supply of arms to the NPFL through Ivorian border towns, Houphoüet complained that his officials may have been acting without his knowledge.[19] The Ivorians also complained of a lack of liaison between Abidjan and the ECOMOG High Command in Monrovia, and Olurin promised to rectify the situation.[20] Abidjan sent more troops to guard the border with Liberia in early September after fighting spread into its territory. Tensions eased after ECOMOG deployed troops along the Ivorian-Liberian border in November 1993 with a mandate to inspect relief convoys.

The Anglophonie: Ghana, Nigeria, and Sierra Leone

Côte d'Ivoire was not the only ECOWAS country to express misgivings about Nigeria's tough approach. Though Ghanaian peacekeepers eventually took part in ECOMOG's military offensive against Taylor, Accra was uncomfortable with renewed enforcement action against the NPFL. The Ghanaian contingent had joined the fray late, only after receiving its opeational orders from Accra.[21] Air Marshal A. H. Dumashie, Ghana's chief of defense staff, later expressed fears that General Olurin, whom he regarded as an ambitious officer keen to establish a reputation in Liberia, was stretching ECOMOG's lines too thin; he felt that peacekeepers should not expand deep into the Liberian countryside.[22] The difference in approaches between Accra and Abuja was further revealed when Ghana's information minister, Koffi Totobi Quakye, told *Africa Report,*

> Ghana is very anxious to find areas of compromise. Compromise lies in the hands of Charles Taylor. . . . There's a Nigerian passion to annihilate Charles Taylor. Charles Taylor is aware that the Ghanaian way of doing things is more accommodating and is looking more at the way of achieving the end of having an election.[23]

The fact that a senior Ghanaian official would publicly accuse Nigeria of adopting Taylor's assassination as official policy was astonishing, even though some Nigerian military officials had made such statements. In the same interview, Quakye distanced Ghana from ECOMOG's enforcement actions and aligned his country closer to a UN peacemaking role.[24] Ghana's increasing ambivalence toward the Liberian quagmire became evident again on 31 January 1994 when Rawlings publicly announced that he was considering withdrawing his troops from Liberia due to growing violence in neighboring Togo. Ghana sought to ensure support from other ECOMOG countries as a way of balancing Nigeria's dominant influence. Rawlings had tremendous influence over the young leader of Sierra Leone, Captain Valentine Strasser, and they met regularly to discuss the situation in Liberia.[25] But with Freetown's heavy dependence on Nigerian troops for additional security amid an increasingly costly civil war, it was hard to imagine Strasser affording less than full support to Nigeria's efforts in Liberia.

In 1993, Sierra Leone's 5,000-man army regained control of most of the southeastern part of the country from the NPFL-backed RUF rebels. But the campaign cost the cash-strapped government $18 million. [26] Diamond- and gold-mining areas, which accounted for 70 percent of Sierra Leone's exports, had also been affected by the civil war. Freetown had a concrete national interest to continue supporting ECOMOG, especially in its campaign to weaken the NPFL. Not only had the Liberian war spilled into its territory, but Sierra Leone was still host to about 7,000 Liberian refugees. As Strasser noted in April 1993,

> We have remained committed to Sierra Leone's participation in ECOMOG because we believe that unless peace is wholly restored to Liberia and Sierra Leone, significant progress cannot be fully realised in the socio-economic spheres of our national and subnational endeavours.[27]

The United States

George Moose, the new U.S. assistant secretary of state for African affairs under the administration of President Bill Clinton, continued his predecessor Herman Cohen's policy: channeling most U.S. aid for Liberia into humanitarian assistance while supporting ECOWAS's mediation efforts. Washington was, however, not fully supportive of ECOMOG's enforcement actions and continued to question its impartiality as a peacekeeper. As

Moose put it, "We do not believe a military solution is possible or desir-able, but we recognise that continuing pressure is an inescapable part of the equation for peace in Liberia."[28] Unwilling to intervene directly, U.S. offi-cials continued to pay lip service to the benefits of a regional solution. William Twadell, the U.S. chargé d'affaires in Liberia, explained: "It seems to me that West African states have a claim to international support for the contribution they have made to stabilise and bring order back to Liberia."[29] But the real feelings of U.S. policymakers about ECOMOG were probably more accurately expressed in the State Department's Intelligence and Re-search Bureau April 1993 report, which accused ECOMOG of assisting the AFL and ULIMO and bluntly stated that the West African force had "aban-doned its neutrality."[30]

After the annulment of democratic elections in Nigeria in June 1993, bilateral relations between Washington and Abuja rapidly deteriorated.[31] The United States immediately announced the suspension of bilateral aid to Nigeria, and direct contacts were broken off between senior officials. Wash-ington had decertified Nigeria in 1992 for its alleged condoning of drug-trafficking, meaning that the United States voted against Nigeria in inter-national financial institutions. With ECOMOG's dominant country having been declared a pariah by Washington, the already inadequate U.S. finan-cial support for ECOMOG became even harder to secure. General Olurin visited Washington in early April 1993 in search of logistical support for ECOMOG—vehicles, communications equipment, spare parts, internal se-curity equipment, and night-vision devices. His visit met with little success. A similar effort by the ECOWAS executive secretary, Abass Bundu, to con-vince the United States to meet the future costs of ECOMOG, during a visit to Washington in June 1993, also resulted in failure.

The United Nations and OAU

Trevor Gordon-Somers had been appointed the UN Secretary-General's special representative in Liberia on 20 November 1992. In the first two months following his appointment, Gordon-Somers visited Abuja, Abidjan, Accra, Banjul, Conakry, Dakar, and Freetown to confer with subregional leaders on the potential UN contribution to the peace process in Liberia. He also met the ECOMOG field commander, General Olurin, in Monrovia be-fore visiting the Liberian faction leaders. Gordon-Somers quickly became embroiled in the cesspit of Liberian politics when ULIMO's original founder, Raleigh Seekie, criticized him for meeting with ULIMO's disputed leader, Alhaji Kromah, in January 1993.

Undeterred, Gordon-Somers continued his diplomatic activities, visiting Accra and Freetown with General Olurin in May. The UN envoy strongly supported ECOMOG's controversial peace enforcement measures against the NPFL, arguing that it was part of ECOMOG's mandate to pursue uncooperative factions and destroy their fighting capabilities.[32] The OAU appointed Reverend Canaan Banana, the former Zimbabwean president (1980–1987), as its eminent person to Liberia in January 1993. Banana visited Abuja and Freetown in February to discuss the dispatch of nonsubregional OAU troops to assist ECOMOG. He was actively involved in other peacemaking activities and, along with Gordon-Somers, discussed the establishment of a cease-fire with Charles Taylor in April.

The Cotonou Agreement

With the signing of the Cotonou agreement on 25 July 1993, ECOMOG had in effect bombed Charles Taylor to the negotiating table. It is no coincidence that the agreement was signed barely two months after ECOMOG's capture of the key port of Buchanan and the expulsion of NPFL combatants from all areas between Buchanan and Monrovia. By July 1993, the NPFL's control of Liberian territory had shrunk from 95 percent in 1990 to 50 percent, even as it faced continued challenges from ULIMO. As Reverend Banana noted, "Previous agreements took place when the NPFL was in a much stronger position. But now the balance of forces has changed and, given this reality on the ground, one hopes that it will cooperate in the completion of the peace agreement."[33]

Peace talks were held at the UN Palais des Nations in Geneva from 10 to 17 July 1993 under the joint chairmanship of the United Nations, ECOWAS, and the OAU; the United Nations essentially financed and organized the talks. ULIMO's presence, after its exclusion from Yamoussoukro in 1991, was a clear sign to potential factions that gaining territory was the most viable way of winning a place at the negotiating table.

In Geneva, the NPFL's Momolu Sirleaf reminded ECOMOG of General Yakubu Gowon's request for other OAU states to stay out of the Nigerian civil war of 1967–1970. ULIMO's Maxwell Kabbah praised ECOMOG, condemned Burkina Faso and Côte d'Ivoire, and promised to crush the NPFL.[34] IGNU's Baccus Matthews tried to stay above the fray by arguing that he did not represent a warring faction but was merely interested in restoring order and democracy to Liberia.

The two most difficult issues in Geneva involved the composition of the Executive Council of State and the procedures for disarming the factions.[35] Even as the warlords squabbled, the death toll in the three-year civil war had reached 150,000; 700,000 Liberian refugees remained in Côte d'Ivoire, Guinea, Sierra Leone, Ghana, and Nigeria.[36] The details of an agreement soon emerged from Geneva: There was to be a cease-fire established by

1 August 1993; a five-member Council of State was to be set up involving nominees from the three parties, with a chairman and two vice chairmen, with decisions taken by consensus; a seventeen-member cabinet was to be established comprising nominees of the three parties; a thirty-five-member legislature was to be created by merging the IGNU legislature in Monrovia with that of the NPFL in Gbarnga; a Liberian National Transitional Government (LNTG) was to be in place by the end of August 1993; presidential elections were to be held in seven months, with council members being ineligible; ECOMOG was to be expanded to include peacekeepers from the United Nations and nonsubregional OAU countries; buffer zones were to be established by ECOMOG on Liberia's borders with Guinea, Côte d'Ivoire, and Sierra Leone; and non-Liberian fighters or mercenaries were to be repatriated from Liberia. ECOMOG and the 368-strong United Nations Observer Mission in Liberia (UNOMIL) consisting of unarmed peacekeepers from outside West Africa were to deploy at all Liberian seaports, airfields, and entry roads, with ECOMOG having the authority to conduct arms searches monitored by UNOMIL. Cotonou also granted a controversial general amnesty to persons and parties who had committed human rights abuses in combat.[37]

This agreement was basically a restatement of Yamoussoukro with more details provided on the interim administration. The real novelty of Cotonou was the involvement of UN and OAU peacekeepers in Liberia. A Joint Cease-Fire Monitoring Committee would meet to investigate and resolve cease-fire violations. The committee would be chaired by UNOMIL and involve ECOMOG and representatives of all the armed factions. ECOMOG had an explicit right of self-defense under Cotonou, which mandated it to exercise peace-enforcement powers with the approval of a UN-chaired Cease-Fire Violations Committee. Cotonou was, however, different from earlier agreements in that the factions had been given center stage in Geneva and were left to resolve their differences; ECOWAS, the OAU, and UN mediators remained in the wings, playing the role of supporting cast.

Charles Taylor refused to attend the signing of the Cotonou agreement personally (which had been negotiated mostly in Geneva with a few outstanding issues left for Cotonou) on 25 July 1993, citing his fear of assassination by Nigeria after he heard that General Babangida would also be attending. He reiterated his refusal to disarm to Nigerian troops. Taylor remained in his Executive Mansion in Gbarnga, watching CNN and listening to loud renditions of Handel's *Messiah* while senior NPFL official Enoch Dogoleah signed the agreement on his behalf. Having failed to achieve his presidential ambitions through two invasions of Monrovia in three years, Taylor finally seemed to have decided to promote his goals through other means: an unprecedented agreement to participate in a transitional government and dropping his insistence on heading the transition.

Yet by refusing to sign peace agreements personally, Taylor could later distance himself from deals that representatives had signed with his consent.

After the signing of the Cotonou agreement, an elated Gordon-Somers exclaimed, "What was fascinating was to see Liberians negotiating face to face. It was very much their meeting. When they get together, they can clearly tackle their own problems."[38] More experienced observers, who had seen at least six previous agreements unravel, remained skeptical.

Even after the signing of Cotonou, there were problems suggesting the agreement would not live up to what optimists were predicting. The familiar deadlock between the IGNU and NPFL reappeared soon after Cotonou: the IGNU called for disarmament before it gave up power while the NPFL, with ULIMO's support, called for a new interim government before disarmament. As was the case at Yamoussoukro in 1991, the task of mediators in Geneva and Cotonou was complicated by the appearance of new factions. Two more armed factions, the Liberia Peace Council and the Lofa Defence Force, joined the fray by the end of 1993.

Notes

1. See Lindsay Barrett, "Why Senegal Withdrew," *West Africa*, no. 3931 (25–31 January 1993).

2. "Enough is Enough" (Interview with Major General Olurin), *West Africa*, no. 3961 (23–29 August 1993): 1486.

3. Quoted in *West Africa,* no. 3936 (1–7 March 1993): 325.

4. Janet Fleischman, "An Uncivil War," *Africa Report* 38, no. 3 (May/June 1993): 57.

5. "The Battle for Gbarnga," *Africa Confidential* 34, no. 11 (28 May 1993): 1.

6. Quoted in Human Rights Watch/Africa, "Waging War to Keep the Peace: The ECOMOG Intervention and Human Rights," *Human Rights Watch/Africa* 5, no. 6 (June 1993): 9.

7. *Africa Confidential* 34, no. 11 (28 May 1993): 2.

8. Human Rights Watch/Africa, "Waging War to Keep the Peace," p. 16.

9. Peter da Costa, "Talking Tough to Taylor," *Africa Report* 38, no. 1 (January/February 1993): 21.

10. Personal interview with General Hezekiah Bowen, former AFL Chief of Staff, Monrovia, 14 July 1999.

11. Human Rights Watch/Africa, "Waging War to Keep the Peace," p. 20.

12. Ibid., p. 3.

13. Personal interview with Ambassador Emmanuel Otaokun, Nigerian Ministry of Foreign Affairs, Abuja, December 1995.

14. United Nations Report of the Secretary-General on the question of Liberia, S/25402 (12 March 1993), reproduced in Marc Weller, *Regional Peacekeeping and International Enforcement: The Liberian Crisis* (Cambridge, UK, and New York: Cambridge University Press, 1994), p. 284.

15. Ibid., p. 282.

16. Personal interview at the Nigerian Ministry of Foreign Affairs, Abuja, December 1995.

17. Personal interview with Matthew Mbu, former Nigerian Foreign Minister, Lagos, 13 January 1997.

18. "Troubleshooting for Africa" (Interview with Chief M. T. Mbu), *West Africa,* no. 3940 (29 March–4 April 1993): 501.

19. Personal interview with General Adetunji Olurin, former ECOMOG commander, Lagos, 9 August 1999.

20. Personal interview with Matthew Mbu.

21. Personal interview with General Victor Malu, Lagos, former ECOMOG commander, 20 October 2001.

22. Personal interview with Air Marshal A. H. Dumashie, former Ghanaian Chief of Defense Staff, Accra, September 1996.

23. Quoted in *Africa Report* 38, no. 4 (July/August 1993): 30.

24. Ibid.

25. *Africa Confidential* 34, no. 16 (13 August 1993): 3.

26. Ibid.

27. Quoted in Earl Conteh-Morgan and Shireen Kadivar, "Sierra Leone's Response to ECOMOG: The Imperative of Geographical Proximity," in Karl Magyar and Earl Conteh-Morgan (eds.), *Peacekeeping in Africa: ECOMOG in Liberia* (Hampshire, UK: Macmillan; and New York, St. Martin's, 1998), p. 145

28. Quoted in *West Africa,* no. 3952 (21–27 June 1993): 1054.

29. Quoted in *Africa Report* 38, no. 4 (July/August 1993): 31.

30. Cited in Human Rights Watch/Africa, "Waging War to Keep the Peace," p. 14.

31. See Omo Omoruyi, *The Tale of June 12: The Betrayal of the Democratic Rights of Nigerians* (Lagos and London: Press Alliance Network, 1999).

32. Cited in *West Africa,* no. 3972 (8–14 November 1993): 2018.

33. Quoted in Weller, *Regional Peacekeeping and International Enforcement,* p. 339.

34. Ibid., pp. 307–312.

35. United Nations Secretary-General, "Further Report on Liberia," S/26200 (2 August 1993), reproduced in Weller, *Regional Peacekeeping and International Enforcement,* p. 340.

36. Ibid., pp. 313–321.

37. For the original texts of Cotonou and other agreements, see Jeremy Armon and Andy Carl (eds.), *Accord: The Liberian Peace Process, 1990–1996,* Issue 1/1996 (London: Conciliation Resources, 1996).

38. Quoted in *Africa Report* 38, no. 5 (September/October 1993): 22.

chapter 7

The Tortuous Road to Akosombo, August 1993–August 1994

There was an orchestrated campaign of calumny against ECOMOG to discredit it, its neutrality, and impartiality. These acts included intimidation, seizure of arms and equipment and commandeering of ECOMOG vehicles. ECOMOG was being described as an army of occupation.
—General John Mark Inienger,
ECOMOG field commander, 1993–1996

In this chapter we examine the failed attempt to implement the Cotonou agreement of July 1993. We argue that the continuing inability of ECOWAS and ECOMOG to secure consensus at the domestic, subregional, and external levels accounted for this failure.

At the domestic level, Charles Taylor was still unwilling to disarm to ECOMOG amid increased military challenges to his control of Liberian territory and resources by other factions. All of Liberia's warlords sought personal gain from the lucrative export of Liberian resources. They struggled to be part of the political spoils of any negotiated settlement by conquering enough territory to win a place at the negotiating table. With factions in control of much of Liberia and with warlords unable to maintain control over their undisciplined fighters, peacekeeping simply became an impossible task; Liberia's new interim government was rendered ineffective. ULIMO split into two factions, again exposing the ethnic roots of Liberia's factions, as well as the irreconcilable personal ambitions of power-seeking warlords.

At the subregional level, Burkina Faso continued to back the NPFL, whereas Nigeria, Guinea, and Sierra Leone continued to be linked to ULIMO, the AFL, and the LPC. ECOWAS states continued to demand international support in recognition of their own logistical and financial shortcomings.

At the external level, the arrival of 368 UN peacekeepers did nothing to improve ECOMOG's logistical shortcomings, and tensions increased as the numerically inferior United Nations declined to share its resources and equipment with ECOMOG. The arrival of 1,500 East African OAU peacekeepers also failed significantly to improve ECOMOG's logistical shortcomings and convince the Liberian factions to disarm to more neutral peacekeepers. The continuing deterioration in Americo-Nigerian relations following the annulment of the presidential election in Nigeria in June 1993, as well as the subsequent return of military rule in Nigeria, also ensured that ECOMOG would continue to be denied the logistical support it needed to fulfill its disarmament tasks. Washington contributed the bulk of its logistical support to the numerically inferior East African peacekeepers, as it had done with the Senegalese contingent in 1992.

We will argue in this chapter that the limits of a hegemonic Pax Nigeriana were again exposed not only by the continuing failure of a Nigerian-dominated ECOMOG to impose its will on Liberia but also by the increasing talk of withdrawing Nigerian troops from Liberia by Nigerian policymakers. Following the failure to achieve peace in Liberia after three years and two attempts at peace enforcement, there was growing recognition that a different approach was needed. In this chapter and the rest of the book, we strongly argue that the ascent to power in Nigeria by General Sani Abacha marked a significant shift in Nigeria's Liberia policy that eventually helped resolve the conflict. Abacha did not have the personal relationship with Liberia's Samuel Doe that had led many to question General Ibrahim Babangida's motives and anti-NPFL stance. Abacha also had far greater domestic problems than did Babangida in establishing his authority within the army and country, reducing his personal stake in the domestically unpopular ECOMOG intervention, though he did profit from ECOMOG-related expenditure.

Ivorian policy continued to distance itself from the NPFL as the destabilizing effects of the Liberian civil war on its territory continued. The death of Félix Houphoüet-Boigny in December 1993 increased the prospect for Abidjan to cooperate closer with ECOMOG to end the war. Houphoüet's death depersonalized the conflict and removed the family reasons for which Abidjan had initially backed Charles Taylor and opposed Samuel Doe. We argue that like Abacha, the new Ivorian leader, Henri Konan Bédié, was more concerned with establishing his domestic authority than embarking on uncertain foreign adventures. Both Abuja and Abidjan now had leaders with a common interest in resolving the Liberian conflict. This increased the chances for an improvement in subregional consensus, as the Liberian policies of ECOWAS's most important anglophone and francophone countries appeared to be converging.

With Ghana, ECOMOG's second largest contingent, showing signs of frustration and threatening to withdraw its peacekeepers from Liberia, Jerry

Rawlings was appointed ECOWAS chairman, giving Accra a greater stake in the resolution of the conflict and raising its international diplomatic profile.

Nigeria: From Babangida to Abacha

The exit from power of General Ibrahim Babangida, a strong supporter of ECOWAS and the leader who had sent Nigerian troops to ECOMOG, led to serious questions about Nigeria's continued commitment to the Liberia mission. On 26 August 1993, having annulled the presidential election of 12 June 1993, Babangida surrendered power to an unelected interim government under businessman Ernest Shonekan, who had been chairman of the British commercial giant United African Company. Babangida had overseen the establishment of interim governments in both Nigeria and Liberia but was unable to move either to full-fledged democracy.

In his inaugural address as Nigeria's interim president, Shonekan urged the United Nations and the international community to come to Liberia's assistance, saying, "We in the subregion have done enough."[1] He noted that Nigeria's economy had suffered as a result of ECOMOG and called for a summit of ECOWAS states to consider the mission's future.[2] A cost-conscious industrialist, Shonekan was signaling his early intention to be rid of Liberia in order to balance Nigeria's books. ECOMOG was costing the Nigerian treasury a reported $500,000 every day.[3] The new leader was a technocrat more concerned with resolving Nigeria's economic problems than with achieving the glory sought by Nigeria's generals. Withdrawal from Liberia seemed an easy way to reduce the strain on Nigeria's finances. In the last week of September 1993, Shonekan asked his defense minister, General Sani Abacha, to prepare plans to bring home Nigeria's 12,000 troops from Liberia by March 1994.[4]

Edouard Benjamin, the former Guinean minister of economy and finance, replaced Abass Bundu as ECOWAS executive secretary on 1 September 1993. One of Benjamin's first tasks was to plead with Shonekan not to withdraw Nigerian troops from Liberia, citing devastating consequences for the subregion.[5] In early September 1993, Liberia's interim government also instructed its ambassador to Nigeria, James Tarpeh, to plead with Abuja not to abandon Liberia without a final resolution of the conflict.

On 18 November 1993, General Sani Abacha took advantage of Shonekan's weak interim government to force his resignation. Abacha then appointed himself head of state. Though it would be an exaggeration to suggest the coup was a direct response to Shonekan's threat to withdraw, the fact that the army had staked its honor and prestige on success in Liberia meant that a withdrawal would be humiliating. Having been undercut by a previous civilian president, Shehu Shagari, who withdrew Nigerian troops from Chad in 1982, the army was keen to avoid another embarrassing exit.

Soon after assuming power, General Abacha proclaimed his unrelenting commitment to ECOMOG. Like Babangida, he felt a humiliating withdrawal would damage the image of the Nigerian army, though Abacha maintained a more pragmatic commitment to ECOMOG. As chief of army staff, Abacha had been the second most powerful military officer and Babangida's loyal deputy for eight years.[6] He was closely involved with Liberia policy, meeting the U.S. ambassador to Nigeria, Lannon Walker, at the start of the conflict, traveling to Freetown in April 1991 to discuss Nigerian military assistance for Sierra Leone after RUF attacks from Liberia,[7] and attempting to convince Charles Taylor to attend the All-Liberia Conference that month.[8] Though unsuccessful, Abacha's early acquaintance with the warlord proved to be one of the most crucial relationships in ending the civil war.

Having assumed power amid reports of splits within the top military brass, Abacha felt that he needed to move quickly to establish his authority over the army. He retired seventeen key army officers and replaced them with more trusted lieutenants. One of the retired officers was the ECOMOG field commander, General John Shagaya. Abacha, as defense minister under Shonekan, had replaced General Olurin, a Babangida loyalist with whom Abacha had a strained personal relationship, as ECOMOG field commander with Shagaya in September 1993. Shagaya was part of the same Langtang mafia of Middle Belt officers to which the first Nigerian field commander, General Dogonyaro, belonged. Shagaya was highly regarded in the Nigerian army and had commanded the 1st Mechanized Division in Kaduna. Touted as a possible successor to Babangida, his appointment was an Abacha ploy to remove Shagaya from influencing events in Nigeria before retiring him from the army upon becoming head of state in November 1993.[9]

Shagaya had barely served three months in Liberia before his removal. During his brief tenure, he strongly advocated disarmament before installation of a new interim government. He had also tried to hasten the arrival of East African peacekeepers under the OAU to assuage NPFL fears about disarming to West African troops. Like former Field Commander General Rufus Kupolati, Shagaya believed that Charles Taylor held the key to any solution and so was conciliatory toward the NPFL leader. Shagaya was replaced in November 1993 by General John Mark Inienger. Inienger himself was considered a Babangida loyalist before he fell out of favor after questioning Babangida's annulment of the presidential election in June 1993 at a senior officers meeting in Abuja. He was reportedly saved from being sacked as commander of the 2d Mechanized Division in Ibadan only by Abacha's timely intervention.[10] Upon assuming power on 18 November 1993, Abacha replaced Shagaya with Inienger as ECOMOG field commander.

Nigeria's chief of army staff, General Chris Alli, visited Monrovia in January 1994. Alli reiterated the Abacha regime's strong commitment to Liberia. But despite his words of support, there was a subtle but discernable change in Nigeria's approach. This was most illustrated by the Nigerian foreign minister, Babagana Kingibe, who noted, "It is time for quiet diplomacy devoid of posturing or gimmickry."[11] The new approach was less confrontational and tried to deemphasize the obvious personal animosity that had existed between Ibrahim Babangida and Charles Taylor. Under General Abacha, Nigeria's military and civilian policymakers started to talk seriously about the financial burden of ECOMOG; outright withdrawal was touted as a serious option. Many policymakers also favored conciliation with Charles Taylor, whose representatives were becoming regular visitors to Abuja.[12]

Nigeria's impatience with the lack of progress in Liberia was becoming obvious. On 23 February 1994, Abacha complained to the visiting Ghanaian envoy and former ECOMOG force commander, General Arnold Quainoo, that the Liberian factions were unnecessarily prolonging the conflict. During the OAU summit in Tunis on 13 June, Abacha also complained to UN Secretary-General Boutros Boutros-Ghali about the heavy financial burden that Nigeria was forced to bear. As Boutros-Ghali noted, "Nigeria specifically said that it would have to withdraw its contingents unless a solution could be found to the problem."[13]

On 24 May 1994, Nigeria announced it would not increase its troops in Liberia and asked that Nigerian soldiers be replaced by other contingents. Growing Nigerian irritation was also evident in the statement of Nigeria's UN ambassador, Ibrahim Gambari, who told a Radio Nigeria reporter in November 1994 that it was grossly unfair that only ECOMOG's new East African contingents benefited logistically from the UN Trust Fund for Liberia. Gambari called for more support for the West African peacekeepers who had endured four difficult years in Liberia. He warned that Abuja might review its participation in ECOMOG if such support was not forthcoming.

To prove these threats were not empty boasts, Abacha ordered a reduction of Nigerian troops in Liberia in November 1994, citing the continued intransigence of the warring factions as the main reason. Nigerian troops were reduced from 10,000 to 6,000, and some heavy equipment and artillery were withdrawn. For good measure, Abacha warned that the attitude of the factions "may yet force Nigeria to reconsider her present position in that country which may compel us to take a more drastic position."[14] However, Abuja retained the option of sending back its troops if the situation improved, and with 6,000 soldiers Nigeria still had a substantial presence— by far the largest ECOMOG contingent in Liberia.

A key factor in Nigeria's growing impatience was Abacha's domestic difficulties. He had to face a crippling prodemocracy oil strike that lasted for nine weeks between July and September 1994. In a further effort to consolidate his grip on the military, Abacha sacked Alli and the naval chief, Commodore Allison Madueke, after both reportedly supported the release from jail of the presumed winner of the 1993 presidential election, Moshood Abiola, at a Supreme Military Council meeting in August 1994.[15] In October, some air force officers were also sacked, and three divisional commanders were redeployed as Abacha swiftly moved to establish his authority.

At the end of 1994, respected Nigerian economist Pius Okigbo released a government-commissioned report revealing that $12.5 billion of Nigeria's oil revenues between 1988 and 1994 could not be accounted for. This revenue included Gulf War profits, some of which the Babangida regime claimed had been used to maintain Nigerian troops in Liberia. In the eyes of many Nigerians, this revelation further tainted a mission already considered to be a profligate foreign adventure.

We now turn to Liberia and the domestic, subregional, and external factors that hampered ECOMOG's peacekeeping efforts.

Of Warlords, Wealth, and War Crimes

After the signing of the Cotonou agreement in July 1993, 60,000 Liberian refugees returned to Monrovia and Bong County from neighboring Côte d'Ivoire, Guinea, and Sierra Leone. Their hopes for peace, however, turned out to be mistaken, for fighting raged throughout Liberia. In October 1993, the Liberia Peace Council was fighting the NPFL in Sinoe and Rivercess Counties in a struggle for control of southeastern Liberia. In November and December 1993, the LDF had captured several towns in northern Lofa County from ULIMO. In the space of one month, two new armed factions had appeared at opposite ends of the country and were wreaking havoc on the sickly body politic. These factions had much to lose and nothing to gain from a successful implementation of Cotonou. Having been excluded from negotiations, they wanted the accord to fail.

The LPC was led by George Boley, who had served as chairman of ULIMO's political affairs committee. The faction described itself as a nonethnic, nonreligious, and nonpartisan movement, but it consisted largely of Krahn refugees from Côte d'Ivoire as well as many Krahn members of Doe's AFL. Nigeria was widely reported to have supported the LPC in its early years.

The LDF, largely Loma citizens, was created in July 1993 to protect the Loma in Lofa County from Mandingo ULIMO fighters, who were accused of looting and burning villages and raping women.[16] The LDF was led by Francois Massaquoi, an economist trained at New York University and self-styled farmer. As Massaquoi noted, "There will never be peace between the Mandingos and the Lomas."[17] Some of the LDF's military equipment had been obtained from the NPFL and Loma soldiers from ECOMOG's Guinean contingent.[18] By early 1994, ULIMO had split into two factions, with the Mandingo-based ULIMO-K controlled by Alhaji Kromah and the Krahn-dominated ULIMO-J controlled by Roosevelt Johnson.

An important aspect of the armed clashes was that battles were fought in areas for control over resources. Alhaji Kromah restored the Mandingo trading links with Sierra Leone, from which his ethnic group had been excluded by the NPFL and RUF in March 1991. Charles Taylor was equally keen to regain control of western Liberia from ULIMO because he had been cut off from his illicit diamond trade in Sierra Leone.[19] Taylor was earning an estimated $200–250 million per year from sales of timber, iron ore, gold, diamonds, and rubber.[20] Roosevelt Johnson was involved in diamond-mining in Bomi County.[21] George Boley captured the Liberian Agriculture Company's rubber plantation near ECOMOG-held Buchanan and enriched himself from these exports.[22]

Even more pernicious were the human rights violations that every faction in Liberia's brutal civil war committed. The most gruesome occurred in the Carter camp near Harbel, where 600 refugees were massacred on 5 June 1993. Although ECOMOG and the IGNU initially blamed the massacre on the NPFL, a UN commission of inquiry placed the blame on members of the AFL in its 10 September 1993 report.[23] There were also reports of ethnic retribution carried out against civilians by the Krahn and Mandingo fighters of the two ULIMO wings in Tubmanburg. LPC fighters were accused of murder, rape, and torture during battles to gain control of the southeast from the NPFL.[24] With this difficult environment, it was clear that the efforts by ECOMOG, UNOMIL, and the OAU to keep peace would encounter serious difficulties.

Keeping Peace Where There Is None

By 28 January 1994, 773 Tanzanian and 796 Ugandan troops arrived in Liberia to join the expanded ECOMOG. They were part of the OAU's contribution to assist the disarmament process but were placed under ECOMOG command. The expected Zimbabwean contingent did not join ECOMOG due to financial disagreements with the UN. Charles Taylor gave a hint of the difficult times ahead for the peacekeepers when he warned that only the Liberian National Transitional Government had the power to supervise disarmament. This was contrary to the terms of the Cotonou agreement, which had given ECOMOG primary responsibility for disarmament.

The ECOMOG field commander, General Mark Inienger, travelled to Gbarnga with Tanzanian Chief of Army Staff General Kiwelu to discuss the disarmament requirements of the Cotonou agreement with Taylor. At this meeting, the NPFL warlord bluntly told both generals that he would not disarm his men to the newly arrived Tanzanian and Ugandan ECOMOG troops until the LNTG had been installed. He also continued to call for a reduction of ECOMOG troops and heavy weapons. Before disarmament in 1992, Taylor had requested the presence of Senegalese troops to avoid disarming to Nigerian soldiers before attaching similar conditions to their deployment to NPFL areas once they arrived, frustrating their efforts.

Despite this early setback, Inienger remained surprisingly optimistic about the prospects for disarmament. His confidence was palpable as he repeatedly assured the international community that disarmament would succeed even without the Zimbabwean contingent. Concomitant with the installation of the LNTG in Monrovia on 7 March 1994, ECOMOG started deploying its troops to the countryside accompanied by unarmed UN military observers: the Ghanaians and Guineans went to Bomi, Grand Cape Mount, Lofa, Margibi, and Montserrado; the Nigerians to Sinoe, Maryland, Grand Kru, Grand Gedeh, Bassa, and Rivercess; and the Ugandans and Tanzanians to the NPFL heartland of Bong and Nimba Counties. As in 1992, ECOMOG had not received the logistical and maintenance support it continuously requested from the international community before deploying.

Despite these deficiencies, the disarmament process started well. Three encampment and demobilization centers were established on 7 March 1994 for NPFL, AFL, and ULIMO combatants. As fighters from the three factions arrived in the camps, ECOMOG soldiers, observed by UNOMIL military personnel, took and registered their weapons before writing down information on the combatants' name, county, ethnic group, and prewar occupation. UNOMIL civilian staff then issued the demobilized combatants identity cards after a brief interview. The combatants underwent a medical examination before receiving clothes, shoes, food, agricultural tools, and transportation to their home communities. In the first month, 2,200 of the estimated 33,000 combatants had been demobilized. But as fighting erupted again and political disagreements among Liberia's factions hampered the implementation of the Cotonou agreement, the initial flood slowed to a trickle. By 22 August 1994, only 3,612 combatants had been disarmed.

ECOMOG went farther in implementing Cotonou than Yamoussoukro in 1992, when it did not even begin disarmament. But its peacekeepers suffered the same frustrating fate in trying to keep the peace in a volatile situation. ECOMOG started to encounter problems in early April 1994, when a hostile NPFL commander told ECOMOG's chief of staff, General Femi Williams, that his Nigerian troops were not welcome in Konola, forcing them to retreat to Kakata.

At the end of May 1994, nine Ugandan soldiers were abducted by the LPC even as ULIMO and the NPFL held six other ECOMOG soldiers captive. Three hundred Tanzanian peacekeepers confronted by the NPFL surrendered all their equipment and weapons rather than resist.[25] In June 1994, General Inienger announced that sixteen Nigerian soldiers were still being held hostage after an ambush by ULIMO combatants two months earlier. In early August, five Nigerian soldiers were wounded during an ambush near the port city of Buchanan. The optimistic Inienger started complaining about the lack of good faith of Liberia's warlords as he suffered the same frustrating fate that had befallen General Ishaya Bakut in 1992. Inienger increasingly issued warnings that he would resort to the peace-enforcement actions undertaken by Generals Joshua Dogonyaro and Adetunji Olurin, but his threats went unheeded.

At the second ECOWAS Committee of Nine foreign ministers meeting, held on the fringes of the OAU's Tunis summit in June 1994, General Inienger described his soldiers' morale as "very low" and complained about the logistical deficiencies of his peacekeepers. He argued that the UN had a "moral responsibility" to take over the full funding of ECOMOG and called for the appointment of a resident ECOWAS political officer in Monrovia to ease the burden of what he described as "cumbersome" political issues.[26] But the field commander's problems grew only worse.

On 14 September 1994, a convoy of Tanzanian soldiers was ambushed by ULIMO-J fighters while traveling between Konola and Kakata in Margibi County, resulting in the murder of three Tanzanian soldiers, the wounding of seven, and the abduction of four. This incident recalled that of Vahun in May 1992 (see Chapter 5), in which six Senegalese peacekeepers had been killed by NPFL fighters. Tanzanian officials, who were threatening to withdraw troops from Liberia unless the United Nations met their financial obligations, were understandably enraged. Tanzanian military spokesman Brigadier Lucas Likongo angrily remarked, "Our troops did not go to Liberia to fight but to keep peace."[27] ECOMOG was becoming a useful scapegoat for the factions in their attempts to resist disarmament: The LPC accused ECOMOG of assisting the NPFL by blocking its routes; the NPFL accused ECOMOG of facilitating LPC successes; ULIMO-K accused ECOMOG of fighting with ULIMO-J against it in Tubmanburg.

The UN military observers also encountered difficulties with the factions. UNOMIL personnel were harassed and their vehicles and radios were confiscated. On 28 June 1994, six UNOMIL observers were kidnapped in Tubmanburg (they were later released). Three months later, NPFL elements detained and mistreated forty-three UNOMIL observers for nine days before releasing them. At about the same time, NPFL fighters shot at a UN helicopter near Harper. These incidents forced the United Nations to withdraw its observers to Monrovia by October and reduce their numbers from 368 to ninety.

In 1994, both wings of ULIMO struggled for control of western Cape Mount and Bomi Counties. Fighting was particularly fierce in Tubmanburg. In the north, the LDF battled ULIMO-K for control of the Liberian-Guinean border. The fighting displaced hundreds of thousands more and hampered humanitarian relief efforts to Liberia's west and southeast. By the end of 1994, 80 percent of all Liberians had been displaced as a result of the war. All the factions continued to experience command-and-control problems, which made it difficult for warlords to control increasingly autonomous groups; human rights abuses and breaches of the UN-imposed arms embargo continued. By the end of 1994, at least seven main factions vied for supremacy in Liberia: two wings of the NPFL (see Chapter 8), two wings of ULIMO, the AFL, the LDF, and the LPC. The LPC controlled parts of the southeast; the NPFL controlled parts of Nimba, Bong, northern Grand Gedeh, and Margibi Counties; ULIMO-J controlled Grand Cape Mount, Bomi, and Lower Lofa Counties; and ULIMO-K controlled Upper Lofa County.

Liberia was effectively partitioned into fiefdoms controlled by rival warlords. UN Secretary-General Boutros Boutros-Ghali best described the chaotic military situation in Liberia in 1994:

> Overall, the military situation remains confused, with groups aligning and realigning themselves depending on their short-term interests and the breakdown of command and control within the factions. . . . The current fighting in Liberia is small-scale bush fighting. The results are not large military victories, but deaths mostly of civilians, the decimation of entire villages and the breakdown of any semblance of law and order.[28]

Policing the Peacekeepers

Illustrating the increasing yet insufficient international attention Liberia attracted at the time, the UN Security Council established the $5.65 million-per-month United Nations Observer Mission in Liberia in September 1993, dispatching 368 unarmed UN peacekeepers to Liberia by early 1994 under General Daniel Opande, its Kenyan chief military observer. Under the Cotonou agreement, UNOMIL was responsible for monitoring the cantonment, disarmament, and demobilization of Liberian combatants, as well as the UN-imposed arms embargo of 1992 (see Chapter 6). UNOMIL was also mandated to work with ECOMOG, which had primary responsibility for disarming the factions.[29]

The Joint Cease-Fire Monitoring Committee held its first meeting on 13 August 1993 to investigate and resolve cease-fire violations. The committee was chaired by UNOMIL and involved ECOMOG and representatives of all the armed factions. UNOMIL's mandate also obliged it to report on human rights violations and to coordinate humanitarian assistance. ECOMOG would be responsible for ensuring the security of UNOMIL's civilian and unarmed military personnel.[30]

But sharp disagreements soon arose between ECOMOG and UNOMIL. Initial friction was already evident after the arrival of the UN military observers. ECOMOG peacekeepers were heard complaining that the United Nations did not make its vehicles and helicopters available for their use and felt that the better-paid UN staff flaunted their status while leaving most of the difficult tasks to ECOMOG. As UN Special Representative Trevor Gordon-Somers later admitted: "You can imagine how we were looked at by the [ECOMOG] soldiers who were fighting and dying, and I am not sure that we were sufficiently sensitive to this issue. That caused a lot of hostility."[31]

These problems were exacerbated by UN Secretary-General Boutros-Ghali's allegations, in an October 1994 report to the UN Security Council, that ECOMOG had collaborated with anti-NPFL combatants during fighting in Gbarnga in September 1994.[32] ECOMOG felt that these accusations detracted from other praiseworthy activities by its peacekeepers, such as escorting humanitarian relief convoys to the countryside and providing security to displaced persons in Monrovia and Tubmanburg. But its cooperation with anti-NPFL factions, dating back to the beginning of its mission in Liberia, was not in dispute.

There were four other key areas of disagreement between ECOMOG and UNOMIL. First, ECOMOG strictly wanted UNOMIL to observe rather than supervise disarmament. As Herbert Howe noted, "ECOMOG co-operated, grudgingly, at best with UNOMIL. Several UNOMIL officials complained that ECOMOG did not want UNOMIL observing activities relating to arms flows, human rights abuses, and food shipments."[33] Second, ECOMOG officials were irritated by what they regarded as Gordon-Somers's unilateral disarmament negotiations with the parties without proper consultation with ECOMOG staff. The third area of disagreement involved UNOMIL's chief military observer, General Opande, and ECOMOG Field Commander Inienger, who held different views about disarmament strategy. Opande asked that Charles Taylor be given the benefit of the doubt in his offer to disarm his combatants unilaterally and talked of the NPFL's good faith. Inienger and his officers considered this view naive and saw Taylor's offer as an attempt to avoid close scrutiny of his arms and military positions. Finally, ECOMOG criticized UNOMIL for deploying military observers without consulting the West Africans, who were mandated to provide them security.[34]

UNOMIL argued that it had obtained the consent of the factions to deploy and that it could not fulfill its mandate by remaining in Monrovia. It also accused ECOMOG of violating its mandate by not protecting UN personnel and restricting their freedom of movement.[35] Despite these military difficulties, there was some progress on the political front in Liberia during this period.

The LNTG's Difficult Birth

Representatives of the three signatories of the Cotonou agreement—the IGNU, NPFL, and ULIMO—went to Cotonou on 3 November 1993 for three days of talks. There they found the terse ECOWAS chairman, Nicéphore Soglo, issuing them a final warning to resolve their differences and establish the interim government they had committed to at Cotonou in July 1993. Having reached agreement on the members of the Council of State, legislature, elections commission, and supreme court, the meeting broke down after three days of strenuous negotiations over nominees for the four remaining (out of seventeen) cabinet posts in the LNTG: foreign affairs, justice, defense, and finance.

The NPFL and ULIMO entered into a marriage of convenience against the IGNU to secure the four posts for themselves. An irritated Soglo gave the factions a ten-day ultimatum to resolve their differences. Soglo was tiring of playing a thankless role that he clearly did not relish. With obvious impatience, which he had demonstrated throughout his two-year stint as ECOWAS chairman, he told the factions: "This time we should not waste time on the path to peace because time is not money but rather blood, suffering and the hope of an entire youth. Today, you must leave Cotonou for good with an established government."[36]

In early December 1993, the parties met again in Monrovia's Hotel Africa for talks that degenerated into heated exchanges and personal attacks. The NPFL objected to the presence of ECOWAS, the United Nations, and the OAU, whose mediators it termed "outsiders." During the acrimonious meeting, ECOMOG Chief of Staff General Williams strongly advocated the disarming of armed factions before the transitional government could be installed.[37] Though this was in strict accordance with the terms of Cotonou, it angered the NPFL and ULIMO. The faction leaders then launched a negative propaganda war against ECOMOG and some opposed the arrival of East African peacekeepers to assist ECOMOG.[38]

On 15 February 1994, the three signatories of Cotonou signed the UN-sponsored Monrovia agreement, pledging them to implement the Cotonou agreement of July 1993. This Monrovia agreement was also referred to as the "Triple 7 agreement," in which three events were meant to occur simultaneously on 7 March 1994: the installation of the LNTG, disarmament, and the deployment of ECOMOG and UNOMIL peacekeepers to all areas of Liberia.

IGNU nominee David Kpomakpor, a law professor, was the surprise choice for chairman of the five-member Council of State, which was installed in Monrovia on 7 March and also included Philip Banks (IGNU), Isaac Musa (NPFL), Mohammed Sherif (ULIMO), and Dexter Tayhor (ULIMO). After its installation, members of the LNTG visited Gbarnga, Buchanan, and Tubmanburg, urging peace and reconciliation. But the LNTG was not only unable to extend its authority to any part of Liberia outside Monrovia, it was financially dependent on contributions from foreign donors as well as the $12–18 million it earned annually from Liberia's issuance of flags of convenience to foreign vessels. Most export resources were still controlled by warlords.

The five members of the Council of State disagreed over appointments to public corporations and autonomous agencies as the factions struggled to share out the wares of Liberia's giant jumble sale. The NPFL forbade its LNTG members from taking up their seats until the four contended ministry posts had been resolved. That problem was finally overcome on 19 April, with the NPFL being granted the foreign affairs and justice portfolios, ULIMO gaining finance, and the IGNU defense. The NPFL took up its seats three days later.

ECOWAS

The instability of the West African subregion was underscored by the 22 July 1994 coup in Gambia, an ECOMOG member state. The young Lieutenant Yaya Jammeh removed Dawda Jawara from power. With the ousting of Jawara, the only ECOMOG founding fathers left in power were Ghana's Jerry Rawlings and Guinea's Lansana Conté. The new Gambian leader had himself served with ECOMOG in Liberia. During the coup, Jammeh complained about the neglect of Gambian troops in Liberia, citing it as one of his key grievances against the Jawara administration. The new military junta pledged to maintain troops in Liberia, and Jammeh attended the ECOWAS summit in Abuja two weeks after the coup to pledge continued support for ECOMOG.

Sierra Leone's interest in resolving the Liberian war was also demonstrated when its military leader, Captain Valentine Strasser, attempted to broker a truce between ULIMO leaders Alhaji Kromah and Roosevelt Johnson in Freetown on 1 April 1994. Kromah went to Freetown again in October 1994 to deny reports of his movement's support for RUF rebels in Sierra Leone. Sierra Leone had 700 troops in Liberia in 1994 and continued to rely on Nigerian, Guinean, and Ghanaian troops for additional internal security.

On 7 August 1994, ECOMOG reported it had apprehended twelve trucks of arms and ammunition on the Liberian-Ivorian border that it said were bound for the NPFL base in Gbarnga. Abidjan and Ouagadougou predictably denied any involvement. Despite claims that he had stopped providing military assistance to Taylor since the end of 1993, Blaise Compaoré was still providing Taylor with arms and bodyguards and was said to be benefiting from Taylor's trade in diamonds, gold, and timber.[39] In a pointed criticism of this policy, Mohammed Chambas, Ghana's deputy foreign minister, complained that "one cannot be part of the peace process if at the same time one is doing things that enable one faction or the other to carry on the war."[40]

Despite such criticism—which seemed accurate at least in the case of Burkina Faso—Côte d'Ivoire seemed increasingly more interested in domestic politics than in fueling conflict in Liberia. Still suffering from the destabilizing effects of the Liberian war, Abidjan continued to distance itself from the NPFL and edged closer to supporting ECOMOG. Addressing the UN General Assembly in October 1993, Ivorian Foreign Minister Amara Essy criticized the NPFL for attacking refugee camps across the Ivorian border and called for more international assistance for ECOWAS efforts in Liberia. Some Ivorian state officials were reportedly profiting from NPFL operations between Buchanan and Ivorian border towns, but it was unlikely that these activities were officially sanctioned.[41]

The death of Ivorian leader Félix Houphoüet-Boigny on 7 December 1993 marked the end of a remarkable era in African politics. Houphoüet had ruled his country since 1960 and was an early NPFL supporter. Regional leaders waited expectantly to see whether his successor would effect any dramatic shift in Abidjan's Liberia policy. The new head of state, Henri Konan Bédié, tried to consolidate his position by changing electoral rules to exclude his rival, Alassane Ouattara, from participation in forthcoming presidential elections. Bédié also had to heal the rift that followed the split of his Parti Démocratique de Côte d'Ivoire.[42] The continuing subregional instability of the Liberian civil war was evidenced by the fact that between September and October 1994, 100,000 Liberian refugees flooded into Côte d'Ivoire and 60,000 into Guinea, giving both countries a continuing incentive to support ECOMOG efforts to resolve the war.

We conclude this chapter by examining U.S. policy in Liberia, its bilateral relations with Nigeria, and the newly acquired prominence of Ghana in peacemaking efforts.

The United States

Washington's continued reluctance to take a high-profile role in Liberia was reflected in a statement by U.S. Secretary of State Warren Christopher, who noted: "Liberia's future will be determined in Monrovia, not in Washington. Only Liberians can create a real and lasting peace, heal the deep scars in Liberian society, and determine who will lead them in the future."[43] Public outcry following the deaths of eighteen U.S. soldiers in Somalia in October 1993 forced Washington to withdraw its peacekeepers from the Horn of Africa. It became clear that U.S. involvement in African conflicts would be kept to the absolute minimum.

Washington contributed $19.8 million to the UN Liberia Trust Fund on 13 October 1993 and another $30 million in December 1993. But most of these funds were set aside specifically to meet the needs of the East African contingents that were to join the expanded ECOMOG, with Uganda and Tanzania receiving eleven trucks, fourteen Humvee vehicles, tents, and radio equipment. Only $2.6 million was provided to the other ECOMOG contingents for medical, transportation, communications, and fuel needs.[44]

ECOMOG officials were upset by this decision. Washington also insisted on retaining a veto over the disbursement of the UN fund. UN Secretary-General Boutros Boutros-Ghali wrote to Warren Christopher on 29 June 1994 requesting greater financial support for ECOMOG. Christopher's reply merely outlined what he described as the "substantial" U.S. contributions to Liberia and urged other countries to contribute more.

U.S. policymakers were becoming increasingly impatient with the continuing political impasse in Liberia. In January 1994, Washington announced that its continued support of the Cotonou agreement would depend on satisfactory progress on disarmament and the seating of the LNTG. Jeffrey Millington, acting director for West Africa at the U.S. State Department, threatened to withdraw U.S. support for the ECOWAS peace plan if an agreement was not reached by 15 February 1994. Millington claimed that the State Department was receiving daily calls from members of Congress asking when Washington was going to end its involvement in Liberia. This reflected the increasingly isolationist mood in the United States after the Somalia debacle.

U.S. diplomats in Liberia, led by the U.S. chargé d'affaires, William Twadell, were pushing for the seating of the LNTG before disarmament on the grounds that it would help build confidence for disarmament. U.S. Assistant Secretary of State for African Affairs George Moose visited Liberia for three days at the end of February 1994 to pressure the factions to cooperate with ECOMOG while uttering the usual platitudes about support for the subregional effort. But even after the installation of the LNTG in March 1994, Washington insisted that it could recognize a government only if it were in effective control of the whole of Liberia.

The prospects of U.S. support for ECOMOG were further diminished by the deterioration in U.S.-Nigeria relations. The Africa director of the U.S. National Security Council, Donald Steinberg, threatened to impose oil sanctions on Nigeria and to freeze illegally acquired Nigerian assets in the United States as a way to pressure General Abacha's military junta to restore the democratic process in Nigeria. But Abuja had its own methods for resisting such pressure. U.S. oil companies in Nigeria opposed oil sanctions, and Nigerian Foreign Minister Babagana Kingibe threatened strong retaliation against the substantial U.S. interests in Nigeria, which included $4 billion in oil investments.

Ghana

Stressing the countless sacrifices that its troops had already made in Liberia, the Ghanaian foreign ministry announced on 8 February 1994 that it would withdraw Ghana's 900 peacekeepers from ECOMOG within thirty days if solid progress was not made toward peace. Foreign Minister Obed Asamoah repeated this threat at the OAU summit in Tunis in June 1994, citing the escalating costs of the mission as the main reason. Ghanaian President Jerry Rawlings's first announcement upon assuming the ECOWAS chairmanship at its August 1994 Abuja summit was a warning that he would withdraw all Ghanaian troops from Liberia if the situation did not improve by the end of the year. Rawlings complained that his parliament did not support the presence of Ghanaian troops in Liberia and that members of parliament were advocating a reconsideration of Liberia policy. He also referred to pressure from domestic public opinion, which increasingly doubted the wisdom of keeping troops in Liberia.

Rawlings tempered his threat with a recognition that ECOMOG could not withdraw from Liberia unless it was prepared to abandon its original goal for embarking on the mission: to prevent a descent into anarchy that could engulf the entire subregion. The Ghanaian president saw the resolution of the Liberian conflict as the key to West African integration, but he also reminded Liberia's armed factions that ECOMOG states were sacrificing resources on the destructive war in Liberia that were better spent on domestic education and health programs.

Both Ghana and Nigeria were threatening to withdraw from Liberia in 1994. The strongest Liberian faction, the NPFL, desired such a withdrawal so it might take advantage of the resulting chaos. The NPFL had, after all, gone to war with ECOMOG in 1990 and 1992 in a bid to defeat the peacekeepers militarily, and throughout the war Charles Taylor had waged a propaganda campaign calling for ECOMOG's withdrawal. These threats were therefore unlikely to elicit good behavior from the factions, because some calculated that a withdrawal of peacekeepers would actually strengthen their positions.

Just as Côte d'Ivoire had been given a prominent peacemaking role at Yamoussoukro in 1991 in order to ensure its commitment to the Liberian peace process, Ghana was given the lead role in peacemaking in 1994, in part to maintain its commitment to ECOMOG. Ghanaians, like Nigerians, have always been proud of their record in international peacekeeping. By

May 1994, Ghana had more than 1,000 peacekeepers working on UN missions in the Balkans, Kuwait, Lebanon, Rwanda, and Western Sahara and could point to a history stretching back to the Congo in 1960. An important part of the historic rivalry between Abuja and Accra has been played on the field of international peacekeeping. Rawlings's appointment as ECOWAS chairman helped ensure Ghana's continued commitment to ECOMOG. It generated more interest in ECOMOG among a Ghanaian public that still looked back nostalgically to the activist days of Kwame Nkrumah, when Accra had briefly been the center of pan-Africanist diplomacy.

* * *

The second phase of ECOMOG's Liberia intervention—from January 1993 to August 1994—revealed how continuing difficulties at the domestic, subregional, and external levels continued to hamper the achievement of a Pax Nigeriana in Liberia. Like the IGNU interim government, the LNTG lacked the ability to enforce anything beyond Monrovia. Even as representatives of factions sat together on the LNTG in Monrovia, their fighters continued to battle one another for control of the countryside. ULIMO split into two factions while the LPC and LDF emerged as independent factions, affecting the smooth functioning of the LNTG. Such instability created tremendous problems for ECOWAS peacemakers and ECOMOG peacekeepers. The appearance of new factions, however, helped facilitate a compromise with Taylor at Cotonou: he now had ECOMOG and three Liberian factions lined up against him, and his control of Liberian territory had shrunk from 90 percent to 50 percent.

This period demonstrated again that other subregional states had a more direct interest than Nigeria in resolving the conflict. With RUF rebels fighting the Freetown regime, Nigerian, Ghanaian, and Guinean troops provided the Sierra Leonean government with additional internal security. Sierra Leone was even more committed to supporting ECOMOG, for its defence policy was closely tied to finding allies who opposed the NPFL-RUF alliance. Military attacks on Ivorian border towns from Liberia led to a continuing shift in Côte d'Ivoire's Liberia policy as it became concerned about its own national security. Fighting forced 100,000 Liberian refugees into Côte d'Ivoire, 60,000 more into Guinea; the LDF and ULIMO-K were fighting for control over Liberia's border with Guinea. All three countries now had a direct interest in a successful resolution of the conflict. Significantly, the main NPFL military and political supporter, Burkina Faso, had no common border with Liberia and was therefore immune to the spillover effects of the war. Senegal, which withdrew its troops from ECOMOG in 1993, also shared no border with Liberia.

The Cotonou agreement of July 1993 attempted to correct the flaws in the Yamoussoukro agreement of 1991 by including ULIMO in the negotiations.

But it committed the same error by excluding two new factions, the LPC and LDF, which eventually had to be included in the peace process in December 1994 (see Chapter 8). ULIMO's success in reaching the negotiating table was a signal to the LPC and LDF that territorial control translated into political power. It was in the interest of the LPC and LDF that Cotonou fail in 1993, just as ULIMO wanted Yamoussoukro to fail in 1991. Cotonou reflected the euphoric planning of the peace agreements; it called for the completion of disarmament and elections in seven months. Like previous agreements, it relied too heavily on the willingness of the warlords to disarm.

The Cotonou agreement failed to resolve the central dilemma that affected all the peace conferences: IGNU insisted on total disarmament prior to the installation of the new interim government while the armed factions (i.e., the NPFL and ULIMO) insisted that the new interim government oversee disarmament. Of the three parties, the IGNU was the only one that lacked a military wing, and thus its interest was to level the playing field before introducing competitive politics. All the factions continued to derive economic benefits from territories under their control, making the resolution of the conflict difficult.

Differences between Ghana and Nigeria continued during this period, with Ghana criticizing ECOMOG's enforcement actions against the NPFL. Ghana's threats to withdraw troops from Liberia contributed to the appointment of Jerry Rawlings as ECOWAS chairman in 1994, giving Accra a greater stake in the resolution of the conflict for reasons of prestige. ECOMOG's dominant contributor, Nigeria, under the Abacha regime was less confrontational toward the NPFL compared to the Babangida regime. Abacha faced more domestic problems and opposition to his rule compared to his predecessor. Babangida's departure from office in August 1993 depersonalized the conflict with Charles Taylor, as Abacha had no personal connection to the late Liberian autocrat Samuel Doe. Under Abacha, NPFL representatives visited Abuja more frequently, and there was more public discussion among senior Nigerian officials about the mounting costs of the ECOMOG intervention.

The widespread fighting in Liberia and ECOMOG's own logistical inadequacies forced the peacekeepers to withdraw from the countryside. The dangers of deploying troops without firm guarantees of cooperation from the factions and without protective logistical support led to similar results as in 1992: ECOMOG peacekeepers were sometimes held hostage, and three Tanzanian peacekeepers were killed. The lack of sustained international attention and support also thwarted ECOMOG efforts in Liberia. The United Nations deployed peacekeepers to monitor ECOMOG's disarmament of the factions to lend more international legitimacy and neutrality to the intervention. But the number of its peacekeepers, already grossly insufficient, was drastically reduced from 368 to ninety following continued fighting.

Friction between ECOMOG and UNOMIL complicated mediation and peacekeeping efforts. UN Special Representative for Liberia Trevor Gordon-Somers played an instrumental role in negotiating the Cotonou agreement. He tried to present himself as a more neutral negotiator than ECOWAS, many of whose members were supporting various Liberian factions. But the United Nations lacked military muscle on the ground to back up its diplomacy.

The OAU envoy, Reverend Canaan Banana, provided diplomatic legitimacy to ECOMOG efforts in Liberia. Although 1,569 Tanzanian and Ugandan peacekeepers were sent to Liberia under OAU auspices in January 1994, they were paid by the United Nations and were not controlled by the OAU. The East African peacekeepers suffered the same fate as the Senegalese contingent in 1992, suggesting that the Liberian warlords were not as interested in disarmament as in pursuing political power through military means while exploiting resources for economic gain.

Finally, U.S. policy in Liberia continued to fluctuate between praise and criticism for ECOMOG. Washington continued to channel the bulk of its resources toward humanitarian rather than peacekeeping efforts. The distrust of ECOMOG's neutrality continued to be a factor in this policy. U.S. bilateral relations with Nigeria deteriorated shortly after the annulment of elections by the Nigerian military in June 1993, virtually killing any prospect for meaningful logistical support.

Having assessed events that hampered ECOMOG's efforts between August 1993 to August 1994, in Part 3 we will examine the final three years of the Liberian conflict. We will describe ECOMOG's more conciliatory approach toward the warlords and analyze the changes in policy among key states that finally led to the (temporary) end of the civil war in Liberia in 1997.

Notes

1. Quoted in *West Africa,* no. 3965 (20–26 September 1993): 1672.
2. Ibid.
3. *Economist Intelligence Unit,* Country Report, "Liberia," no. 1 (1994): 39.
4. *Economist Intelligence Unit,* Country Report, "Liberia," no. 4 (1993): 29.
5. Personal interview with Edouard Benjamin at the ECOWAS Secretariat, Lagos, December 1995.
6. See Ifeanyi Ezieugo, *Abacha: Another Evil Genius?* (Lagos: El-Rophekah International, 1998); and Chuks Iloegbunam, "A Stubborn Dictator," *The Guardian* (London) (9 June 1998): 16.
7. *Newswatch* 13 no. 19 (6 May 1991): 34.
8. *Jeune Afrique,* no. 1580 (10–16 April 1991): 27.
9. *Africa Confidential* 33, no. 4 (21 February 1992): 3.
10. *Africa Confidential* 34, no. 15 (30 July 1993): 7.
11. Quoted in *West Africa,* no. 4024 (14–20 November 1994): 1953.
12. Personal interview at the Nigerian Ministry of Foreign Affairs, Abuja, December 1996.

13. Fifth Progress Report of the Secretary-General on the United Nations Observer Mission in Liberia, S/1994/260 (24 June 1994), p. 4.

14. Quoted in *West Africa,* no. 4028 (18–24 December 1994): 2127.

15. *Africa Confidential* 35, no. 17 (26 August 1994): 8.

16. Personal interview with Francois Massaquoi, LDF leader, Monrovia, 16 July 1999.

17. Ibid.

18. Ibid.

19. See William Reno, "The Business of War in Liberia," *Current History* 95, no. 601 (May 1996): 211–215.

20. William Reno, *Warlord Politics and African States* (Boulder and London: Lynne Rienner, 1998), p. 99.

21. Ibid., p. 104.

22. Ibid., p. 105.

23. For the full report, see Marc Weller (ed.), *Regional Peacekeeping and International Enforcement: The Liberian Crisis* (Cambridge, UK: Cambridge University Press, 1994), pp. 382–394.

24. Cited in "U.S. Policy in Liberia," Hearing Before the Subcommittee on Africa of the Committee on Foreign Affairs, House of Representatives, 18 May 1994 (Washington, D.C.: U.S. Government Printing Office, 1995), pp. 64–65.

25. Herbert Howe, "Lessons of Liberia: ECOMOG and Regional Peacekeeping," *International Security* 21, no. 3 (Winter 1996/1997): 69.

26. "Final Report," Second Meeting of Ministers of Foreign Affairs of the Committee of Nine on Liberia. Tunis, ECW/MINFA/CTTE9/II/3, 10 June 1994, pp. 6–9.

27. Quoted in *West Africa,* no. 4018 (3–9 October 1994): 1717.

28. Seventh Progress Report of the Secretary-General on the United Nations Mission in Liberia, S/1994/1167, 14 October 1994, pp. 6–7.

29. See Margaret Carey, "Peacekeeping in Africa: Recent Evolution and Prospects," in Oliver Furley and Roy May (eds.), *Peacekeeping in Africa* (Aldershot, UK, and Vermont: Ashgate, 1998), pp. 23–25.

30. See Report of the Secretary-General on Liberia, S/26422, 9 September 1993.

31. Personal interview with Trevor Gordon-Somers, UNDP, New York, May 1997.

32. See Seventh Progress Report of the Secretary-General on Liberia.

33. Howe, "Lessons of Liberia," p. 163.

34. See Clement Adibe, "The Liberian Conflict and the ECOWAS-UN partnership," *Third World Quarterly* 18, no. 3 (1997); "Problematic Peacekeeping," *Africa Confidential* 35, no. 5 (4 March 1994): 2–3; Binaifir Nowrojee, "Joining Forces: UN and Regional Peacekeeping, Lessons from Liberia," *Harvard Human Rights Journal* 18 (Spring 1995); Funmi Olonisakin, "UN Co-operation with Regional Organizations in Peacekeeping: The Experience of ECOMOG and UNOMIL in Liberia," *International Peacekeeping* 3, no. 3 (Autumn 1996); and United Nations, *The United Nations and the Situation in Liberia,* revision 1 (New York: Department of Public Information, February 1997).

35. Personal interview with Trevor Gordon-Somers.

36. Quoted in *West Africa,* no. 3974 (22–28 November 1993): 2122.

37. *West Africa,* no. 3979, 27 December 1993–9 January 1994): 2350.

38. General John Shagaya, The ECOMOG Experience: September–December 1993, in "Militaries, Democracies, and Security in Sub-Saharan Africa." Papers presented at a conference in Abuja, Nigeria, 1–4 December 1997, p. 111.

39. Personal interview with Ambassador William Twadell, U.S. Chargé d'Affaires to Liberia, 1992–1995, U.S. State Department, Washington, D.C., June 1997.

40. "We Are Making Headway" (interview with Dr. Mohammed Chambas), *West Africa*, no. 4028 (12–18 December 1994): 2116.

41. See William Reno, "Re-invention of an African Patrimonial State: Charles Taylor's Liberia," *Third World Quarterly* 16, no. 1 (1995): 109–120.

42. See Robert Mundt, "Côte d'Ivoire: Continuity and Change in a Semi-Democracy," in John Clark and David Gardinier (eds.), *Political Reform in Francophone Africa* (Boulder and Oxford: Westview, 1997), p. 194.

43. Warren Christopher, "A New Relationship," *Africa Report* 38, no. 4 (July/August 1993): 39.

44. "U.S. Policy in Liberia," Hearing Before the Subcommittee on Africa of the Committee on Foreign Affairs, House of Representatives, 18 May 1994 (Washington, D.C.: U.S. Government Printing Office, 1995), p. 103.

part **3**

A Banquet for the Warlords, September 1994–July 1997

chapter 8

The Pied Piper of Accra,
September 1994–August 1995

We cannot help being struck by the fact that the international community is
willing to spend $5 million a day on UN peacekeeping in Bosnia-Herzegovina
. . . but when we have asked for a sum that represents 10 to 15 days of that bill
to help those of us in Africa making every possible effort to assist ourselves
with our meagre resources, there is deafening silence.
—Jerry Rawlings, president of Ghana

In this chapter we examine the complex negotiations among Liberia's various parties, involving three peace conferences—at Akosombo, Accra, and
Abuja—that led to the direct and unprecedented inclusion of the warlords
in the executive Council of State in a triumph of Ghanaian diplomacy. As
we have consistently argued throughout this study, the lack of consensus at
all three levels of analysis (domestic, subregional, and external) hampered
efforts to resolve the conflict. The emerging consensus at the domestic and
subregional levels suggested, however, that prospects for ending the war
were improving. The warlords joined the Council of State, and Ghana
played an important role in encouraging the rapprochement between Nigeria and Charles Taylor.

We argue that the key to resolving the Liberian civil war was the convergence of policies between Nigeria and the NPFL, on the one hand, and
between Nigeria and Ghana on the other. Nigeria was the dominant contingent within ECOMOG. Having spent five frustrating years opposing Taylor's ambitions, Nigeria finally accepted Ghana's idea that only the direct
inclusion of the warlords in an interim government could bring peace to
Liberia. The Akosombo agreement was the first one to allow the warlords
to serve on the Council of State without being disqualified from contesting
elections. As personal relations were an important factor that perpetuated

Liberia's civil war, we will demonstrate how they were also important to re-solving the war. The relationship between General Abacha and Charles Tay-lor, and that between Abacha and Rawlings, were crucial to the August 1995 Abuja agreement.

The negotiations between Liberia's warring factions and political and civic groups reflected the difficulties of achieving a Pax Nigeriana at the domestic level. Political and civic groups insisted on disarmament and op-posed the direct inclusion of the warlords in the interim government. These groups lacked military muscle and relied on ECOWAS mediators to curtail the ambitions of the faction leaders. They attempted to exploit the rivalry between Nigeria and Ghana to their own advantage. For their part, the war-lords insisted on exchanging disarmament for political power and attempted to use Ghana against Nigeria to promote their own interests. The NPFL split into two factions while Liberia's smaller factions formed a loose anti-NPFL alliance to promote their military and diplomatic goals. This un-wieldy alliance successfully won a place at the negotiating table by captur-ing territory largely from the NPFL. However, it lacked the cohesion to champion a common political agenda and further complicated ECOWAS peacemaking tasks.

External support for efforts to resolve the conflict remained weak. The United Nations increased its role in mediation efforts in a bid to build con-sensus in a divided subregion. But the small, unarmed UN contingent lacked the leverage to enforce its will on the warlords. Tension continued between UNOMIL and ECOMOG as the West Africans complained about the lack of logistical and financial support from the United Nations as well as the lack of diplomatic consultation. But the United Nations did provide important humanitarian relief, something the subregion could not provide. The United States could not resolve the tension between supporting ECOWAS peace efforts in Liberia without directly supporting its largest contributor of troops, Nigeria. Washington's bilateral relations with Abuja continued to af-fect its multilateral support for ECOMOG.

The Akosombo Agreement

Barely a month after becoming ECOWAS chairman in August 1994, Ghanaian President Jerry Rawlings summoned Liberia's factions to Ako-sombo, Ghana, a small town on the Volta River. Only the NPFL's Charles Taylor, ULIMO-K's Alhaji Kromah, and AFL Chief of Staff Hezekiah Bowen attended the negotiations (7–12 September). The UN special representative for Liberia, Trevor Gordon-Somers, was also present. Leaders from the other factions refused to attend, arguing that the initiative should be led by the United Nations rather than ECOWAS.[1]

The Akosombo agreement created a new five-member Council of State with a rotating chairman; the three faction leaders would personally sit on the council along with one representative jointly nominated by Taylor and Kromah. The remaining seat would go to a nominee from the ongoing Liberian National Conference of political and civic groups. The agreement also gave joint responsibility for disarmament, monitoring of borders, and arms searches to ECOMOG and a reconstituted Liberian National Transitional Government, which would now be dominated by the warlords. Bowen later complained that he had been misled by Taylor and Kromah into believing that he would become chairman of the Council of State, and there were unconfirmed rumors that Taylor had paid Bowen $65,000 to sign off on the deal.[2]

Akosombo granted the LNTG the right "to use the necessary force available to compel compliance . . . in collaboration with ECOMOG." Akosombo amended the Cotonou agreement of 1993 by making council decisions enforceable by a simple majority rather than the previous unanimity requirement, thought to have paralyzed the David Kpomakpor–led council inaugurated in March 1994. The agreement further broadened the Transitional Legislative Assembly from thirty-five to forty-nine members and scheduled national elections for October 1995.

Akosombo was clearly a warlords agreement. It was a blatant attempt to appease the faction leaders by asking them to correct grievances surrounding earlier agreements. In a sense, warlords were being invited to feast at a sumptuous banquet: having plundered Liberia's crown jewels during the war, the warlords were now invited to help themselves to the rest of the national treasure. Charles Taylor, who had struck up a rapport with Rawlings since the start of the war, had long argued that the leaders of the warring factions should be directly represented on the Council of State and that the LNTG be allowed to supervise disarmament. Akosombo fulfilled both wishes. Taylor exclaimed shortly after the agreement, "When the three of us [Taylor, Kromah, and Bowen] say there will be no more war in Liberia, there will be no more war."[3]

But Akosombo had little prospect for success. At the time the agreement was signed, fighting was raging throughout Liberia, and two of its three signatories had been expelled from their headquarters by rival factions—Taylor from Gbarnga, Kromah from Tubmanburg. The warlords not surprisingly insisted on a clause in the Akosombo agreement that no new factions be recognized; ECOMOG, in fact, would disarm any such factions. A military coup was attempted in Monrovia just three days after the signing of Akosombo (see discussion below).

It soon became clear that Akosombo had accorded its signatories a political role that was far from commensurate with their military strength. The fact that the LPC and LDF were excluded from the agreement, despite their control over parts of southeastern and northern Liberia, meant that Akosombo bore no resemblance to military and political realities. Just as Yamoussoukro had unraveled in 1992 with the exclusion of ULIMO, so would Akosombo unravel in 1994. Like other Liberian peace agreements, Akosombo was hastily drafted, riddled with ambiguous loopholes, and open to tendentious interpretation by opportunistic faction leaders. Asking the warlords to help disarm their own factions was like asking an arsonist to help douse a fire.

The Liberian National Conference, which was meeting at the time in Monrovia, attacked Akosombo's midwives for replacing the LNTG with a government of warlords after ECOMOG had struggled for four years to prevent that very outcome. The conference questioned the participation of Bowen and the classification of the AFL, which the LNTG had been trying to convert into a national army, as a warring faction. Krahn political leaders like Roosevelt Johnson and George Boley opposed Akosombo because it accorded their rival, Hezekiah Bowen, political preeminence. Delegate after delegate at the Liberian National Conference accused UN Special Representative Gordon-Somers of perfidy and called for his immediate replacement. As Gordon-Somers later recognized, "They would have cut my throat if they could have done so."[4] Rawlings and Gordon-Somers were accused of appeasement, of brandishing an agreement that was as worthless as the paper it was written on. Delegations were sent to ECOWAS capitals to campaign against Akosombo.

Rawlings was forced to abandon the controversial agreement in the face of mounting criticism from Liberia as well as the subregion. Stunned by the negative reactions to Akosombo, Rawlings later admitted:

> The lack of support and enthusiasm with which some member countries of our subregional organisation . . . greeted the agreement . . . undermined its acceptability. Our own Executive Secretary of ECOWAS . . . also challenged the legal basis of the Akosombo Agreement.[5]

The ECOWAS executive secretary, Edouard Benjamin, was unhappy about the lack of prior consultation and considered the agreement a unilaterally imposed accord.[6]

Ghana Deputy Foreign Minister at the time and current ECOWAS Executive Secretary Mohammed Chambas later admitted that the strong reaction against Akosombo had come as a surprise. Chambas summed up the philosophy behind Akosombo and his country's consistent belief that peace would come to Liberia only by accommodating the most powerful warlords: "In order to achieve effective disarmament one has to engage and deal directly with the leaders who, in the first instance, [are] the various armed groups, various factions and their followers."[7]

Rawlings, who moved from radical socialism to conservative economic reform backed by the World Bank and IMF, had always been the ultimate pragmatist. This was displayed by his swift move to rectify the flaws in Akosombo. The Ghanaian president dispatched a high-powered delegation to Monrovia on 17 September 1994, led by Kojo Tsikata, his trusted national security chief. He then ordered his air force to conduct shuttle flights between Accra and Monrovia to bring Liberian civic and political groups to discuss their grievances. During these two-week consultations, Rawlings tried to explain his own rationale for crafting the agreement. Following these meetings, a set of compromise proposals emerged that were submitted to Liberians for further deliberation.

Nigerian foreign ministry officials confirmed that they had been surprised by Akosombo and regarded it as a unilateral fait accompli on the part of Ghanaian authorities.[8] In late October, Rawlings met General Abacha for five hours of discussions on ways to build a credible interim government in Liberia. The meeting took place in the presidential wing of Abuja International Airport; the ECOMOG field commander, General Mark Inienger, Nigerian Foreign Minister Babagana Kingibe, and Mohammed Chambas were also present. At this meeting, Rawlings sought Nigeria's support for the Akosombo agreement. Abacha expressed doubts about the formula and stressed that the key issue was disarmament rather than the constitution of the Council of State.[9] The meeting underlined the two countries' different approaches: whereas Accra believed that if the faction leaders could run the government, disarmament would automatically follow, Abuja believed that if the faction leaders could be convinced to disarm, an effective interim government would be the inevitable result. Two incidents in September 1994 revealed the fluidity of the Liberian situation.

Gunboat Diplomacy

Fighting intensified in the Liberian countryside in September 1994, and by the end of the year it had engulfed more than 80 percent of the country. Even ECOMOG-protected Monrovia was not immune, experiencing its first serious breach of the peace since Operation Octopus in October 1992. This occurred on 15 September 1994 when General Charles Julu, a former AFL commander, attempted to stage a military coup in Monrovia. Returning from four years of U.S. exile, Julu entered Monrovia disguised as a marabout on 14 September 1994. Within twenty-four hours, he had mobilized 300 renegade AFL soldiers, who stormed the poorly guarded Executive Mansion in the early hours of 15 September. ECOMOG soldiers managed to prevent them from taking over the radio station at the top of Monrovia's Ducor Hotel to announce the coup.

Julu arrived at the Executive Mansion in camouflage and occupied Samuel Doe's former presidential chair on the fourth floor. He conducted phone interviews with the BBC, conversed by telephone with General Inienger at ECOMOG headquarters, declared himself president of Liberia, and invited Liberian journalists and photographers to meet with him. After a final warning from Inienger to Julu to desist from his antics, ECOMOG stormed the mansion on 16 September using armored cars, tanks, and frigates. Within an hour and a half, ECOMOG had overwhelmed the rebels with superior firepower.[10] The Nigerian army's experience with six successful, and at least four attempted, coups served ECOMOG well in foiling this latest attempt.

This was one of the most bizarre incidents of the Liberian civil war. With thousands of ECOMOG peacekeepers in Monrovia and with a civil war raging between seven major Liberian factions throughout the country, a band of 300 men took over the seat of power for twelve hours, declaring rather implausibly that they were in full control of the country. It was difficult to understand the reason for Julu's mysterious coup attempt. He may have been attempting to establish himself as the leading Krahn political figure in Liberia. The coup had been planned to coincide with the fourth anniversary of the murder of Samuel Doe, and it dovetailed with the LNTG's attempts to ensure a better ethnic balance in the Krahn-dominated AFL. Julu and eighteen followers were tried and jailed. Like Doe's arrest from ECOMOG headquarters in 1990 and Taylor's invasion of Monrovia in 1992, the Julu coup exposed ECOMOG's security lapses and lack of military intelligence.

The NPFL Split

The second dramatic incident, which occurred in the same month, was a split among the ranks of the NPFL. In a stunning blow to Charles Taylor, three NPFL cabinet ministers in the LNTG—Tom Woewiyu, Laveli Supuwood, and Sam Dokie—broke ranks. The trio was widely considered to be the NPFL's intellectual backbone. In a statement in late September, Woewiyu, who was the LNTG labor minister, launched a personal attack on his leader, saying: "Mr. Taylor is an enemy to this society. He is an enemy to the NPFL. He has distorted our ideals and wasted blood on the noble goals of the people of this country."[11] Woewiyu called for the speedy disarmament of all factions; advised the NPFL to give up its armed struggle for peaceful competition in the political arena; accused Taylor of continuing the war because he feared electoral defeat; personally implicated the NPFL leader in the murders of politicians like Jackson Doe, Alfred Flomo, Stephen Daniels, and Cooper Teah; and praised ECOMOG's efforts at resolving the civil war.[12] Woewiyu later described Taylor as a "deranged and confused person," saying that the NPFL leader "must be arrested and killed like a snake."[13] Dokie and Supuwood reiterated their support for Woewiyu's position.

Charles Taylor accused his three former stalwarts of mutiny and tried unsuccessfully to replace them on the LNTG with more loyal lieutenants. Under Woewiyu's leadership, the trio organized the Central Revolutionary Council (CRC-NPFL), taking away some of Taylor's combatants. The CRC-NPFL formed a loose coalition with other anti-NPFL factions like the LPC and the LDF to expel the NPFL from Gbarnga. The NPFL became a house divided against itself as NPFL factions battled one another in Margibi, Nimba, and Maryland Counties.

The Accra Agreement

In order to address Abuja's complaint about not being consulted on Akosombo, Nigerian Foreign Minister Babagana Kingibe was invited by his Ghanaian counterpart, Obed Asamoah, to play a prominent part in the Accra peace negotiations of 22–24 November 1994. The meeting was convened to rectify the flaws of Akosombo. Members of the ECOWAS Committee of Nine (Benin, Burkina Faso, Côte d'Ivoire, Gambia, Ghana, Guinea, Nigeria, Senegal, and Togo), as well as representatives from Tanzania and Uganda, attended.

During this meeting the so-called Coalition (LPC, LDF, and CRC-NPFL) failed to isolate Charles Taylor by attempting to recruit Alhaji Kromah to its side. Kromah withdrew from the talks after alleging that ECOMOG had killed nine of his men, and it took a plea by Rawlings to lure him back to the negotiating table. Ghanaian mediators pressured Roosevelt Johnson to join either ULIMO-K or the Coalition. Obed Asamoah dismissed the complaints of political and civic groups that Akosombo had turned the Council of State into a military junta as "politically motivated hysteria" and argued that the views of the LPC, which failed to attend the meeting (it was part of the Coalition), were similar to the AFL's and that its interests would therefore be represented in Accra.[14]

The outlines of an agreement started to emerge in Accra. There would be a five-member Council of State with seats divided between the NPFL, ULIMO, the Coalition and AFL, the Liberian National Conference, and one member elected by the electoral college of the LNTG. Warlords could serve on the Council of State without being disqualified from elections, and council decisionmaking would be by consensus, although majority decisions could arise if consensus failed. The council chairman would have executive powers, and the council would appoint the cabinet. The agreement also mandated that ECOMOG-protected safe havens be established in Monrovia, Gbarnga, Buchanan, Greenville, Harper, Totota, Tubmanburg, Voinjama, and

Zwedru that the peacekeepers could defend by force. The AFL would be restructured to include all factions. The Council of State would sit ten days after ECOMOG and UNOMIL had certified the creation of safe havens.[15]

A team of facilitators was established under the OAU's eminent person, Reverend Canaan Banana, on 24 November in a bid to address a disagreement over the composition and decisionmaking powers of the council, reluctance by warlords to disarm before an interim government was established, and warlords' concerns about the emergence of new factions.[16] Following the discrediting of Caribbean technocrat Gordon-Somers at Akosombo, Banana gained more prominence as a mediator and played the role of wise African elder. But even he could not convince the parties to agree, and they were sent packing from Accra on 30 November for two weeks of consultation in Liberia.

On 21 December 1994, all factions returned to the Ghanaian capital to sign the Accra agreement. It called for a cease-fire by 28 December 1994, the installation of a new Council of State in two weeks, disarmament within four months, the establishment of safe havens, elections on 14 November 1995, and the installation of an elected government by 1 January 1996. Akosombo had effectively legitimized the direct participation of the warlords in government.

As with previous negotiations, however, problems developed even before the ink was dry. Two days after the scheduled date of the cease-fire, fighting continued to rage in the southeast between the NPFL and LPC and in central Liberia between the NPFL and ULIMO-J. The LDF leader, Francois Massaquoi, was ominously complaining that the Ghanaians had pressured him into signing an unacceptable agreement. To make matters worse, the Coalition could not agree on a joint candidate to represent it on the Council of State.

Yet Accra did produce a glimmer of hope. At the December conference, Charles Taylor approached Nigerian Foreign Minister Kingibe to ask whether he could visit Nigeria. Taylor had also made the same request through OAU Secretary-General Salim Ahmed Salim in October 1994. Kingibe requested that the visit be kept secret, but Taylor insisted that he first had to confer with Blaise Compaoré, who reportedly opposed the visit.[17] After another secret meeting in Accra between Taylor and Edouard Benjamin, the ECOWAS executive secretary prodded Kingibe to arrange a meeting between Taylor and General Sani Abacha.[18]

From Accra to Abuja

The Accra agreement had called for a cease-fire by 28 December 1994 and the installation of a new Council of State by 11 January 1995. Neither event happened. The Liberian parties met in Accra under ECOWAS auspices in early January 1995 in a bid to agree on the composition and chairmanship of the Council of State. But the talks deadlocked. On 24 January, an ECOWAS minisummit was hosted again in Accra by the indefatigable ECOWAS chairman, Jerry Rawlings—the Pied Piper of Accra, who continued to play diplomatic tunes to which Liberia's warlords often refused to dance. General Abacha ventured on a rare foreign trip to attend the Accra minisummit. Rawlings met with Abacha, Guinea's Lansana Conté, and Burkina Faso's Blaise Compaoré for a whole day in Accra before deciding that the proposed Council of State be enlarged from five to six members to allow for Coalition and AFL representation.

Charles Taylor was insisting on being chairman of the council, a recurring demand based on his belief that political power should be in direct proportion to military control of territory. When Taylor's demand was rejected, he insisted on being made the sole vice chairman, but this too was rejected.[19] Taylor was adamant that he would not sit on the same council with Tom Woewiyu, the leader of the trio that broke ranks.[20] Taylor publicly accused Nigeria of trying to manipulate the new council against his interests and repeated his request that ECOMOG troops leave Liberia.

A further difficulty was the LNTG's continued insistence that the AFL should not be represented on the council because it was in fact the former national army. The LNTG called for restructuring the former national army to ensure ethnic balance (eight of the top eleven AFL posts were still held by Krahns).[21] Kwame E. Amoa-Awua, the director of the Africa and OAU bureau in the Ghanaian foreign ministry who played an important role at the summit, attributed the breakdown of the Accra talks to a clash of personalities between the two leading Krahns, George Boley and Hezekiah Bowen, both of whom wanted seats on the council.[22] The outcome of this personality conflict would determine who would assume political leadership of the late Samuel Doe's Krahn ethnic group. The CRC-NPFL, LPC, and most Krahn elements backed Boley over Bowen.[23] Bowen then decided to support Charles Taylor's candidacy on the council to spite the Coalition.[24]

Chief Tamba Tailor, a ninety-year-old patriarch who had been a paramount chief in Lofa County since 1955, was nominated as chairman of the Council of State. Tailor, an unabashed polygamist with twenty wives and countless children, was pious and widely respected but lacked a formal Western education.[25] Nicknamed "Tamba the Tailor" because he once made and repaired garments professionally, his skills were now needed to stitch together political compromises among Liberia's factions.

In the absence of any universally recognized national authority, faction leaders and politicians continued to appeal to outside authority in the form of ECOWAS mediators. LNTG politicians and CRC-NPFL leaders continued to insist that disarmament be made a priority before installing a government of warlords. There were also concerns expressed, most vociferously by Hezekiah Bowen and the Liberian National Conference representative, Oscar Quiah, about Tamba Tailor's age and health and the danger of the chairmanship falling into the hands of the warlords in the event of Tailor's death. Furthermore, internal squabbles plagued almost every faction: the AFL and the Coalition could still not agree on a joint representative to the council; members of the Coalition wrote to Jerry Rawlings objecting to the inclusion of ULIMO-J in their alliance;[26] some of Alhaji Kromah's members published a protest note rejecting his leadership; and some ULIMO-J members complained of a lack of consultation over representation on the council.[27]

Reports later filtered out that the Ghanaian facilitators had pushed Bowen to vote for Charles Taylor as council chairman.[28] Oscar Quiah rejected the proposed formula at Accra and allied with the Coalition to oppose what they complained was a Ghanaian diktat. There had been reports that Ghanaian Foreign Minister Asamoah was pressuring the Coalition to accept Taylor's membership on the council.[29] Senior Nigerian diplomats also noted that some of the anti-NPFL factions refused to return to Accra, preferring instead to shift talks to Abuja.[30] Rawlings, whose government had spent more than $10 million on ECOMOG since the start of the conflict, regarded these accusations as profound ingratitude.[31] Out of frustration he sent the squabbling factions packing on 30 January 1995, urging them to continue their deliberations in Liberia.

After the failure at Accra, Alhaji Kromah and Hezekiah Bowen proposed to Rawlings that the five-member Council of State be retained with Chief Tailor as chairman, three vice chairmen of equal status from the NPFL, AFL, and ULIMO-K, and a fifth representative from the LNC. They further proposed that the three vice chairmen and the LNC nominee, Oscar Quiah, be given oversight responsibilities for Liberia's ministries and that the Coalition be allowed to appoint some ministers.[32] Rawlings advised Kromah and Bowen to consult with other parties to reach a common agreement.[33] On 22 March, the ECOWAS chairman invited Tamba Tailor and the lame-duck LNTG chairman, David Kpomakpor, to Accra for two days of talks on how to revive the peace process. After the meeting, Rawlings sent his security chief, Kojo Tsikata, to Abuja to deliver a message to General Abacha. In the aftermath of Nigeria's adverse reaction to Akosombo, Accra was realizing the importance of consulting closely with Abuja.

On 15 and 16 May, the fifth meeting of the foreign ministers of the ECOWAS Committee of Nine took place in Abuja. It was hosted by the new Nigerian foreign minister, Tom Ikimi, a former political adviser to General Abacha. Ikimi's arrogance and abrasive style infuriated many of his own Nigerian diplomats and alienated Western diplomats at a time of growing international pressure against General Abacha's military junta. The foreign ministers proposed several recommendations to be considered by the ECOWAS summit: A six-member Council of State should be constituted with Chief Tamba Tailor as chairman; the council should draw up its own rules of procedure and agree on the sharing of ministerial posts and other public offices; the Coalition should decide its own representation on the council; and the two wings of ULIMO should decide between themselves on the distribution of posts, with ECOWAS assistance if necessary.[34] The ministers failed to agree on the status of the vice chairman, with some countries calling for a single powerful vice chairman and others favoring five vice chairmen of equal status. The matter was referred to the ECOWAS summit of heads of state for final resolution.[35]

From 17 to 21 May 1995, the third summit of the heads of state and government of the ECOWAS Committee of Nine took place in Abuja. All Liberia's faction leaders attended with the notable exception of Charles Taylor. At the summit, Jerry Rawlings called for the harmonization of ECOWAS policies, noting that the pursuit of separate agendas by members was undermining ECOWAS efforts to resolve the crisis.[36] Rawlings and Abacha met with each faction leader to review the recommendations of the ECOWAS foreign ministers. No final agreement was reached, but ECOWAS leaders reported substantial agreement on the outstanding issues. They asked the Liberian factions to consult further and requested the ECOWAS foreign ministers to reconvene a meeting with the factions to resolve outstanding issues.[37] But differences in diplomatic approaches were still evident between Abuja and Accra despite the outward appearance of consensus. Nigeria appeared less than fully convinced about the efficacy of a Council of State controlled by warlords. Rawlings went to Abuja on two additional occasions in the weeks following the summit in a bid to harmonize subregional policy on Liberia.

The ECOWAS foreign ministers also met with the Liberian parties on 19 May to discuss the status of the Council of State. A six-member council was proposed, to be chaired by Tamba Tailor, with five vice chairmen enjoying equal status. The ECOWAS Committee of Nine would decide on the succession to the chairmanship in consultation with Liberia's parties. All the parties except the LPC supported Tailor's candidacy, and all except the NPFL backed the role of the Committee of Nine in choosing a successor. ULIMO-K argued for three vice chairmen; the NPFL and LPC favored two vice chairmen.[38]

On 2 June 1995, a historic breakthrough occurred between the Nigerian government and Charles Taylor, something that many thought would lead to a final resolution to end the Liberian civil war. Taylor arrived in Abuja at the head of a seventy-six-member entourage for the first direct meeting between Taylor—the leader of Liberia's strongest faction—and General Abacha, the leader of the dominant ECOMOG contingent who had twice thwarted Taylor's attempts to capture Monrovia. The warlord spent four days with Abacha, in a rapprochement recalling that between Washington and Somali warlord Mohammed Farah Aideed: in both cases, policy changed from pursuing to protecting the warlords. Apparently overwhelmed by Abacha's hospitality, Taylor tried to atone for the killing of Nigerian citizens by his fighters in 1990 by donating money to a church and a mosque in Abuja.[39] Taylor was to visit Nigeria two more times before August 1995.

The background to these meetings was shrouded in secrecy. Beforehand, Burkina Faso and Côte d'Ivoire had pressured Taylor to settle his differences with Nigeria,[40] and Rawlings and Abacha personally assured Taylor of his safety if he visited Nigeria.[41] Blaise Compaoré, the Burkinabè leader, was intimately involved in these negotiations, and NPFL and Nigerian envoys met in Ouagadougou to discuss the details of the visit.[42] The Taylor-Abacha meeting had apparently been arranged during ECOWAS's Accra minisummit in January 1995 when the senior NPFL official and LNTG Information Minister Victoria Refell approached the Nigerian delegation and arranged a secret meeting between a middle-ranking Nigerian diplomat and Taylor. Taylor later met in Accra with Nigerian Foreign Minister Kingibe in a meeting witnessed by both Rawlings and Abacha. The Nigerians assured Taylor of his personal safety and their willingness to receive him in Abuja.[43] NPFL senior officials Enoch Dogoleah and Momolu Sirleaf went to Abuja to meet Kingibe to arrange the visit.[44] Reflecting profound fears for his personal safety in Nigeria, Taylor requested to be accompanied by former U.S. President Jimmy Carter or OAU Secretary-General Salim Ahmed Salim.[45]

Eventually, Taylor and Abacha recognized the reality of the situation: neither could achieve anything without the other, and each side could frustrate the other's goals. As the former Nigerian ambassador to Liberia, Ayo Ajakaiye, put it, "We realized the most formidable force in the Liberian context was Taylor's NPFL."[46] Nigeria could not achieve its peacekeeping objectives in Liberia without NPFL cooperation, and Taylor could not achieve his presidential ambitions without Nigerian cooperation.

From 19 to 22 July, ECOWAS foreign ministers held a consultative meeting with Liberian parties in Monrovia. At this meeting, Liberia's interim President, David Kpomakpor, called for a revision of the Accra agreement and a possible return to the 1993 Cotonou agreement, which had excluded the warlords from direct participation in the Council of State.[47] The NPFL walked out after unsuccessfully trying to limit the size of the Coalition's delegation. Ghana's astute deputy foreign minister, Mohammed Chambas, had to reassure delegates that visits by Charles Taylor and Amos Sawyer to Accra were not an attempt to conduct parallel talks that would undermine the consultative meeting.[48] Members of the meeting agreed that the chairman of the Council of State should have voting power and cast the deciding vote in the event of a tie. It called for the suspension from the LNTG of any party against which ECOMOG was to take enforcement action for violating the Accra agreement.[49] Neither the NPFL nor ULIMO-J signed the final agreement.

The Abuja Agreement

The ECOWAS diplomatic roadshow returned to Abuja, where the sixth meeting of the ECOWAS Committee of Nine foreign ministers took place on 16–17 August 1995. A day before the talks, Rawlings held a closed-door meeting with Abacha that lasted five hours. Both leaders decided to break the political impasse by including General Bowen on the council and by convincing the Coalition's new nominee, Tom Woewiyu, to relinquish his seat on the council to LPC leader George Boley.[50]

This time Charles Taylor personally attended the meeting, arriving in Abuja with a thirty-strong retinue that included bodyguards, protocol officers, and a personal physician. Taylor again criticized ECOWAS for seeking consensus from every faction on every issue, reiterating his argument that the factions were not equal in military strength and that ECOWAS therefore needed to use more discretion in arriving at a majority position. The civilian groups again urged disarmament before seating the Council of State, and Roosevelt Johnson stressed the need to resolve the status of the vice chairmen as well as the question of ULIMO representation on the council.[51] Nigerian Foreign Minister Tom Ikimi called for a council that could provide strong and effective leadership and would be able to control all territory in Liberia.[52] This was the first sign that Abuja was finally coming around to Accra's position: only the inclusion of warlords who controlled most of Liberia's territory could ensure peace in Liberia.

During the meeting with the ECOWAS heads of state on 18–19 August, the realpolitik of the decisionmaking stood in stark contrast to the earlier idealism of excluding warlords from government and propping up civilian-chosen candidates. The powerful warlords Taylor, Kromah, and Boley were nominated to be vice chairmen and asked to suggest names for chairman.[53] Abuja and Accra decided that Bowen, a military man, should not sit on the council.[54] This process also produced the candidacy and chairmanship of a political neophyte, Wilton Sankawulo, a former English professor from Bong County whose claim to fame was his published folktales and storybooks. In the end, the old, unlettered Tamba Tailor was forced to give way to a younger man of letters as council chairman. In the political horsetrading that followed, both General Bowen and Tom Woewiyu were dropped from the council. The spirit of Abuja was vividly captured by Charles Taylor's extension of a hand of reconciliation to his two NPFL defectors, Tom Woewiyu and Laveli Supuwood.

Along with the three powerful warlords, three civilians were nominated to the Council of State: Chairman Sankawulo and two vice chairmen of equal status with the three warlords: the venerable patriarch Tamba Tailor and Liberian National Conference representative Oscar Quiah. But of the three, only Quiah had intimate experience in Liberian politics, leading to fears that faction leaders would dominate the council. Quiah was also considered close to George Boley, one of the warlords on the council.[55] The Abuja agreement stipulated that council members wishing to run for president would have to resign three months before the election, scheduled for 20 August 1996, and barred the council chairman from entering the first presidential election. Ministerial posts were shared on an equitable basis with Roosevelt Johnson, Hezekiah Bowen, Tom Woewiyu, Sam Dokie, and Francois Massaquoi obtaining cabinet posts. Positions to the supreme court, autonomous agencies, and public corporations were also shared among the armed factions and political parties; consultations were held to fill the remaining posts in the Transitional Legislative Assembly and the electoral commission. Significantly, the Abuja agreement also reversed the Akosombo agreement of 1994 by restoring to ECOMOG the exclusive enforcement powers that it had enjoyed since the Cotonou agreement of 1993.

The Abuja agreement was signed on 19 August 1995. It modified the Cotonou and Akosombo agreements and clarified the Accra agreements. A cease-fire was to come into effect on 26 August 1995; ECOMOG and UNOMIL would deploy throughout the country between 2 October and 14 December 1995; combatants were to move to assembly points between 9 November and 31 December 1995; and disarmament of the belligerents was to occur between 1 December 1995 and 30 January 1996. Shortly after the agreement was reached, the factions provided a list of 59,370 fighters; these inflated figures were reduced to an overall total of 33,000 fighters in January 1997.

On 1 September, the Council of State was inaugurated in Monrovia's grand Centennial Hall. The day before, Charles Taylor had received a rapturous reception from large crowds keen to catch a glimpse of his return to the capital. Alhaji Kromah received a similar response upon his return from his base in Conakry. All six councilmen swore an oath to defend Liberia's constitution in a ceremony witnessed by Jerry Rawlings. The elated ECOWAS chairman exclaimed, "It is time for Liberians to drop their guns and embrace each other."[56]

Even after the failure of nine previous peace agreements, the widespread optimism that Abuja would finally bring peace to Liberia was based on several factors. All the faction leaders were directly involved in the council for the first time and were therefore thought to have a direct stake in keeping the peace. Also, the warlords would now have to portray themselves as peace-loving statesmen if they were to win votes in national elections.

And finally, after six years of civil war, war-weariness began to affect the 33,000 faction fighters; some voluntarily disarmed to ECOMOG even before the Abuja agreement had been signed.

Abuja was indeed a lavish banquet, something to whet the appetites of Liberian warlords. Put simply, it was a desperate attempt to buy peace by offering the faction leaders the spoils of office. The thinking was that political power could be exchanged for military peace. It was the same idea behind the hastily arranged Akosombo agreement, from which Accra had learned the lesson of not consulting closely with Abuja before making important decisions. As Ambassador A. O. Esan, former director of the West Africa division of the Nigerian foreign ministry, put it, "Rawlings knew the engine room was Nigeria and he kept close to it."[57]

But Nigeria also needed Ghana's support to keep it all running. The relationship between Ghana and Nigeria was clearly one of mutual dependence. The Abuja agreement was, however, a triumph of Ghanaian diplomacy. Rawlings had established a close relationship with General Abacha, which he used to good effect. The Ghanaian chief of defense staff, Air Marshal A. H. Dumashie, put it this way: "Rawlings has a special respect for the leader of Nigeria and will always yield a lot."[58] Both leaders frequently spoke on the telephone.[59] Rawlings finally convinced Abacha of the wisdom of the government of warlords he first proposed at Akosombo in September 1994. With the signing of Abuja, then, Ghana's policy of appeasement toward Taylor had triumphed over Nigeria's policy of isolating him. Despite Nigeria's strong reaction against Akosombo, Abuja was based on similar logic: the need to include the warlords in government to ensure success in the peace process. It seemed that Nigeria had not rejected the substance of what Ghana had proposed at Akosombo but instead opposed the unilateral style that led to it.

The United Nations

At the end of November 1994, UN Secretary-General Boutros Boutros-Ghali sent assistant secretary-general for political affairs and ECOWAS executive secretary between 1996 and 2001, Lansana Kouyaté, to Côte d'Ivoire, Ghana, Guinea, Liberia, Nigeria, and Sierra Leone. Kouyaté met ECOWAS ministers at a peace conference on Liberia in Accra, where he urged them to harmonize their policies on Liberia and to desist from contravening the UN-imposed arms embargo. Kouyaté made three key recommendations at the end of his visit: the convening of an extraordinary ECOWAS summit to harmonize subregional Liberia policy; the expansion of ECOMOG to include more extraregional troops; and the provision of financial and logistical support to ECOMOG.[60]

But the most dramatic event concerning the United Nations was the departure of Special Representative Trevor Gordon-Somers in December 1994. During his two-year stint the Jamaican diplomat became despised among Liberian political actors for what they saw as his reckless push for a premature installation of an interim government—that is, before disarmament—as well as his apparent willingness to appease faction leaders like Charles Taylor and Alhaji Kromah. Gordon-Somers also alienated the ECOMOG High Command due to, according to several generals, lack of consultation. He offended regional diplomats who complained that he conferred more with the U.S. chargé d'affaires, William Twadell, and did not keep them sufficiently informed about his negotiations.

After the Akosombo debacle in September 1994, Gordon-Somers wrote to the UN Secretary-General and requested to be withdrawn from his post, saying he had achieved as much as he could in Liberia. He later admitted: "I had become part of the problem. If my objectivity was no longer accepted and if they [Liberian parties] thought I was biased, I could no longer be effective."[61] The Jamaican envoy thus left Monrovia on 11 December 1994 amid controversy. On 28 December, Anthony Nyakyi, Tanzania's former permanent representative to the UN, arrived in Monrovia to replace Gordon-Somers. Nyakyi attended all the ECOWAS meetings with the Liberian factions and consulted regularly with subregional leaders and Liberian parties.

In February 1995, Boutros-Ghali suggested to the Security Council that it establish a large UN peacekeeping force under which ECOMOG would be subsumed.[62] But with the most powerful members of the UN Security Council wary of proliferating peacekeeping missions amid the debacles in Bosnia, Rwanda, and Somalia, the proposal met only silence. A month later, Boutros-Ghali met the ECOWAS chairman, Jerry Rawlings, in Copenhagen and repeated his suggestion for an ECOWAS summit to harmonize subregional Liberia policy. The Liberian parties would be expected to participate in the proposed summit.[63] On 23 March 1995, the UN Secretary-General sent a message to General Abacha suggesting Abuja, and Abacha quickly agreed to host the meeting.

During the Committee of Nine foreign ministers meeting held in May 1995, Anthony Nyakyi promised that all violations of the arms embargo would be reported to the UN commission on sanctions.[64] In a Committee of Nine meeting three months later, Nyakyi reminded the warlords of Boutros-Ghali's June 1995 threat to withdraw the sixty-three remaining UN observers from Liberia by 30 September 1995 unless the following conditions were met: a comprehensive cease-fire; the installation of the Council of State; and agreement on a timetable for implementing other aspects of the peace agreements, especially the disarmament process.[65] Nervous ECOWAS states reacted by warning that the withdrawal of UN observers would compromise

ECOMOG efforts and could lead to further destabilization within the West African subregion.[66] This again underscored the importance, for reasons of international legitimacy and attention, of the largely symbolic UN presence to ECOMOG efforts.

UN humanitarian agencies remained active, providing social and economic assistance. In 1995, the UN's consolidated interagency appeal raised $49 million (out of $65 million it requested), mostly to meet food needs.[67] The UNDP awarded small grants to restart businesses; the United Nations Children's Fund (UNICEF) provided essential drugs and trained health personnel to immunize children; the Office of the United Nations High Commissioner for Refugees repatriated 7,000 Liberian refugees from neighboring countries in the first nine months of the year; the Food and Agricultural Organization provided handtools and vegetable seeds to farmers; the World Health Organization provided health-care services; and the World Food Programme distributed food.[68] But these efforts were merely a drop in the ocean. They only marginally alleviated the suffering of Liberians, many of whom still suffered from the deleterious effects of fighting in inaccessible parts of the countryside. UN support, then, helped keep the Liberian patient on life-support but did not treat the main afflictions.

Nigeria

The five-year ECOMOG intervention continued to be criticized in Nigeria. Nigerian media questioned the huge costs of what many often dismissively termed the "Liberian adventure." The *Vanguard* described Nigerian military spending in Liberia as "mind-boggling," asking rhetorically: "Is the Nigerian economy buoyant enough to sustain the 660,000 naira spent daily feeding about 6,000 soldiers in Liberia?"[69] The *Tribune* dismissed the mission as "monstrous" concluding that "Nigeria's involvement in ECOMOG in Liberia is one too much for her healthy existence. . . . So, enough of Nigeria in Liberia."[70]

The defense of the mission was left to military spokesmen like the director of defense information, General Fred Chijuka, who argued that it was in Nigeria's interest to maintain stability in the subregion, to which many goods were exported. As Chijuka put it, "If you have resources and your region is boiling, what kind of resources do you have?"[71] The government-owned *Daily Times* also justified the continued deployment of Nigerian troops in Liberia: "What we have done in Liberia is to show the world that when a nation is disturbed, it is not fair to leave it to kill itself on the excuse that no one needs to interfere in its domestic issues."[72]

But General Abacha faced a multitude of domestic problems that made the Liberian imbroglio pale in comparison. Amid rumors of growing unrest and deep divisions in the middle and lower ranks of the army, Abacha increased the number of military officers in his cabinet.[73] The insecurity of the junta was further exposed with the arrest, in February 1995, and subsequent trial of thirty-nine alleged coup-plotters, including Brigadier Lawan Gwadabe, commander of the 31st Armored Brigade in Yola, the former military head of state and current civilian president, General Olusegun Obasanjo, and his former chief of staff, General Shehu Musa Yar'Adua who died in detention in December 1997.[74]

Many opponents of the regime, including journalists and human rights activists, were put on trial with accused putschists, which led to suspicions that the entire plot was a fallacy and that Abacha was using the trial to silence domestic critics. Mounting international pressure on Abacha to commute the death sentences of fourteen defendants to prison terms caused divisions in the upper echelons of the Nigerian military. Further exacerbating the general insecurity in Nigeria was a spate of bombings that rocked parts of the country: in early 1995, oil installations at the Bonny terminal were bombed, as was a section of the Murtala Muhammed International Airport and the Lagos office of an Abacha associate, oil trader Gilbert Chagouri. On 31 May 1995, there was an explosion at Ilorin Stadium in Kwara state during a rally attended by Abacha's wife and two of his senior officers. The bomb killed one person and injured forty.

During his first visit to Abuja in June 1995, Charles Taylor saw firsthand the magnitude of Abacha's domestic problems. This may have led Taylor to conclude that Liberia was not a priority for Abacha but rather a distraction.[75] Abacha's determination to consolidate his power within the army led him to devote most of his time to domestic power struggles. He rarely ventured abroad on foreign trips, content simply to host peace conferences on Liberia to raise his own image as the subregion's preeminent statesman. Unlike General Babangida, a personal friend of the late Samuel Doe, Abacha was able to depersonalize the conflict with Taylor. His main priority was the survival of his regime; any glory that derived from a breakthrough in Liberia would be incidental. Still struggling to establish his domestic legitimacy, Abacha knew that Babangida had won no domestic political support for the highly unpopular ECOMOG intervention.

However, as international pressure intensified on Abacha's human rights record, Nigeria's participation in Liberia became an important but unstated negotiating tool. With little appetite for direct humanitarian intervention in Africa, Western countries were grateful to Nigerians for their stamina and endurance in Liberia. Washington, given its historical links to Liberia and earlier support for Samuel Doe (see Chapter 2), knew that the precipitate withdrawal of ECOMOG from Liberia would result in pressure for U.S. intervention in the likely event of a humanitarian catastrophe. Leonard Robinson, the former U.S. deputy assistant secretary of state for

African affairs, noted in November 1992: "A precipitous ECOMOG with-drawal from Liberia would lead to resumption of warfare and probably hu-manitarian catastrophe . . . pressure will build rapidly for direct U.S. or UN intervention."[76] We now turn to U.S. policy during this period.

The United States

Relations between Washington and Abuja remained strained during this period. The unwillingness of the United States to rescind its decision to decertify Nigeria for the government's alleged failure to control drug-trafficking meant that Washington voted against any multilateral financial assistance for Nigeria. By 13 February 1995, the United States had donated $16.5 million of the $18.4 million contributed to the UN Trust Fund for Liberia. Ninety percent of this money was, however, set aside for the Tan-zanian and Ugandan contingents, which joined ECOMOG in 1994. Only 10 percent of the funds went to ECOMOG's more numerous West African con-tingents.[77] In June 1995, Washington cut off funding to the rest of the ECOMOG contingents, citing a lack of accountability.[78] This strained the already poor relations between Washington and Abuja, with Nigerian offi-cials complaining that their sacrifices were not being appreciated by a country that had abandoned its responsibilities in Liberia. Some Nigerian officials also felt that the United States was attempting to work with Ghana as an ally in Liberia, praising Ghanaian efforts while ignoring or criticizing those of Nigeria.[79]

U.S. Special Envoy for Liberia Dane Smith attended all the ECOWAS peace meetings. Smith also visited Nigeria before Charles Taylor's trip to Abuja to obtain an assurance that his security would be guaranteed.[80] But several Nigerian officials found Smith patronizing, and Nigerian Foreign Minister Ikimi asked him to leave an ECOWAS meeting until he obtained proper accreditation.[81] Former U.S. President Jimmy Carter visited Nigeria in April 1995 to obtain a similar guarantee for Taylor and to plead for the re-lease of his friend, General Olusegun Obasanjo.[82] Carter also telephoned Tay-lor in June 1995 to encourage him to settle his differences with Nigeria.[83]

The U.S. State Department's annual report of 1995 reflected the depth of U.S. skepticism regarding ECOMOG's professionalism. The report ac-cused Nigerian soldiers of drug-trafficking and Ghanaian soldiers of child prostitution. It also alleged that ECOMOG soldiers systematically looted goods and stripped entire buildings of scrap metals for sale abroad. The iron ore factory in ECOMOG-protected Buchanan was said to have been completely stripped of its machinery, fittings, and scrap metal, its contents loaded onto a ship bound for Nigeria. In Monrovia, the same was said to have been done to the Bong Mining Company.[84] Senior ECOMOG officials confirmed some of these damaging allegations, which led Liberians to give ECOMOG the rather unflattering sobriquet "Every Car Or Moveable Object Gone."[85]

Shortly before his arrest for alleged involvement in a coup plot, Olusegun Obasanjo visited Washington and met with members of the influential Congressional Black Caucus, some of whom were leading a campaign to impose oil sanctions on Nigeria. After death sentences were passed on some of the alleged coup-plotters, Washington sent a strong protest letter to Abuja urging restraint, and President Bill Clinton telephoned General Abacha to warn him that Americo-Nigerian relations would deteriorate further if any of the defendants were executed.[86] TransAfrica, headed by the dynamic African American lawyer Randall Robinson, who had led an effective campaign for sanctions against apartheid South Africa, was now leading efforts to pressure Congress to impose an oil embargo on Abacha's regime.[87]

Abuja's strategy for dealing with such threats was twofold. First, the Nigerian ambassador to Washington, Alhaji Z.M. Kazaure, hired no fewer than nine U.S. public relations and lobbying firms to counter efforts to isolate the regime. Washington and Christian, the Washington, D.C.–based lobbying group of liberal black Democrats, received $600,000 in the first six months of the year; Symms, Lehn and Associates received $300,000 in the same period. Randall Robinson reported he had been offered $1 million by a businessman with close ties to the Nigerian military regime to drop his criticism.[88]

The second strategy was to tie U.S. oil companies in Nigeria in an increasingly intricate web of mutual dependence. U.S. companies like Coastal and Sun were offered oil-lifting contracts.[89] Oil giants Mobil and Chevron were already well-established producers in the Nigerian market. Abuja used the threat of retaliation against U.S. oil companies to forestall any talk of Washington imposing oil sanctions on the military junta. In the aftermath of the sentencing of alleged coup-plotters in Nigeria, U.S. oil companies like Chevron and Mobil warned President Clinton that imposing an oil embargo on Nigeria would be disastrous.[90] These oil companies publicly voiced doubts about the efficacy of a unilateral U.S. oil embargo and tirelessly reiterated fears that European companies would simply move in to fill the vacuum. Senior U.S. officials quietly dropped their threats, and African American members of Congress like Senator Carol Mosely-Braun and Representative William Jefferson started to speak out against sanctions and in favor of a policy of constructive dialogue with the Abacha regime.

In the end, U.S. strategic interests proved enough to ward off the threat of oil sanctions. Since the mid-1970s, Nigeria has remained between the second and fifth largest supplier of oil to the United States, providing 600,000 barrels of oil per day and accounting for 8 percent of total U.S. oil imports.[91] U.S. investment in the Nigerian oil sector in 1995 was estimated at $4 billion.[92] As Adonis Hoffman put it, "While U.S. policy involves a tenuous mixture of quiet diplomacy and limited sanctions, it is evident that Washington does not quite know what to do about Nigeria."[93] A former U.S. ambassador to the United Nations, Donald McHenry, became the Clinton administration's tireless special envoy for Nigeria. He traveled to Nigeria seven times in 1995 and won the respect of Abacha and his senior advisers, who attempted to use him to counter the hostility of U.S. Ambassador to Nigeria Walter Carrington. But mutual suspicion and antagonism continued to dominate Americo-Nigerian relations, denying ECOMOG crucial logistical support from Washington.

Peacekeeping

In concluding this chapter, we will briefly assess the difficult security situation that ECOMOG and UN peacekeepers faced in Liberia before the Abuja agreement was signed in August 1995. At the beginning of 1995, ECOMOG had 8,430 troops in Liberia organized in ten infantry battalions: 4,908 Nigerians, 1,028 Ghanaians, 760 Ugandans, 747 Tanzanians, 609 Guineans, 359 Sierra Leoneans, ten Gambians and ten Malians.[94] ECOMOG's inability to deploy troops at major points along Liberia's borders led to continuous breaches of the arms embargo. ECOMOG was deployed only in Monrovia, Buchanan, Kakata, and Tubmanburg, representing less than 15 percent of Liberia's territory.[95] The eighty-six UNOMIL military observers were deployed in Monrovia, Buchanan, and Kakata.

With the peacekeepers so thinly dispersed, factional fighting continued in the countryside: In the first eight months of the year, the NPFL fought the LPC in Grand Bassa, Maryland, Sinoe, and River Cess Counties; ULIMO-J and the NPFL clashed in Bong and Margibi Counties; ULIMO-K and ULIMO-J battled in Grand Cape Mount, Lower Lofa, and Bomi Counties; the NPFL and ULIMO-K warred in northern Lofa County; and the Coalition seized territory from the NPFL in Nimba County. A major factor in all these battles was to control mineral-rich areas. In 1995, the warlords exported an estimated $300–500 million in diamonds and gold and $53 million in timber.[96]

The fighting spilled over the Liberian border into the Ivorian town of Danané in April 1995. Two months later, fighting between the LPC and NPFL spilled into the Ivorian border town of Tai, resulting in the deaths of Ivorian citizens and the flight of an additional 16,000–35,000 refugees into Côte d'Ivoire.[97] Arms were still reaching Liberia through the porous Ivorian border, and the LPC claimed that the NPFL maintained training camps and bases in the Ivorian border towns of Tai, Tabou, and Grabo.[98]

Guinea also accused the NPFL of launching crossborder raids into its territory on 2–3 July 1995.[99] The fighting in this period resulted in thousands of Liberians seeking refuge in ECOMOG-controlled areas like Monrovia, Buchanan, Kakata, and Tubmanburg. Monrovia's population increased threefold from its prewar level to 1.3 million inhabitants by the end of 1995. An estimated 727,000 Liberian refugees remained in the subregion: 395,000 in Guinea, 367,300 in Côte d'Ivoire, 14,000 in Ghana, 4,600 in Sierra Leone, and 4,000 in Nigeria.[100]

The ECOMOG field commander, General Mark Inienger, and the UNOMIL chief military observer, General Daniel Opande, held frequent meetings with the Liberian faction leaders, but they failed to curb the fighting. The peacekeepers were reduced to reporting on the frequent cease-fire violations and providing security and logistical support for humanitarian relief convoys. Tension continued between ECOMOG and UNOMIL peacekeepers, leading UN Secretary-General Boutros Boutros-Ghali to recommend the establishment of a joint ECOMOG-UNOMIL Liaison and Coordination Cell in February 1995.[101] As the Secretary-General noted, "While ECOMOG and UNOMIL continue to enjoy close working relations, especially between the top levels of their command structures, the cooperation required to carry out its task has not always been satisfactory at the working level."[102]

Relations were also strained by the fact that UNOMIL's military and civilian officials had to abide by an ECOMOG-imposed curfew restricting their ability to monitor aspects of the peace process. Even after UN Special Representative Anthony Nyakyi obtained a promise from General Inienger to respect UNOMIL's freedom of movement, there were reports of UNOMIL staff being stopped and harassed at ECOMOG checkpoints.[103]

In his report to the ECOWAS Committee of Nine foreign ministers meeting in May 1995, Inienger complained about attacks on ECOMOG and UNOMIL peacekeepers by both wings of ULIMO, as well as the continued use of antipersonnel and antivehicle landmines by Liberian factions. He noted that 1,000 fighters had voluntarily surrendered to ECOMOG between August 1994 and May 1995 and reported that the creation of ECOMOG safe havens had allowed the LNTG to establish civil administration in Bomi and Grand Cape Mount Counties. Inienger concluded his report by calling for logistical support for his peacekeepers, explaining that ECOMOG would need a troop strength of 12,000–18,000 soldiers to fulfill its disarmament tasks effectively.[104]

The high costs of maintaining ECOMOG in Liberia for five years were imposing an increasingly intolerable burden on its member states. Twenty-five percent of the ECOMOG budget was going toward paying the peacekeepers' $5 stipends, and the rest was used for logistical and other needs.[105] By August 1995, ECOMOG suffered the loss of its Tanzanian and Ugandan contingents: both countries cited the lack of financial support for troops in addition to the lack of diplomatic progress.

The signing of the Abuja agreement in August 1995, however, introduced a glimmer of hope that the end of the protracted Liberian civil war was near after six years of fighting. Following the Abuja agreement, the moribund Disarmament and Cease-Fire Committees, involving ECOMOG, UNOMIL, and all of the Liberian factions, were revived. Humanitarian assistance was resumed to areas in central and northern Liberia that had been cut off by the fighting. With peace apparently having broken out, 12,000 Liberian refugees returned to Liberia in the first month after the signing of the Abuja agreement.[106]

Notes

1. Personal interview with Francois Massaquoi, former LDF leader, Monrovia, 16 July 1999.

2. Personal interview with General Hezekiah Bowen, former AFL Chief of Staff, Monrovia, 14 July 1999.

3. Quoted in *West Africa,* no. 4016 (19–25 September 1994): 1637.

4. Personal interview with Trevor Gordon-Somers, UNDP, New York, May 1997.

5. Quoted in *West Africa,* no. 4028 (12–18 December 1994): 2114.

6. Personal interview with Edouard Benjamin, ECOWAS Secretariat, Lagos, December 1995.

7. "We Are Making Headway" (interview with Dr. Mohammed Chambas), p. 2116.

8. Personal interview at the Nigerian Ministry of Foreign Affairs, Abuja, December 1995.

9. Ibid.

10. See Ben Asante, "The Coup That Went Badly Wrong," *West Africa,* no. 4017 (26 September–2 October 1994).

11. Quoted in *West Africa,* no. 4009 (1–7 August 1994): 1343.

12. Ibid., pp. 1342–1343.

13. Quoted in *West Africa,* no. 4012 (22–28 August 1994): 1476.

14. "Final Report," Fourth Meeting of ECOWAS Ministers of Foreign Affairs of the Committee of Nine on Liberia, Accra, 22–24 November 1994, pp. 9–10.

15. Ibid., pp. 1–4, annex.

16. Ibid., pp. 1–5.

17. Personal interview at the Nigerian Ministry of Foreign Affairs, Abuja, December 1995.

18. Personal interview with Edouard Benjamin at the ECOWAS Secretariat, Lagos, December 1995.

19. *West Africa,* no. 4041 (20–26 March 1995): 424.

20. Ninth Progress Report of the Secretary-General on the United Nations Observer Mission in Liberia, S/1995/158, 24 February 1995, p. 2.

21. Max Ahmadu Sesay, "Politics and Society in Post-war Liberia," *Journal of Modern African Studies* 34, no. 3 (September 1996): 415.

22. "Peace Talks Deadlock" (Interview with Kwame E. Amoa-Awua), *West Africa,* no. 4033 (23–29 January 1995): 105.

23. *West Africa,* no. 4031 (9–15 January 1995): 12.

24. *Africa Confidential* 36, no. 1 (6 January 1995): 8.

25. "Who Is Tamba Tailor?," *West Africa*, no. 4037 (20–26 February 1995): 254.

26. "Peace Talks Deadlock" (interview with Kwame E. Amoa-Awua), *West Africa*, no. 4033 (23–29 January 1995): 105.

27. *West Africa*, no. 4031 (9–15 January 1995): 13.

28. *West Africa*, no. 4036 (13–19 February 1995): 222.

29. "Taylor Wins Out," *Africa Confidential* 36, no. 1 (6 January 1995): 8.

30. Personal interview at the Nigerian Ministry of Foreign Affairs, Abuja, 30 November 1995.

31. Max Ahmadu Sesay, "Civil War and Collective Intervention in Liberia," *Review of African Political Economy* 23, no. 67 (March 1996): 47.

32. Ninth Progress Report of the Secretary-General on the United Nations Observer Mission in Liberia, 24 February 1995, S/1995/158, p. 3.

33. Ibid.

34. "Final Report," Economic Community of West African States, Fifth Meeting of Foreign Ministers of the Committee of Nine on Liberia, 15–16 May 1995. ECW/MINFA/CTTE.9/VI/2 Rev.2 (Restricted), p. 11.

35. Ibid.

36. Eleventh Progress Report of the Secretary-General on the United Nations Observer Mission in Liberia, 10 June 1995, S/1995/473, p. 3. See also "Final Communiqué," Third meeting of ECOWAS Heads of State and Government of the Committee of Nine on Liberia, 20 May 1995.

37. Ibid., p. 3.

38. "Final Report," Meeting of the Foreign Ministers of the ECOWAS Committee of Nine and the Liberian Parties, Abuja, 19 May 1995, pp. 4–8.

39. Personal interview at the Nigerian Ministry of Foreign Affairs, Abuja, 10 December 1995.

40. *Africa Confidential* 36, no. 12 (9 June 1995): 8; and Emmanuel Wotany, "The Hawk Starts to Coo," *Africa Today* (September/October 1995): 26.

41. Personal interview at the Nigerian Ministry of Foreign Affairs, Abuja, 30 November 1995.

42. Personal interview with Bruno Zidouemba, Ambassador of Burkina Faso to the United States, Washington, D.C., 27 October 1999.

43. Personal interview at the Nigerian Ministry of Foreign Affairs, Abuja, 10 December 1995.

44. Personal interview with Victoria Refell, LNTG Information Officer, Monrovia, 15 July 1999.

45. Personal interview with Joshua Iroha, Nigerian Ambassador to Liberia, 1995–1999, Lagos, 28 July 1999.

46. Personal interview with Ambassador Ayo Ajakaiye, Nigerian Ministry of Foreign Affairs, Abuja, 6 December 1995.

47. "Final Report," ECOWAS Consultative Meeting on the Liberian Peace Process, Virginia, Liberia, 19–22 July 1995, p. 3.

48. Ibid., pp. 8–10.

49. Ibid., pp. 13–14.

50. *West Africa*, no. 4067 (18–24 September 1995): 1477.

51. "Final Report," Economic Community of West African States Consultative Meeting on the Liberian Peace Process, 16–19 August 1995, ECW/MINFA/CTTEE9/VI/2, p. 8.

52. Ibid., p. 8.

53. Ibid., p. 10.

54. Personal interview with General Hezekiah Bowen, former AFL Chief of Staff, Monrovia, 14 July 1999.

55. I thank Augustine Toure for bringing this point to my attention.

56. Quoted in *West Africa,* no. 4065 (4–10 September 1995): 1476.

57. Personal interview with Ambassador A. O. Esan, Nigerian Ministry of Foreign Affairs, Abuja, 6 December 1995.

58. Personal interview with Air Marshal A. H. Dumashie, Accra, September 1996.

59. Personal interview with Kwame Amoa-Awua, Ghanaian Foreign Ministry, Accra, September 1996.

60. See Eighth Progress Report of the Secretary-General on the United Nations Observer Mission in Liberia, 6 January 1995 S/1995/9, pp. 1–2.

61. Personal interview with Trevor Gordon-Somers.

62. Ninth Progress Report of the Secretary-General on the United Nations Observer Mission in Liberia, p. 12.

63. Tenth Progress Report of the Secretary-General on the United Nations Observer Mission in Liberia, 10 April 1995, S/1995/279, p. 2.

64. "Final Report," Economic Community of West African States, Fifth Meeting of Foreign Ministers of the Committee of Nine on Liberia, 15–16 May 1995 (Restricted), ECW/MINFA/CTTE 9/V/2. Rev. 2, p. 11.

65. See Eleventh Progress Report of the Secretary-General on the United Nations Observer Mission in Liberia, p. 9.

66. Twelfth Progress Report of the Secretary-General on the United Nations Observer Mission in Liberia, 13 September 1995, S/1995/781, p. 2.

67. Eleventh Progress Report of the Secretary-General on the United Nations Observer Mission in Liberia, p. 7.

68. Twelfth Progress Report of the Secretary-General on the United Nations Observer Mission in Liberia, pp. 6–7.

69. Quoted in *West Africa,* no. 4045 (17–23 April 1995): 586.

70. Ibid.

71. Ibid.

72. Ibid.

73. "Abacha Digs In," *Africa Confidential* 36, no. 5 (3 March 1995): 8.

74. See Shehu Othman and Gavin Williams, "Power, Politics, and Democracy in Nigeria," in Jonathan Hyslop (ed.), *African Democracy in the Era of Globalisation* (Johannesburg: Witwatersrand University Press, 1999), pp. 15–71.

75. *Africa Confidential* 36, no. 15 (21 July 1995): 4.

76. "The Ongoing Civil War and Crisis in Liberia," Hearing Before the Subcommittee on Africa of the Committee on Foreign Affairs, House of Representatives, 19 November 1992 (Washington, D.C.: U.S. Government Printing Office), p. 5.

77. Ninth Progress Report of the Secretary-General on the United Nations Observer Mission in Liberia, 24 February 1995, pp. 6–10.

78. *Africa Confidential* 36, no. 12 (9 June 1995): 8.

79. Personal interview at the Nigerian Ministry of Foreign Affairs, Abuja, 30 November 1995.

80. Personal interview at the Nigerian Ministry of Foreign Affairs, Abuja, 10 December 1995.

81. Personal interview with Joshua Iroha, former Nigerian Ambassador to Liberia, 1995–1999, Lagos, 28 July 1999.

82. Personal interview at the Nigerian Ministry of Foreign Affairs, Abuja, 10 December 1995.

83. *Africa Confidential* 36, no. 12 (9 June 1995): 8.

84. Cited in Wotany, "The Hawk Starts to Coo," p. 26.

85. Personal interview with ECOMOG officials, Accra, 5 September 1996.

86. Adonis Hoffman, "Nigeria: The Policy Conundrum," *Foreign Policy*, no. 101 (Winter 1995/1996): 151.

87. See Randall Robinson, *Defending the Spirit: A Black Life in America* (New York and London: Penguin, 1998), pp. 225–239.

88. Glenn Frankel, "Nigeria Mixes Oil and Money," *Washington Post*, 24 November 1996, p. C4. See also Robinson, *Defending the Spirit,* p. 225.

89. *Africa Confidential* 36, no. 5 (3 March 1995): 8.

90. *Africa Confidential* 36, no. 13 (23 June 1995): 2.

91. Frankel, "Nigeria Mixes Oil and Money," p. C4.

92. Hoffman, "Nigeria," p. 149.

93. Ibid., p. 146.

94. Ninth Progress Report of the Secretary-General on the United Nations Observer Mission in Liberia, pp. 4–5.

95. Eighth Progress Report of the Secretary-General on the United Nations Observer Mission in Liberia, p. 5.

96. Philippa Atkinson, *The War Economy in Liberia: A Political Economy* (London: Overseas Development Institute, 1997), p. 9.

97. Amnesty International, *Annual Report on Liberia* (London: Amnesty International, 1996), p. 2.

98. "Report of the Liberia Peace Council on the Liberian-Ivorian Border Incident 13th June 1995 and Its Aftermath," 26 July 1995, Liberia.

99. *West Africa,* no. 4058 (17–23 July 1995): 1107.

100. Thirteenth Progress Report of the Secretary-General on the United Nations Observer Mission in Liberia, 23 October 1995, S/1995/881, p. 9.

101. Ninth Progress Report of the Secretary-General on the United Nations Observer Mission in Liberia, p. 8.

102. Eleventh Progress Report of the Secretary-General on the United Nations Observer Mission in Liberia, p. 5.

103. Ibid.

104. "Final Report," Economic Community of West African States, Fifth Meeting of Foreign Ministers of the Committee of Nine on Liberia, 15–16 May 1995, pp. 7–8.

105. Ninth Progress Report of the Secretary-General on the United Nations Observer Mission in Liberia, p. 8.

106. Twelfth Progress Report of the Secretary-General on the United Nations Observer Mission in Liberia, p. 7.

chapter 9

Two Weddings and a Funeral, September 1995–August 1996

Don't put your mouth when Council people are making palava. It is just like husband and wife business. When they make their peace and settle everything you would become the common enemy.
—*Alhaji Kromah, ULIMO-K leader, 1994–1997*

In this chapter we provide a detailed accounting of the reasons leading to the failure of the 1995 Abuja agreement. We argue that despite growing subregional consensus in support of ECOMOG, problems continued at the domestic and external levels that led to the failure of Abuja.

At the domestic level, the executive Council of State was divided as warlords entered into two marriages of convenience that eventually resulted in the death of Abuja. The irreconcilable differences and personal ambitions of the warlords led to divisions within ULIMO-J. ECOWAS members were forced to negotiate a second Abuja agreement in which they attempted to exercise more supervisory control over the Council of State.

At the subregional level, consensus continued to increase following the rapprochement between Nigeria and Charles Taylor in 1995. Burkina Faso, the strongest NPFL supporter throughout the civil war, started to play a more constructive role in support of ECOMOG. Côte d'Ivoire, the other erstwhile backer of the NPFL, took further steps to play a neutral role in the conflict as the instability from the Liberian civil war continued to spill over into its territory. Both countries attended ECOWAS military chiefs of staff meetings and, along with francophone Benin and Niger, offered to contribute troops to an expanded ECOMOG. Francophone opposition to the Nigerian-led peacekeeping mission was finally giving way to a more cooperative approach and to an acceptance of ECOMOG as a neutral force with no intention of blocking Taylor's presidential ambitions. The appointment of Nigeria's General Sani Abacha as ECOWAS chairman was another sign of a growing acceptance of its leadership role in Liberia. Following factional fighting in Monrovia in April 1996, a second Abuja agreement was signed in a bid to correct the perceived flaws of the first agreement of 1995.

At the external level, West African states again recognized the limitations of Pax Nigeriana, pleading for a larger UN role in Liberia. Financial assistance was sought from international donors to implement the Abuja agreement at a conference in 1995. The response was lackluster, reflecting yet again the low priority accorded Liberia and donor governments' lack of confidence after the failure of nine peace agreements in five years. The United Nations continued to support ECOMOG efforts without addressing its logistical deficiencies. The OAU continued to lend ECOWAS diplomatic support by threatening recalcitrant Liberian warlords with sanctions. However, it lacked the resources to correct ECOMOG's military and financial deficiencies.

The most important development at the external level occurred after the outbreak of fighting in Monrovia in April 1996. The United States promised substantial logistical support for ECOMOG for the first time since its deployment. This was a major shift in U.S. policy, which had until then denied meaningful logistical support for ECOMOG's Nigerian-led contingents. Belgium and Denmark also promised support to an expanded ECOMOG. These changes would prove significant to the resolution of the Liberian civil war. ECOMOG's logistical deficiencies were again exposed by attacks that resulted in the killing of sixteen peacekeepers by Liberian factions in 1995.

The Council of Warlords

In early September 1995, Jerry Rawlings, the ECOWAS chairman, appointed Victor Gbeho as his special representative for Liberia. Gbeho had been Ghana's permanent representative to the United Nations and had previously worked as an adviser to Rawlings at Osu Castle. Upon assuming office, he described his task thus: "My mandate is to reflect the concerns and attitudes of the member states of ECOWAS in respect to the peace process . . . to act as a catalyst for bringing together all the various factions' views and ideology . . . to ensure that the various stages prescribed by the Abuja Agreement are adhered to."[1]

Plain-spoken and articulate, Gbeho often offered cogent analyses of the Liberian situation. He was not afraid to criticize the leadership of the council for creating an impression of wasting money on foreign trips and cultivating lavish lifestyles. Gbeho's friendship with UN Special Representative Anthony Nyakyi, with whom he had served in New York as their countries'

UN ambassadors, improved coordination between ECOMOG and UNOMIL. For three years, ever since the departure of Joshua Iroha, ECOWAS had lacked a high-profile political figure in Liberia, leaving delicate diplomacy in the hands of ECOMOG military commanders who did not always possess the necessary training or tact. Gbeho was appointed to fill this void.

In line with the provisions of the first Abuja agreement, the Liberian National Transitional Government appointed its cabinet and swore in new ministers by 26 September. Council of State Chairman Wilton Sankawulo's first major announcement was that the LNTG would submit a comprehensive plan for the long-overdue restructuring of the Krahn-dominated Armed Forces of Liberia to reflect better ethnic and geographical realities. It soon became clear, however, that all the warlords saw the council as part of the hustings for the presidential campaign. There was a growing crescendo of complaints about Sankawulo's weak and ineffectual leadership. Without an army or popular support base, he was constantly outmaneuvered by the warlords.[2] Charles Taylor took every opportunity to portray himself as de facto council chairman. As John Stewart wrote, "[Taylor] has spared no effort to provide himself with the accoutrements, pomp and pageantry associated with the highest office in the land."[3] Taylor's superior financial power was a source of concern to other faction leaders, especially Alhaji Kromah.[4]

The presence of the warlords in government did not, however, have the expected result of achieving peace in Liberia. Fighting continued between the LPC and NPFL in the southeast; between the two wings of ULIMO in the west around the Lofa Bridge; and between the NPFL and ULIMO-K in Gbarnga, Suacoco, and St. Paul River Bridge in Bong County. In September 1995, Rawlings dispatched Deputy Foreign Minister Mohammed Chambas, Army Chief of Staff Francis Agyemfra, and ECOWAS Executive Secretary Edouard Benjamin on a trip to New York, Washington, Brussels, Paris, and London in search of international assistance to implement the Abuja peace process.

On 27 October 1995, a donor conference on assistance to Liberia was held at UN Headquarters in New York. The conference sought support for humanitarian assistance, disarmament and demobilization, recovery and rehabilitation, and assistance to ECOMOG. In opening the conference, UN Secretary-General Boutros Boutros-Ghali described Liberia as a "forgotten emergency." The low priority that Western donors accorded Liberia meant that only $145.7 million was pledged for Liberia's reconstruction; Rawlings had asked for $195 million for ECOMOG and UNOMIL's disarmament and demobilization tasks alone.[5] By contrast, the international community had pledged $6 billion for the reconstruction of Bosnia.

Boutros-Ghali visited Jerry Rawlings in Accra from 26 to 29 November 1995 to keep up the momentum for implementing the first Abuja agreement. During the UN Secretary-General's visit, Rawlings expressed disappointment at the inadequate international assistance for Liberia.[6] Leaving Ghana, Boutros-Ghali went to Monrovia, where he met with members of the Council of State and stressed the importance of demonstrating total commitment to the peace process and implementing Abuja on schedule. During this meeting at the Executive Mansion, the UN Secretary-General highlighted the importance of disarmament and demobilization, arguing that such actions would encourage donors to fulfill their pledges to Liberia.[7]

On 30 November, Charles Taylor and Alhaji Kromah signed a memorandum of understanding in which they agreed to cease hostilities, create a buffer zone between their forces in Lofa County, and guarantee the free movement of civilian and commercial activity in areas under their control. Taylor and Kromah, both trained economists and strong-willed political leaders, were fierce political rivals, and many doubted the new alliance would last. Just six weeks before the memorandum of understanding, Taylor had accused Kromah of launching fresh attacks on his Gbarnga base. Taylor also accused Kromah of planning a jihad to Islamize Liberia and preparing to import ethnic Mandingos from Guinea and Mali to boost his electoral chances.[8] Kromah, for his part, accused Taylor's Gio and Mano fighters of killing 10,000 Mandingos in 1990. Despite the widespread skepticism, this was the start of a surprisingly durable marriage of convenience between two strange political bedfellows. Kromah and Boley, whose forces had been fighting the NPFL under the ULIMO umbrella, had earlier been expected to form an alliance on the Council of State. Kromah probably felt that Taylor would be a more useful military ally against his arch-enemy and former alliance partner, Roosevelt Johnson. (Boley would eventually draw closer to his fellow Krahn Johnson in the second marriage of warlords.)

Between September and December 1995, 1,500 Liberian refugees from eastern Guinea and 3,000 from Sierra Leone returned.[9] According to the Abuja peace plan, ECOMOG was to have completed its deployment to the Liberian countryside by 14 December 1995; in fact, this was the date that ECOMOG *started* its deployment. ECOMOG deployed to Gbarnga (Bong County), Greenville (Sinoe County), Suehn (Lofa County), and Lofa Bridge (Bomi/Grand Cape Mount County). In late December, members of the Council of State traveled to the countryside to explain the peace process and to prepare combatants for disarmament and demobilization. Nigeria's ECOMOG field commander, General Mark Inienger, and the UN special representative, Anthony Nyakyi, also undertook extensive consultations with the parties in a bid to facilitate the deployment of peacekeepers.

The Tubmanburg Troubles

As the year drew to a close, another fatal event exposed the dangers facing ECOMOG's ill-equipped peacekeepers. On 28 December 1995, ULIMO-J combatants attacked ECOMOG troops in the Bomi County town of Tub-manburg, killing sixteen Nigerian peacekeepers, wounding seventy-eight others, and capturing some of ECOMOG's heavy weapons and other equipment. In the fighting, ULIMO-J used civilians seeking refuge in a hospital as human shields in a bid to defend Tubmanburg.[10] One hundred and thirty ECOMOG peacekeepers were trapped in an area where they had been clearing landmines.[11] ECOMOG also held some ULIMO-J fighters captive and refused to release them until its men and heavy weapons were returned. The fighting in Tubmanburg continued for a week, with ULIMO-J fighters attacking ECOMOG positions; there were civilian casualties.

The background for this dispute remains confused. It seems that trouble started after clashes between the two wings of ULIMO in Gbaama, fifteen kilometers north of Tubmanburg, and Lofa Bridge on 16 December 1995. On 24 and 25 December, ULIMO-K and ULIMO-J fighters separately attacked ECOMOG forces in Gbaama, wounding five peacekeepers. After ECOMOG arrested some ULIMO-J fighters, whom it claimed were entering ECOMOG-protected Tubmanburg with arms and harassing civilians, the ULIMO-J commander in Tubmanburg accused ECOMOG of siding with ULIMO-K. ULIMO-J fighters overran ECOMOG positions in the area, and ECOMOG reinforcements were ambushed on their way to Tubmanburg. Some LDF fighters were also involved in the fighting against ECOMOG.[12] There were unsubstantiated allegations that the conflict had resulted from diamond deals involving ECOMOG officers.[13]

On 6 January 1996, a Nigerian delegation arrived in Monrovia led by Tom Ikimi, Nigeria's foreign minister, and the chief of defense staff, General Abdulsalam Abubakar. The Nigerian delegation saw the Tubmanburg incident as proof of the dangers inherent in deploying troops without the requisite logistical resources.[14] In a two-hour meeting with the Council of State, Ikimi scolded council members like a schoolmaster. He demanded and obtained apologies from each member for the attacks on ECOMOG. He then asked them to avoid a repetition of the incident.[15]

On 9 January, ULIMO-J released an ECOMOG prisoner and the mutilated corpses of several ECOMOG soldiers. A week later, it became clear that ULIMO-J was experiencing internal divisions when its chief of staff, Arma Youlou, ordered the release of all ECOMOG peacekeepers and the return of ECOMOG's heavy weapons. Troops loyal to Roosevelt Johnson responded the same day by attacking an ECOMOG checkpoint and a displaced-persons camp in Be Goba near Kakata. The attacks were repeated a day later. ECOMOG successfully repelled the attacks, but they led to the displacement of 6,000 additional people. On 17 January, Arma Youlou escorted an ECOMOG-protected humanitarian relief convoy to distribute relief in Tubmanburg.[16] ECOMOG would withdraw its peacekeepers from Tubmanburg by early March.

ULIMO-K, the NPFL, and the AFL offered to send troops to help ECOMOG fight ULIMO-J. Rawlings politely declined. An incensed Taylor accused ECOMOG of inconsistency, pointing out that ECOMOG had received help from ULIMO and the AFL during the NPFL siege of Monrovia in 1992. ECOMOG suspended plans to deploy in Voinjama (Upper Lofa County), Zwedru (Grand Gedeh County), Tappita (Nimba County), and Harper (Maryland County). It withdrew its troops from the Lofa Bridge area and Bong Mines and removed its checkpoints from the Kakata–Bong Mines road. General Inienger refused to deploy any more troops until he could secure guarantees for the safety of his troops from the warring factions.

History had repeated itself once again. ECOMOG's deployment over six years followed the same predictable pattern: warlords sign binding agreements committing themselves to peace; they invite ECOMOG into their areas to disarm their fighters; ECOMOG deploys troops to the countryside despite inadequate logistical support; ECOMOG's troops are killed by faction fighters and forced to beat a speedy retreat from the countryside. In 1992, it was Senegalese troops that were killed. In 1994, it was Tanzanian troops. In 1996, it was Nigerian troops. ECOMOG had tragically failed to learn the lessons of previous deployments: it continued to deliver peacekeepers into the traps of ruthless warlords.

The Gathering Storm

The warlords squabbled over the signing of a status-of-forces agreement that would have given the LNTG authority over the renewal of ECOMOG's mandate: Charles Taylor and Alhaji Kromah were in favor, whereas George Boley, supported by Oscar Quiah, felt it unnecessary until after disarmament.[17] Taylor and Kromah had pushed for such powers since the Akosombo agreement of September 1994. They insisted that the LNTG be responsible for disarming fighters and approve all of ECOMOG's deployment plans.[18] In violation of the Abuja agreement, the three warlords argued that the council was a collective presidency and insisted that the five vice chairmen were of equal status with the chairman. The illiterate council vice chairman, Chief Tamba Tailor, was totally ineffective. No one interpreted proceedings for him, and he was often left nodding politely.[19]

In late February, the Liberian war spilled over into Côte d'Ivoire again when suspected LPC fighters launched a crossborder raid on the Ivorian plantation of Palm Industries near the village of Weka, killing five people.[20] The Ivorian capital of Abidjan was becoming an entrepôt for guns and drugs from Liberia, increasing the incidence of violent crime in Côte d'Ivoire.[21] On 7 June 1996, another crossborder raid by suspected NPFL combatants took place in Basobly village, where eight Ivorian and seven Liberian refugees were hacked to death; domestic animals were also stolen. This was at least the fifth such raid in three years.[22]

A month later, Ivorian leader Henri Konan Bédié declared the western region of his country a military zone to be controlled by military *préfets*. He also sacked his powerful minister of security, General Gaston Ouessanan Koné, and provided 2.4 billion Communauté Financière Africaine (CFA) francs for border security.[23] Some Liberian refugees were forcibly moved from border areas to facilitate monitoring.[24] There were reports of Liberian refugees being killed by heavy-handed Ivorian security forces.[25] Ivorians were finally feeling the social effects of their earlier military and political support for the NPFL. Abidjan now realized that it had a concrete interest in stopping a war it had done so much to fuel.

Regarding the domestic difficulties in Liberia, the idea of a council of warlords that would bring peace was rapidly becoming an embarrassing fiasco. The cantankerous council of warlords continued to squabble. Boley accused Kromah of unilaterally appointing his supporters to two key posts in the finance ministry and the National Bank of Liberia and threatened grave consequences. Kromah accused Boley of improperly installing Ignatius Clay, an LPC ally, as governor of the same National Bank of Liberia.[26] These political differences hampered the smooth functioning of the Council of State.

On 2 March 1996, the executive council of ULIMO-J removed Roosevelt Johnson as chairman and replaced him with William Karyee while insisting that Johnson retain his LNTG post as minister for rural development. Two days later, the Council of State held an emergency meeting. Council members condemned ULIMO-J's attack on ECOMOG in Tubmanburg, ordered it to return the peacekeepers' confiscated heavy weapons, and invited Johnson and Karyee to a meeting at the Executive Mansion the next day. Though Karyee attended, Johnson did not. Charles Taylor and Alhaji Kromah led the council to recognize Karyee as ULIMO-J's new chairman, suspended Johnson from his cabinet post, and requested that ECOMOG search Johnson's Monrovia home for weapons.[27] The council also removed Ignatius Clay, the ULIMO-J nominee who had George Boley's backing, from his post as governor of the National Bank of Liberia.

On 7 March, the ECOMOG High Command, still smarting from the events in Tubmanburg, acceded to the council's request to send troops to Johnson's home. Johnson loyalists abducted a UN observer and threatened to kill him if Johnson was harmed. Two foreigners were also abducted. The hostages were released following negotiations between UN Special Representative Anthony Nyakyi and Johnson.[28]

By March 1996, ECOMOG's 7,500 troops were deployed in Monrovia, Gbarnga, Buchanan, Greenville, Kakata, Suehn, and Konola; UNOMIL's ninety-three military observers were deployed in Monrovia, Buchanan, and Suehn. But logistical support for ECOMOG remained elusive: in the six months after the October 1995 pledging conference, the peacekeepers received only three helicopters and twenty trucks. ECOMOG had failed to meet its Abuja-mandated deadlines. Its troops had not fully deployed in Liberia by 14 December, and disarmament, which was to have been completed by 30 January 1996, had not even begun.

On 22 March, fighting erupted in Monrovia between ULIMO-J elements; Johnson loyalists killed three bodyguards of ULIMO-J Chief of Staff Arma Youlou. One day later, the Council of State made yet another controversial decision, issuing an arrest warrant for Roosevelt Johnson on murder charges, alleging that a man had been found dead on his property. Amid the increasingly tense security situation, Boutros Boutros-Ghali included a warning in his 1 April 1996 report to the UN Security Council:

> The international community may ultimately face a major humanitarian disaster that could destabilize the subregion. Such a disaster would be far more costly, in the long run, than providing ECOMOG with the means to carry out its responsibilities under the Abuja Agreement.[29]

These words would soon prove prophetic.

Dog Days in Monrovia

After the Council of State issued its arrest warrant for Roosevelt Johnson, Charles Taylor and Alhaji Kromah ordered the Rapid Reaction Unit of the national police, backed by NPFL and ULIMO-K fighters, to carry out the order. On 6 April, this motley crew of enforcers marched to Johnson's home in the Sinkor district of Monrovia. Predictably, Johnson refused to give himself up, and some of the fiercest fighting in the capital since 1990 erupted between NPFL and ULIMO-K forces, on the one hand, and ULIMO-J elements supported by the AFL and LPC on the other.[30]

Many fighters flooded into Monrovia from the countryside with the purported aim of protecting their leaders. The fighting spread quickly to central Monrovia, trapping thousands of civilians in the cross fire. NPFL and ULIMO-K forces took over many areas of the city, while a combined force of the largely Krahn ULIMO-J, LPC, and AFL retreated to the AFL's Barclay Training Center (BTC), taking civilians, including some foreign nationals, at gunpoint for use as human shields. As they had done during fighting in 1990 and 1992, U.S. Marines evacuated 2,300 foreigners to safety following the outbreak of fighting in Monrovia.

During the first week of fighting in the Liberian capital, there was a complete breakdown of law and order as fighters moved into the commercial district, systematically looting offices and warehouses, setting buildings

ablaze, looting homes, commandeering UN and other vehicles, and disarming ECOMOG soldiers at checkpoints. AFL and ULIMO-J forces stormed
Monrovia prison and released fellow Krahn Charles Julu, the ringleader of
the botched September 1994 coup attempt in Monrovia (see Chapter 8).
Spriggs Payne airport was attacked by ULIMO-J fighters, who killed
two ECOMOG soldiers and damaged two commercial aircraft and three
ECOMOG helicopters.

Soon after the fighting broke out in Monrovia, the ambassadors of
Guinea, Nigeria, Sierra Leone, and the United States, as well as the UN special representative, formed a mediation team to broker a cease-fire. They
soon reached an agreement with Taylor and Kromah on the terms of a cease-
fire: the deployment of ECOMOG in Monrovia and around the BTC, the disarming of fighters at the BTC, the delivery of humanitarian assistance, and
the withdrawal of fighters from Monrovia.[31] After this agreement, the NPFL
and ULIMO-K temporarily stopped shelling the BTC, permitting the mediators to meet with representatives of ULIMO-J, the NPFL, and the AFL on 18
April. The BTC commanders also agreed to the terms of the cease-fire, which
came into effect the next day, and 226 foreign nationals were released from
the barracks. ECOMOG then deployed its troops and established checkpoints
in Monrovia as fighters started withdrawing from the capital.

On 29 April, the tenuous cease-fire broke down after an attempted
meeting of the Council of State, attended by Sankawulo, Taylor, and Kromah,
was interrupted by fighting between ULIMO-J and NPFL/ULIMO-K forces
near the Executive Mansion. Violence soon spread throughout central Monrovia. Fighters who had left the city soon reentered, and ECOMOG withdrew its troops from the city center. The NPFL and ULIMO-K resumed
shelling of the AFL's BTC and Camp Schefflin on alternate days.[32]

After strenuous negotiations at the U.S. Embassy in Monrovia, the mediators were able to convince Roosevelt Johnson to leave the country in
order to defuse tensions. Johnson was offered political asylum in Ghana
and Nigeria. Perhaps remembering the fate of Prince Yeduo Johnson, who
had been forcibly bundled onto a ship in 1992 and taken to exile in Nigeria,
he declined both offers. On 4 May, Johnson was flown out of Monrovia by
U.S. Marines to attend an ECOWAS Committee of Nine meeting in Accra.
In the middle of the fighting, council member Oscar Quiah suffered a
stroke and had to be evacuated to Accra. With Boley and Quiah out of the
country, Taylor and Kromah could impose their will on the Council of
State. The neophyte chairman, Sankawulo, was marginalized and failed to
make any formal statement for several weeks. He was reported to have condemned ULIMO-J and taken shelter in Taylor's home during the fighting.[33]

A full month after the fighting began, the ECOWAS Committee of
Nine foreign ministers met in Accra on 7 May to discuss ways to end the

fighting. George Boley, Oscar Quiah, and Tamba Tailor attended; Taylor and Kromah declined. Rawlings presented three options: continue searching for an elusive peace; create a more credible ECOMOG force that could undertake peace enforcement; or withdraw ECOMOG from Liberia. Rawlings backed the second option, welcoming offers of increased support for ECOMOG following the fighting in Monrovia. A U.S.-led international contact group, consisting of donor countries and subregional states, met in Geneva on 26 April. Washington promised $30 million to support ECOMOG with disarmament tasks, and Belgium and Denmark promised to finance the deployment of battalions from Burkina Faso and Ghana to an expanded ECOMOG.[34] These important promises would be the first substantial logistical contributions to ECOMOG's main contingents.

The ECOMOG commander, General Inienger, concluded his report to the meeting of ECOWAS foreign ministers in Accra by calling for the withdrawal of ECOMOG from Liberia if its logistical and manpower needs were not met.[35] The meeting also approved a status-of-forces agreement to govern relations between ECOMOG and the LNTG, with a warning that ECOMOG would never be under LNTG control.[36] ECOWAS foreign ministers adopted a document entitled "Mechanism for Returning Liberia to the Abuja Agreement," which reaffirmed the Abuja agreement as the only basis for peace and set out six conditions for the Liberian factions to fulfill: restoring the cease-fire; withdrawing factional fighters from Monrovia, thereby allowing the deployment of ECOMOG; removing arms from Monrovia and restoring its safe-haven status; guaranteeing the freedom of movement of civilians; returning weapons seized from ECOMOG and vehicles looted from UNOMIL, UN agencies, and nongovernmental organizations (NGOs); and reactivating the moribund Cease-Fire Violations Committee.[37]

In Accra, the ECOWAS foreign ministers insisted that the transitional government be inclusive and refused to recognize any government that came to power by force. The foreign ministers further called for Roosevelt Johnson to be reinstated in his ministerial post and requested that safe passage be guaranteed to fighters withdrawing from the BTC.[38] There was increasing talk of elections being held before total disarmament and of the creation of a postelection government of national unity.[39]

International press reports of looting by ECOMOG soldiers during fighting in Monrovia, though not uncommon in international peacekeeping, again damaged ECOMOG's reputation.[40] There were reports that some UN equipment was loaded onto ships destined for West Africa.[41] Some looted hardware was reportedly shipped to Guinea and Nigeria, and the Guinean ambassador in Liberia was said to have been complicit in the looting.[42] A Nigerian colonel was also sent home in August 1996 for shipping looted goods like cars and television sets to Nigeria.[43] Equally damaging were reports that Guinean members of the ECOMOG contingent were assisting Alhaji Kromah's forces in the early days of the assault on the BTC.[44]

Many observers have wondered why ECOMOG did not intervene to prevent fighting in Monrovia as it had in 1992 when the NPFL attacked. But the situations were different: In 1992, ECOMOG had been forced to defend itself from a direct attack; in 1996, the factions were attacking each other and ECOMOG had made peace with Charles Taylor. But it was obvious that the breakdown of law and order in the ECOMOG-protected capital damaged its peacekeeping credentials. It seems also that Inienger, still angry from the humiliation of his peacekeepers at Tubmanburg at the hands of ULIMO-J, was not averse to seeing Roosevelt Johnson given a bloody nose in Monrovia.

ECOMOG claimed that it could not intervene in the fighting, first because it was a neutral peacekeeper that could not become embroiled in conflicts between factions, and second because it lacked the manpower and resources to stem the mayhem.[45] However, it seems that by refusing to act ECOMOG wanted to highlight its plight to the international community, which had failed to provide the logistical and financial resources needed to operate effectively. The promised communications equipment, all-terrain vehicles, and armored personnel carriers failed to arrive. An unresolved conundrum thus remained: the donors refused to give ECOMOG the promised support until they were sure that a peaceful environment existed for its use; ECOMOG argued that this peaceful environment would not come about until it was given the resources to deploy throughout Liberia and disarm the factions. In short, without disarmament there would be no peace and therefore no resources; without resources, there would be no disarmament and therefore no peace.[46]

By the end of May 1996, ECOMOG troops were deployed in Monrovia, Buchanan, and Kakata, but the peacekeepers had withdrawn completely from Bo, Gbarnga, Tienne, and Sinje to reinforce their presence in Monrovia. The strategy of safe havens had collapsed as a result of the fighting in Monrovia, and this most important of safe havens had been rendered wholly unsafe. ECOMOG's inability to control the situation was expressed with brutal frankness by Victor Gbeho:

> The present cease-fire . . . resulted as and when individual factions arbitrarily curtailed further hostilities and not necessarily when ECOWAS and the mediators demanded a cease-fire. This suggests that the cease-fire was rather the product of factional fatigue and the debilitating and steady diminution in resources for sustaining the armed clashes.[47]

Ghana's deputy foreign minister, Mohammed Chambas, went further, actually demanding that the United States provide a "limited humanitarian force" to quell the fighting in Monrovia.[48]

By the end of the mayhem, 3,000 people had died in Monrovia.[49] The fighting marked the funeral of the first Abuja agreement as ECOWAS priests recited obsequies for yet another of their *abiku* children on Liberia's famished road.[50] Monrovia eventually returned to relative calm by the end of May 1996 following a bloodbath unleashed by warlords who refused to accept the responsibility that goes with power. It was hardly an edifying spectacle for politicians hoping to win electoral support from their citizens.

The Peace Train Returns to Abuja

During the OAU summit in Yaoundé from 8–10 July 1995, heads of state called for sanctions against recalcitrant faction leaders in Liberia and passed a resolution warning that

> should the ECOWAS assessment of the Liberian peace process . . . turn out to be negative, the OAU will help sponsor a draft resolution in the UN Security Council for the imposition of severe sanctions on them including the possibility of the setting up of a war crimes tribunal to try the leadership of the Liberian factions on the gross violations of the human rights of Liberians.[51]

From 26 to 27 July, ECOWAS heads of state met in Abuja for their nineteenth ordinary session. Subregional leaders expressed irritation and impatience with the protracted Liberian situation, even as they committed to finding a peaceful solution to the conflict.[52] Liberia was like a political boomerang: every time ECOWAS leaders tried to throw it away, it would come back to hit them on the head. The perennial fear of a wider subregional conflagration ensured that the Liberian crisis could not be ignored. The Liberian civil war had spilled 750,000 Liberian refugees into five subregional states; it also instigated a civil war in Sierra Leone that resulted in the death of 15,000 people and the displacement of 40 percent of the population by 1996 and spilled over sporadically into Côte d'Ivoire and Guinea.[53]

During the July 1996 ECOWAS meeting, subregional leaders called for restructuring Liberia's Council of State, disarming the factions, and holding early elections. ECOWAS leaders also threatened the warlords with sanctions.[54] The highlight of the summit involved the vitriolic attack on Liberia's warlords and their backers by the Gambian military leader, Captain Yaya Jammeh, who bluntly told the faction leaders:

> You are a disgrace to Africa. Your roles have brought more suffering to the Liberian people you claim to liberate, causing death and suffering in the wake of destruction. These bandits see ECOMOG as their enemies but they are enemies of themselves. . . . Maybe they will plant trees all over Liberia and rule over them.[55]

In what appeared to be pointed criticism of Burkina Faso and Côte d'Ivoire, Jammeh further noted, "Some of you sitting here are responsible for the carnage in Liberia. . . . While we are talking, some of your territories are being used by some of the warlords to ship arms and ammunition into Liberia."[56] But with Nigeria having made peace with Charles Taylor, making clear it would not obstruct his presidential ambitions, Blaise Compaoré started to support ECOMOG. By early 1996, Burkina Faso offered to send two battalions to ECOMOG, subject to the provision of logistical support by the international community.

The Ivorian government had started distancing itself from the NPFL since the failure of the Yamoussoukro agreement in 1992. Abidjan's changed Liberia policy was evident during the ECOWAS Committee of Nine Meeting in Abuja in August 1996, when Côte d'Ivoire was at the forefront of countries pushing for sanctions against the warlords and urging Burkina Faso to discontinue military support to the NPFL.[57] A month earlier, Abidjan denied Taylor permission to overfly its airspace to travel to Nigeria.[58] At the ECOWAS meeting, Ivorian leader Henri Konan Bédié refused Charles Taylor's invitation to meet alone, insisting that Taylor must meet him with Kromah and Boley, who were becoming increasingly frequent visitors to Abidjan.[59] Bédié had won a controversial presidential election in October 1995 marred by violence and an opposition boycott.[60] He was more interested in consolidating his position at home than in embarking on a risky foreign adventure that was causing instability on his border. Ivorian opposition parties added to the pressure by complaining about the destabilizing effects of the Liberian civil war on Côte d'Ivoire.[61]

At the end of the ECOWAS summit on 27 July 1996, Ghana's Jerry Rawlings was replaced as ECOWAS chairman by Nigeria's General Sani Abacha. Rawlings proved to be the most dynamic ECOWAS chairman on the Liberian issue. But even his efforts could not achieve a breakthrough. With difficult presidential elections in Ghana scheduled for 7 December 1995, Rawlings was relieved to cede the ECOWAS chair to Abacha after two tireless but thankless years. He took a backseat in the labyrinth of Liberian politics to concentrate on the most difficult election of his career, which in the end he comfortably won.

Some intricate politics surrounded the election of General Abacha as ECOWAS chairman. After Rawlings, tradition dictated that the next in line should come from a francophone country. Malian President Alpha Konaré, who reportedly had Washington's backing, was expected to be nominated. Rawlings communicated to other ECOWAS states that Konaré would be succeeding him. The Ghanaian president strongly supported his Malian counterpart due to experience in dealing with the Tuareg problem in Mali. But Nigeria had other plans.

General Abacha sent a note to ECOWAS leaders suggesting that Togo's Gnassingbé Eyadéma become ECOWAS chairman due to his role as cofounder of the subregional body. Senegal's Abdou Diouf alerted Konaré to

Abuja's intrigue. Abacha's suggestion of Eyadéma was, in fact, a diplomatic ruse: he knew that Rawlings would never accept Eyadéma's candidacy due to the known antagonism between the two leaders. Abacha courted several leaders, particularly Sierra Leone's Ahmad Tejan Kabbah, and was eventually able to present himself as the compromise candidate after an acrimonious debate had failed to agree on either Konaré or Eyadéma.[62]

Liberian politicians did not take part in the ECOWAS summit of 26 July 1996 but met with General Abacha four days later. It was clear that most of the six conditions of the May 1996 Accra mechanism had not yet been met: The cease-fire had not been restored; arms had not been fully removed from Monrovia; stolen ECOMOG weapons and looted UN equipment had not been returned; the NPFL still refused to participate in the Cease-Fire Violations Committee; and the freedom of movement of civilians was far from guaranteed. Furthermore, disagreements continued among members of the Council of State regarding total disarmament prior to elections: Taylor favored elections without full disarmament, whereas Boley insisted on disarmament before any elections. Boley was also calling for ECOWAS to take strong action against Taylor and Kromah for the events of April 1996.

From 13 to 14 August 1996, the ECOWAS chiefs of staff held their thirteenth meeting in Abuja. Countries represented included Nigeria, Benin, Burkina Faso, Côte d'Ivoire, Gambia, Ghana, Guinea, Liberia, Niger, and Togo. At this meeting ECOMOG's longest-serving field commander, Mark Inienger (who later died of illness in March 2002), handed over the reins to another Nigerian general, Victor Malu, after nearly three years of service. General Malu had served as ECOMOG chief of staff between 1992 to 1993 and was well acquainted with the Liberian dossier. Before his appointment, Malu had commanded the 82d Division of the Nigerian army and was a member of the Provisional Ruling Council. His reputation was that of a tough soldier in the mold of the second and fifth ECOMOG commanders, Generals Joshua Dogonyaro and Adetunji Olurin.

During his opening address at the August 1996 chiefs of staff meeting, the Nigerian chief of defense staff, General Abdulsalam Abubakar, reiterated the usual complaints about ECOMOG's lack of logistical support and its pernicious impact on the peace process. Abubakar suggested that it would be ill-advised for ECOWAS to organize elections with the enormous, undiscovered arms caches that still existed in Liberia. He recommended the creation of safe havens in which to organize elections.[63]

During the meeting General Malu said he would need 18,000 troops and adequate logistics to perform disarmament tasks effectively. He also stressed the importance of Liberian government officials submitting to searches by ECOMOG troops in Monrovia to prevent arms-smuggling.[64] During further deliberations, the Ivorian chief of staff, Admiral Timite Lassana, reported that his country had stationed 1,000 troops to protect its border with Liberia in order to stem the flow of arms into that country. He also announced Abidjan's decision to send a contingent of fifty medical and paramedical staff to Liberia to strengthen ECOMOG.[65]

The chiefs of staff concluded their meeting with a series of recommendations to the ECOWAS Authority suggesting, among other things, that disarmament should precede elections; that ECOWAS member states should report breaches of the arms embargo to the UN Sanctions Committee; that the status-of-forces agreement should increase ECOMOG's powers to operate effectively; that all ECOWAS states should contribute troops to ECOMOG; and that the title of ECOMOG field commander be changed back to force commander.[66] The title of force commander had not been used since the first ECOMOG commander, Arnold Quainoo, was replaced by Joshua Dogonyaro in September 1990.

From 15 and 16 August 1996, the eighth meeting of the ECOWAS Committee of Nine foreign ministers took place in Abuja. During the meeting, Nigerian Foreign Minister Ikimi called for a revision of the Abuja timetable backed by a set of guarantees to ensure strict compliance. He suggested a monitoring mechanism to assess compliance.[67] The meeting of the ECOWAS Committee of Nine on 17 August extended the Abuja timetable by postponing elections from 20 August 1996 to 30 May 1997, with the new Liberian government to be installed by 15 June 1997. The disengagement of Liberian factions would occur between 20 and 31 August 1996 after the expected cease-fire came into effect. Logistical support would be provided to ECOMOG between 1 and 30 September 1996. Disarmament, demobilization, and repatriation of fighters would occur between 22 November 1996 and 31 January 1997. Council members and other public officials wishing to contest elections would resign by 28 February 1997. UN assistance would be requested for conducting the elections.[68] This agreement came to be known as Abuja II.

The implementation schedule of Abuja II was divided into five stages, with monitoring visits to Monrovia during each stage between October 1996 and April 1997. The monitoring team was authorized to recommend sanctions against violators of the cease-fire.[69] Sanctions for recalcitrant faction leaders would involve: travel and residence restrictions; freezing of business activities and assets; exclusion from the electoral process; restriction on the use of the airspace and territorial waters of ECOWAS states; expulsion of family members from ECOWAS states; request for the UN Security Council to impose visa sanctions; restrictions on Liberian imports; and invoking the OAU 1996 summit resolution that threatened a war crimes tribunal.[70] It was somewhat ironic that Nigeria, one of the most vociferous advocates of these sanctions, was itself placed under mild international sanctions after the hanging of nine Ogoni environmental activists, including Ken

Saro-Wiwa, on 10 November 1995. This incident further worsened already strained bilateral relations between Washington and Abuja.

Offering a report card on the council of warlords at its August 1996 meeting, ECOWAS foreign ministers ruled that it had performed well below expectations. In a barely concealed criticism of Sankawulo's ineffectual leadership, the ministers noted that stronger leadership could have helped the council perform better. They suggested that the Committee of Nine be empowered to replace errant council members and called for a new code of conduct to guide its activities. The ECOWAS heads of state endorsed the decisions of their foreign ministers on 17 August and designated Ruth Perry, a former Liberian senator (1986–1990), as the new council chairperson. West African leaders also praised the steps taken by the Ivorian government to prevent the flow of arms supplies through its territory, showing a clear recognition within ECOWAS that Abidjan had changed its Liberia policy.[71]

In an encouraging development, six ECOWAS states offered to contribute troops to ECOMOG: Ghana offered a 750-man battalion; Niger promised a company and a battalion; Benin and Togo promised an unspecified number of troops; Burkina Faso offered a reduced battalion; and Côte d'Ivoire repeated its earlier offer of fifty medical and paramedical personnel.[72] It was significant that this list included four new francophone members, including those who supported the NPFL: Burkina Faso and Côte d'Ivoire.

By the end of August 1996, ECOMOG had deployed troops in Kakata, the Po River, and Buchanan. Abuja II called for a new cease-fire by 31 August 1996, but peace still remained elusive in many parts of Liberia. Both wings of ULIMO were fighting in Bomi and Grand Cape Mount Counties; the LPC battled the NPFL in the southeast, with the NPFL capturing the LPC stronghold of Greenville; and to exacerbate further an already complicated civil war, yet another faction emerged, calling itself the Congo Defense Force. It joined the fighting between the two ULIMOs in Liberia's western counties.[73]

As Liberians awaited the inauguration of yet another transitional government, they pondered the death of Abuja I, which seemed to offer the best hope for peace in six years. Ten peace agreements had now been signed and broken. The ECOWAS peace train meandered its way along a tortuous, winding route through Banjul, Bamako, Lomé, Yamoussoukro, Geneva, Cotonou, Akosombo, Accra, and Abuja. Its cargo of warlords had disembarked once again in Abuja, guided by ECOWAS's weary locomotive drivers. Now, yet another agreement had been signed—Abuja II—which looked like another respite that would give factions enough time to gather their strength before waging more war. The eleventh peace agreement in the Liberian civil war was now signed. This incredible journey without maps looked as if it would end only when the exhausted warlords bid a final farewell to arms, or when ECOMOG's exasperated peacekeepers bid a final farewell to Liberia.

Notes

1. "Here to Ensure Lasting Peace (interview with Ambassador Victor Gbeho)," *West Africa,* no. 4078 (11–17 December 1995): 1920.

2. *West Africa,* no. 4085 (5–11 February 1996): 260.

3. John H.T. Stewart, "Teething Problems for Ruling Council," *West Africa,* no. 4069 (9–15 October 1995): 1564.

4. Ibid.

5. *West Africa,* no. 4073 (6–12 November 1995): 1717.

6. Fourteenth Progress Report of the Secretary-General on the United Nations Observer Mission in Liberia, 18 December 1995, S/1995/1042, p. 1.

7. Ibid., p. 2.

8. Ben Asante, "Another Peace Pact," *West Africa,* no. 4075 (20–26 November 1995): 1802.

9. Fourteenth Progress Report of the Secretary-General on the United Nations Observer Mission in Liberia, p. 5.

10. Fifteenth Progress Report of the Secretary-General on the United Nations Observer Mission in Liberia, 23 January 1996, S/1996/47, p. 6.

11. See *The Guardian* (London), 5 January 1996, p. 8.

12. Fifteenth Progress Report of the Secretary-General on the United Nations Observer Mission in Liberia, pp. 3–4.

13. William Reno, "The Business of War in Liberia," *Current History* 95, no. 601 (May 1996): 213–215; and *The Economist,* "The Way Ahead?" 20 January 1996, pp. 61–62.

14. Fifteenth Progress Report of the Secretary-General on the United Nations Observer Mission in Liberia, p. 2.

15. *West Africa,* no. 4083 (22–28 January 1996): 98–99.

16. Fifteenth Progress Report of the Secretary-General on the United Nations Observer Mission in Liberia, p. 4.

17. "Keeping What Peace?" *Africa Confidential* 37, no. 4 (16 February 1996): 1.

18. "Final Report," Seventh Meeting of the Ministers of Foreign Affairs of the ECOWAS Committee of Nine on Liberia, Accra, 7 May 1996, ECW/MINFA/CTTE9/VII/2/Rev.1 (Restricted), p. 4.

19. Personal interview at the British Embassy, Abidjan, 31 July 1996.

20. *West Africa,* no. 4089 (4–10 March 1996): 331.

21. Personal interview at the United Nations Development Programme office, Abidjan, 1 August 1996.

22. Personal interview at the Office of the United Nations High Commissioner for Refugees, Abidjan, 1 August 1996.

23. *West Africa,* no. 4113 (19–25 August 1996): 1299.

24. Personal interview at the UNHCR office, Abidjan, 1 August 1996.

25. See, for example, "Report of the Liberia Peace Council on the Liberian-Ivorian Border Incident 13th June 1995 and Its Aftermath," 26 July 1995, Liberia.

26. See Ben Asante, "Power Tussle in Monrovia," *West Africa,* no. 4090 (11–17 March 1996).

27. Sixteenth Progress Report of the Secretary-General on the United Nations Observer Mission in Liberia, 1 April 1996, S/1996/232, p. 2.

28. Ibid.

29. Ibid., p. 10.

30. My account of the events in Monrovia that follows is based largely on the Seventeenth Progress Report of the Secretary-General on the United Nations Observer Mission in Liberia, 21 May 1996, S/1996/362; see also Annex 1 of this report, which provides a detailed account of the fighting.

31. Seventeenth Progress Report of the Secretary-General on the United Nations Observer Mission in Liberia, p. 13.

32. Report of the Special Representative of the Chairman of ECOWAS, Monrovia, 12 July 1996, pp. 2–3.

33. Personal interview at the Ghanaian Foreign Ministry, Accra, September 1996.

34. "Final Report," Seventh Meeting of the Ministers of Foreign Affairs of the ECOWAS Committee of Nine on Liberia, pp. 5–6.

35. Ibid., p. 17.

36. Ibid., p. 18.

37. Seventeenth Progress Report of the Secretary-General on the United Nations Observer Mission in Liberia, p. 2.

38. Ibid., p. 3.

39. Ajoa Yeboah-Afari, "The Aborted Accra Summit," *West Africa,* no. 4100 (20–26 May 1996): 787.

40. Peacekeepers were accused of looting in Bosnia and Cambodia; accusations of child prostitution and corruption have also been leveled at peacekeepers in Somalia and Mozambique.

41. Seventeenth Progress Report of the Secretary-General on the United Nations Observer Mission in Liberia, p. 7.

42. Personal interview at the Ghanaian Foreign Ministry, Accra, September 1996.

43. Personal interview with a senior military official, Accra, September 1996.

44. Lindsay Barrett, "Confusion Reigns Supreme," *West Africa,* no. 4101 (27 May–2 June 1996): 823.

45. Seventeenth Progress Report of the Secretary-General on the United Nations Observer Mission in Liberia, p. 5.

46. Adekeye Adebajo, "Rich Man's War, Poor Man's War," *World Today* 52, nos. 8–9 (August/September 1996): 224.

47. Report of the Special Representative of the Chairman of ECOWAS, 12 July 1996, p. 2.

48. *West Africa,* no. 4098 (6–12 May 1996): 691.

49. Eighteenth Progress Report of the Secretary-General on the United Nations Observer Mission in Liberia, 22 August 1996, S/1996/684, p. 7.

50. To understand this reference, see Ben Okri, *The Famished Road* (New York, London, Sydney: Anchor Books, 1992).

51. Quoted in Kaye Whiteman, "The OAU Summit," *West Africa,* no. 4109 (22–28 July 1996): 1139.

52. Eighteenth Progress Report of the Secretary-General on the United Nations Observer Mission in Liberia, p. 2.

53. Paul Richards, *Fighting for the Rainforest: War, Youth, and Resources in Sierra Leone* (Oxford: James Currey, 1996), p. xix.

54. Eighteenth Progress Report of the Secretary-General on the United Nations Observer Mission in Liberia, p. 2.

55. Quoted in *West Africa,* no. 4113 (19–25 August 1996): 1307.

56. Quoted in Moffat Ekoriko, "Summit Dashes Peace Hopes," *Africa Today* 2, no. 5 (September/October 1996): 16.

57. Personal interview at the British Embassy, Abidjan, September 1996.

58. Personal interview with Kwame Amoa-Awua, Director for Africa and OAU Bureau, Ghanaian Foreign Ministry, Accra, September 1996.

59. Personal interview with Aidara Abdoulaye, Head of Conflict Division, Côte d'Ivoire Ministry of Foreign Affairs, Abidjan, September 1996.

60. See Robert Mundt, "Côte d'Ivoire: Continuity and Change in a Semi-democracy," in John Clark and David Gardinier (eds.), *Political Reform in Francophone Africa* (Boulder and Oxford: Westview, 1997), p. 197.

61. Personal interview with J. Coker, Nigerian Ambassador to Côte d'Ivoire, Abidjan, August 1996.

62. This account is from a personal interview in Accra, in September 1996, with Air Marshal A. H. Dumashie, Ghanaian Chief of Defense Staff.

63. "Final Report," Economic Community of West African States, Thirteenth meeting of Chiefs of Staff of ECOWAS Member States, Abuja, 13–14 August 1996 (Restricted), pp. 2–13.

64. Ibid., pp. 4–6.

65. Ibid., p. 9.

66. Ibid., pp. 15–16.

67. "Final Report," Eighth Meeting of Ministers of Foreign Affairs of the ECOWAS Committee of Nine on Liberia. Abuja, 15–17 August 1996, ECW/MFA/C9-8/8/96/rev.1, pp. 4–5.

68. See "Final Communiqué," Fourth Meeting of Heads of State and Government of the ECOWAS Committee of Nine on Liberia, Abuja, 17 August 1996.

69. ECOWAS Decision HSGC9-2/8/96 relating to the implementation of the arms embargo in Liberia, Abuja, 17 August 1996, p. 4.

70. "Final Report," Eighth Meeting of Ministers of Foreign Affairs of the ECOWAS Committee of Nine on Liberia, Abuja, 15–17 August 1996, pp. 10–14.

71. Ibid., pp. 7–12.

72. Ibid., p. 15.

73. "Final Report," Economic Community of West African States, Thirteenth meeting of Chiefs of Staff of ECOWAS Member States, Abuja, 13–14 August 1996 (Restricted), p. 7.

chapter 10

Farewell to Arms?
September 1996–July 1997

The time has come for us to put the past behind us and move our country
forward. —Ruth Perry, Liberian head of state (August 1996–August 1997)

In this chapter we cover the events surrounding the disarmament and demobilization of the Liberian factions that led to the end of Liberia's seven-year civil war and culminated in a national election on 19 July 1997. We highlight two main arguments. The first is that the outcome of the Liberian civil war ultimately depended on contingent developments and on consensus being reached at three levels of analysis: domestic, subregional, and external. The lack of consensus at these three levels hampered efforts to achieve a Pax Nigeriana in Liberia. The unprecedented attainment of consensus at all three levels came together in a way that facilitated a solution to the Liberian civil war through Charles Taylor's electoral victory. The second argument, outlined farther below, is that the limits and constraints of Pax Nigeriana were glaringly exposed during the conflict.

At the domestic level, the warlords' decision to enter directly the political process in August 1995 led them to cooperate with disarmament. The strongest Liberian faction, Charles Taylor's NPFL, made peace with Nigeria, which under General Sani Abacha's leadership was no longer obstructing Taylor's political ambitions. Taylor calculated correctly that he had the financial resources, acquired through the control of much of Liberia's territory during the war, to mount the most effective electoral campaign against a divided opposition. Most Liberian voters also concluded that a Taylor presidential victory was the best guarantee for preventing a return to war. At the subregional level, former NPFL backers Burkina Faso and Côte d'Ivoire saw no reason to continue obstructing ECOMOG and, along with francophone

Benin and Niger, contributed troops to ECOMOG. This forged a genuinely subregional peacekeeping force for the first time since the start of the conflict.

At the external level, the United States decided for the first time to separate its strained bilateral relationship with Nigeria, ECOMOG's dominant contingent, from its multilateral support for ECOMOG, as well as to provide all peacekeepers with logistical support they previously lacked. This problem of inadequate logistics had thwarted three previous efforts at disarmament. The European Union also played an important role in providing logistical support to ECOMOG; the United States, European Union, and United Nations assisted demobilization, reintegration programs for former combatants, and the electoral process.

The second main argument is this: contrary to more conventional explanations, which contend that a hegemonic Nigeria imposed its will on the subregion in order to resolve the Liberian crisis, the limits of and constraints on Pax Nigeriana were exposed during the conflict. Put simply, Nigeria lacked the logistical and financial resources—eventually provided by external actors—to end the civil war. It also needed the cooperation of the warlords, as well as subregional assistance from francophone countries to help end the war. Although Nigeria was the most influential actor in this process, it lacked the means to impose a Pax Nigeriana on Liberia. It had hegemonic aspirations but lacked hegemonic abilities and therefore needed crucial Liberian, subregional, and external support to resolve the conflict.

Mother Courage and Her Children

German playwright Bertolt Brecht's epic *Mother Courage and Her Children* depicted the efforts of a tragic heroine-widow who fought bravely but unsuccessfully to save her children from Europe's Thirty Years' War (1618–1648). Ruth Perry, Liberia's head of state and Africa's first female leader, was also a widow, the mother of seven children. She was also the courageous matriarch of a nation struggling to save its children from death and destruction. Perry frequently referred to Liberians as "my children"; even the warlords on the Council of State referred to her as "mother."

On 3 September 1996, Ruth Perry was inaugurated as chair of the Council of State. A week later, she chaired the first meeting of the council since the fighting of April-May 1996. Charles Taylor generated more controversy by missing Perry's inauguration, preferring instead to travel to Tripoli to attend celebrations marking the twenty-seventh anniversary of the coup that brought his ally, Muammar Qaddafi, to power. Roosevelt Johnson, the source of the outbreak of fighting in April 1996, was appointed minister of transport. In stark contrast to the lackadaisical neophyte Wilton

Sankawulo, Perry proved to be an energetic council chair: in September 1996, she traveled to Bomi and Grand Cape Mount Counties to highlight the suffering there and urged speedy humanitarian assistance; she rallied support for the Liberian peace process during an impassioned address at the UN General Assembly in New York on 9 October 1996; and she traversed the country prior to disarmament to urge fighters to lay down their arms.

But deep divisions persisted within the Council of State. Oscar Quiah, one of three civilian council members, noted that serious dialogue on key issues of the peace process was blocked by the three warlords; this political gridlock was exacerbated by the warlords' ongoing control of Liberia's ministries, which were run by their appointees.[1] In a telling incident, Taylor demanded that Perry make changes to her UN speech before he voted to approve funding for the trip to New York. Apparently, she made the changes.[2]

Government agencies continued to be dominated by sometimes incompetent factional representatives. Factionalism within deprived these agencies of neutrality, with consequences impacting sensitive areas like justice and security. Corruption continued, with the finance ministry and the National Bank of Liberia blaming one another in January 1997 for the disappearance of $3 million. The Liberian National Transitional Government continued to experience financial difficulties: the $16–20 million it collected from the registration of Liberian ships was virtually its only source of income, and civil servants went unpaid between March and December 1996.[3]

ECOWAS showed a new determination and seriousness in implementing Abuja II, consulting with the Liberian parties on electoral issues during its regular assessment meetings. The ECOWAS chairman, General Sani Abacha, summoned Ruth Perry to Abuja for a meeting between 24 and 26 September 1996 to review implementation of Abuja II. The first assessment meeting to review implementation of the agreement was held in Monrovia from 16 to 17 October 1996. It was chaired by Tom Ikimi, Nigeria's foreign minister and the new special envoy of the ECOWAS chairman, and involved representatives of ECOWAS, UNOMIL, the LNTG, and donor countries.

In one of the most dramatic conversions since the biblical Paul tumbled off his horse on the road to Damascus, Charles Taylor announced in September 1996 that he had found solace in Jesus Christ and become a born-again Christian. Taylor told stunned and incredulous Liberians: "Let us look closely at the teachings of Christ and try to emulate him. I have a share of the blame in the massacre that took place recently but my people must forgive me."[4] His newfound faith would prove crucial during the next major episode of the war.

On 31 October 1996, Taylor narrowly escaped an assassination attempt. Upon entering his office on the sixth floor of the Executive Mansion in Monrovia, he was attacked by a grenade followed by a burst of machine-gun fire from the office of George Boley, who was not in the office at the time. Five persons were killed, including Taylor's personal aide, and several injured. ECOMOG troops in the vicinity whisked Taylor to safety and arrested twenty assailants, mostly LPC members. The ECOMOG force commander, General Victor Malu, responded by sending ECOMOG reinforcements to seal off the area and deploying troops, tanks, and helicopters at strategic points in the capital. Taylor demonstrated political maturity in urging his followers not to retaliate but pointedly accused three leading politicians—George Boley, Roosevelt Johnson, and Oscar Quiah—of complicity. All three had opposed Taylor during the April 1996 fighting and denied the allegation, with Boley and Johnson accusing Taylor of having staged the event to draw attention to himself. Taylor later apologized to Quiah, absolving him of any blame in the incident.

General Malu demonstrated his lack of diplomatic tact by agreeing with Taylor's assessment, even before an investigation had been conducted, that the LPC had been behind it all. He also argued, somewhat implausibly, that Boley personally may not have been involved.[5] Boley predictably accused ECOMOG of bias and asked that it be excluded from any investigation. ECOMOG, UNOMIL, and the justice ministry were, however, assigned to investigate the incident. Tensions heightened when several factions threatened to take hostages if any arrests were made.

Despite the assassination attempt, Taylor continued to play the extravagant showman and president-in-waiting. Even before the election of July 1997, he began erecting a huge mansion in Monrovia with a large wall and luxurious banquet rooms for visiting dignitaries. With pomp and pageantry, he remarried Jewel Howard, mother of one of his eight children and deputy governor of the National Bank of Liberia, on his forty-ninth birthday (28 January 1997). He threw a lavish wedding party in Gbarnga, attended by Victor Malu and Tom Ikimi. The bridal gowns and wedding souvenirs had been ordered from Macy's in New Jersey, the bridegroom's cream-colored suit was tailored in Abidjan, and there was a spectacular three-layer wedding cake.[6]

General Malu, Chief Ikimi, and the Warlords

ECOWAS adopted a more assertive and sometimes intrusive role in the Liberian peace process, imposing decisions related to sensitive electoral issues on Liberia's fractious parties, which were too disunited to resist. Some of the parties actually welcomed ECOWAS's role of arbiter as a balance against powerful warlords. The foreign ministers of the ECOWAS Committee of Nine met in Monrovia on 8–9 November 1996, along with representatives from Mali, Niger, and Sierra Leone. The attendance by nearly all ECOWAS members demonstrated a new subregional consensus in settling the Liberian conflict. The meeting adopted a code of conduct for the Council of State to ensure that its members complied with Abuja II and gave the ECOWAS chair authority to impose sanctions on violators.[7] The foreign ministers' attempt to convene a Council of State meeting to reconcile Liberia's parties following the assassination attempt in October, however, proved unsuccessful; no venue was considered safe by all parties.

General Victor Malu was acquiring a reputation for hyperactivity and ruthless dynamism. He managed to win almost universal respect among Liberians, West Africans, and members of the international community, and the Liberian press nicknamed him "the strongman of Liberia." Malu seemed to revel in his reputation as a no-nonsense general, saying: "I will try to be a good soldier, and if that is being tough, then I am."[8] The force commander won the crucial respect of the warlords, with even Charles Taylor praising his "astute handling of the ECOWAS mandate." Taylor asked ECOMOG to stay on for eighteen months after elections to help train a new national army.[9] Malu was also tough with his own Nigerian soldiers. Amid growing reports of Liberian women being impregnated by ECOMOG soldiers, he warned that any peacekeeper engaging in such relations would be immediately discharged from the army. As Malu memorably put it, "We are here to make peace, not babies."[10]

Malu's strategy for creating a secure environment for elections was to ensure security in Monrovia, where at least half of Liberia's population lived; to increase gradually ECOMOG's presence in the countryside; and to disarm the factions while simultaneously conducting random cordon-and-search raids for arms and arms caches. There were some early signs of optimism in the disarmament process on 7 September 1996, when the NPFL encamped 500 fighters in Nimba County and ULIMO-K surrendered arms, ammunition, and 119 antitank mines to ECOMOG in Voinjama. The two largest factions undertook these acts unilaterally before the formal start of disarmament on 22 November. However, fighting continued in the southeast between the NPFL and LPC and in the northwest between the two wings of ULIMO in violation of Abuja II, which had called for a cease-fire by 31 August. Diamond, timber, and rubber were still being exported from areas under the control of the factions. On 6 September, both wings of ULIMO agreed to a cease-fire in Bomi County, but ULIMO-J increased its presence in Tubmanburg, and clashes resumed between both factions in neighboring Grand Cape Mount County by the middle of October, especially in Sinje, Wengokor, Gbesse, and Tienne.

The NPFL's capture of Greenville, a port city used for timber exports, from the LPC in September 1996 angered Boley, and he threatened to stop cooperating with the disarmament process unless the NPFL withdrew its fighters. The NPFL recaptured most of the territory it had earlier lost in Grand Bassa, Grand Gedeh, Maryland, River Cess, and Sinoe Counties.

Boley, alone among the faction leaders, refused to provide ECOMOG with information on potential sites for collecting arms. This drew a sharp warning from General Malu, who implored the warlord to cooperate with ECOMOG in monitoring LPC areas. Malu eventually arranged a reconciliation meeting between Boley and Taylor, which eased tensions.

In another gruesome incident, at least twenty-one civilians were killed in Sinje, Grand Cape Mount County, when the village was attacked on 28 September by ULIMO-K fighters just after it had received food relief. The victims were decapitated, castrated, and shot. There were reports of other killings in Bomi and parts of Grand Cape Mount around the same time, believed to be linked to the Sinje killings. Such incidents were reported up until the end of disarmament: on 7 December 1996, eleven civilians were hacked to death by alleged ULIMO-J fighters in the so-called Bloun Town massacre following fighting in the northwest between ULIMO-J and the Congo Defense Force, a militia allied with ULIMO-K.[11] The discovery of 100 skeletons at Greenville hospital in December 1996 suggested that the full horror of this ghastly civil war was still being unearthed.

On 7 October, General Malu issued a two-day ultimatum to ULIMO-J to remove its roadblocks from the highways to Tubmanburg and Grand Cape Mount County. He sent troops to ensure his order was carried out after the expiration of the ultimatum, allowing humanitarian relief to resume to Bo Waterside for the first time in a year. On 27 October, both wings of ULIMO agreed to yet another cease-fire in the northwest, and a buffer zone was created between the factions, with ECOMOG and UNOMIL increasing patrols in Bomi and Grand Cape Mount Counties. The southeast reported fewer incidents of violence, allowing ECOMOG to redeploy a battalion to Greenville and Harper. Joint ECOMOG and UNOMIL patrols were undertaken in Bong and Nimba Counties. On the eve of disarmament, scheduled to begin on 22 November, several areas in four of Liberia's thirteen counties still remained inaccessible to ECOMOG, fighters continued to loot food relief, and civilians and humanitarian relief groups still suffered harassment at the hands of armed factions.

Though ECOMOG still needed vehicle maintenance and spare parts for its vehicles, the arrival of 119 trucks, some helicopters, as well as communications equipment between August and October 1996 gave peacekeepers the logistical support to deploy to the countryside with confidence for the first time since the start of its mission in 1990. It also enabled ECOMOG to respond swiftly to security problems. Donors were finally delivering on pledges they had made since October 1995. Earlier attempts at disarmament by ECOMOG peacekeepers in 1992, 1994, and 1995 had all ended tragically after the killing of ill-equipped peacekeepers and their subsequent withdrawal back to Monrovia and its environs. ECOMOG's 7,500 troops had previously been deployed only to Monrovia, Kakata, Buchanan, and the

Po River area. By November 1996, Malu dispatched more troops to Voin-jama, Bo Waterside, SOS Village, Zwedru, and Tubmanburg, all of which were to be used as disarmament sites. Within two months, more peace-keepers were also deployed to disarmament sites near Monrovia at the Bar-clay Training Center, Camp Schiefflin, Camp Nama, and Tapeta.

ECOMOG's deployment allowed humanitarian relief to reach previously inaccessible and insecure parts of Bomi and Grand Cape Mount Counties. Tubmanburg, for example, had not been provided with humanitarian relief for seven months between March and September 1996, and 82 percent of its children were suffering from severe malnutrition.[12] An estimated 4,000 civilians had died of starvation and disease in Tubmanburg in 1996. Davidetta Browne provided a graphic eyewitness description after a visit to the area:

> Village after village and town after town held thousands of starving people, some of them no different from walking skeletons and corpses. It is a shocking tale of human suffering, disease, malnutrition and death of unparalleled occurrence anywhere in the subregion.[13]

Despite provision of food and medicines to Tubmanburg by UN agencies and other international relief agencies, parts of Bomi, Grand Cape Mount, and Lofa Counties remained inaccessible until early January 1997 due to continued clashes between the warring factions.

On 16 January 1997, Tom Ikimi led a delegation that included Guinean Foreign Minister Lamine Camara and Ghanaian Deputy Foreign Minister Mohammed Chambas to Monrovia for the second ECOWAS verification and assessment meeting. Each met separately with the Council of State, and they were finally able to persuade the council to reconvene. The council meeting of 16 January, attended by ECOWAS delegates, was the first one held since the Taylor assassination attempt two months earlier.

Ikimi continued to treat Liberia's squabbling politicians like schoolboys in his hectoring, haughty, headmasterly manner. He publicly berated Liberia's election commissioners and reminded them that he was in charge. During a meeting on the election law, he presented his own amendments as the final word, leaving no room for negotiation.[14] As Victor Tanner noted, "Chief Ikimi's outbursts during his periodical visits to Liberia acquired such a reputation that a new expression was coined in Monrovia: to be *ikimied,* that is, to be dressed down in public usually in loud, unequivocal language."[15] ECOWAS foreign ministers complained that they were often kept waiting for hours by Ikimi, and some Liberian journalists noted that he was arrogant, ignored civilian politicians, and dealt only with the faction leaders.[16]

But there was another side to Ikimi's abrasiveness: though he was blunt in public, he was less confrontational with the faction leaders in private.

His failure to support sanctions against the warlords, despite such calls after the Sinje massacre, showed he was keenly aware of the limits of his power and the importance of maintaining the cooperation of the warlords. As Howard Jeter, the U.S. special envoy for Liberia at the time and the current ambassador to Nigeria, put it: "Ikimi's bluster and Malu's determination have been a key to the process."[17]

Disarming the Factions

Liberia's disarmament process started on schedule on 22 November 1996. First, fighters were provided food rations and transportation to chosen destinations in exchange for surrendering a serviceable weapon or 100 rounds of ammunition. LPC fighters disarmed in Zwedru; ULIMO-K in Voinjama and Bo Waterside; NPFL in Gbarnga and Saniquellie; ULIMO-J in Tubmanburg; and AFL at Barclay Training Center and Camp Schiefflin. Fighters surrendered howitzers, rocket-launchers, antiaircraft machine guns, antitank weapons, mortars, grenades, pistols, rifles, submachine guns, artillery shells, and mines.

Despite the impressive and unprecedented scale of disarmament, there were worrisome signs that disgruntled warlords were keeping arms in reserve in the event their electoral fortunes dimmed. Many of the arms surrendered in the early stages were unserviceable, and some fighters even surrendered bows and arrows. Some local commanders actively discouraged disarmament, intimidating and punishing fighters who had disarmed without permission and forcing some to disarm surreptitiously under cover of darkness. Abuja II did not provide small assistance packages for former combatants, and demobilized combatants complained about the meager food rations. Unlike the first Abuja agreement, which envisaged demobilized fighters spending one week at encampment centers, demobilization under Abuja II saw disarmed fighters moving into bridging activities within twenty-four hours of registering at demobilization centers.

By the end of disarmament on 31 January 1997, ECOMOG had established buffer zones between the two ULIMO factions in Bomi and Grand Cape Mount Counties and between the NPFL and LPC in Grand Gedeh County. General Malu left no doubt about his seriousness, warning that any fighter found in possession of weapons after the official end of disarmament would be chased down like a common criminal. The force commander extended the disarmament deadline by one week to allow more fighters to come forward, and ten of the fifteen disarmament centers were kept open even after the official end of the process.

By 9 February, 24,500 of the estimated 33,000 fighters (74 percent) had been disarmed and demobilized.[18] These included 4,306 child fighters and 250 adult female fighters. More than 9,570 weapons and 1.2 million rounds of ammunition were also surrendered, and ECOMOG's cordon-and-search operations yielded another 917 weapons and 122,162 rounds of ammunition.[19] Initially, 21,315 people were disarmed (11,553 of 12,500 NPFL fighters; 5,622 of 6,800 ULIMO-K fighters; 571 of 7,000 AFL fighters; 1,114 of 3,800 ULIMO-J fighters; 1,223 of 2,500 LPC fighters; and 249 of 400 LDF fighters).[20] Smaller factions like ULIMO-J and the LPC seemed more reluctant, fearing they had more to lose if fighting in fact resumed. The low disarmament figure for the AFL reflected the fact that many of its fighters were near ECOMOG-dominated Monrovia and were therefore not treated with as much urgency. Some AFL fighters would also be needed for the restructuring of the new national army.

Though some pockets of armed fighters remained in Grand Kru and Maryland Counties, success can be measured by the fact that no cease-fire violations were reported between 12 January and 19 March 1997.[21] Most roadblocks were cleared and manned by ECOMOG soldiers. Even after the end of disarmament, 132 fighters voluntarily disarmed to ECOMOG in Grand Kru, Grand Gedeh, and River Cess Counties, and cordon-and-search operations recovered heavy artillery in Nimba County, antitank guns in Lofa County, and small arms in Bong Mines, Bo Waterside, Buchanan, Monrovia, Tubmanburg, and Voinjama.

There were, however, fatal consequences resulting from ECOMOG's tough disarmament tactics, which yet again soiled the image of the peacekeepers: on 10 May 1997, one person was allegedly killed and several injured by ECOMOG soldiers during a cordon-and-search operation at the Lajoy gold mine in Grand Cape Mount County; eight days later, another man was allegedly beaten to death in Bong County by ECOMOG soldiers during an interrogation.[22] In a controversial decision, the United Nations shelved its plans to investigate the two incidents. ECOMOG's image was further damaged by charges that its soldiers, whose stipends were often late, extorted money from civilians at checkpoints. This was especially common among the Nigerian contingent.

On 28 February, in accordance with Abuja II, faction leaders Charles Taylor, Alhaji Kromah, and George Boley resigned from the Council of State to run in the presidential elections. They were replaced on the council by handpicked successors from their own factions: Victoria Refell replaced Taylor; Weade Kobbah Wureh replaced Boley; and Vamba Kanneh replaced Kromah. With Taylor and Boley both choosing female candidates, half of the six members on Ruth Perry's Council of State were now women.

On 6 March, ECOMOG seized some weapons in the Executive Mansion. The next day, it conducted a simultaneous search of the Monrovia residences of warlords Boley, Taylor, Kromah, and Johnson. The discovery of three truckloads of weapons and ammunition in Kromah's home led to his arrest by ECOMOG; General Malu warned that he would be treated like a common criminal. Amid concerns expressed by prominent Liberian politicians about the effect such an arrest could have on the fragile peace process, and after several attacks on Mandingo taxi-drivers and money-changers in Monrovia, Malu recommended that all charges be dropped against Kromah on 14 March. A remorseful Kromah publicly acknowledged his error in violating the terms of Abuja II. So as not to appear to place the warlords above the law, Malu asked the LNTG to extend a general amnesty to everyone arrested for possessing arms after the end of the disarmament process.

Between February and April 1997 with the arrival of 650 Malian, 500 Ghanaian, 320 Burkinabè, 321 Nigerien, and 250 Beninois peacekeepers, along with a thirty-five-member medical team from Côte d'Ivoire and an additional 1,000 Nigerian troops, ECOMOG's troop strength grew from 7,500 to 10,500. Malu assured his political masters that this figure was sufficient to provide security for elections despite his earlier calls for 18,000 troops. U.S. military planes transported troops from Mali and Ghana, and Nigeria airlifted Niger's contingent to Liberia. EU member states Belgium, Denmark, and the Netherlands helped defray the costs of the new contingents. Their arrival diversified the force's composition to include six francophone and four anglophone states, though Nigeria still provided 7,000 of the 10,500 troops. For the first time since its establishment in 1990, ECOMOG's francophone contingents outnumbered their anglophone counterparts.

In another clear sign that subregional divisions were being bridged, the Burkinabè leader, Blaise Compaoré, visited General Abacha in Abuja for two days in early April 1997. Both leaders promised closer cooperation and consultation on Liberia, and Compaoré, previously the most vociferous critic of ECOMOG, praised Nigeria's role in Liberia. Côte d'Ivoire had demonstrated its commitment to subregional stability with its successful role in the signing of the Abidjan agreement by Sierra Leone's factions on 30 November 1996. Abidjan had thus played an instrumental role in brokering a peace agreement in an anglophone country. Côte d'Ivoire also demonstrated its commitment to a more evenhanded Liberia policy by controlling the flow of arms through its border with Liberia and publicly denying Taylor's claims that he had secured its support for his presidency.

The continuing strength of the Abuja-Accra axis was confirmed by General Abacha's attendance, as special guest, at Jerry Rawlings's presidential inauguration in Accra in January 1997. Nigeria also sought to win new friends and keep old ones by selling oil to neighboring states at concessionary rates. Six francophone states—Benin, Burkina Faso, Côte d'Ivoire, Guinea, Mali, and Niger—were allocated oil contracts for 20,000 barrels per day each by the Nigerian National Petroleum Company. Ghana, Gambia, and Togo already enjoyed concessionary supplies. Because only Accra and

Abidjan had oil refineries, this was in essence a gift to subregional leaders, who could then sell the oil for huge profits.[23] In another gesture, Nigeria took over payment of the $3 daily salaries and the feeding of the 368 Sierra Leonean soldiers in Liberia.[24] The Sierra Leonean contingent had not been paid since March 1996; Nigeria paid their arrears as well, despite frequent delays in paying its own troops.

The strengthening of the ECOMOG force allowed Malu to maintain a presence in all parts of Liberia except Grand Kru and River Cess Counties, though the peacekeepers still remained under strength in Lofa, Maryland, and Sinoe Counties. ECOMOG eventually deployed to all thirteen Liberian counties and along the country's borders with neighboring Guinea, Côte d'Ivoire, and Sierra Leone, improving security in the areas and allowing humanitarian relief to reach the entire country for the first time since the start of the civil war.

UNOMIL, ECOWAS, and ECOMOG

The ECOWAS chairman, General Abacha, wrote to UN Secretary-General Boutros Boutros-Ghali on 15 September 1996, informing him that "the United Nations would be requested to work with ECOWAS to provide necessary assistance and support in the process leading to the conduct of free and fair elections in Liberia."[25] ECOWAS established a committee to consult with UNOMIL and the LNTG on the electoral process in November 1996. Based on a request from the Council of State to help develop an electoral framework, a UN technical survey team visited Monrovia on 8 December 1996, consulting with ECOWAS and Liberia's civic and political groups. Kofi Annan, a Ghanaian who became the new UN Secretary-General, dispatched his special envoy for Liberia (and later ECOWAS executive secretary), Lansana Kouyaté, to Abuja on 14 January 1997 to discuss the electoral recommendations of the technical survey team with General Abacha. At this meeting, Kouyaté proposed a so-called provisional electoral package that retained Liberia's 1986 constitution and electoral system while allowing for the installation of a government of national unity. The Guinean UN envoy suggested that this proposal be enacted at a special ECOWAS Committee of Nine meeting involving the Liberian parties. Abacha accepted the proposal and scheduled a Committee of Nine meeting for February 1997.[26]

Abacha then wrote to Kofi Annan on 18 February 1997, confirming ECOWAS's endorsement of the five UN recommendations: the date for elections should remain 30 May; the elections should be organized by the Liberian Independent Elections Commission (IEC), comprising seven Liberians chosen by civic and political groups, in consultation with ECOWAS, and three nonvoting technical advisers from ECOWAS, the United Nations, and the OAU; electoral disputes should be adjudicated by the supreme court, whose members would be appointed in consultation with the justice ministry and the Liberian Bar Association, subject to review by ECOWAS; the bicameral parliament should contain a sixty-four-member House of Assembly and twenty-six-member Senate, with elections conducted based on proportional representation under a single constituency system; and the 660,000 Liberian refugees in neighboring countries wishing to participate in elections should return to Liberia to vote.[27] Guinea and Côte d'Ivoire objected strongly to the idea of Liberian refugees voting within their territory. Due to the fact that 750,000 Liberians had been internally displaced by the civil war, it was also decided that a system of proportional representation would be more appropriate, with parties choosing representatives to the thirteen counties from a party list based on their electoral strength.[28]

Military cooperation between UNOMIL and ECOMOG saw continued joint investigations of cease-fire violations and UNOMIL's verification of the arms and ammunition secured during ECOMOG's cordon-and-search operations. The United Nations increased its number of peacekeepers from twenty-three to ninety-three by March 1997 in preparation for elections. UNOMIL was, however, still suffering from its own logistical and communications problems, having recovered only thirty-two of its 489 vehicles looted during the fighting in Monrovia in April-May 1996. It also had only one helicopter for transportation.

Tensions renewed between UNOMIL and ECOMOG in February 1997 when General Malu seized eighteen UNOMIL containers at Monrovia's Freeport, arguing that ECOMOG had the authority to search the goods to ensure that no arms were being smuggled into Liberia. In May 1997, Kofi Annan requested that a clear understanding be reached with ECOMOG concerning its responsibilities for protecting UN and other international personnel during the electoral process. This was a source of tension between ECOMOG and the United Nations ever since the arrival of UNOMIL peacekeepers in 1993. The guaranteed protection of UNOMIL personnel had always been understood as part of ECOMOG's mandate even before the arrival of UN peacekeepers in Liberia, but UNOMIL felt that ECOMOG was deficient in this area. Annan's reiteration of this concern was an obvious sign of UN nervousness and lack of confidence in ECOMOG's ability to fulfill this role during the upcoming elections.

Kofi Annan's decision to dismiss his special representative in Liberia, Anthony Nyakyi, three months before the elections raised some eyebrows. Nyakyi had spent more than two years in Liberia as head of mission and was familiar with the main events and actors. Annan, who had served as UN undersecretary-general for peacekeeping before becoming Secretary-General, felt he needed dynamic leadership in the run-up to elections amid criticism that the UN actors in Liberia lacked proper coordination and planning. On 28 April, Tuliameni Kalomoh, Namibia's former ambassador to Washington, arrived in Monrovia to replace the embittered Nyakyi.

Before elections, UNOMIL's thirty-four medium-term civilian electoral observers undertook reconnaissance missions into the countryside to gather information—some of which they shared with the IEC—regarding terrain and infrastructure, population centers, and the activities of political parties. UNOMIL also produced a radio program, published a newsletter, provided civic information on registration and voting, and shared its helicopters, vehicles, and communications equipment with the IEC. Two weeks before elections, the United Nations deployed 200 observers to Liberia to monitor the poll. The four-year UNOMIL presence in Liberia eventually cost the international community no more than $115 million.[29]

General Abacha and Uncle Sam

Shocked by the scale of fighting in Monrovia during April-May 1996, Washington finally decided to hold its nose at the stench of the Nigerian military junta's human rights record and separate its troubled bilateral relations with Abuja from its support for the multilateral peacekeeping mission in Liberia. This decision proved crucial to the success of the disarmament process in Liberia. Between August and December 1996, Washington provided the logistical support that it had long denied ECOMOG peacekeepers. It released $40 million for three helicopters, communications equipment, footwear, uniforms, blankets, tents, water tankers, water rehabilitation units, insect repellent, medical supplies, and concrete guardhouses for peacekeepers deployed at roadblocks.

As Ibrahim Gambari, the Nigerian permanent representative to the United Nations, noted between 1990 and 1999:

> The [United States] made a conscious decision to separate multilateral relations with Nigeria over this matter and are dealing very closely with us now. . . . They have come to the realization that the only credible force for peace in Liberia is ECOMOG and that if they are unwilling or unable to contribute in any big way, the best way is to help ECOMOG.[30]

To alleviate U.S. concerns that none of the new equipment would become the property of the Nigerian military, the ECOWAS Committee of Nine promised in November 1996 that this equipment would be handed over to a new Liberian army before ECOMOG's departure.

The appointment of Ambassador Howard Jeter as President Clinton's special envoy for Liberia in late 1996 did much to improve the frosty relations between Washington and Abuja. Jeter, an African American and former ambassador to Namibia, struck up a good personal relationship with Tom Ikimi, and Nigerian officials spoke of Jeter in glowing terms. Jeter attended ECOWAS meetings on Liberia during this period and met several times with the ECOWAS chairman, Sani Abacha. Though Washington had made the decision to provide ECOMOG with logistical support before Jeter's appointment, the fact that it arrived during his tenure strengthened his credibility with Nigerian diplomatic and military officials.

During a speech to the Nigeria-American Chamber of Commerce, Ikimi was conciliatory, calling for improved trade relations and urging better understanding of Nigeria's political problems. He even asked Washington to reconsider the decertification of Nigeria, which led Washington to vote against debt relief for Nigeria for what the United States saw as Abuja's failure to crack down on drug trafficking. A month later, Ikimi described Americo-Nigerian relations as "excellent" and called for continued cooperation. As Donald McHenry, President Clinton's special envoy to Nigeria, noted, "Liberia helped save U.S.-Nigeria relations."[31]

Washington airlifted West African contingents that joined ECOMOG between February and April 1997. In June, the United States announced a further contribution of $7.4 million to support the electoral process and pledged additional support for ECOMOG, including communications equipment and two helicopters.[32] A continuing source of friction was the fact that ECOMOG still had to seek the authorization of the U.S.-based Pacific Architects and Engineers to lease helicopters and obtain flying hours. This private firm helped maintain ECOMOG helicopters and vehicles. In the course of the Liberian civil war, Washington contributed $500 million in humanitarian assistance and $75 million to ECOMOG contingents, particularly the Senegalese, Tanzanians, and Ugandans.[33]

Washington donated $1 million to UNICEF to reintegrate children into civilian life and $500,000 for bridging activities to reintegrate demobilized fighters. A U.S. Justice Department delegation visited Monrovia in November 1996 to assess the training requirements of the Liberian civil police force, with Washington eventually providing $725,000 and some training personnel. USAID provided technical and logistical support to the IEC, funded the International Foundation for Election Systems to provide technical assistance and purchase electoral material, and paid for the electoral observation missions of the Carter Center and Friends of Liberia. Total U.S. funding to Liberia between January and August 1997 was $25 million.

The warm relationship between Ikimi and Jeter was, however, in stark contrast to the mistreatment of the U.S. ambassador to Nigeria, Walter Carrington. On 24 December 1996, Tom Ikimi summoned Carrington to the foreign ministry in Abuja to explain what Ikimi described as the U.S. role in a spate of bombings in Lagos. The Nigerian foreign minister noted that the United States had issued a travel advisory warning its citizens to avoid

Nigeria during the period of the bombings. Ikimi constantly accused Carrington of fraternizing with enemies of the government, referring to meetings with Nigeria's prodemocracy groups. Abuja was also irked by Carrington's constant questioning of the credibility of the regime's transition process and by his frequent calls for the release of political prisoners.

As the U.S. ambassador prepared to leave Nigeria at the end of his tenure in September 1997, Nigerian Minister for Special Duties Alhaji Wada Nas described Carrington's tenure as "four wasted years" and "a diplomatic disaster for the two countries." Nas also accused Carrington of disregarding Abuja's views and of siding with Nigeria's prodemocracy opposition groups. These opposition groups were based in the southwest, the location of the main U.S. diplomatic presence after closing its consulates in Kano and Kaduna for cost-saving reasons. Some senior Nigerian officials thus regarded Carrington as the U.S. ambassador to Southwest Nigeria.[34] Abuja refused to extend the departing Carrington the traditional courtesy call on the head of state. A farewell party hosted for him by Nigeria's prodemocracy groups was disrupted by gun-wielding policemen, who implausibly claimed to be searching for weapons.

Before his visit to Africa in October 1996, U.S. Secretary of State Warren Christopher had quietly reassured U.S. oil giants Mobil and Exxon that there would be no push for oil sanctions against Nigeria.[35] Mobil was importing oil to Nigeria from Saudi Arabia in June 1997, following fuel shortages, and Texaco was purchasing offshore oil rights in Nigeria in October 1997.[36] Christopher did not visit Nigeria but criticized the military junta's human rights record and threatened new sanctions. He also promoted the idea of a 10,000-strong African Crisis Response Force to help civilians trapped in civil wars, with Washington promising funds and logistics for the African peacekeepers.[37] Although a few African states agreed to contribute troops, Nigeria was not asked, despite its dominant role in the ECOMOG operation in Liberia. This reflected U.S. discomfort with close military cooperation with the existing Nigerian regime.

Former U.S. President Jimmy Carter reopened his Carter Center in Monrovia in April 1997 to assist in the Liberian electoral process. He traveled to Monrovia from 26 to 29 June and met with Liberian groups and ECOWAS officials. Carter then went to Abuja to meet with General Abacha. Both men called for an improvement in relations between Abuja and Washington. During his visit, Carter told reporters he had counseled President Clinton against imposing sanctions on Nigeria and called for a lessening of tensions and an improvement in relations between Washington and Abuja. The former president demonstrated his continuing commitment to Liberia by returning to Monrovia to monitor the Liberian election in July 1997.

Washington's aversion to intervening in African conflicts, as well as its desire to see a democratically elected government restored to power in

Freetown, eventually resulted in U.S. officials publicly supporting the Nigerian military intervention in Sierra Leone in February 1998 to reverse the coup of 25 May 1997. This was a reluctant recognition of Nigeria's leadership role in the subregion and another step toward delinking the Nigerian regime's domestic policies from its foreign policies. Nigerian troops assisted U.S. Marines in evacuating Western citizens from Freetown.

Domestic opinion in the United States, however, remained divided over Nigeria. In mid-1997, African American Congressman Donald Payne introduced the Nigeria Democracy Act, proposing a freezing of U.S. investments and imposing an oil embargo. But some members of the Congressional Black Caucus opposed the measure. African American Representative William Jefferson, wrote to the Black Caucus in June 1997, urging members not to support sanctions against Nigeria, which he described as "unimaginative" and "wrong-headed." He later argued before the U.S. House of Representatives Subcommittee on Africa that Washington should pursue a "multi-pronged approach that included government-to-government dialogue; aid to Nigerian institutions implementing democratization and to pro-democracy and civil society groups."[38] He also criticized U.S. double standards in condemning Nigeria while remaining silent on China, Kuwait, and Saudi Arabia, which had no democratic transitions.

There was, in any case, insufficient political support for oil sanctions against Nigeria in the U.S. Congress; senior administration officials, diplomats, and oil company executives opposed such actions. Thomas Pickering, the U.S. undersecretary of state and former U.S. ambassador to Nigeria, had an intimate understanding of the country's strategic importance and volatility. Complaining that U.S. policy toward Nigeria was "getting tougher and tougher with fewer and fewer results," he ordered a policy review on Nigeria in August 1997. Pickering felt that more communication should accompany any measures taken against Nigeria. William Twadell, the former U.S. envoy in Liberia, was dispatched to Nigeria as the new U.S. ambassador with a mandate to seek a détente in Americo-Nigerian relations. Constructive engagement had seemingly triumphed over diplomatic isolation.

General Abacha's domestic problems persisted during this period. In September 1996, bloody religious riots in Kaduna led to scores of deaths. A bomb blast in Lagos in December 1996 narrowly missed the convoy of the Lagos governor, Colonel Mohamed Marwa. In January 1997, a bomb blast on a military bus in Lagos killed two soldiers and injured several others. In May, there were bomb blasts in Lagos, Ibadan, and Onitsha within weeks of each other in which civilians were killed and soldiers injured. Growing discontent following three months of fuel shortages caused by dilapidated oil refineries forced the importation of oil in June 1997. Concerns continued to be voiced about the credibility of General Abacha's transition program amid pervasive rumors that he was suffering from cirrhosis of the liver. Foreign visitors to Abuja painted a picture of Abacha as a leader surrounded by a coterie of sycophantic advisers who did not pass along unpleasant news and who restricted access to him.[39] Abacha seemed like a reclusive, beleaguered leader holed up in the fortress of Aso Rock, getting little sleep and rarely venturing abroad.

United Nations, Divided Country

The European Union played a belated but important role in the success of disarmament and elections in Liberia. The European Commission in Brussels donated $2 million to UNICEF for primary education. It provided offices and logistical support for the IEC. The Netherlands and Germany supplied ECOMOG with 119 trucks to facilitate its deployment to the countryside. The Dutch government provided an additional $3 million for disarmament. France contributed $679,611 to the UN Trust Fund for Liberia. During elections, the European Union funded civic education programs, paid election workers, and provided technical and logistical support to the IEC.

Jan Pronk, minister for development cooperation of the Netherlands at the time, launched an important initiative that helped support Liberia's disarmament, demobilization, and electoral processes.[40] The first ministerial meeting of the ad hoc special conference on Liberia was held in New York on 22 October 1996 under the auspices of ECOWAS, the United Nations, and donor countries to discuss external support for peacekeeping and peacebuilding activities. In December 1996, a UN interagency program for community reintegration and peacebuilding obtained pledges of only $3.04 million—far short of the $46.91 million requested.

A second ministerial meeting of the ad hoc special conference was held in New York on 20 February 1997 and involved more than 140 participants. Donors reiterated their preparedness to contribute resources to the electoral process if progress continued on disarmament and demobilization. On 12 June, ECOWAS and OAU representatives met again with major donors in Geneva at the third ministerial meeting of the ad hoc special conference on Liberia. Participants pledged $15 million toward the peace process, including $3.7 million from the European Union and $200,000 from the OAU. Denmark promised to provide and transport ballot boxes.

UN agencies and international NGOs continued to provide humanitarian relief and social and economic support to Liberia. The World Food Programme distributed food to 252,000 displaced persons and refugees and conducted feeding programs for other vulnerable groups. The UNDP provided technical assistance to the IEC on electoral management, voter estimates, voter registration, polling, and civic education; it also funded the purchase of seed rice, groundnuts, and vegetable seeds to revive agricultural production.

It provided vehicles, computers, office supplies, motorcycles, and communications equipment to government agencies, as well as a mobile control tower for Monrovia's Spriggs Payne airport. The Food and Agricultural Organization distributed agricultural products and provided jobs to war-affected farmers. UNICEF provided community centers for vocational and literacy training as well as shelters, transit homes, and trauma counseling to the 4,306 demobilized child fighters. The World Health Organization controlled an outbreak of cholera in Monrovia in October 1996, undertook a national vaccination campaign, and continued to provide medical equipment and medicines. The International Labour Organization launched a vocational training program to increase trained manpower. International NGOs that provided humanitarian relief included Catholic Relief Services, Médecins du Monde, International Rescue Committee, Save the Children Fund, Action Contre la Faim, and Oxfam.

The World Food Programme, European Union, and UNDP established a Civil Reconstruction Team bridging program to support demobilization. The United Nations spent $3.3 million on bridging activities; the UNDP's 110 public works projects created 10,000 jobs for civilians and former fighters; and the UN Humanitarian Coordination Office funded forty-four projects involving 8,352 temporary jobs. The European Union's 128 micro-projects also provided short-term employment for nearly 8,000 civilians and former combatants. By June 1997, 30,000 former fighters and civilians had benefited from short-term employment and training opportunities, which included rehabilitating rural roads and bridges; restoring health and education infrastructure; building latrines, wells, bridges, and shelters; farming; civic education; and skills development.

Though these programs sound impressive, it must be noted that they fell far short of the resources and long-term assistance needed to restore economic and social life and ensure a durable postwar political order. By June 1997, only 25 percent of Liberia's public and private health facilities were functioning; electricity supply was nonexistent in most parts of the country; less than 12 percent of rural Liberians enjoyed access to safe drinking water; less than 1 percent of rural Liberians had access to proper sanitation; and 60 percent of children were absent from school.[41] The hopes of an entire generation had been destroyed by the civil war, and the tasks ahead did not appear easily surmountable. It was clear that Liberia would have to rely on international charity for years to come.

From Bullets to Ballots

As early as 22 February 1996, the Liberian opposition decided to unite in a common front in order to defeat Charles Taylor's National Patriotic Party

(NPP) at the polls. Amos Sawyer, Liberia's interim president from 1990 to 1994, was the moving spirit behind a seven-party alliance that included the Liberia Action Party (LAP), the Liberia People's Party (LPP), the Liberia Unification Party (LUP), the Unity Party (UP), the True Whig Party (TWP), the United People's Party (UPP), and Samuel Doe's old National Democratic Party of Liberia (NDPL). Most of these parties were resurrected from the late 1970s and mid-1980s and many were led by politicians who had served under William Tolbert and Samuel Doe: Togba-Nah Tipoteh (LPP), Gabriel Baccus Matthews (UPP), George Boley (NDPL), Cletus Wotorson (LAP), Rudolph Sherman (TWP), and Laveli Supuwood (LUP). Other politicians, like Chea Cheapoo and Boima Fahnbulleh, both of them ministers under Doe, also contested the presidency. Alhaji Kromah led the Mandingo-based All-Liberia Coalition Party.

At the seven-party alliance convention on 25–27 March 1997, delegates elected Cletus Wotorson, an unassuming geologist from Grand Kru County and former minister of mines under President Tolbert, as its presidential candidate. Baccus Matthews and Togba Nah-Tipoteh, ministers under the Doe regime, regarded the relatively unknown Wotorson as an upstart. Alleging that the party primary had been rigged and that Charles Taylor paid delegates to elect Wotorson, Matthews and Nah-Tipoteh withdrew their parties from the alliance rather than accept Wotorson as their presidential candidate. By the time of the election, the seven-party alliance had been whittled down to an alliance of two.

This incident revealed the insincerity and opportunism of Liberian politicians. Politicians wanted power at all costs, and narrow self-interests prevented them from abiding by rules they had previously agreed to. In another sign of persisting historical divisions between former pro- and anti-Doe forces, Baccus Matthews asked his delegates to abstain from the second round of voting during the alliance convention in March rather than support Togba Nah-Tipoteh. Members of George Boley's NDPL continued to blame Doe's death on some of the alliance partners.[42]

By 7 April 1997, the Independent Elections Commission and the supreme court were installed in Monrovia, one month behind schedule. Both had to be restructured to make them more neutral (previously they had been dominated by nominees of the former armed factions). The month-long delay was caused by disputes over nominations. Charles Taylor was angry at Ruth Perry for the selection of Henry Andrews as IEC chairman while Taylor was away in Taipei. ECOWAS eventually stepped in to resolve the dispute by approving Andrews's appointment.

After much vacillation and several visits to Liberia, Ellen Johnson-Sirleaf, a former finance minister and prominent exile, finally decided on 18 April 1997 to give up her senior position as director of the UNDP's Africa bureau to run for president of Liberia as the UP's candidate. The TWP,

LUP, and some LPP elements immediately threw their weight behind her candidacy. Her entry into the race added another dimension to the strained relations between Washington and Abuja. With her probusiness views and strong U.S. contacts, Johnson-Sirleaf was considered the favored candidate of the United States. Johnson-Sirleaf had opposed ECOMOG intervention in 1990 (see Chapter 3), criticizing it as a Nigerian attempt to save Samuel Doe and calling instead for a U.S.-led intervention. Taylor and some Nigerian officials accused Washington of funding her presidential campaign. For his part, Taylor was considered Nigeria's favored candidate, a clear sign that relations had improved between Abuja and the warlord it had twice waged war against. Tom Ikimi was said to have hosted a reception in Abuja at which he introduced Taylor as Liberia's future president,[43] and it was alleged that Taylor's campaign received financial support from Abuja.[44]

Between 24 and 27 April, Ikimi led another ECOWAS assessment team to Monrovia, comprised of Guinean Foreign Minister Camara and the Ghanaian deputy foreign minister (and President Rawlings's former special envoy to Liberia), Victor Gbeho. The delegation met with the IEC and Liberia's political parties to discuss the draft election law, the code of conduct for political parties, the timetable for electoral activities, and the IEC budget. During the meeting, the ECOWAS delegation reduced the proposed IEC budget from $9.5 million to $5.4 million and decided that ECOWAS should take greater responsibility in logistical aspects of the electoral process, including the procurement and transportation of electoral material.[45]

ECOWAS's assertiveness reflected the tension that pervaded the election preparations with Nigeria, especially anxious to see that the United Nations or any other external actor did not steal the glory after ECOMOG had sacrificed so many men, matériel, and money during seven years of lonely peacekeeping. Ikimi, not renowned for his diplomatic tact at the best of times, often reminded people that these were ECOWAS elections and urged international donors to provide funding but not to interfere.

Holding elections on 30 May 1997 would have meant enacting the election law and regulations by March, registering voters in April, and conducting the campaign in May—a tight and ultimately impossible schedule. The IEC called for polling to be postponed from March to July 1997; most politicians, with the notable and noisy exception of the better-organized Charles Taylor, called for a six-month postponement. Ghana threatened to withdraw its peacekeepers if elections were postponed. Kofi Annan wrote to General Abacha on 1 May 1997 asking for a two-month postponement. Four days later, Abacha responded to Annan, informing him that the ECOWAS assessment team had recommended a thirty-day postponement of elections.

On 21 May, the ECOWAS Committee of Nine heads of state held an extraordinary summit meeting in Abuja. The meeting postponed Liberia's election from 30 May to 19 July 1997, approved the new Liberian election law, and accepted the recommendations of Liberia's political parties to employ a single ballot system for presidential and legislative candidates and to count ballots at polling stations and not at a centralized location. ECOWAS states had finally accepted Charles Taylor's repeated assertions that total disarmament before elections would be impossible and that a future government would have to complete disarmament. Sierra Leone's election in February 1996 was instrumental in convincing ECOMOG that such a scenario could be replicated in Liberia. George Boley, Alhaji Kromah, and civilian politicians continued to insist on total disarmament before elections. But ECOWAS calculated that ECOMOG, in light of the fact that three-quarters of the fighters had been disarmed, would be able to secure the country for voting and control any postelectoral violence.

Nigeria provided vehicles for the election commissioners and sent some of its own helicopters to Liberia. A minimum $100,000 levy was imposed on ECOWAS members to help pay for the election in a bid to raise $1.5 million on top of the $5.4 million earlier approved. ECOWAS and the United Nations established a Joint Electoral Coordination Mechanism, which met regularly with the IEC to discuss operational and other issues. ECOWAS sent its own observers to Liberia, and Tom Ikimi, Lansana Camara, Amara Essy, and Victor Gbeho—respectively, the foreign ministers of Nigeria, Guinea, Côte d'Ivoire, and the deputy foreign minister of Ghana—arrived in Monrovia a week before elections to oversee the process.

Only 70,000–80,000 refugees returned home to participate in elections, leaving more than 550,000 disenfranchised refugees, nearly one-quarter of the population, in neighboring countries. Since elections were held in the middle of the rainy season, there was a pressing need for helicopters and communications equipment. Some roads were flooded and impassable particularly in Grand Gedeh, Grand Kru, Maryland, Sinoe, and Upper Lofa Counties. ECOMOG, UNOMIL, and the European Union provided the logistical support for transporting ballot materials and provided communications and transportation support to IEC officials.

The campaign started on 16 June 1997 with thirteen parties competing. Malu left no one in doubt that ECOMOG would deal ruthlessly with any faction that tried to disrupt the process. As he put it, "While ECOMOG is escorting anyone to campaign, if you throw stones at that person, you will be throwing stones at ECOMOG and, as such, ECOMOG will retaliate by throwing bullets [at you]."[46] No major acts of violence or intimidation were reported, and all parties were able to travel freely and to open offices throughout the country. The few disruptive acts included an attack on Mandingo worshippers by nineteen NPP supporters in a mosque in Gbarnga in May, and a clash between supporters of Taylor and Kromah during Johnson-Sirleaf's rally in Ganta in June that left several people injured.

Six days before the elections, Charles Taylor paid $23,500 for the Liberian soccer team to travel to an African Nations Cup qualifying game against Togo; he donated ambulances to Monrovia's John F. Kennedy Memorial Hospital; established the philanthropic Charles Ghankay Taylor Educational and Humanitarian Relief Foundation to rehabilitate war victims and to resettle unemployed Liberians; and established the Charles Taylor Relief Agency, which distributed rice, milk, and bread to needy Liberians. Playing the archetypal African Big Man, Taylor's strategy was to portray himself as the biggest and richest chief with the most patronage to dole out to loyal subjects.

On the hustings, Taylor arrived in a helicopter for rallies and distributed rice, T-shirts, and other gifts to electors. He used Land Rovers, buses, and motorcycles, and his rallies were a glitzy carnival of music, dance, fashion, and games. Taylor countered accusations that he had destroyed the country by asking for a chance to rebuild it. In contrast, Johnson-Sirleaf, his closest rival, drove around in a convoy of battered old vehicles, condemned the violence and greed of the warlords (especially Charles Taylor), and blamed them for destroying the country. She called for a government of national unity to rebuild Liberia and flaunted her international credentials for attracting economic assistance to the country. Baccus Matthews promised free and compulsory universal primary education. Cletus Wotorson touted his reliable judgment and character. Harry Moniba, Samuel Doe's former vice president, promised peace and stability.

On 19 July 1997, Liberian voters cast their ballots as ECOMOG soldiers provided security at the 1,864 voting stations. ECOMOG also provided trucks, helicopters, and ships to transport personnel and equipment around the country. The peacekeepers put their communications equipment at the disposal of election officials. The United Nations had 330 observers; the European Union sent sixty, the OAU thirty-five, the Carter Center forty, and Friends of Liberia thirty-four. More than 500 international and 1,300 local observers from the Liberian Elections Observer Network monitored the election. On the eve of the election, Malu put on a show of military strength in Monrovia, with ECOMOG tanks and armored cars patrolling the streets and fighter jets flying overhead.

Final results were announced on 24 July, with Charles Taylor scoring a stunning landslide victory. He won 75.3 percent of the presidential vote, making a runoff unnecessary, and was thereby elected to a six-year term; Ellen Johnson-Sirleaf won 9.6 percent, Alhaji Kromah 4 percent, Baccus Matthews 3 percent, Cletus Wotorson less than 2 percent, and Togba-Nah Tipoteh 1.6 percent. The NPP also won twenty-one of the twenty-six seats in the Senate and forty-nine of the sixty-four seats in the House of Representatives. The UP won three Senate and seven House seats.[47] Even in Montserrado County, where nearly half the population lived and where access to newspapers and radio was most equal for all parties, Taylor won 55 percent of the vote. An impressive 85 percent of the 750,000 registered voters turned out to cast their ballots on polling day. ECOWAS and the United Nations issued a joint statement on 24 July declaring the elections free and fair. There were some logistical and technical deficiencies: voter education had been inadequate; there was no census conducted; and the secrecy of the ballot was compromised by assistance given to illiterate voters. But some of these difficulties were to be expected after seven years of civil war; it was the first Liberian election in eleven years.

After the vote, Johnson-Sirleaf, Kromah, and Boley alleged that ECOMOG soldiers had intervened in the election in favor of Taylor by assisting illiterate voters to cast their ballots. There were some confirmed cases, but the IEC determined that they did not compromise voters' choices. Johnson-Sirleaf and Kromah also complained about the procedure for allocating parliamentary seats that had earlier been agreed to by all parties. These complaints were later withdrawn, and Johnson-Sirleaf urged her supporters to prepare for the role of constructive opposition.

Several reasons explain Taylor's stunning victory. Liberians saw Taylor as a guarantor of peace and stability and feared a return to war if he lost. As Terrence Lyons, a senior program adviser for the Carter Center in Liberia, put it: "The issue of peace dominated the July 1997 election and most voters seemed determined to use their franchise to maximise the chances of stability. Many Liberians believed that if Taylor lost the election, the country would return to war."[48] The genuine fear that Taylor would "do a Savimbi" by reverting to bullets if ballots failed was a significant factor in propelling him to victory, something many Liberians openly admitted. One frequently quoted voter said, "He killed my father but I'll vote for him. He started all this and he's going to fix it."[49] Like Angolan warlord Jonas Savimbi (who was killed by government troops in February 2002) in 1992, Taylor repeatedly told journalists that he could not imagine himself losing the election and that accepting electoral defeat was irrelevant.

Taylor's victory also had a financial aspect. With an estimated $450 million per year in earnings from natural resources in areas he controlled during the war, Taylor built up a war chest that his rivals could not match. This enabled him to reach more voters, even in the remotest parts of Liberia, through private radio stations and newspapers. He had the means to distribute largesse.

Taylor's rivals were also perceived as disunited and opportunistic. Their failure to run a convention and abide by its rules was an undignifying spectacle. Matthews, Tipoteh, and Fahnbulleh, who in a bygone era had made their marks by opposing the True Whigs, found out they lived in a different Liberia. The country was a political jungle where warlords and firepower, not the tired rhetoric of old-time politicians, guaranteed stability.

The veterans of yesteryear were humbled and humiliated. After seven years of weak and squabbling interim governments that featured civilian politicians, not faction leaders, until 1995, Liberians voted for a strong government that could control the whole country and make swift decisions that had a chance of being implemented.

Finally, Taylor's main rival, Johnson-Sirleaf, was seen as out of touch with the suffering of ordinary Liberians, having spent eleven years outside Liberia and returning from her cushy UN job in New York. Her position was not helped by her vacillation and belated decision to run, which made people unsure of her commitment and willingness to sacrifice. There was also a gender bias in Liberia's male-dominated society, and despite Ruth Perry's impressive energy as interim leader, it was clear that the warlords on the Council of State called the shots. Johnson-Sirleaf's strong criticism of Taylor on the hustings were partly blunted by her own admission that she had supported him at the start of the conflict.

On 2 August 1997, Charles Taylor was inaugurated as Liberia's twenty-first president. He had finally won the prize that eluded him for seven years. But he faced a daunting task. Taylor inherited an empty national treasury with a domestic debt of $200 million and an external debt of $3 billion.[50] In his inaugural address, President Taylor stressed reconciliation, the protection of human rights, national unity, and the urgent need to reconstruct Liberia's infrastructure and institutions. He assured Liberians that there would be no witch hunts in his efforts to build a new nation from the ashes of war.

Taylor also praised ECOWAS, ECOMOG, and the United Nations for their efforts in bringing peace to Liberia. Eight ECOWAS leaders, including Nigeria's Sani Abacha, Burkina Faso's Blaise Compaoré, Côte d'Ivoire's Henri Konan Bédié, Guinea's Lansana Conté, and Mali's Alpha Konaré, traveled to Monrovia to attend the inauguration. At one point during his address, Taylor turned to Abacha and revealed that a defining moment in resolving the Liberian crisis was his trip to Abuja in June 1995, when Abacha had assured Taylor of his personal safety. In another irony, three Nigerian jets flew overhead as part of the inauguration ceremonies—jets that had earlier been used to bomb Charles Taylor to the negotiating table. It was a fitting end to the final diplomatic banquet for Liberia's most lavish warlord.

* * *

The final phase of the ECOMOG intervention in Liberia (September 1994–July 1997) saw cooperation at the domestic, subregional, and external levels that resulted in the achievement of ECOMOG's goals after seven tortuous years. The importance of contingencies and personal relationships was evident in the shifting alliances and policies that brought about this outcome. Rapprochement between Nigeria, the dominant ECOMOG state, and the NPFL—the most powerful Liberian faction—was crucial in resolving the civil war. There was a final realization by both sides that each could frustrate the goals of the other and that each needed the other to achieve its objectives. Nigeria wanted a diplomatic triumph by ending the war. Charles Taylor wanted the Liberian presidency. Both Nigeria and the NPFL lacked the military strength for the pacification of Liberia, and the resulting military stalemate eventually forced a political accommodation. Taylor correctly calculated that he could outspend his divided rivals during the election of July 1997, and the fear of a return to war among Liberians if Taylor lost the election carried him to victory.

The difference in approach between Nigeria and Ghana was also resolved during this period, as Abuja finally accepted Accra's consistent policy of securing the cooperation of Liberia's warlords for disarmament by offering them political power. The fighting in Monrovia in April 1996 revealed the dangers inherent in Accra's policy of appeasing the faction leaders to ensure disarmament. After four years of attempting to give the francophone states the lead role in peacemaking efforts, the diplomatic pendulum swung back to the anglophones, with General Abacha replacing Jerry Rawlings as ECOWAS chairman. The last three years of the conflict saw Nigeria and Ghana directing the peace negotiations in Liberia.

Several subregional states had a greater stake in the resolution of the conflict than did Nigeria. Fear of instability closer to home finally forced ECOWAS states to develop a common interest in supporting ECOMOG efforts to resolve the conflict. Continuing incursions into Ivorian territory by Liberian warlords led Côte d'Ivoire to conclude that the easiest and cheapest way to contain the worsening situation was to support ECOMOG's efforts. The death of Félix Houphoüet-Boigny in December 1993 had helped depersonalize the Ivorian involvement in Liberia. His successor, Henri Konan Bédié, wanted to consolidate his power at home and stop border incursions. Guinea, part of the ECOMOG force since 1990, also complained about Liberian crossborder raids into its territory. With Charles Taylor having made peace with Nigeria and now being protected by ECOMOG peacekeepers, Burkina Faso no longer had any reason to frustrate ECOMOG efforts.

Burkina Faso, Côte d'Ivoire, Niger, and Togo all sent their military chiefs of staff to attend ECOWAS meetings, a recognition by francophone states that they needed to adopt a higher profile in military decisionmaking. The introduction of four new francophone contingents to ECOMOG gave unprecedented political balance to the peacekeeping mission and made it a truly subregional effort involving eleven of ECOWAS's sixteen members. The external level of analysis was also important in the final resolution of the Liberian conflict. With ECOMOG now a united, neutral force, the

United States finally delinked its support for ECOMOG from its acrimonious bilateral relations with Nigeria and provided ECOMOG the logistical support that enabled it to disarm Liberia's factions. The United Nations and European Union also played important roles in providing additional military, financial, and technical support that Pax Nigeriana could not provide.

Notes

1. Cited in Friends of Liberia, "Liberia: Opportunities and Obstacles for Peace," report given in Washington, D.C., December 1996, p. 28.

2. Ibid., p. 28.

3. *Economist Intelligence Unit,* Country Report, "Liberia," no. 4 (3 October 1996): 46–47.

4. Quoted in *West Africa,* no. 4115 (2–8 September 1996): 1380.

5. *West Africa,* no. 4124 (11–17 November 1996): 1753.

6. Ofeibea Quist-Arcton, "Warlord and Wife," *Focus on Africa* 8, no. 2 (April-June 1997): 20.

7. Twentieth Progress Report of the Secretary-General on the United Nations Observer Mission in Liberia, 19 November 1996, S/1996/962, p. 2.

8. Ben Asante, "The Ace Commander," *West Africa,* no. 4128 (9–15 December 1996): 1969.

9. Quoted in *West Africa,* no. 4132 (13–19 January 1997): 48.

10. Quoted in *West Africa,* no. 4144 (7–13 April 1997): 543.

11. Twenty-first Progress Report of the Secretary-General on the United Nations Observer Mission in Liberia, 29 January 1997, S/1997/90, p. 7.

12. Nineteenth Progress Report of the Secretary-General on the United Nations Observer mission in Liberia, 17 October 1996, S/1996/858, p. 9.

13. Davidetta Browne, "Human Tragedy in Bomi," *West Africa,* no. 4120 (14–20 October 1996): 1598.

14. *Africa Confidential* 38, no. 13 (20 June 1997): 6.

15. Victor Tanner, "Liberia: Railroading Peace," *Review of African Political Ecomony* 75, no. 25 (March 1998): 134.

16. See, for example, John H.T. Stewart, "Assessing Chief Ikimi's Role in the Liberian Peace Process," *Daily Observer,* 24–27 April 1997.

17. Personal interview with Ambassador Howard Jeter, U.S. Department of State, Washington, D.C., 3 April 1997.

18. "A No-Nonsense Commander" (interview with Victor Malu), *West Africa* no. 4142 (24–30 March 1997): 464.

19. Twenty-second Progress Report of the Secretary-General on the United Nations Observer Mission in Liberia, 19 March 1997, S/1997/237, pp. 3–4.

20. Ibid., p. 14.

21. Ibid., p. 3.

22. Twenty-fourth Progress Report of the Secretary-General on the United Nations Observer Mission in Liberia, 13 August 1997, S/1997/643, p. 7.

23. "Oil Glistens," *Africa Confidential* 38, no. 19 (26 September 1997): 8.

24. Dotun Oladipo, "War and Peace," *Newswatch* 26, no. 6 (11 August 1997): 16.

25. Quoted in the Nineteenth Progress Report of the Secretary-General on the United Nations Observer mission in Liberia, p. 2.

26. Twenty-first Progress Report of the Secretary-General on the United Nations Observer Mission in Liberia, p. 6.

27. Twenty-second Progress Report of the Secretary-General on the United Nations Observer Mission in Liberia, pp. 4–5.

28. For more details, see Independent Elections Commission, *Special Elections Law for the 1997 Elections* (Monrovia: Sabanoh, 1997).

29. Final Report of the Secretary-General on the United Nations Observer Mission in Liberia, 12 September 1997, S/1997/712, p. 4.

30. Personal interview with Ambassador Ibrahim Gambari, Nigerian Mission to the United Nations, New York, 17 March 1997.

31. Personal interview with U.S. Ambassador Donald McHenry, Washington, D.C., 14 July 1997.

32. See Howard Jeter, ECOMOG: An American Perspective on a Successful Peacekeeping Operation, in "Militaries, Democracies, and Security in Sub-Saharan Africa." Papers presented at a conference in Abuja, 1–4 December 1997, pp. 175–189.

33. Herbert Howe, "Lessons of Liberia: ECOMOG and Regional Peacekeeping," *International Security* 21, no. 3 (Winter 1996/1997): 150.

34. Personal interview with Ambassador Donald McHenry, Washington, D.C., 14 July 1997.

35. *The Economist,* 9 November 1996, p. 46.

36. *Africa Confidential* 38, no. 21 (24 October 1997): 4.

37. See Adekeye Adebajo and Michael O'Hanlon, "Africa: Toward a Rapid-Reaction Force," *SAIS Review* 17, no. 2 (Summer-Fall 1997): 153–164; and Jendayi Frazer, "The Africa Crisis Response Initiative: Self-Interested Humanitarianism," *Brown Journal of World Affairs* 4, no. 2 (Summer/Fall 1997): 103–118; and Paul Omach, "The African Crisis Response Initiative: Domestic Politics and Convergence of National Interests," *African Affairs* 99, no. 394 (January 2000): 73–95.

38. Quoted in *Africa Today* 44, no. 4 (October–December 1997): 12.

39. Personal interview with Ambassador Donald McHenry, Washington, D.C., 14 July 1997.

40. See Klass Van Walraven, *The Netherlands and Liberia: Dutch Policies and Interventions with Respect to the Liberian Civil War* (The Hague: Netherlands Institute of International Relations, 1999).

41. Twenty-third Progress Report of the Secretary-General on the United Nations Observer Mission in Liberia, 19 June 1997, S/1997/478, p. 9.

42. James Butty, "Waiting for the Alliance," *West Africa,* no. 4146 (21–27 April 1997): 634.

43. *Africa Confidential* 38, no. 16 (4 August 1997): 3.

44. *Tell,* no. 31 (4 August 1997): 27.

45. Twenty-third Progress Report of the Secretary-General on the United Nations Observer Mission in Liberia, p. 2.

46. Quoted in Terrence Lyons, *Voting for Peace: Post-conflict Elections in Liberia* (Washington, D.C.: Brookings Institution, 1999), p. 51.

47. Ibid., p. 57.

48. Ibid., p. 59.

49. Quoted in *Economist Intelligence Unit,* Country Report, "Liberia," no. 3 (28 July 1997): 31.

50. *West Africa,* no. 4175 (24–30 November 1997): 1839.

part **4**

The Bloody Waters of the Mano River, July 1997–August 2001

chapter 11

A Warlord's Bazaar,
July 1997–August 2001

In some modern countries, you have a political opposition. In Africa, you are
not just an adversary if you lose an election; you become almost an enemy.
—*Charles Taylor, president of Liberia*

In this chapter we will assess President Charles Taylor's first four years in office, focusing on five key issues. We will briefly assess the controversial UN peacebuilding role in Liberia and then examine Taylor's crackdown on internal rivals to stifle any opposition to his rule through autocratic means. Next, we examine the instability on Liberia's borders with Guinea and Sierra Leone, which continues to destabilize the entire Mano River Basin. We also assess the likely consequences of Taylor's decision to fill his security forces with former NPFL combatants. Finally, we analyze the increasing external pressure on Taylor's regime following the imposition of limited economic sanctions on Liberia by the UN Security Council in May 2001.

Taylor's election victory accorded him the trappings of sovereignty, allowing him to have a monopoly over the legitimate use of force, to cut deals with more legitimate business partners, and to have access to international lending institutions. Taylor's entry into the political kingdom is akin to a warlord entering a giant bazaar where he could feast to his heart's desire. Achieving political power through popular election did not, however, mean that the warlord was reformed. It merely gave him political, legal, and military cover to pursue looting by other means. But the security that Taylor hoped sovereignty would bring proved elusive in postwar Liberia, as armed rebels started a second civil war in 1999 and as donors withheld funds for reconstruction and even imposed limited economic sanctions to protest Taylor's domestic and foreign policies.

The UN in Liberia: Building Peace or Avoiding Trouble?

Taylor's years in office have been financially difficult and marred by controversy over human rights violations.[1] After the 1997 elections, the United Nations established its first small peacebuilding support office in Liberia to coordinate postconflict programs of various UN agencies, support the rehabilitation of demobilized soldiers, and promote international assistance for reconstruction efforts. The head of the UN office until early 2002, Felix Downes-Thomas, was criticized by Liberian civil society groups, opposition parties, and some national media for being too close to Taylor, for not supporting human rights efforts, and for interpreting the UN mandate too narrowly. Domestic actors complained they had no contact with Downes-Thomas and many regarded him as an apologist for the Taylor regime.[2] As an internal UN report of July 2001 admitted, the UN peacebuilding office was poorly resourced; its mandate was weak and not politically intrusive due to the initial reluctance of the UN Security Council to establish the office. The Liberian government had accepted the office as the lesser evil to a continued ECOMOG presence with the full knowledge that the United Nations would not interfere with its running of the country.[3]

Bad Governance

Taylor has been unable to attract much foreign assistance to rebuild his shattered country. Liberia's National Reconstruction Program sought $433 million over the first two postelection years to revive government institutions, provide essential social services, rehabilitate public infrastructure, repatriate and resettle refugees and internally displaced persons, and reintegrate demobilized fighters into society. The program talked of "transparency," "accountability," and "broad-based participation."[4] But the reality of postwar Liberia scarcely matched such noble objectives.

Though Taylor at first embarked on a policy of national reconciliation, even inviting members of rival parties to join his cabinet, he soon cracked down on opposition and attempted to institutionalize his dominance. Former Taylor ally (and later opponent) Sam Dokie and members of his family were murdered in November 1997 after being arrested by Taylor's security forces. The suspects were acquitted in April 1998 as a result of an apparent lack of evidence. Liberia's journalists and human rights activists have been harassed and jailed for criticizing the government. Two radio stations were closed down in March 2000, and four newspapers were closed down and several journalists of the *News* arrested in February 2001. Taylor now controls most of the media through his private radio stations and newspapers.

In November 2000, 300 armed men vandalized the office of the Center for Democratic Empowerment in Monrovia and injured its directors, Amos Sawyer and Commany Wesseh, forcing both into exile shortly afterward. Members of the Catholic Justice and Peace Commission, like its director James Verdier and his exiled predecessor Samuel Kofi Woods, and the deputy director of Liberia Democracy Watch, Augustine Toure, have complained about threats on their lives.

Liberia's security situation remains precarious more than four years after the end of the war. Armed robbery, looting of food aid, and banditry have thrived in rural Liberia. Crime and insecurity plague Monrovia. The mobilization of armed ethnic groups in support of the agendas of rival warlords during the civil war has led to continuing political problems in postwar Liberia. Following intense fighting in Monrovia, a shooting incident involving Taylor's security men and his former Krahn minister of rural development, Roosevelt Johnson, at the U.S. Embassy in Monrovia in September 1998 led to fifty-two deaths and the evacuation of Johnson from Liberia. There were reports of the harassment of Krahns in Monrovia following this incident, forcing more than 4,000 Krahns to flee to Côte d'Ivoire.[5] Another disturbing trend involved reports of Mandingos being violently attacked by Lomas in Lofa County and by Gios and Manos in Nimba County. These clashes are related to disputes over land and resources as refugees return to areas they abandoned during the civil war. By June 1998, arsonists had burned six mosques throughout the country. Liberia's ethnic and religious powderkegs may yet be reignited, with disastrous results, if these conflicts are not carefully managed.

Problems Abroad Come Home

Following the 1997 elections, instability on Liberia's borders soured relations between Taylor and ECOMOG. ECOMOG, along with the United States, Britain and others, criticized Taylor's continued military support of RUF rebels and dissident soldiers, who killed dozens of Nigerian troops in Freetown following the military coup on 25 May 1997. For his part, Taylor accused ECOMOG of supporting some of his rivals in Sierra Leone; refused ECOMOG jets permission to use Liberian airfields for missions into Sierra Leone; criticized ECOWAS and UN sanctions against the AFRC/RUF military junta in Freetown; and publicly opposed the Nigerian-led intervention in Freetown to restore the elected government of Ahmed Tejan Kabbah in February 1998.[6] Taylor successfully pressured Abacha to remove ECOMOG Force Commander Victor Malu, who had resisted Taylor's plans to bring ECOMOG under his own command and insisted forcefully that

ECOMOG restructure Liberia's army.[7] Malu was replaced by the mild-mannered General Timothy Shelpidi in January 1998. By the end of 1998, ECOMOG finally withdrew its peacekeepers from Liberia.

Following ECOMOG's departure, insecurity continued along Liberia's borders with Guinea and Sierra Leone. After 200,000 Sierra Leonean refugees flooded into Liberia after September 1997 following fighting in that country, Taylor sent troops to guard his border with Sierra Leone. Taylor had been hypersensitive about his borders ever since ULIMO launched its invasion against the NPFL from Sierra Leone; Taylor himself had invaded Liberia from Côte d'Ivoire. In an outbreak of violence that signified the start of Liberia's second civil war in a decade and reversal of ECOMOG's gains and sacrifices, Liberian dissidents invaded the towns of Voinjama and Kolahun, Lofa County, in April and August 1999. These attacks were launched from Guinea by a group calling themselves Liberians United for Reconciliation and Democracy (LURD), thought to be mostly Mandingo and Krahn fighters of the former ULIMO-K and ULIMO-J militias. ULIMO-K leader Alhaji Kromah had close ties to Conakry during Liberia's seven-year civil war. Former ULIMO-J leader Roosevelt Johnson left Liberia after intense fighting with Taylor's security forces in 1998. Shortly before May 1999, Taylor-supported RUF rebels launched attacks into Guinea, destroying property and lives.[8]

In September 1999, two Guinean villages on the border with Liberia were attacked by Guinean rebels believed to be backed by Taylor.[9] The acrimonious relationship between Taylor and the Guinean leader, Lansana Conté, dates to 1990, before the ECOMOG intervention, when Conté threatened to invade Liberia unilaterally following the NPFL invasion.[10] In March 2001, Taylor announced the expulsion of the Guinean and Sierra Leonean ambassadors from Monrovia, accusing them of aiding rebels. He had withdrawn his own ambassador from Conakry three months earlier. The relationship between Liberia and Guinea worsened following renewed attacks into Lofa County by LURD rebels between July and November 2000, forcing thousands of refugees to flee the area. Guinea issued inflammatory statements against Liberian and Sierra Leonean refugees, which led to xenophobic attacks against nationals of those two countries. Like Taylor, General Conté has scarcely been a paragon of democratic leadership: he had conducted deeply flawed elections and jailed his political rivals. By April 2001, heavy fighting raged between Taylor's army and Guinean-backed Liberian rebels near the Lofa towns of Foya and Kolahun, and violence spread into Nimba County.

Having already deployed troops in Lofa County, Taylor was forced to mobilize 15,000 former NPFL fighters to repel the rebels. The fighting and lack of funding made it impossible for ECOWAS to implement a plan to deploy 1,700 troops along the borders of Liberia, Sierra Leone, and Guinea. Taylor's claims that his army was controlling the situation in Lofa County rang especially hollow when suspected LURD rebels killed Francois Massaquoi, the minister for youth and sports and former leader of the LDF faction, by shooting down his helicopter while landing in Lofa County. Daniel Chea, Liberia's defense minister, warned that his troops would pursue the rebels across the border into Guinea, threatening a further escalation of the conflict. By February 2002, LURD rebels were attacking Kle, barely twenty-two miles from Monrovia, forcing Taylor to declare a state of emergency. There are genuine fears that instability in Liberia could threaten progress in Sierra Leone with the completion of disarmament in January 2002 and elections scheduled for May 2002.

A Private Army

An especially disturbing aspect of post-1997 Liberia is Taylor's failure to restructure the Armed Forces of Liberia and other security forces, with the assistance of ECOMOG and the United Nations, as envisaged in the Accra agreement of 1994. After his election in 1997, Taylor refused to permit peacekeepers any role in restructuring and training his security forces. He ordered the demobilization and retirement of 2,628 soldiers from the AFL, including many Krahn officers, in January 1998. Taylor has included thousands of his former NPFL fighters in the new Liberian army and created the notorious Anti-terrorist Unit as a private army reporting directly to him.[11] The restructuring process has been criticized as partisan and lacking transparency.

Taylor's decision to fill his security forces with loyal lieutenants is hardly unique in contemporary African politics; leaders in Burundi, Rwanda, Côte d'Ivoire, Togo, and Zaire have followed tradition by placing kinsmen in strategic military positions. The fragile state of Liberia and the continuing sources of insecurity, however, suggest that Taylor is repeating Doe's fatal mistake: by filling the army with ethnic loyalists and using it as a tool against political opponents, Taylor has created conditions for the mobilization of ethnic groups to protect their own people against a partisan army. The institutionalization of violence—a hallmark of the Doe regime that became a way of life during the civil war—seems to be continuing into the Taylor era.[12] Liberian security forces historically served as an instrument of partisan rule, first defending the interests of the Americo-Liberian oligarchy, then keeping the autocratic regime of Doe in power, and now attempting to ensure the survival of Taylor's regime.

Most of Taylor's opponents view the state apparatus as an extension of his personal power; justice is not perceived to be neutral. As Taylor continues to use state power to silence critics, and tries to control a growing insurgency by rebels by removing all opposition prior to the next election, scheduled for 2003, he has created a situation similar to that produced by Doe's fraudulent election of 1985, in which opponents were left with no alternative but violence. All of Taylor's main political rivals now live out-side the country. On 12 November 1998, Taylor accused thirty-two people, including Alhaji Kromah, Roosevelt Johnson, George Boley, and Ellen Johnson-Sirleaf, of involvement in a plot to overthrow his government. Fol-lowing a court trial in Liberia, many of the suspects were convicted, some in absentia, and several were jailed.

Once a Warlord . . .

Having waged a guerrilla campaign for seven years, Taylor retains the psy-chology of a warlord. He has failed to transform himself from a ruthless warlord to a responsible statesman. Good governance in a democratic set-ting has been far more difficult than the unencumbered autocracy of war-lord politics. During the civil war, Taylor briefly lost his headquarters in Gbarnga to his enemies, saw other factions gang up against him, witnessed Nigeria, Sierra Leone, and Guinea providing assistance to rival factions, and heard calls by several Nigerian generals for his assassination. He is still profoundly scarred by these experiences. Having himself led an ultimately successful rebellion into Liberia based on the exploitation of ethnic griev-ances, and having witnessed Doe's grisly end, Taylor is deeply aware of his own vulnerability in Liberia's political cesspit.

Taylor's paranoia and obsession with security are not altogether sur-prising. Within days after the assassination of Congolese leader Laurent Kabila by one of his bodyguards in January 2001, Taylor replaced his own personal security detail.[13] As the Liberian leader candidly admitted, "Once you are in, because of the chaos created from outside, you become undemo-cratic in the preservation of power. It is almost like the survival of the fittest."[14] Having amassed so much illicit wealth and gathered so many en-emies in his bloody ascent to power, Taylor, like Doe before him, is deter-mined to retain his position to prevent any vindictive rival from probing his past practices.

The lack of security, the collapse of public infrastructure, and the ab-sence of the rule of law in Liberia have made international donors stingy and deterred foreign investors. A few South African and Canadian firms are involved in prospecting for Liberian minerals, but such interest has been rare. Taylor has tried to maintain close political relations with Burkina Faso and Libya and sought to court Taiwanese and French investors. But tradi-tional trading partners like the United States, Japan, and Germany continue to stay away. Liberian diamonds are still being smuggled out of the country despite a UN embargo, and there are reports of lucrative contracts being awarded to Taylor's close political associates.[15] The Liberian president has asked the National Assembly to grant him sole power to conclude commercial contracts for exploiting strategic commodities, the clearest sign of his determination to use the trappings of sovereignty to plunder resources. A donor conference for Liberia's reconstruction held in Paris in April 1998 led to pledges of $200 million. But these funds were made conditional on progress on security and human rights and never arrived. Four years after a devastating civil war, Liberia's shattered infrastructure has not been revived even as a new war in the north causes further damage.

Pressure from Abroad

Amid these domestic difficulties, Taylor faces unprecedented external pressure. In March 2001, the UN Security Council, led by the United States and Britain, demanded that Liberia halt the import of Sierra Leonean diamonds, end Liberian support for the RUF, and pressure the rebels to allow the UN mission in Sierra Leone access to rebel-controlled territory. Liberia's support for the rebels reportedly included the training of RUF rebels in Liberia; strategy meetings with the RUF in Monrovia; and supply of military assistance to the RUF from Liberia. All were documented by a panel of experts on Sierra Leone diamonds and arms, established by the UN Security Council, in a report dated 20 December 2000.[16] Taylor made frantic efforts to comply with the Security Council's requests by grounding all Liberian aircraft, inviting international monitoring of Liberia's diamond trade, calling for the deployment of UN monitors along Liberia's land and sea borders, and announcing the expulsion of former RUF commander Sam Bockarie and the closure of the RUF office in Monrovia.

But there were reports of continuing collaboration between Taylor and the RUF, and Bockarie's expulsion, which was vociferously supported by Liberia's religious and civic groups, could not be independently verified.[17] Deciding that Taylor's efforts lacked conviction, the UN Security Council on 7 May 2001 imposed a ban on the export of diamonds from Liberia as well as travel sanctions on senior government officials and their spouses. The Security Council also tightened an existing arms embargo by prohibiting the sale or supply of arms and related material to Liberia and banning the provision of military training to the government. These sanctions, which many civil groups and opposition politicians supported on the basis that they would hurt the leadership in Liberia more than the people, are to be reassessed every fourteen months.

The UN Security Council delayed the imposition of sanctions for three months at the urging of most ECOWAS states with the notable exceptions of Guinea and Sierra Leone. The sanctions debate between the Security Council and ECOWAS reflected a continuing difference in approaches. Most ECOWAS states argued against what they saw as a policy of sticks without carrots and criticized the Security Council's policy as contradictory. The Security Council imposed sanctions on Liberia even while seeking Taylor's assistance in gaining RUF compliance to implement the Lomé peace plan in Sierra Leone.[18]

ECOWAS's own policy may not be entirely free of contradiction. Nigerian President Olusegun Obasanjo has actively courted Taylor and worked closely with him in negotiating the Lomé agreement to end Sierra Leone's war.[19] Although Obasanjo told a visiting UN Security Council mission in October 2000 that he believed Taylor was behind the destabilization of the subregion, he and many colleagues also seem to believe that the former warlord can be transformed into a responsible statesman through diplomatic means.[20] ECOWAS leaders, several of whom have demonstrated undemocratic and destabilizing behavior, doubtless fear the precedent of the UN Security Council imposing sanctions on Liberia for bad behavior.

In order for UN sanctions to be effective, it is important that the Security Council secure ECOWAS cooperation. The diamond sanctions may not be watertight, for Liberian gems can be smuggled easily through third countries, and no effective enforcement mechanism exists on the ground. The travel sanctions and arms embargo will need the support of ECOWAS states to be implemented. But the sanctions have rattled Taylor. He has accused their main architects—the United States and Britain—of attempting to overthrow his regime and of providing military support to Guinea. More devastating economic sanctions on Liberia's $13 million annual timber trade were blocked in the UN Security Council by France and China, which together import about 45 percent of Liberia's timber.[21]

Today, Taylor faces the greatest challenge to the survival of his regime. Liberia's total government revenue for 2000 was estimated to have been only $85 million, even as Taylor announced that $15 million of it had been diverted to the war effort in Lofa County.[22] Meanwhile, civil-service salaries went unpaid for almost a year. The situation in postwar Liberia parallels that in prewar Liberia: widespread insecurity, a weak economy, patronage-fueled corruption, government harassment of the press and civic groups, interethnic clashes, trumped-up coup plots, and external sanctions. The current cycle of violence that began with master-sergeant Samuel Doe's bloody coup in 1980 has certainly not been broken by Taylor's 1997 election victory. As General Timothy Shelpidi, ECOMOG's last force commander in Liberia, noted, "Taylor believes in swimming in troubled waters."[23] The Liberian warlord-turned-president may yet end up drowning in the bloody waters of the Mano River which he has done so much to pollute.

Notes

1. See Jon Lee Anderson, "The Devil They Know," *New Yorker* (27 July 1998); and Baffour Ankomah, "Knives Out for Taylor," *New African* (September 1998).

2. Report of the Joint Review Mission on the United Nations Post-conflict Peacebuilding Offices, Department of Political Affairs/United Nations Development Programme, 20 July 2001, p. 14.

3. Ibid., p. 11.

4. See Norwood Langley, "The National Reconstruction Program in Liberia," in *State Rebuilding after State Collapse: Security, Democracy, and Development in Post-War Liberia* (Report of the Strategic Planning Workshop on Liberia dated 19 June 1998) (London: Center for Democracy and Development, 1998).

5. *Economist Intelligence Unit,* Country Report, "Liberia" (First Quarter 1999): 8.

6. On Sierra Leone, see Adekeye Adebajo, *Building Peace in West Africa: Liberia, Sierra Leone, and Guinea-Bissau* (Boulder, Colo.: Lynne Rienner, 2002), pp. 79–109; Eric Berman and Katie Sams, *Peacebuilding in Africa: Capabilities and Culpabilities* (Pretoria: Institute for Security Studies, 2001), pp. 111–128; and Robert Mortimer, "From ECOMOG to ECOMOG II: Intervention in Sierra Leone," in John W. Harbeson and Donald Rothchild, eds., *Africa in World Politics: The African State System in Flux,* 3d ed. (Boulder, Colo.: Westview Press, 2000), pp. 188–207.

7. Personal interview with General Victor Malu, former ECOMOG force commander, Lagos, 2 October 2001.

8. "Final Communiqué," Meeting of ECOWAS Ministers of Foreign Affairs, Lomé, 24–25 May 1999, p. 5.

9. *Economist Intelligence Unit,* Country Report, "Liberia" (Fourth Quarter 1999): 36–40; and *Economist Intelligence Unit,* Country Report, "Liberia" (Second Quarter 1999): 36.

10. Personal interview with Professor Amos Sawyer, former President of Liberia, 1990–1994, Monrovia, 14 July 1999.

11. *Africa Confidential* 40, no. 4 (19 February 1999): 7.

12. Amos Sawyer, "Foundations for Reconstruction in Liberia: Challenges and Responses," in *State Rebuilding after State Collapse,* p. 69.

13. Jeffrey Bartholet, "Liberia's Charles Taylor—Inside the Mind of a Tyrant," *Newsweek,* 14 May 2001, p. 31.

14. "The West Wants to Suffocate Liberia" (Interview with Charles Taylor), *West Africa,* no. 4251 (6–12 November 2000): 11.

15. *Economist Intelligence Unit,* Country Report, "Liberia" (Third Quarter 1998): 11.

16. See Report of the Panel of Experts appointed pursuant to Security Council Resolution 1306 (2000), Paragraph 19, in Relation to Sierra Leone, 20 December 2000, S/2000/1195, pp. 32–34.

17. First Report of the Secretary-General Pursuant to Security Council Resolution 1343 (2001) Regarding Liberia, 30 April 2001, S/2001/424, p. 3.

18. Ibid., p. 6.

19. See Ismail Rashid, "The Lomé Peace Negotiations," in David Lord, ed., *Paying the Price: The Sierra Leone Peace Process, Accord No. 9 (2000),* pp. 26–35.

20. Report of the Security Council Mission to Sierra Leone, 16 October 2000, S/2000/992, p. 8.

21. *Economist Intelligence Unit,* Country Report, "Liberia" (March 2001): 49.

22. Ibid., p. 42.

23. Personal interview with General Timothy Shelpidi, former ECOMOG Force Commander, Abuja, 10 July 2001.

chapter **12**

CONCLUSION

> *ECOMOG has achieved more success than expected by its founders and the international community. It has provided clear proof of what is possible if African states pool their resources to address a problem.*
> —*General Maxwell Khobe, former ECOMOG task force commander*

The Contingencies, Complexities, and Ironies of the Liberian Civil War

Pax Nigeriana, as exhibited through ECOMOG, reflected the efforts of an aspiring hegemon to manage regional security in West Africa. Nigeria was the most significant actor in determining the policies that ECOMOG pursued. Liberia provided a stage for Nigeria to play out its aspirations as regional hegemon; Ghana, Gambia, Guinea, and Sierra Leone played the role of supporting cast; and Liberia's warlords and political actors provided important props in a tragedy of epic proportions. We have argued that the Nigerian-led ECOMOG intervention was consistent with Nigeria's foreign policy ambitions since its independence in 1960. We have explained the factors that triggered the Liberian civil war by examining the important events of the preceding decade under Samuel Doe. We have analyzed the domestic, subregional, and external factors that first hampered, but eventually helped, the attainment of a Pax Nigeriana in Liberia.

In this study we have used an empirical and historical narrative to demonstrate how contingencies and changes over time explained the outcomes of the Liberian civil war. No real pattern of alliances was established during ECOMOG's seven-year presence, and personal relationships and the

241

impact of the war on neighbors were more important factors in determining the policies pursued by the various actors. Personalities like Generals Ibrahim Babangida and Sani Abacha, Jerry Rawlings, Félix Houphoüet-Boigny, Blaise Compaoré, Henri Konan Bédié, Samuel Doe, and Charles Taylor—all made a difference in the course of events in a subregion where institutions are generally weak and leaders generally strong. The choices of these actors shaped how the conflict started, developed, and ended. By examining motivations and policies in detail, this historical narrative has explained the complex processes through which the conflict was eventually terminated in 1997.

We have also focused on interactions: between Nigeria and important ECOWAS states; between Nigeria and the United States; between ECOMOG and various Liberian factions; between ECOMOG and UNOMIL; and among Liberian factions and civilian political groups. These complex interactions produced outcomes that were often different from the ones originally intended or anticipated by the parties. Interactions among interested parties produced systemic consequences that generated improvised structures—like the various ECOWAS mediation committees and Liberian interim governments—that tended to be fragile. Structures were therefore a result of immediate contingencies rather than of long-term intentions.

Intraregional relations depended as much on contingent circumstances as on long-standing patterns of interests and alignments. Geographic contiguity and the destabilizing effects of war eventually determined the policies of several subregional states. The termination of the conflict in 1997 did depend on the Nigerian military's ambition and willingness to bear most of the burden for the intervention, and Nigeria acted as a pivotal state in directing the process and accepting the terms under which Taylor came to power. But it was also crucial that various actors changed their stances. This often resulted from a change of leadership in key countries like Nigeria and Côte d'Ivoire.

These contingencies produced ironic consequences: Nigeria crowned Taylor president after obstructing his ambitions for five years; General Abacha, less interested in foreign policy than domestic survival, achieved the foreign policy success that his legacy-conscious predecessor, General Babangida, failed to achieve; Côte d'Ivoire, among the NPFL's earliest backers, and the crucial staging post for its 1989 invasion, halted support for the NPFL and became an important supporter of ECOMOG; the United States eventually supported the Nigerian-dominated force to which it had denied logistical support for six years; Charles Taylor entered into an alliance with his bitter rival, Alhaji Kromah, on the executive Council of State; and ECOWAS spurned ECOMOG but eventually succeeded in creating an instrument of collective (albeit Nigerian-dominated) military action without making any significant progress in regional economic integration.

The structures that emerged were more often the outcome of complex interactions rather than being determined by any existing structure of alignments and interests. We will illustrate these points with a synopsis of the narrative sequence leading to the achievement of peace in Liberia in 1997.

The Tortuous Road to Peace

ECOMOG's overconfident soldiers entered Liberia in 1990 assuming they could achieve a quick cease-fire. They soon discovered they had overestimated their military capabilities against the largely untrained Liberian factions, and the putative peacekeepers had to increase their troops to enforce peace. This reflected the confusion of the initial mandate and the improvised nature of the intervention. The dangers of deploying troops without firm guarantees of cooperation from the factions and without the provision of logistical support led to the killing and hostage-taking of ECOMOG peacekeepers, most notably in 1992, 1994, and 1995.

The ECOMOG intervention exacerbated existing subregional divisions between francophone and anglophone states. Guinea was the only francophone member of the initial ECOMOG force. The two francophone members of the ECOWAS Standing Mediation Committee, Togo and Mali, refused to contribute troops to ECOMOG. The animosity that Houphoüet-Boigny and Compaoré felt toward Samuel Doe, as well as Compaoré's friendship with Taylor, the strained relations between Jerry Rawlings and Compaoré, and the historical rivalry between Côte d'Ivoire and Nigeria further deepened these divisions. This led ECOWAS states to back different Liberian factions: Côte d'Ivoire and Burkina Faso supported the NPFL; Sierra Leone and Guinea cooperated militarily with ULIMO; Nigeria supported several anti-NPFL factions and pursued an aggressive stance against Charles Taylor; and Ghana favored political accommodation with the NPFL. ECOMOG states sought to heal these divisions by belatedly including francophone states in efforts to resolve the conflict.

Charles Taylor's support for the invasion of Sierra Leone in 1991 triggered a ten-year civil war in that country and had the effect of strengthening the commitments of Sierra Leone, Gambia, Guinea, and eventually Côte d'Ivoire to ECOMOG, for they feared a similar result in their countries. Guinea, Côte d'Ivoire, and Sierra Leone suffered the most destabilizing effects, including refugees and military incursions. All three countries had a direct interest in a successful resolution of the conflict. Significantly, the main NPFL military and political supporter, Burkina Faso, had no common border with Liberia and was therefore immune to the spillover effects of the war. Compaoré could continue his support for the NPFL in the full knowledge that his national security would not be directly threatened by the war. The same was not true of Abidjan, Conakry, and Freetown.

The appearance of new factions like ULIMO, the LPC, and LDF, as well as the split of the NPFL and ULIMO into four factions, made outright NPFL military victory—which Burkina Faso and Côte d'Ivoire hoped for at the start of the conflict—more difficult and ensured a protracted struggle. The military challenges that Taylor faced greatly reduced his control of Liberian territory by 1993 and forced him to the negotiating table. But peace agreements lacked viable implementation mechanisms, and there was no incentive for the warlords, who earned lucrative profits from resources exported from their territories, to disarm. Ironically, the warlords were politicians and not military men, but their militarization of politics intensified the war.

ULIMO's success in reaching the negotiating table was a clear sign to the LPC and LDF that territorial control was essential to gaining a share of political power. The most powerful factions attempted to cut a deal that would exclude others: the IGNU and NPFL excluded ULIMO from Yamoussoukro in 1991; ULIMO joined both parties to exclude the LPC and LDF from Cotonou in 1993. Shifting alliances among the warlords further complicated peacemaking. Such alliances were inherently unstable, as the factions themselves lacked coherence and discipline. Efforts to involve UN and OAU peacekeepers in mediation and disarmament efforts in 1993 failed to secure the cooperation of the warlords.

A crucial event that eventually accelerated the resolution of the conflict was the ascent to power in Nigeria of General Sani Abacha in November 1993. The death of Houphouët-Boigny a month later triggered the shift of Côte d'Ivoire's Liberia policy under the leadership of Henri Konan Bédié. Both Abacha and Bédié had less of a personal stake in the outcome of the conflict and lacked the close ties, real or imagined, of their predecessors to Doe and Taylor. Both had more pressing domestic concerns of establishing their political authority, as they were less popular than their predecessors. Taylor visited General Abacha in Abuja in 1995, marking a rapprochement between the dominant ECOMOG state and the most powerful Liberian faction. Rawlings's close friendship with Abacha was also important in securing Nigeria's agreement to include the warlords in the Council of State at Abuja in 1995.

Burkina Faso offered ECOMOG two battalions five months after Nigeria's rapprochement with Taylor. With Taylor having made peace with Nigeria, Compaoré no longer had a reason to frustrate ECOMOG's efforts: he could support ECOMOG and the NPFL simultaneously. Burkina Faso, Côte d'Ivoire, Niger, and Benin sent troops to ECOMOG by 1997. The introduction of four new francophone contingents restored political balance to ECOMOG and made it a truly subregional effort for the first time.

With Taylor convinced that Nigeria no longer obstructed his presidential ambitions and confident of electoral victory, and having amassed a fortune from lucrative exports of Liberian resources, the largest faction—the NPFL—led the way in disarmament. The United States led the international community to provide ECOMOG with crucial logistical support for disarmament tasks, encouraged by the increased cooperation of the warlords, the wider subregional composition of ECOMOG, and the restoration of neutrality to the peacekeeping force.

ECOMOG: Pax Nigeriana?

We have pursued three main arguments with regard to the question of whether ECOMOG was a Pax Nigeriana. Nigeria intervened in Liberia due to the image its military leaders have historically had of the country as a regional leader and their perception of the importance of their own place in Nigerian history. We thus challenge the widespread view expressed in the academic literature that explains Nigeria's intervention in terms of regional rivalries with Burkina Faso, Côte d'Ivoire, Libya, and France; our explanation is rooted in Nigeria's historical aspirations for regional hegemony. General Babangida and General Abacha were fully committed to a continued Nigerian role in ECOMOG despite strong opposition from the Nigerian public. Babangida, having established the most personalized style of leadership seen in Nigeria, saw ECOMOG as a chance to leave a historical legacy in the subregion. Lacking Babangida's popularity in the army and facing greater domestic and international opposition to his regime, Abacha was more pragmatic in seeking a solution to Liberia. Both generals, supported by the military top brass, viewed the prospect of a humiliating withdrawal from Liberia as an unacceptable blow to Nigerian prestige.

But the reasons Nigeria intervened in Liberia were not necessarily the same as the reasons for its extended stay. Other interests developed as the intervention continued. Aside from attempting to pursue Nigeria's consistent foreign policy goals in the subregion, the ECOMOG intervention served at least three additional purposes. Under the regime of General Abacha, ECOMOG became a useful bargaining tool to ward off international sanctions by implicitly threatening to withdraw Nigerian troops from Liberia. It was widely believed that Nigeria's generals illicitly diverted funds from ECOMOG to private bank accounts, helping to explain ECOMOG's continuing logistical problems despite Nigerian claims of having spent $3.5 billion on the intervention;[1] other estimates have put ECOMOG's spending closer to $1.2 billion.[2] Recent revelations by Nigeria's civilian regime under Olusegun Obasanjo—that Sani Abacha, who died in office in June 1998, stole billions of dollars in government revenue—lend credence to these reports. Obasanjo's regime recovered the lost money by April 2002.

Finally, the position of ECOMOG commander was used by Nigerian military rulers to reward loyal lieutenants. The first four Nigerian ECOMOG field commanders (Generals Dogonyaro, Kupolati, Bakut, and Olurin) were all trusted allies of the Nigerian head of state, General Babangida. The arrival of the fifth Commander, General John Shagaya, marked the first and only time that a field commander did not enjoy the total support of his military superior. At the time of Shagaya's appointment in September 1993, Nigeria had a weak interim government under Ernest Shonekan. The defense minister at the time, General Sani Abacha himself, sent Shagaya to Liberia in order to sideline his potential rival and then retired Shagaya from the army upon becoming head of state two months later. The appointment of the sixth Nigerian field commander, General Mark Inienger, restored the previous pattern, with Inienger, an Abacha loyalist, going on to become the longest-serving ECOMOG commander.

Our second argument is that Nigeria did not have parochial or expansionist interests in Liberia and in fact lost more than it gained in military and financial terms in the quest for subregional grandeur. We have sought to disprove claims that Nigeria was using ECOMOG purely as a self-serving instrument of its own foreign policy by demonstrating that other states had far more direct interests in resolving the conflict. Sierra Leone suffered a decade-long civil war triggered from Liberia; Côte d'Ivoire suffered increased Liberian factional incursions into its territory; the Liberian war spilled over sporadically into Guinea. The three countries hosted more than 500,000 Liberian refugees during the war. The fact that Charles Taylor's NPFL contained Gambian, Guinean, and Sierra Leonean dissidents also helps explain those countries' sustained military commitment to ECOMOG.

Contrary to the popular portrayal of other ECOMOG states as mere pawns on Nigeria's geostrategic chessboard, these states were not simply bullied into joining ECOMOG but saw the importance of the peacekeepers' presence in Liberia in promoting subregional stability; they accepted Nigerian leadership as an inevitable, if sometimes uncomfortable, necessity. Pax Nigeriana was constrained in the management of the conflict through Ghana's influence within ECOMOG and the influence of francophone countries in peacemaking. Nigeria could not always determine what policies ECOWAS and ECOMOG pursued and often had to compromise to retain the support of its neighbors. For example, Nigeria surrendered peacemaking leadership to Côte d'Ivoire in 1991 and acceded to Ghana's insistence on including the warlords in government in 1995.

Finally, contradicting the frequent claims of a bullying Nigerian hegemone in Liberia, we have demonstrated that ECOMOG represented Nigeria's hegemonic *ambitions* rather than its hegemonic *abilities*. We have consistently shown the limits of Pax Nigeriana in Liberia. This case study does not support claims of Nigerian hegemony if it is defined in terms of power and capability. Nigeria was unable to pacify Liberia militarily due to its own logistical shortcomings as well as the ability of Liberian warlords to control much of the country outside Monrovia. Nigeria's failure to secure subregional consensus earlier in the conflict also hampered its efforts.

ECOMOG needed logistical support from the United States and European Union even while the United Nations and NGOs provided the humanitarian relief that Nigeria and the rest of the subregion lacked the means to provide. This important external support underpinned Pax Nigeriana, complementing but not supplanting Nigeria's efforts. Pax Nigeriana was in effect hegemony on a shoestring: Nigeria simply lacked the economic resources, military capacity, and diplomatic support to impose peace in Liberia. In order to achieve its objectives, it had to rely on external assistance for logistics and legitimacy, subregional assistance for political consensus, and cooperation in disarmament from Liberian warlords.

ECOMOG:
Domestic, Subregional, and External Dimensions

Throughout this book, we pursued two main arguments regarding the interactions between the domestic, subregional, and external levels of analysis.

We have demonstrated that difficulties at the domestic, subregional, and external levels prevented the achievement of ECOMOG's goals for six years. We have stressed the importance of the underanalyzed security interdependence of these three levels, but we have not formally adopted or tested Barry Buzan's concept of the regional security complex due to its limitations in this case. This case study instead shows that contingencies, rather than any established security patterns, were the most crucial factors in explaining the outcomes of the civil war. Internally, the situation was complicated by the unwillingness of the strongest faction, the NPFL, to share power with other groups and by the determination of other factions to gain a stake in power through territorial conquest. Liberia's warlords profited from the economic resources derived from territory under their control. They were unable to agree on disarmament due to the mutual fear of rival factions gaining military superiority and the risk of losing economic benefits from areas under their control.

At the subregional level, ECOWAS members failed to reach consensus on how to resolve the conflict. Even after the francophone states were given more representation in peacemaking activities, Burkina Faso, Libya, and to a lesser extent Côte d'Ivoire continued to support the NPFL, rendering ECOWAS's attempts to impose trade and arms embargos on Liberia's warlords ineffective. Ghana and Nigeria disagreed over fundamental issues like the participation of warlords on the Council of State and whether ECOMOG should remain a strictly peacekeeping force or adopt a more aggressive enforcement role.

At the external level, the United States denied ECOMOG meaningful logistical support and channeled its resources largely toward the less controversial humanitarian effort. Washington's difficult bilateral relations with Nigeria and its distrust of ECOMOG's neutrality led it to continue this policy for six years. As for other external actors, the United Nations for most of its four years in Liberia (1993–1997) had less than 100 peacekeepers. Its unarmed soldiers relied entirely on ECOMOG for security. Because their mandate depended on the existence of a peaceful environment to help monitor ECOMOG's disarmament of the factions, the UN peacekeepers were unable to influence events significantly in a civil war situation. The OAU also lacked the financial and logistical resources to alleviate ECOMOG's shortcomings.

We have also demonstrated that only by achieving consensus at all three levels was the Liberian conflict finally resolved in 1997. This case calls attention to the need for more scholars to study the complex interaction at all three levels in order to capture the dynamics that led to the temporary end of the conflict. All three levels were interdependent: Without the commitment of Liberian warlords to disarmament, it proved difficult for ECOMOG to achieve peace in Liberia; without the healing of subregional divisions, the ECOMOG intervention lacked subregional legitimacy and the NPFL continued to enjoy military support, especially from Burkina Faso; without external support from the United States and European Union, ECOMOG lacked adequate logistical resources. Put simply, the end of animosity between Nigeria and the NPFL led the warlords to cooperate with ECOMOG; this in turn led Burkina Faso, Côte d'Ivoire, Niger, and Benin to contribute troops to ECOMOG. The cooperation of warlords and subregional unity allayed fears of ECOMOG's partiality and eventually convinced the United States and European Union to contribute logistical support to ECOMOG. Success at these three levels was crucial to the implementation of Abuja II.

* * *

We now turn to the broader implications of the ECOMOG intervention in Liberia for three key issues: the emerging realignment of relations among West African states; the future of ECOMOG itself; and the prospects of Pax Nigeriana.

ECOMOG as Region-builder

Despite the unprecedented subregional cooperation at the end of the ECOMOG mission in Liberia, deep-seated fears still exist among francophone states regarding Nigeria's possible intentions to dominate West Africa, as evidenced by the reaction to Nigeria's unilateral intervention to reverse a coup in Sierra Leone in February 1998.[3] The continuing divisions in West Africa are symbolized by the proliferation of some forty intergovernmental organizations, the continued existence of ten separate currencies, and the creation of the eight-member, almost exclusively francophone, West African Monetary and Economic Union in January 1994.[4]

Article 58 of the revised ECOWAS treaty of July 1993 called for the establishment of a regional peace and security observation system and a peacekeeping force.[5] ECOMOG's success in Liberia in terminating the war in 1997 added impetus to the historic decision to create such a force. In West Africa, the new regionalism seems to be more successful in the military sphere than in the economic domain. Intraregional trade in ECOWAS remains no more than about 10 percent of officially recorded trade. In the military sphere, however, ECOWAS could achieve more results because practical success in Liberia has preceded theory. Whereas postwar European integration in the European Economic Community was accomplished by spillover from economic cooperation to the political sphere, the situation could be reversed in West Africa: improved political relations may eventually lead to greater economic cooperation.[6]

ECOMOG as a Future Peacekeeping Force

At the ECOWAS summit in Abuja at the end of October 1998, an ECOWAS draft security mechanism calling for an ECOMOG peacekeeping force, based on standby troops from national armies, was finally adopted.[7] The ECOWAS protocol relating to the Mechanism for Conflict Prevention, Management, Resolution, Peacekeeping, and Security was later signed in Lomé on 10 December 1999.[8] The protocol called for the establishment of the following organs to implement security decisions: Mediation and Security Council, Defense and Security Commission, and Council of Elders.[9] Many of these suggestions were based on the Liberia experience.

ECOWAS states have now agreed to establish a brigade-size standby force consisting of specially trained and equipped units of national armies ready to be deployed at short notice. The force will be called ECOMOG, and its main tasks will involve observation and monitoring, peacekeeping, humanitarian intervention, enforcement of sanctions and embargos, preventive deployment, peacebuilding operations, disarmament and demobilization, and policing activities, including antismuggling and anticrime activities.

The Liberia case cautions, however, that there are several important policy lessons to be learned before this effort can succeed. ECOWAS states must first recognize that decisions to intervene in countries will be inherently political in subregional conflicts where member states often have concrete interests. Unlike the collective security system of the United Nations, whose universal membership often allows it to send peacekeepers from countries that have no direct stake in the conflicts to be resolved, ECOWAS does not have this luxury. ECOWAS will have to find a way to exclude countries whose presence is strongly opposed by the disputing parties, and it may sometimes have to borrow troops from outside the subregion, as it did in Liberia with OAU and UN peacekeepers and as it did with the UN mission in Sierra Leone (UNAMSIL) between 1999 and 2002. Political discretion will always have to be exercised in decisions to intervene in conflicts, even when the criteria for intervention have been met.

In addition, military interventions like ECOMOG's action in Liberia will always have to be determined on a case-by-case basis. The requirement of a two-thirds majority of ten states—required under the new ECOWAS security protocol—is an important check that allows for a blocking minority. But this still leaves ECOWAS with a dilemma: if the need for intervention is pressing on humanitarian grounds but subregional states on the Mediation and Security Council veto intervention due to self-interest, ECOMOG can be blocked from undertaking action as a result of parochial, partisan interests; the interests of the wider community would suffer.

Finally, the ECOMOG intervention in Liberia exposed ECOWAS's logistical and financial weaknesses. For the foreseeable future, logistical support for subregional peacekeeping missions will have to come from external actors like the United States, United Nations, and European Union until ECOWAS develops its own capabilities. The Liberia mission clearly demonstrated the importance of securing financial support *before* embarking on an intervention. Costs like those borne by Nigeria in Liberia can become a disincentive to any future intervention. In 1997, only Nigeria, Benin, and Côte d'Ivoire had paid their ECOWAS dues in full; unpaid ECOWAS dues stood at $38.1 million in December 1999. This is not an encouraging record for building the financial foundations to support future military interventions.

The Future of Pax Nigeriana

Several Western analysts have attempted to deny the Nigerian military government any credit for its successful intervention in Liberia, as well as the subsequent intervention in Sierra Leone that restored the democratically elected government of Ahmad Tejan Kabbah to power in March 1998 following a military putsch.[10] These interventions could, however, come to represent Nigeria's most notable foreign policy triumphs. In both cases, Nigeria was able to play a leadership role in the achievement of important subregional goals. Unlike the Nigerian-led creation of ECOWAS in 1975, which has so far failed to achieve its integrationist goals in West Africa, ECOMOG eventually achieved the goals set out in Liberia and Sierra Leone: ending civil war and military rule and restoring elected governments in both countries. However, a note of caution is necessary. Despite the euphoria of ECOWAS leaders following these two interventions, it is unclear how durable these successes will be. They could well prove to be ephemeral. Sources of instability remain in both countries, as recent events have demonstrated, and the leaders of Liberia and Sierra Leone lack the resources for rapid socioeconomic transformation that could help entrench democracy and prevent a return to conflict.

The ECOMOG interventions in Liberia and Sierra Leone, however, demonstrated the indispensability of Nigeria to subregional peacekeeping: no other country in West Africa has the military and economic resources to mount such operations. Difficulties encountered in the ECOMOG military mission to Guinea-Bissau—involving peacekeepers from Benin, Gambia, Niger, and Togo—led to the withdrawal of the force in May 1999 after only four months, underlining the importance of Nigeria's financial and military resources to subregional peacekeeping.[11]

Even though Nigeria's military leaders pursued a Pax Nigeriana, the reactions of ordinary Nigerians to the missions in Liberia and Sierra Leone have ranged from lukewarm to hostile. On the premise that charity begins at home, there have been widespread demands to resolve internal problems before helping neighbors, and the sacrifices incurred in both interventions have been widely condemned as wasteful. This stands in stark contrast to the exhilaration of the 1970s oil boom, when Nigerians took great pride in their country's exploits in Angola and the liberation struggles in southern Africa. While Nigerians have become more isolationist, their military leaders seem to have grown more interventionist.

Nigeria's military leaders, who made decisions on Liberia in powerful cliques, have been largely immune from domestic pressures in foreign policy. The civilian government of Olusegun Obasanjo, which was elected in February 1999, has faced greater pressure from parliament, the press, and the public. Unlike the Babangida and Abacha military regimes, it has been unable to avoid the scrutiny of costs and casualties resulting from foreign military missions like those in Liberia and Sierra Leone. Significantly, three of Nigeria's four major military interventions—Chad, Liberia, and Sierra Leone—have been undertaken by military regimes. The domestic unpopularity of the ECOMOG mission in Liberia might well have forced a withdrawal of troops by an elected civilian government, as occurred under the presidency of Shehu Shagari, who withdrew Nigerian peacekeepers from Chad in 1982, and as threatened by the unelected civilian government of Ernest Shonekan in 1993. ECOMOG casualties in Liberia were estimated at 500, of which about 400 were Nigerian.[12]

It is unlikely that a civilian government in Nigeria will be able to sustain the casualties and costs like those incurred in Liberia without some loss of political support for the mission. Nigeria's refusal to contribute peacekeepers to the ECOMOG mission in Guinea-Bissau in 1999, and its decision to withdraw about 8,500 peacekeepers (out of 12,000) from Sierra Leone by 2000 and to subsume the rest under a UN force, are clear signs of growing wariness with the disproportionate costs of subregional peacekeeping. As Obasanjo noted during an address to the United Nations General Assembly in September 1999,

> The time has come . . . for the Security Council to assume its full responsibility, specifically in Sierra Leone and other flash points in Africa. For too long, the burden of preserving international peace and security in West Africa has been left almost entirely to a few states in our subregion. . . . Nigeria's continual burden in Sierra Leone is unacceptably draining Nigeria financially. For our economy to take off, this bleeding has to stop.[13]

But if the post-Somalia aversion of Western countries to sanction and contribute to UN missions in Africa continues, the ECOMOG mission in Liberia suggests that Pax Nigeriana may eventually result in an attempt by Nigeria to establish a West African sphere of influence, a *domaine réservé* where trespassers are forbidden and members resolve their own problems free of external interference.[14] A subregional Monroe Doctrine may be in gestation. This would allow West African states to define their own subsystem of international law that does not require prior UN or OAU legitimation but rather legitimation from a Nigeria-dominated ECOWAS. The United Nations did not give prior approval to the military interventions in Liberia and Sierra Leone, though it later expressed support for both. The ECOMOG intervention in Liberia revealed that if Nigeria can lead subregional states to take genuine united action and show stamina and commitment to resolving local problems, then it may eventually obtain diplomatic, military, and financial support from external actors.

But in order to fulfill its hegemonic ambitions in West Africa, Nigeria will have to be able to provide not only military muscle for subregional peacekeeping but also a domestic market that can sustain economic integration, provide economic assistance to its neighbors, and ease the acceptance of Nigerian leadership in West Africa. Nigeria is facing political and social instability that has resulted in more than 6,000 deaths between 1999 and 2002. These problems could well end Nigeria's hegemonic aspirations in West Africa. A democratic and stable Nigeria will be important for guaranteeing international legitimacy and support for future interventions, as well as for avoiding the charges of hypocrisy faced by General Abacha in restoring democracy to Liberia and Sierra Leone while denying it to Nigerians at home. Nigeria will also have to be careful not to arouse the fears of neighbors through unilateral military interventions that make it appear to be pursuing parochial policies in an attempt to dominate its subregion.

In the post–Cold War era, the slogan "African solutions to African problems" is now being expressed out of necessity; it is no longer wishful thinking, as during the era of superpower rivalry. During the Cold War, this ideal was expressed from a position of passive impotence, reflecting the frustration of Africans at their inability to prevent external intervention on their continent. After the Cold War, African solutions to African problems is an idea that is expressed from a position of greater strength, albeit with the sober realization that Africa has lost its strategic value to the external world and that few former Cold War actors are interested in intervening in Africa. Africans are being forced by changed circumstances to keep their own peace.

During the Cold War, Africa lacked the military strength to enforce continental peace; today, Nigeria has demonstrated the military potential to enforce a subregional peace. The impotent embodiment of continental peacemaking during the Cold War was the OAU, whereas the embodiment of subregional peacemaking in post–Cold War West Africa is ECOMOG. In post–Cold War Africa, Pax Africana may have found its most eloquent expression in West Africa, giving rise to the regionalization of the concept in the form of Pax Nigeriana.

Notes

1. See, for example, Agwuncha Arthur Nwankwo, *Nigeria: The Stolen Billions* (Enugu, Nigeria: Fouth Dimension, 1999).

2. See *Economist Intelligence Unit*, Country Report, "Liberia," no. 1 (1994): 39; Herman Cohen, *Intervening in Africa: Superpower Peacemaking in a Troubled Continent* (New York, N.Y.: St. Martin's Press, 2000), p. 160; Herbert Howe, "Lessons of Liberia: ECOMOG and Regional Peacekeeping," *International Security* 21, no. 3 (Winter 1996/1997): 68; and Karl Magyar, "ECOMOG's Operations: Lessons For Peacekeeping," in Karl Magyar and Earl Conteh-Morgan (eds.), *Peacekeeping in Africa: ECOMOG in Liberia* (Hampshire, UK: Macmillan; and New York: St. Martin's, 1998), p. 56. The figure of $1.2 billion is based on projections of these figures cited at various stages of the intervention. These estimates are almost exactly the same.

3. Colonel Festus Aboagye, *ECOMOG: A Sub-Regional Experience in Conflict Resolution, Management, and Peacekeeping in Liberia* (Accra: SEDCO, 1999), pp. 229–266; Adekeye Adebajo, *Building Peace in West Africa: Liberia, Sierra Leone, and Guinea-Bissau* (Boulder and London: Lynne Rienner, 2002); Comfort Ero, "The Future of ECOMOG in West Africa," in Jakkie Cilliers and Greg Mills (eds.), *From Peacekeeping to Complex Emergencies: Peace Support Missions in Africa* (Johannesburg and Pretoria: South African Institute of International Affairs and the Institute for Security Studies, 1999), pp. 55–74; and Robert Mortimer, "From ECOMOG to ECOMOG II: Intervention in Sierra Leone," in John W. Harbeson and Donald Rothchild (eds.), *Africa in World Politics: The African State System in Flux*, 3rd ed. (Colorado and Oxford: Westview, 2000), pp. 188–207.

4. Members include Benin, Burkina Faso, Côte d'Ivoire, Guinea-Bissau, Mali, Niger, Senegal, and Togo.

5. See *Economic Community of West African States Revised Treaty* (Lagos: ECOWAS Secretariat, 1993).

6. Ibrahim Gambari, *Political and Comparative Dimensions of Regional Integration: The Case of ECOWAS* (Atlantic Highlands, N. J., and London: Humanities Press International, 1991), p. 63.

7. "Final Report," Meeting of ECOWAS Ministers of Foreign Affairs, 26–29 October 1998, Abuja, p. 17.

8. See Protocol Relating to the Mechanism for Conflict Prevention, Management, Resolution, Peacekeeping, and Security, Lomé, 10 December 1999; and Adebajo, *Building Peace in West Africa*.

9. Protocol Relating to the Mechanism for Conflict Prevention, Management, Resolution, Peacekeeping, and Security.

10.See, for example, "Nigeria Does It Again," *The Economist*, 21 February 1998, pp. 16–17; and Howard French, "A Muscular Nigeria Proves a Flawed Peacekeeper," *New York Times*, 26 June 1997, p. A12.

11.See Adebajo, *Building Peace in West Africa*, pp. 111–136; and Eric G. Berman and Katie E. Sams, *Peacekeeping in Africa: Capabilities and Culpabilities* (Geneva: UN Institute for Disarmament Research; and Pretoria: Institute for Security Studies, 2000), pp. 128–138.

12. *Newswatch* 26, no. 6 (11 August 1997): 17.

13. Olusegun Obasanjo, "Nigeria, Africa, and the World in the Next Millennium," Address to the Fifty-Fourth Session of the United Nations General Assembly, New York, 23 September 1999, p. 6.

14.See Adekeye Adebajo, "Nigeria: Africa's New Gendarme?" *Security Dialogue* 31, no. 2 (June 2000): 185–199.

ACRONYMS & ABBREVIATIONS

ACDL	Association for Constitutional Democracy in Liberia
AFL	Armed Forces of Liberia
AFRC	Armed Forces Ruling Council (Nigeria)
BTC	Barclay Training Center
CIA	Central Intelligence Agency
CRC-NPFL	Central Revolutionary Council
ECOMOG	ECOWAS Cease-Fire Monitoring Group
ECOWAS	Economic Community of West African States
EEC	European Economic Community (now the EU)
EU	European Union
GNP	gross national product
IEC	Independent Elections Commission
IGNU	Interim Government of National Unity
IMF	International Monetary Fund
INPFL	Independent National Patriotic Front of Liberia
IPA	International Peace Academy
LAP	Liberia Action Party
LNTG	Liberian National Transitional Government
LPC	Liberia Peace Council
LPP	Liberia People's Party
LUP	Liberia Unification Party
LURD	Liberians United for Reconciliation and Democracy
MOJA	Movement for Justice in Africa
NDPL	National Democratic Party of Liberia
NGO	nongovernmental organization
NPFL	National Patriotic Front of Liberia

NPP	National Patriotic Party
OAU	Organization of African Unity
PAL	Progressive Alliance of Liberians
PRC	People's Redemption Council
RUF	Revolutionary United Front
SECOM	Special Elections Commission
SMC	Standing Mediation Committee
TWP	True Whig Party
ULIMO	United Liberation Movement of Liberia for Democracy
UN	United Nations
UNDP	United Nations Development Programme
UNICEF	United Nations Children's Fund
UP	Unity Party
UPP	United People's Party
USAID	U.S. Agency for International Development
VOA	Voice of America

BIBLIOGRAPHY

Interviews

Aidara Abdoulaye, Head of Conflict Division, Ivorian Foreign Ministry. Abidjan, July 1996.

Olu Adeniji, former Nigerian Ambassador to France. Lagos, 13 January 1997.

Brigadier Francis Agyemfra, former chief of Staff of Ghana. Monrovia, 18 July 1999.

Admiral Augustus Aikhomu, former Nigerian Chief of General Staff. Lagos, December 1996.

Ayo Ajakaiye, former Nigerian Ambassador to Liberia. Abuja, December 1995.

Cyril Allen, Secretary General, National Patrotic Party. Monrovia, 12 July 1999.

Kwame Amoa-Awua, Director for Africa and OAU Bureau, Ghanaian Foreign Ministry. Accra, September 1996.

Colonal Kayode Are, former ECOMOG Chief Military Intellingence Officer. Abuja, 4 August 1999.

Edouard Benjamin, former ECOWAS Executive Secretary. Lagos, December 1995.

James Bishop, former U.S. Ambassador to Liberia. Washington, D.C., July 1997.

Yéro Boly, Minister of the Interior of Burkina Faso. Ouagadougou, 22 July 1999.

General Hezekiah Bowen, former Chief of Staff, Armed Forces of Liberia. Monrovia, 14 July 1999.

British Embassy, Abidjan. 31 July 1996.

Mary Brownell, Liberia Women Initiative. Monrovia, 15 July 1999.

Burkinabè Permanent Mission in New York, July 1998.

Monie Captan, Foreign Minister of Liberia. Monrovia, 15 July 1999.

Mohammed ibn Chambas, former Deputy Foreign Minister of Ghana. New York, September 1996.

Daniel Chea, Defense Minister of Liberia. Monrovia, 13 July 1999.

Herman Cohen, former U.S. Assistant Secretary of State for African Affairs. Washington, D.C., July 1997.

J. Coker, former Nigerian Ambassador to Côte d'Ivoire. Abidjan, August 1996.

General Theophilus Danjuna, Defense Minister of Nigeria. Abuja, 7 July 1999.

Alexandre Diam, ANAD Secretary-General. Abidjan, 19 July 1999.

General Cheick Diarra, Ecowas Deputy Executive Secretary. Abuja, 10 July 2001.

Felix Downes-Thomas, former UN Special Representative of the Secretary General in Liberia. New York, 15 March 1999.

Air Marshal A. H. Dumashie, Chief of Defense Staff, Ghanaian army. Accra, September 1996.

General Emmanuel Erskine, former Commander of the UN Mission in Lebanon. Accra, 13 August 1996.

A. O. Esan, former Director of West Africa Division, Nigerian Ministry of Foreign Affairs. Abuja, 6 December 1995.

Ibrahima Fall, former Senegalese Foreign Minister. New York, July 1998.

Colonel O. Folorunso, former ECOMOG Chief Military Public Information Officer. 5 July 1999.

Michael Francis, Archbishop of Monrovia. Monrovia, 13 July 1999.

Ibrahim Gambari, Permanent Representative of Nigeria to the United Nations. New York, 17 March 1997.

Trevor Gordon-Somers, former UN Special Representative to Liberia. New York, May 1997.

Baffour Assasie-Gyimah, former Ambassador of Ghana to Burkina Faso. Ouagadougou, 20 July 1999.

Joshua Iroha, former Nigerian Ambassador to Liberia. Lagos, 28 July 1999.

Brigadier Cyril Iweze, former ECOMOG Chief of Staff. Lagos, December 1996.

Baboucarr Jagne, Foreign Minister of Gambia. New York, 30 July 2001.

Colonel Ibrahim Jalloh, former Deputy Force Commander. Conakry, 7 July 1999.

Howard Jeter, U.S. Presidential Envoy to Liberia. Washington, D.C., 3 April 1997.

General Prince Johnson II, former Chief of Staff, Armed Forces of Liberia. Monrovia, 14 July 1999.

James Jonah, former UN Special Envoy for Liberia. New York, May 1997.

Colonel Daprou Kambou, Director General, Ministry of Defense of Burkina Faso. Ouagadougou, 22 July 1999.

Dieliman Osman Kouyaté, Head of the Department of Africa, Asia and the Middle East; Foreign Ministry of Guinea. Conakry, 30 June 1999.

Maes Kouamé, Chief of the Division of African Conflicts, Foreign Ministry of Côte D'Ivoire. Abidjan, 9 July 1999.

General Rufus Kupollati, former ECOMOG Force Commander. Lagos, 13 July 2001.

Sule Lamido, Foreign Minister of Nigeria. Lomé, 8 December 1999.

General Julius Maada Bio, former Head of State Sierra Leone. Washington, D.C., 19 January 2001.

General Victor Malu, former ECOMOG Force Commander. Lagos, 2 October 2001.

Francois Massaquoi, former Head of the Lofa Defense Force. Monrovia, 10 July 1999.

Gabriel Baccus Matthews, former Interim Foreign Minister of Liberia. Monrovia, 17 July 1999.

Matthew Mbu, former Nigerian Foreign Minister. Lagos, 13 January 1997.

Donald McHenry, U.S. Presidential Envoy to Nigeria. Washington, D.C., 14 July 1997.

Albert Millogo, Defense Minister of Burkina Faso. Ouagadougoy, 22 July 1999.

General Ike Nwachukwu, former Nigerian Foreign Minister. New York, 3 August 2001.

General Felix Mujakpero, former ECOMOG Force Commander. Freetown, 3 July 1999.
Colonel Chris Olukolade, former ECOMOG Military Information Officer. Freetown, 3 July 1999.
Youssouf Ouedraogo, Foreign Minister of Burkina Faso. Ouagadougou, 20 July 1999.
Domba Jean-Marc Palm, former Foreign Minister of Burkina Faso. Ouagadougou, 21 July 1999.
General Arnold Quainoo, first ECOMOG Force Commander. Accra, 7 August 1996.
Victoria Refell, Chairman, National Reconciliation Commission. Monrovia, 15 July 1999.
Amos Sawyer, former Interim President of Liberia. Monrovia, 14 July 1999.
Mamadou Sermé, Director-General, Foreign Ministry of Burkina Faso. Ouagadougoy, 22 July 1999.
General Mamadou Seck, former Chief of Staff of the Senegalese army. Washington, D.C., 21 July 1997.
Omar Sey, former Gambian Foreign Minister. Baghdad, 14 December 1997.
General Timothy Shelpidi, former ECOMOG Force Commander Abuja. 10, July 2001.
John Stewart, Regional Director, Justice and Peace Commission. Monrovia, 16 July 1999.
Ahmadou Touré, ANAD Director of Studies. Abidjan, 19 July 1999.
Augustine Toure, former Deputy Director, Liberia Democracy Watch. Monrovia, 16 July 1999.
Ambassador Ahmadou Traoré, Director of Africa, Asia, and the Middle East, Ivorian Foreign Ministry. Abidjan, July 1996.
William Twadell, former U.S. Chargé d'Affaires in Liberia. Washington, D.C., June 1997.
United Nations Development Programme Office. Abidjan, 1 August 1996.
Office of the United Nations High Commissioner for Refugees, Abidjan. 1 August 1996.
James Verdier, Justice and Peace Commission. Monrovia, 16 July 1999.
Prosper Vokouma, former Foreign Minister of Burkina Faso. Ouagadougou, 22 July 1999.
Lannon Walker, former U.S. Ambassador to Nigeria. Abidjan, August 1996.
General Ishola Williams, former Commander, Nigerian Training and Doctrine Command. Lagos, 6 January 1997.
Stephen Wreh-Wilson, Justice and Peace Commission. Monrovia, 16 July 1999.
Bruno Zidouemba, Ambassador of Burkina Faso to the United States. Washington, D.C., 27 October 1999.

References

Abdullah, Ibrahim, and Patrick Muana, "The Revolutionary United Front of Sierra Leone: A Revolt of the Lumpenproletariat," in Christopher Clapham (ed.), *African Guerrillas* (Oxford, Kampala, and Bloomington: James Currey, Fountain Publishers, and Indiana University Press, 1998).
Adamolekun, Ladipo, *Sékou Touré's Guinea: An Experiment in Nation Building* (London: Methuen, 1976).

Adebajo, Adekeye, "Rich Man's War, Poor Man's War," *The World Today* 52, nos. 8–9 (August/September 1996).
———, "Towards a New Pax Africana: Three Decades of the OAU," *Praxis* 10, no. 1 (Spring 1993).
Adebajo, Adekeye, and Michael O'Hanlon, "Africa: Toward A Rapid-Reaction Force," *SAIS Review* 17, no. 2 (Summer-Fall 1997).
Adefuye, Ade, et al., *Seven Years of IBB,* 7 vols. (Lagos: Daily Times of Nigeria, 1993).
Adeleke, Ademola, "The Politics and Diplomacy of Peacekeeping in West Africa: The ECOWAS Operation in Liberia," *Journal of Modern African Studies* 33, no. 4 (1995).
Adeniji, Olu, "Mechanisms for Conflict Management in West Africa: Politics of Harmonization," *ACCORD* Occasional Paper, January 1997.
Adibe, Clement, "Hegemony, Security, and West African Integration: Nigeria, Ghana, and the Transformation of ECOWAS," Ph.D., Queens University, Canada (December 1994).
Agetua, Nkem, *Operation Liberty: The Story of Major-General Joshua Nimyel Dogonyaro* (Lagos: Hona Communications, 1992).
Akinrinade, Olusola, "From Hostility to Accommodation: Nigeria's West African Policy, 1984–1990," *Nigerian Journal of International Affairs*, 18, no. 1 (1992).
Akinyemi, Bolaji, *Foreign Policy and Federalism* (Ibadan: Ibadan University Press, 1974).
Alao, Abiodun, *The Burden of Collective Goodwill: The International Involvement in the Liberian Civil War* (Aldershot, UK: Ashgate, 1998).
Aluko, Olajide, "Nigerian Foreign Policy under the Second Republic," Centre d'Etude d'Afrique Noire, Université de Bordeaux, Travaux et Documents no. 18, 1988.
———, *Ghana and Nigeria, 1957–1970: A Study of Inter-African Discord* (London: Rex Collings, 1976).
———, "The Expulsion of Illegal Aliens from Nigeria: A Study in Decision-making," *African Affairs* 84, no. 337 (October 1985).
Aluko, Olajide (ed.), *Africa and the Great Powers* (Lanham, Md.: University Press of America, 1987).
Aminu, L. S., *Nigeria's Weapons Procurement Process: Its Implications for Her Defence Policy* (Lagos: Nigerian Institute for International Affairs, Monograph series no. 15, n.d.).
Amnesty International, *Annual Report on Liberia* (London: Amnesty International, 1996).
Amuta, Chidi, *Prince of the Niger: The Babangida Years* (Lagos: Tanus Communications, 1992).
Andrews, Christopher M., "France: Adjustment to Change," in Hedley Bull (ed.), *The Expansion of International Society* (Oxford: Clarendon, 1984).
Aning, Emmanuel Kwezi, "Managing Regional Security in West Africa: ECOWAS, ECOMOG, and Liberia" (Centre for Development Research, Copenhagen, Working Paper 94.2, February 1994).
Armon, Jeremy, and Andy Carl (eds.), *Accord: The Liberian Peace Process, 1990–1996*, Issue 1/1996 (London: Conciliation Resources, 1996).
Ate, Bassey, and Bola Akinterinwa (eds.), *Nigeria and Its Immediate Neighbours* (Lagos: Nigerian Institute of International Affairs, 1992).
Atkinson, Philippa, *The War Economy in Liberia: A Political Economy* (London: Overseas Development Institute, 1997).

Azikiwe, Nnamdi, *Zik* (Cambridge: Cambridge University Press, 1960).

Bach, Daniel, "Francophone Regional Organisations and ECOWAS," in Julius Okolo and Stephen Wright (eds.), *West African Regional Cooperation and Development* (Boulder: Westview, 1990).

———, "The Politics of West African Economic Cooperation: CEAO and ECOWAS," *Journal of Modern African Studies* 21, no. 4 (1983).

Berkeley, Bill, "Between Repression and Slaughter," *Atlantic Monthly* (December 1992).

Bienen, Henry, *Armed Forces, Conflict, and Change in Africa* (Boulder: Westview, 1989).

Boley, G. E. Saigbe, *Liberia: The Rise and Fall of the First Republic* (New York: St. Martin's, 1983).

Boutros-Ghali, Boutros, *An Agenda for Peace,* 2nd ed. (New York: UN Department of Public Information, 1995).

Briggs, Wenike, "Negotiations Between the Enlarged European Economic Community and the African, Caribbean, and Pacific Countries," *Nigerian Journal of International Affairs* 1, no. 1 July 1975).

Buzan, Barry, *People, States, and Fear: An Agenda for International Security Studies in the Post–Cold War Era,* 2nd ed. (Boulder: Lynne Rienner, 1991).

Carey, Margaret, "Peacekeeping in Africa: Recent Evolution and Prospects," in Oliver Furley and Roy May (eds.), *Peacekeeping in Africa* (Aldershot, UK: Ashgate, 1998).

Chipman, John, *French Power in Africa* (Oxford: Basil Blackwell, 1989).

Clapham, Christopher, *Africa and the International System: The Politics of State Survival* (Cambridge, UK: Cambridge University Press, 1996).

Clapham, Christopher (ed.), *Private Patronage and Public Power: Political Clientelism in the Modern State* (London: Frances Pinter, 1982).

Clough, Michael, *Free at Last? U.S. Policy Toward Africa and the End of the Cold War* (New York: Council on Foreign Relations, 1992).

Cohen, Herman, *Intervening in Africa: Superpower Peacemaking in a Troubled Continent* (New York: St. Martin's, 2000).

Damrosch, Lori Fisler (ed.), *Enforcing Restraint: Collective Intervention in Internal Conflicts* (New York: Council on Foreign Relations, 1993).

De St. Jorre, John, *The Brothers' War* (Boston: Houghton Mifflin, 1972).

Deng, Francis, "Africa and the New World Dis-order: Rethinking Colonial Borders," *Brookings Review* 11, no. 2 (Spring 1993).

———, "Africa's Dilemmas in Sudan," *World Today* 54, no. 3 (March 1998).

Diamond, Larry, Anthony Kirk-Greene, and Oyeleye Oyediran (eds.), *Transition Without End: Nigerian Politics and Civil Society Under Babangida* (Boulder: Lynne Rienner, 1997).

Dolo, Emmanuel, *Democracy versus Dictatorship: The Quest for Freedom and Justice in Africa's Oldest Republic* (Lanham, Md.: University Press of America, 1996).

Dunn, D. Elwood, and S. Byron Tarr, *Liberia: A National Polity in Transition* (Metuchen, N.J.: Scarecrow, 1988).

Elaigwu, J. Isawa, *Gowon* (Ibadan: West Books Publisher, 1986).

El-Ayouty, Yassin, and I. William Zartman (eds.), *The OAU after Twenty Years* (New York: Praeger, 1984).

Ellis, Stephen, "Liberia, 1989–1994: A Study of Ethnic and Spiritual Violence," *African Affairs* 94, no. 375 (April 1995).

———, "Liberia's Warlord Insurgency," in Christopher Clapham (ed.), *African Guerrillas* (Oxford: James Currey; Bloomington: Indiana University Press; and Kampala: Fountain, 1998).

Englebert, Pierre, *Burkina Faso: Unsteady Statehood in West Africa* (Boulder: Westview, 1996).

Evans, Graham, and Jeffrey Newnham, *The Dictionary of World Politics* (New York: Harvester Wheatsheaf, 1990).

Falola, Toyin, and Julius Ihonvbere (eds.), *The Rise and Fall of Nigeria's Second Republic* (London: Zed, 1985).

Fawcett, Louise, and Andrew Hurrell (eds.), *Regionalism in World Politics* (Oxford: Oxford University Press, 1995).

Forsyth, Frederick, *Emeka* (Ibadan: Spectrum, 1982).

Friends of Liberia, "Liberia: Opportunities and Obstacles for Peace," Washington, D.C., December 1996.

Gambari, Ibrahim, *Political and Comparative Dimensions of Regional Integration: The Case of ECOWAS* (London: Humanities Press International, 1991).

————, *Theory and Reality in Foreign Policy Making: Nigeria after the Second Republic* (Atlantic Highlands, N.J.: Humanities, 1989).

Garba, Joseph, *Diplomatic Soldiering: Nigerian Foreign Policy, 1975–1979* (Ibadan: Spectrum, 1987).

Gifford, Paul, *Christianity and Politics in Doe's Liberia* (Cambridge, UK: Cambridge University Press, 1993).

Gilpin, Robert, *War and Change in World Politics* (Cambridge, UK: Cambridge University Press, 1981).

Gowon, Yakubu, *The Economic Community of West African States: A Study of Political and Economic Integration* (Ph.d. Thesis, Warwick University, February 1984).

Greene, Graham, *Journey Without Maps* (London: Penguin, 1978).

Harris, Katherine, *African and American Values: Liberia and West Africa* (Lanham, Md.: University Press of America, 1985).

Herbst, Jeffrey, *U.S. Economic Policy Toward Africa* (New York: Council on Foreign Relations, 1992).

Herskovits, Jean, *Africans Solving African Problems: Militaries, Democracies, and Security in West and Southern Africa* (New York: International Peace Academy, 1998).

Hoffman, Adonis, "Nigeria: The Policy Conundrum," *Foreign Policy*, no. 101 (Winter 1995/1996).

Howe, Herbert, "Lessons of Liberia: ECOMOG and Regional Peacekeeping," *International Security* 21, no. 3 (Winter 1996/1997).

Huband, Mark, *The Liberian Civil War* (London: Frank Cass, 1998).

Human Rights Watch/Africa, "Waging War to Keep the Peace: The ECOMOG Intervention and Human Rights," 5, no. 6 (June 1993).

Idang, Gordon, *Nigeria: Internal Politics and Foreign Policy, 1960–1966* (Ibadan: Ibadan University Press, 1973).

Independent Elections Commission, *Special Elections Law for the 1997 Elections* (Monrovia: Sabanoh, 1997).

Inegbedion, E. John, "ECOMOG in Comparative Perspective," in Timothy M. Shaw and Julius Emeka Okolo (eds.), *The Political Economy of Foreign Policy in ECOWAS* (London: Macmillan, 1994).

International Peace Academy, "The OAU Mechanism for Conflict Prevention, Management, and Resolution," report of a conference cosponsored by the International Peace Academy and Organization of African Unity, Cairo, 7–11 May 1994.

James, Alan, *Peacekeeping in International Politics* (London: Chatto and Windus, 1990).

Job, Brian (ed.), *The Insecurity Dilemma: National Security of Third World States* (Boulder: Lynne Rienner, 1992).

Jolaoso, Olujimi, *In the Shadows: Recollections of a Pioneer Diplomat* (Lagos: Malthouse, 1991).

Joseph, Richard, *Democracy and Prebendal Politics in Nigeria* (Cambridge: Cambridge University Press, 1987).

———, "The International Community and Armed Conflict in Africa: Post–Cold War Dilemmas," in Gunnar Sørbø and Peter Vale (eds.), *Out of Conflict: From War to Peace in Africa* (Uppsala: Nordiska Afrikainstitutet, 1997).

Kappel, Robert, and Werner Korte (eds.), *Human Rights Violations in Liberia, 1980–1990: A Documentation* (Bremen, Germany: Liberia Working Group, 1990).

Keen, David, "'Sell-game': The Economics of Conflict in Sierra Leone," paper presented at University College of London, 21 October 1995.

Kennedy, Paul, *The Rise and Fall of the Great Powers: Economic Change and Military Conflict from 1500–2000* (New York: Random House, 1987).

Keohane, Robert, *After Hegemony: Cooperation and Discord in World Political Economy* (Princeton, N.J.: Princeton University Press, 1984).

Kirk-Greene, A.H.M., *Crisis and Conflict in Nigeria*, 2 vols. (London: Oxford University Press, 1971).

———, A.H.M., *"Stay by Your Radios"* (Leiden and Cambridge: African Studies Centre, 1981).

———, "West Africa: Nigeria and Ghana," in Peter Duignan and Robert H. Jackson (eds.), *Politics and Government in African States, 1960–1985* (Stanford: Hoover Institution, 1986).

Kirk-Greene, Anthony, and Douglas Rimmer, *Nigeria since 1970: A Political and Economic Outline* (London: Hodder and Stoughton, 1981).

Kornegay, Francis, and Chris Landsberg, *Mayivuke!Afrika! Can South Africa Lead an African Renaissance?* (Johannesburg: Centre for Policy Studies, International Relations Series 11, no. 1, January 1998).

Kramer, Reed, "Liberia: A Casualty of the Cold War's End?," *CSIS Africa Notes*, no. 174 (July 1995).

Kupolati, R. M., "Strategic Doctrines: Joint Operations," in A. E. Ekoko and M. A. Vogt (eds.), *Nigerian Defence Policy: Issues and Problems* (Lagos and Oxford: Malthouse, 1990).

Lawyers Committee for Human Rights, *Liberia: A Promise Betrayed* (New York: Lawyers Committee For Human Rights, 1986).

Liebenow, Gus, *The Evolution of Privilege* (Ithaca: Cornell University Press, 1969).

———, *Liberia: The Quest for Democracy* (Bloomington: Indiana University Press, 1987).

Luckham, Robin, *The Nigerian Military: A Sociological Analysis of Authority and Revolt, 1960–1967* (London: Cambridge University Press, 1971).

Lyons, Terrence, *Voting for Peace: Postconflict Elections in Liberia* (Washington, D.C.: Brookings Institution, 1999).

Macfarlane, Neil, and Thomas Weiss, "Regional Organizations and Regional Security," *Security Studies* 2, no. 1 (Autumn 1992).

Magyar, Karl, and Earl Conteh-Morgan, *Peacekeeping in Africa: ECOMOG in Liberia* (Hampshire, UK: Macmillan; and New York: St. Martin's, 1998).

Martin, Guy, "Continuity and Change in Franco-African Relations," *Journal of Modern African Studies* 33, no. 1 (March 1995).

Mayall, James, "Oil and Nigerian Foreign Policy," *African Affairs* 75, no. 300 (July 1976).

Mazrui, Ali, *Towards a Pax Africana* (Chicago: University of Chicago Press, 1967).

Miners, N.J., *The Nigerian Army, 1956–1966* (London: Methuen, 1971).

Mortimer, Robert, "Senegal's Role in ECOMOG: The Francophone Dimension," *Journal of Modern African Studies* 34, no. 2 (1996).

Mundt, Robert, "Côte d'Ivoire: Continuity and Change in a Semi-Democracy," in John Clark and David Gardinier (eds.), *Political Reform in Francophone Africa* (Boulder: Westview, 1997).

Myers, David (ed.), *Regional Hegemons: Threat, Perception, and Strategic Response* (Boulder: Westview, 1991).

Nowrojee, Binaifir, "Joining Forces: UN and Regional Peacekeeping Lessons from Liberia," *Harvard Human Rights Journal* 18 (Spring 1995).

Nwokedi, Emeka, "Regional Integration and Regional Security: ECOMOG, Nigeria, and the Liberian Crisis," Travaux et Documents no. 35 (Bordeaux, France: Centre d'Etude d'Afrique Noire, 1992).

Obasanjo, Olusegun, *My Command* (London: Heinemann, 1980).

———. *Not My Will* (Ibadan: University Press, 1990).

O'Brien, Donal Cruise, John Dunn, and Richard Rathbone (eds.), *Contemporary West African States* (Cambridge: Cambridge University Press, 1989).

Ofuatey-Kodjoe, W., "Regional Organizations and the Resolution of Internal conflicts: The ECOWAS Intervention in Liberia," *International Peacekeeping* 1, no. 3 (Autumn 1994).

Ohaegbulam, Festus Ugboaja, *Nigeria and the UN Mission to the Democratic Republic of the Congo* (Gainesville: University Press of Florida, 1982).

Ojo, Olatunde, "Nigeria and the Formation of ECOWAS," *International Organization* 34, no. 4 (Autumn 1980).

Olonisakin, Funmi, "UN Co-operation with Regional Organisations in Peacekeeping: The Experience of ECOMOG and UNOMIL in Liberia," *International Peacekeeping* 3, no. 3 (Autumn 1996).

Olukoshi, Adebayo, Omotayo Olaniyan, and Femi Aribisala (eds.), *Structural Adjustment in West Africa* (Lagos: Nigerian Institute of International Affairs, 1994).

Olusanya, G. O., and R. A. Akindele (eds.), *Nigeria's External Relations: The First Twenty-Five Years* (Ibadan: University Press, 1986).

Omede, Adedoyin Jolaade, "Nigeria's Military-Security Role in Liberia," *African Journal of International Affairs and Development* 1, no. 1 (1995).

Omonijo, Mobolade, *Doe: The Liberian Tragedy* (Lagos: Sahel, 1990).

Onwuka, Ralph, *Development and Integration in Africa: The Case of the Economic Community of West African States* (Ile-Ife, Nigeria: University of Ife Press, 1982).

Onwuka, Ralph, and Amadou Sesay (eds.), *The Future of Regionalism in Africa* (London: Macmillan, 1985).

Osaghae, Eghosa, *Ethnicity, Class, and the Struggle for State Power in Liberia* (Dakar: CODESRIA, 1996).

Othman, Shehu, "Classes, Crises, and Coups: The Demise of Shagari's Regime," *African Affairs* 83, no. 333 (October 1984).

———, "Nigeria: Power for Profit—Class, Corporatism, and Factionalism in the Military" in Donal Cruise O'Brien, et al. (eds.), *Contemporary West African States* (Cambridge: Cambridge University Press, 1989).

Othman, Shehu, and Gavin Williams, "Power, Politics, and Democracy in Nigeria," in Jonathan Hyslop (ed.), *African Democracy in the Era of Globalisation* (Johannesburg: Witwatersrand University Press, 1999.)

Pellow, Deborah, and Naomi Chazan, *Ghana: Coping with Uncertainty* (Boulder: Westview,1986).

Person, Yves, "French West Africa and Decolonization," in P. Gifford and W. R. Lewis (eds.), *The Transfer of Power in Africa: Decolonization 1940–1960* (New Haven: Yale University Press, 1982).

Polhemus, James, "Nigeria and Southern Africa: Interest, Policy, and Means," *Canadian Journal of African Studies* 11, no. 1 (1977).

Reno, William, "The Business of War in Liberia," *Current History* 95, no. 601 (May 1996).

———, "Reinvention of an African Patrimonial State: Charles Taylor's Liberia," *Third World Quarterly* 16, no. 1 (1995).

———, *Warlord Politics and African States* (Boulder: Lynne Rienner, 1998).

Richards, Paul, *Fighting for the Rainforest: War, Youth, and Resources in Sierra Leone* (Oxford: James Currey, 1996).

———, "Rebellion in Liberia and Sierra Leone: A Crisis of Youth?," in Oliver Furley (ed.), *Conflict in Africa* (New York: Tauris Academic Studies, 1995).

Rivière, Claude, *Guinea: The Mobilization of a People* (Ithaca: Cornell University Press, 1978).

Saleem, Ali Ahmed, "An Introduction to IGADD," in Martin Doornbos, et al. (eds.), *Beyond Conflict in the Horn* (The Hague: Institute of Social Studies, 1992).

Sawyer, Amos, *Effective Immediately: Dictatorship in Liberia, 1980–1986—A Personal Perspective* (Bremen, Germany: Liberia Working Group, 1987).

———, *The Emergence of Autocracy in Liberia: Tragedy and Challenge* (San Francisco: ICS, 1992).

Schraeder, Peter, "Senegal's Foreign Policy: Challenges of Democratization and Marginalization," *African Affairs* 96, no. 385 (1997).

Sesay, Amadou (ed.), *The OAU after Twenty-Five Years* (Cambridge: St. Martin's, 1990).

Sesay, Max, "Civil War and Collective Intervention in Liberia," *Review of African Political Economy* 23, no. 67 (March 1996).

Sesay, Max, "Politics and Society in Post-War Liberia," *Journal of Modern African Studies* 34, no. 3 (September 1996).

Shagari, Shehu, *My Vision of Nigeria* (London: Frank Cass, 1981).

Shaw, Timothy, and Olajide Aluko (eds.), *The Political Economy of African Foreign Policy* (Aldershot, UK: Gower, 1984).

Sisay, Hassan B., *Big Powers and Small Nations: A Case Study of United States–Liberian Relations* (Lanham, Md.: University Press of America, 1985).

Skinner, Elliot, "Sankara and the Burkinabe Revolution: Charisma and Power—Local and External Dimensions," *Journal of Modern African Studies* 26, no. 3 (1988).

Sotumbi, Abiodun O., *Nigeria's Recognition of the MPLA Government of Angola: A Case-Study in Decision-making and Implementation* (Lagos: Nigerian Institute of International Affairs, 1981).

Soyinka, Wole, *The Open Sore of a Continent: A Personal Narrative of the Nigerian Crisis* (Oxford: Oxford University Press, 1996).

Stedman, Stephen John, "Conflict and Conciliation in Sub-Saharan Africa," in Michael Brown (ed.), *The International Dimensions of Internal Conflict* (Cambridge, Mass.: Center for Science and International Affairs, 1996).

Stremlau, John, *The International Politics of the Nigerian Civil War, 1967–1970* (Princeton, N.J.: Princeton University Press, 1977).

Tanner, Victor, "Liberia: Railroading Peace," *Review of African Political Economy* 75, no. 25 (March 1998).

Thompson, W. Scott, *Ghana's Foreign Policy, 1957–1966* (Princeton, N.J.: Princeton University Press, 1969).

United Nations, *The United Nations and the Situation in Liberia*, revision no. 1 (New York: UN Department of Public Information, February 1997).

Vogt, Margaret, "Nigeria's Participation in the ECOWAS Monitoring Group (ECOMOG)," *Nigerian Journal of International Affairs* 17, no. 1 (1991).

Vogt, M. A. (ed.), *The Liberian Crisis and ECOMOG: A Bold Attempt at Regional Peacekeeping* (Lagos: Gabumo, 1992).

Vogt, M. A., and A. E. Ekoko (eds.), *Nigeria in International Peacekeeping, 1960–1992* (Lagos: Malthouse, 1993).

Vogt, M. A., and L. S. Aminu (eds.), *Peacekeeping as a Security Strategy in Africa: Chad and Liberia as Case Studies,* 2 vols. (Enugu: Fourth Dimension, 1996).

Wayas, Joseph, *Nigeria's Leadership Role in Africa* (London: Macmillan, 1979).

Weller, Marc, *Regional Peacekeeping and International Enforcement: The Liberian Crisis* (Cambridge: Cambridge University Press, 1994).

Williams, David, *President and Power in Nigeria: The Life of Shehu Shagari* (London: Frank Cass, 1982).

Wippman, David, "Enforcing Peace: ECOWAS and the Liberian Civil War," in Lori Fisler Damrosch (ed.), *Enforcing Restraint: Collective Intervention in Internal Conflicts* (New York: Council on Foreign Relations, 1993).

Yates, Douglas, *The Rentier State in Africa: Oil Rent Dependency and Neocolonialism in the Republic of Gabon* (Trenton, N.J.: Africa World, 1995).

INDEX

267

ABOUT THE BOOK

Liberia's Civil War offers the most in-depth account available of one of the most baffling and intractable of Africa's conflicts.

Adekeye Adebajo unravels the tangled web of the conflict by addressing four questions: Why did Nigeria intervene in Liberia and remain committed throughout the seven-year civil war? To what extent was ECOMOG's intervention shaped by Nigeria's hegemonic aspirations? What domestic, regional, and external factors prevented ECOMOG from achieving its objectives for so long? And what factors led eventually to the end of the war? In answering these questions—drawing on previously restricted ECOWAS and UN reports and numerous interviews with key actors—he sheds much-needed light on security issues in West Africa.

The concluding chapter of the book assesses the continuing insecurity in Liberia under the repressive presidency of Charles Taylor and its destabalizing effect on the entire West Africa region.

Adekeye Adebajo is director of the Africa Program at the International Peace Academy and adjunct professor at Columbia University's School of International and Public Affairs. Dr. Adebajo has served on UN missions in South Africa, Western Sahara, and Iraq. His most recent publication is *Building Peace in West Africa: Liberia, Sierra Leone, and Guinea-Bissau.*